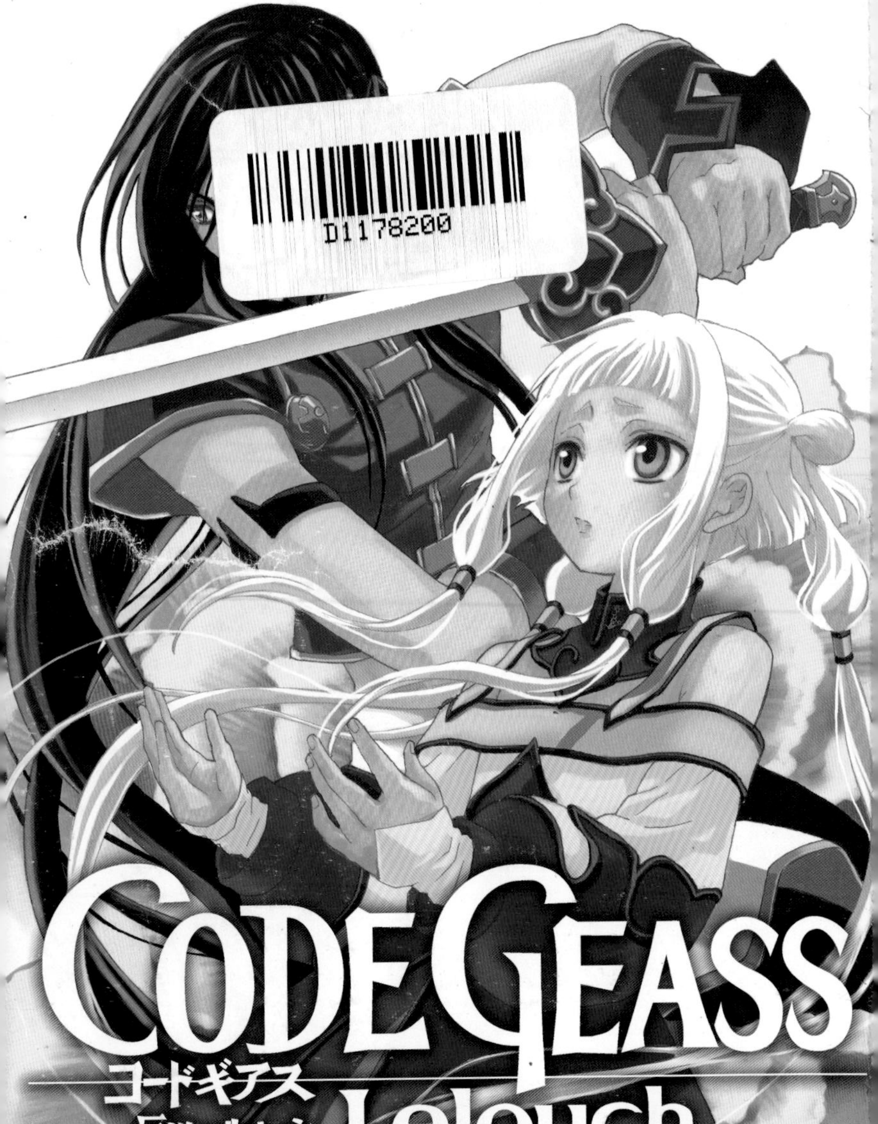

CODE GEASS
コードギアス
反逆のルルーシュ
Lelouch of the Rebellion

BY MAJIKO! ORIGINAL STORY BY ICHIROU OHKOUCHI / GORO TANIGUCHI

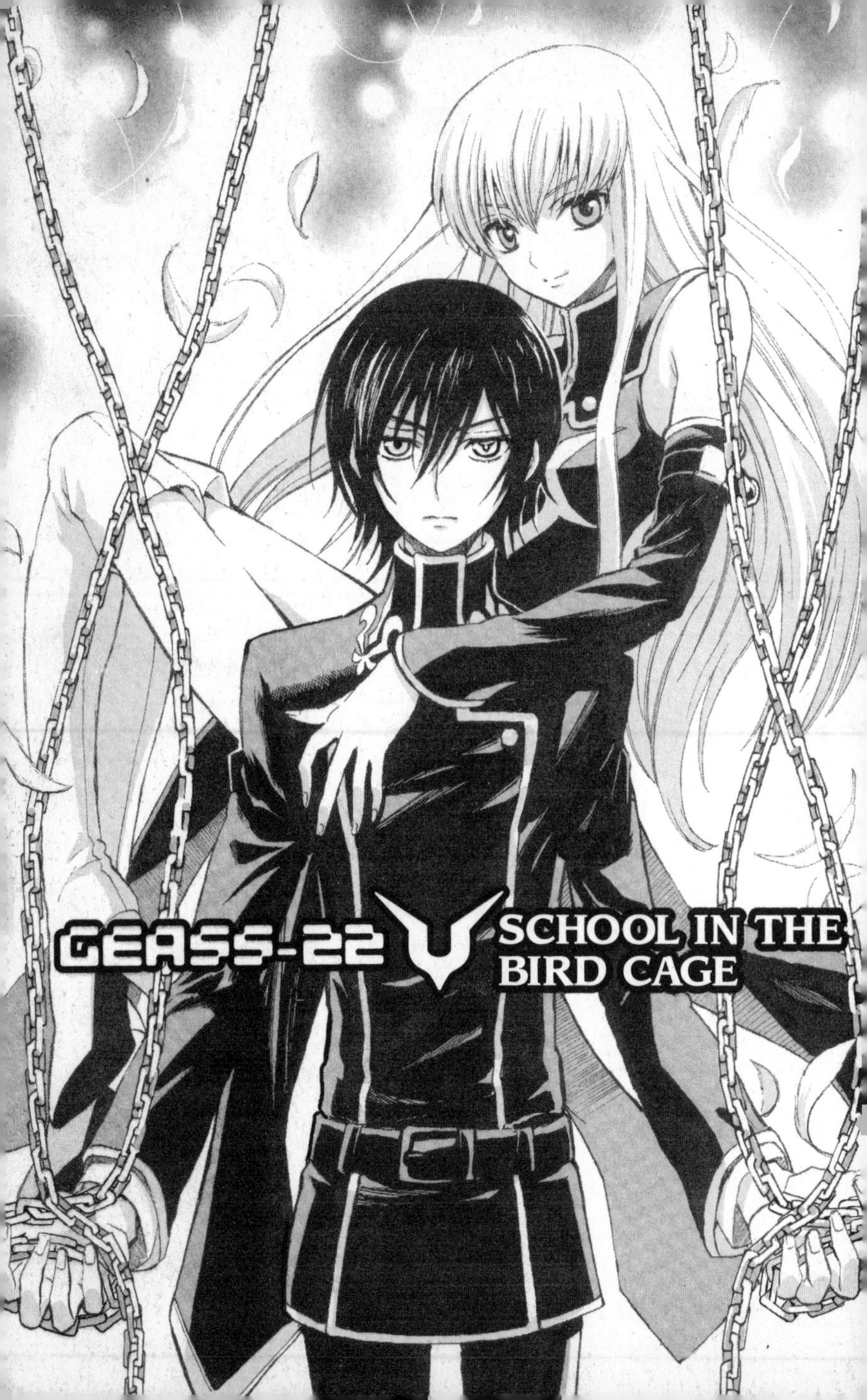
GEASS-22
SCHOOL IN THE BIRD CAGE

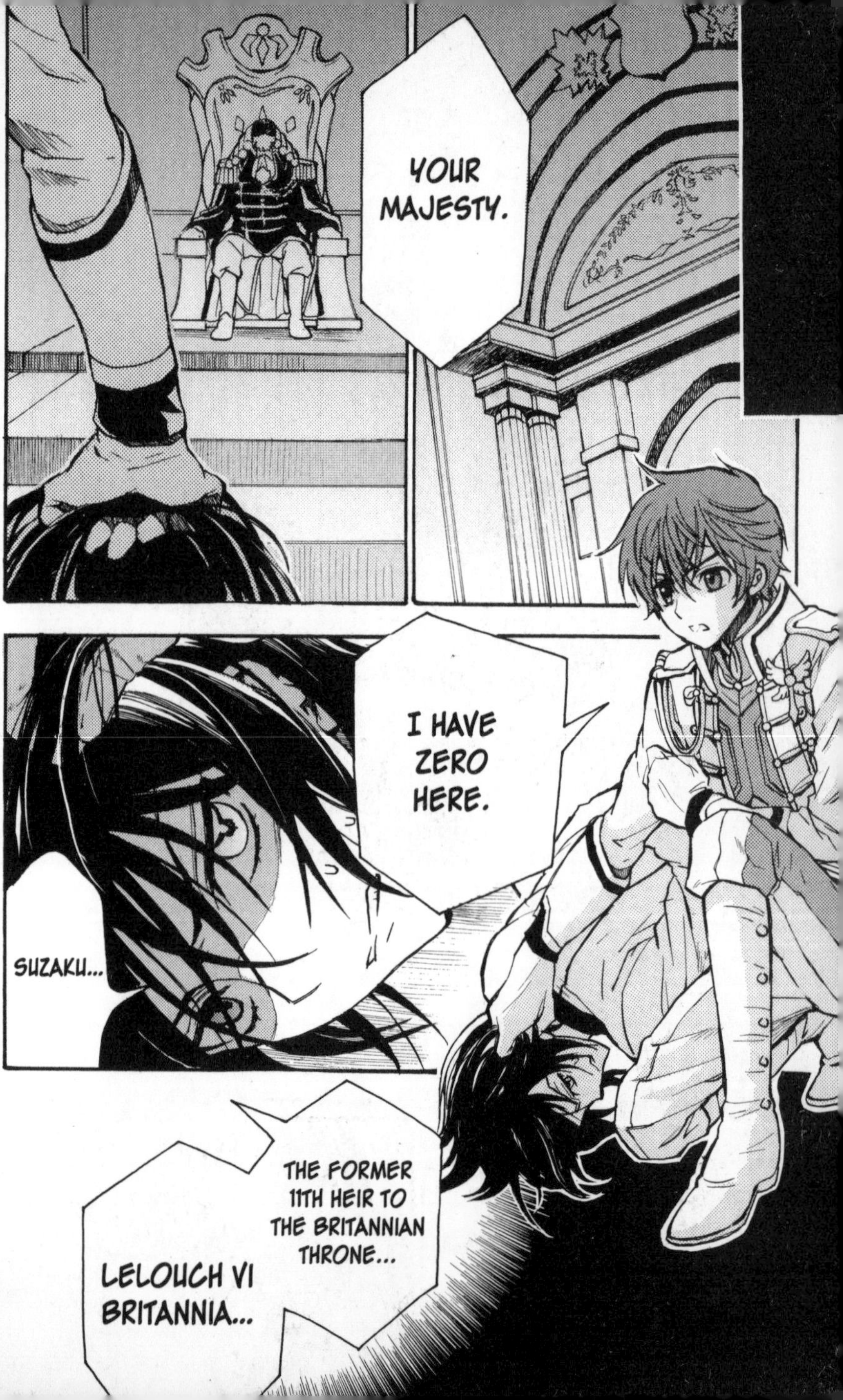
YOUR MAJESTY.
I HAVE ZERO HERE.
SUZAKU...
THE FORMER 11TH HEIR TO THE BRITANNIAN THRONE...
LELOUCH VI BRITANNIA...

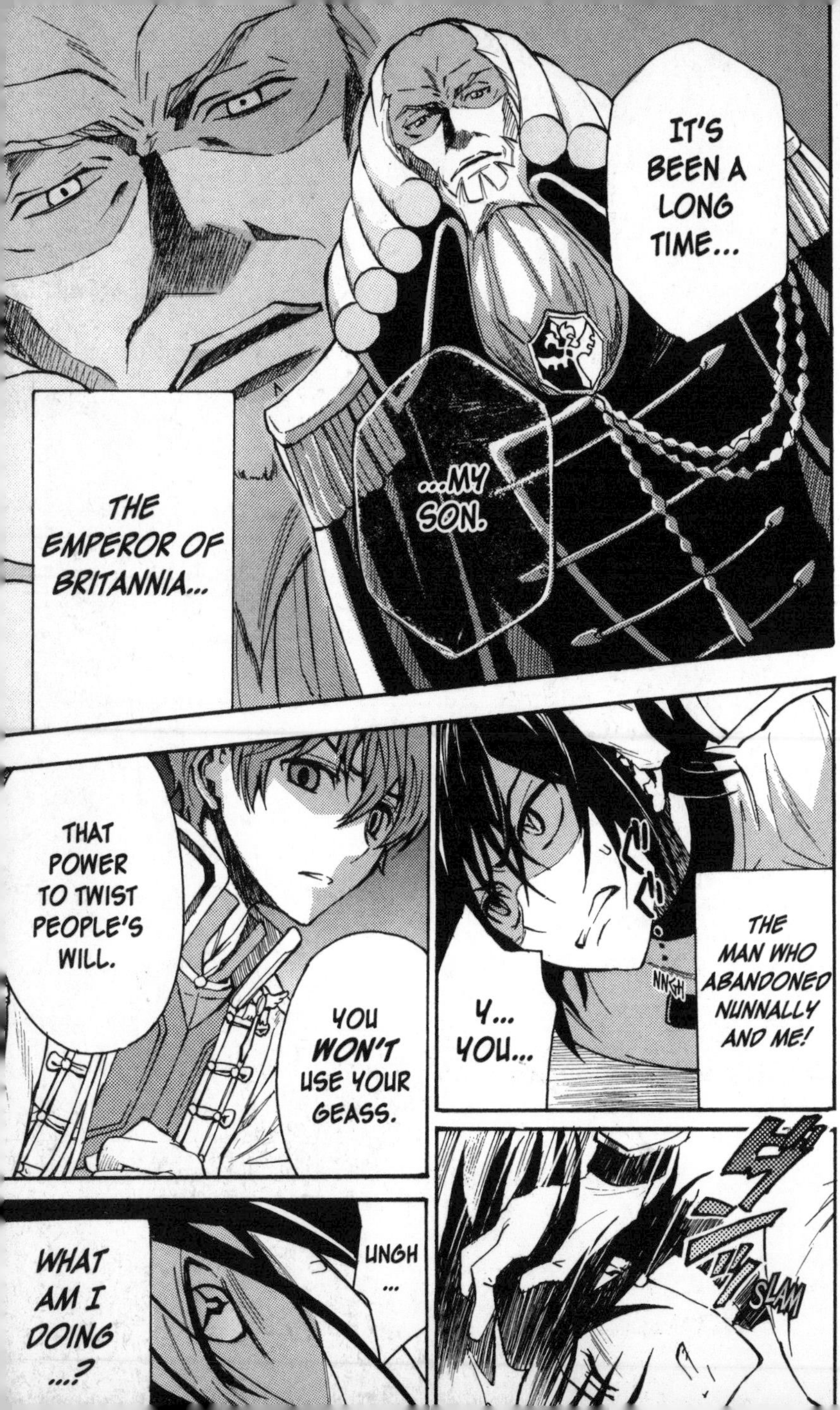
IT'S BEEN A LONG TIME...
...MY SON.
THE EMPEROR OF BRITANNIA...
THE MAN WHO ABANDONED NUNNALLY AND ME!
NNGH
Y... YOU...
THAT POWER TO TWIST PEOPLE'S WILL.
YOU *WON'T* USE YOUR GEASS.
SLAM
UNGH ...
WHAT AM I DOING ...?

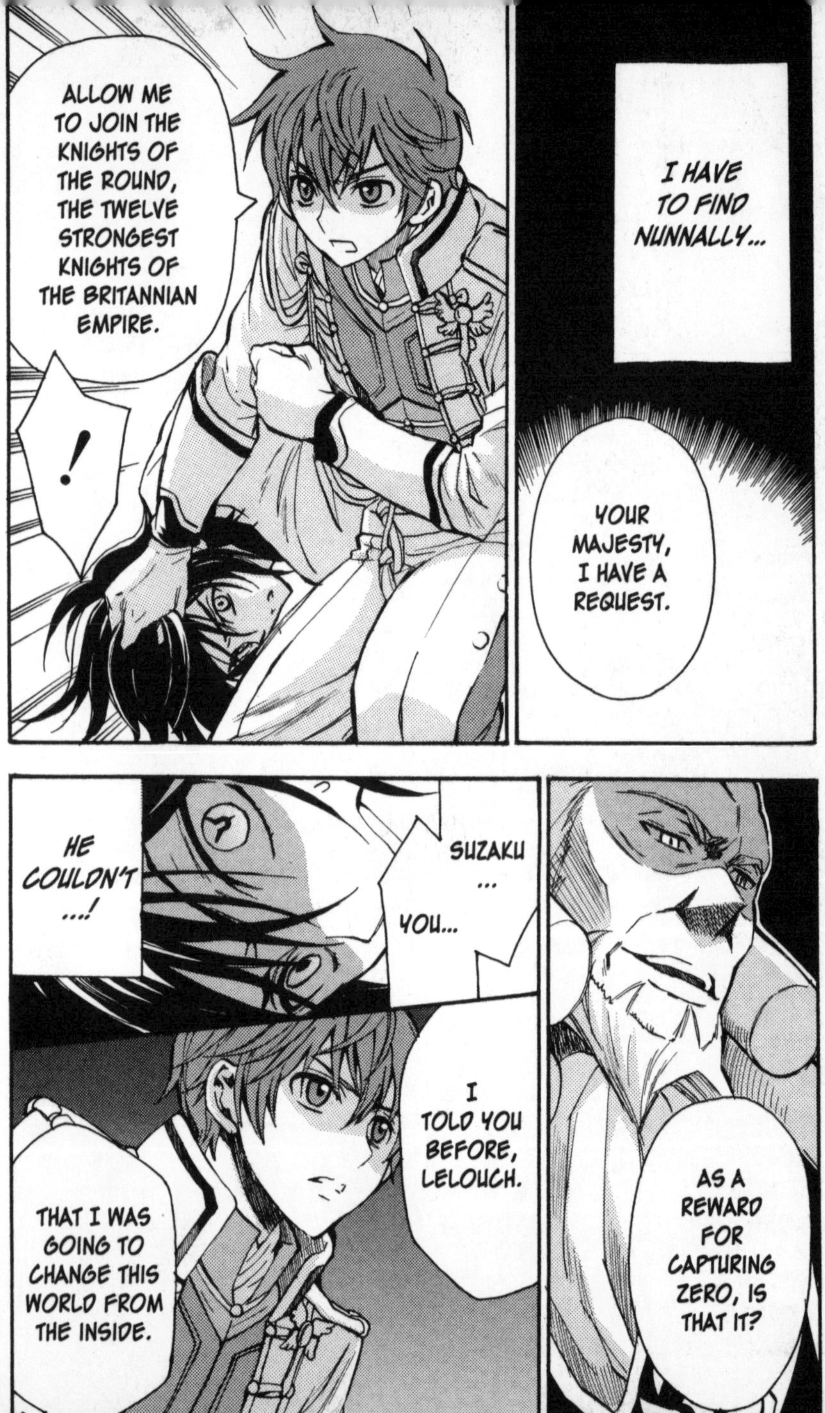
I HAVE TO FIND NUNNALLY...
YOUR MAJESTY, I HAVE A REQUEST.
ALLOW ME TO JOIN THE KNIGHTS OF THE ROUND, THE TWELVE STRONGEST KNIGHTS OF THE BRITANNIAN EMPIRE.
!
AS A REWARD FOR CAPTURING ZERO, IS THAT IT?
SUZAKU ...
YOU...
HE COULDN'T ...!
I TOLD YOU BEFORE, LELOUCH.
THAT I WAS GOING TO CHANGE THIS WORLD FROM THE INSIDE.

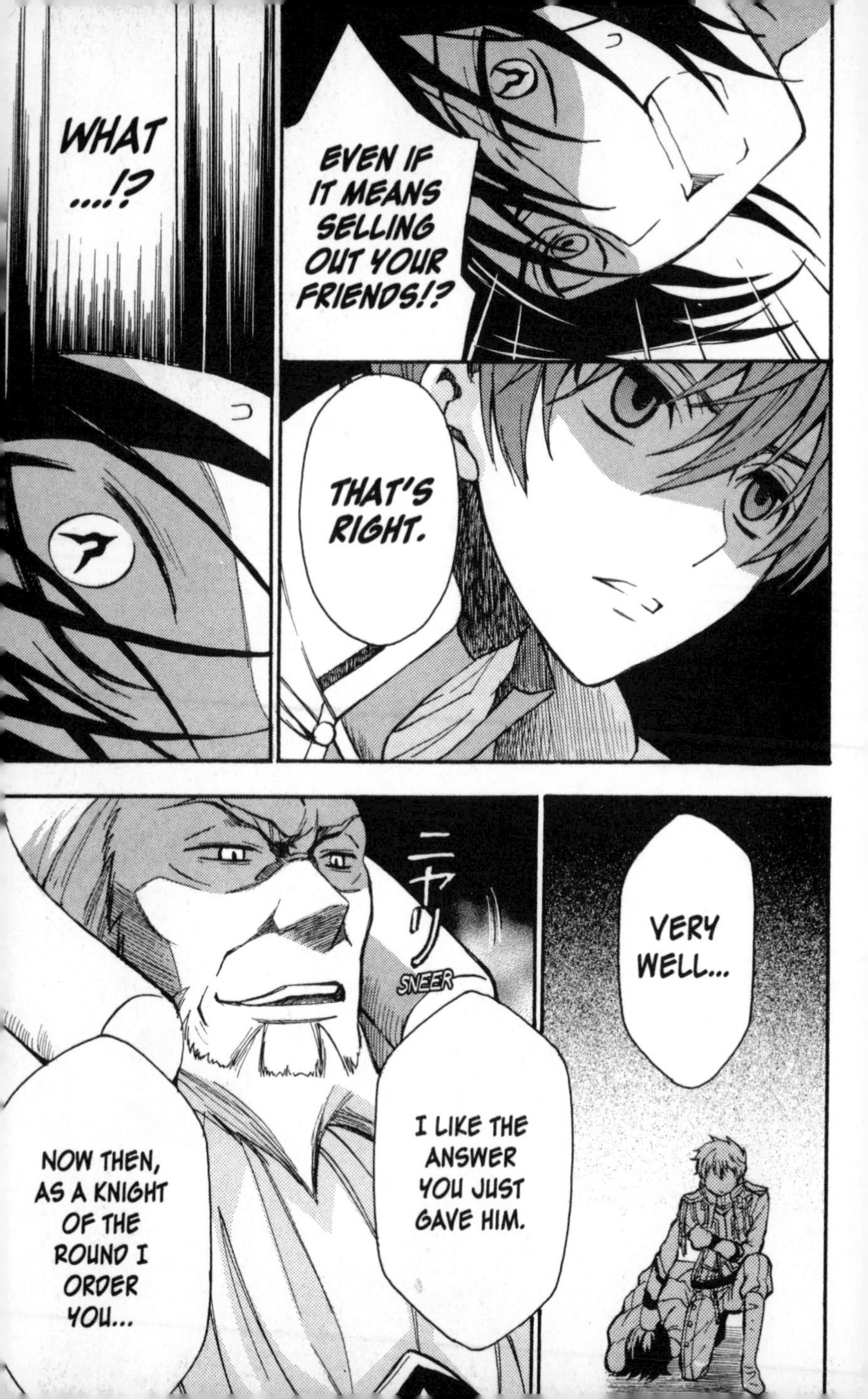
EVEN IF IT MEANS SELLING OUT YOUR FRIENDS!?
WHAT ...!?
THAT'S RIGHT.
VERY WELL...
ニヤリ
SNEER
I LIKE THE ANSWER YOU JUST GAVE HIM.
NOW THEN, AS A KNIGHT OF THE ROUND I ORDER YOU...

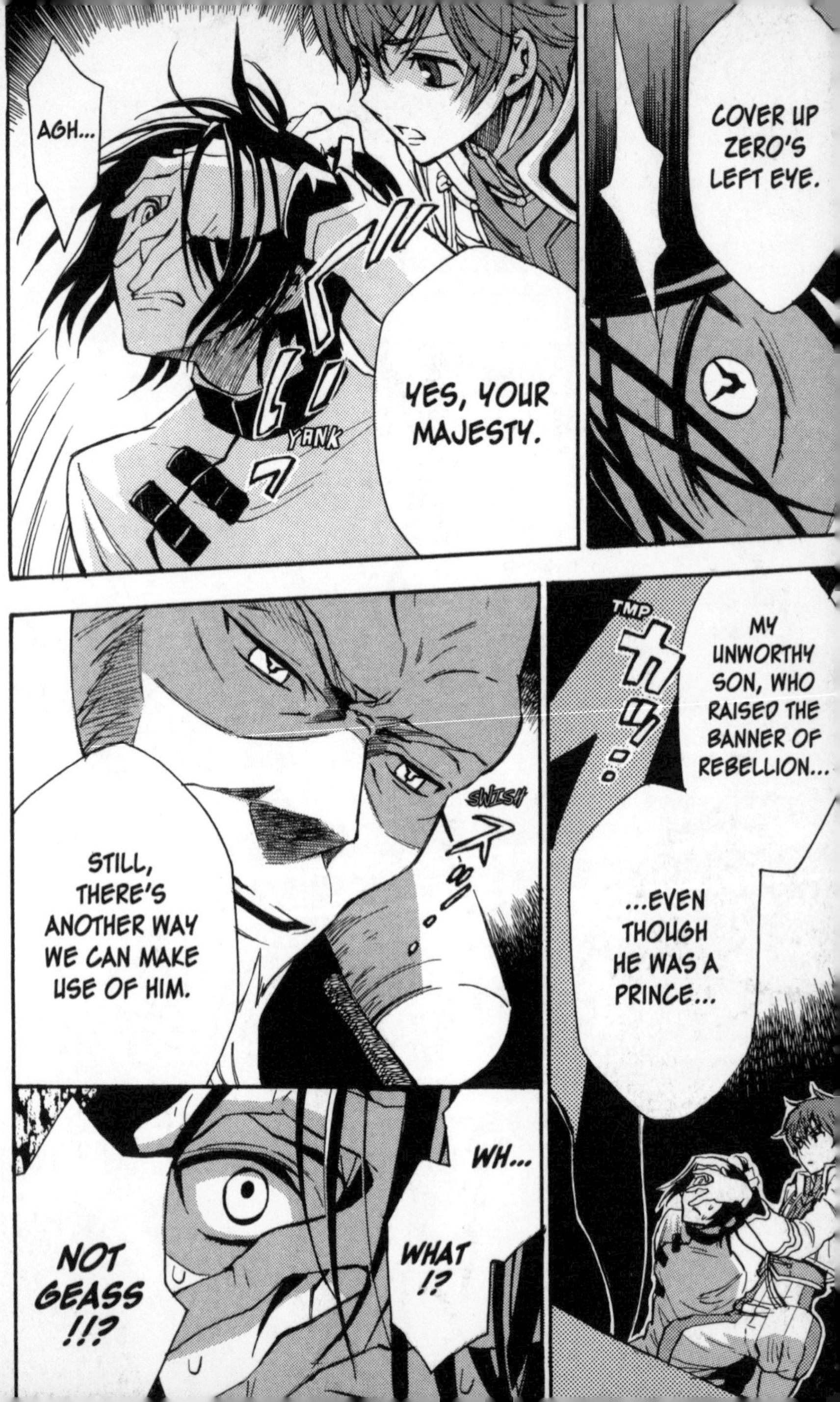
COVER UP ZERO'S LEFT EYE.
YES, YOUR MAJESTY.
YANK
AGH...
TMP
MY UNWORTHY SON, WHO RAISED THE BANNER OF REBELLION...
...EVEN THOUGH HE WAS A PRINCE...
SWISH
STILL, THERE'S ANOTHER WAY WE CAN MAKE USE OF HIM.
WH...
WHAT !?
NOT GEASS !!?

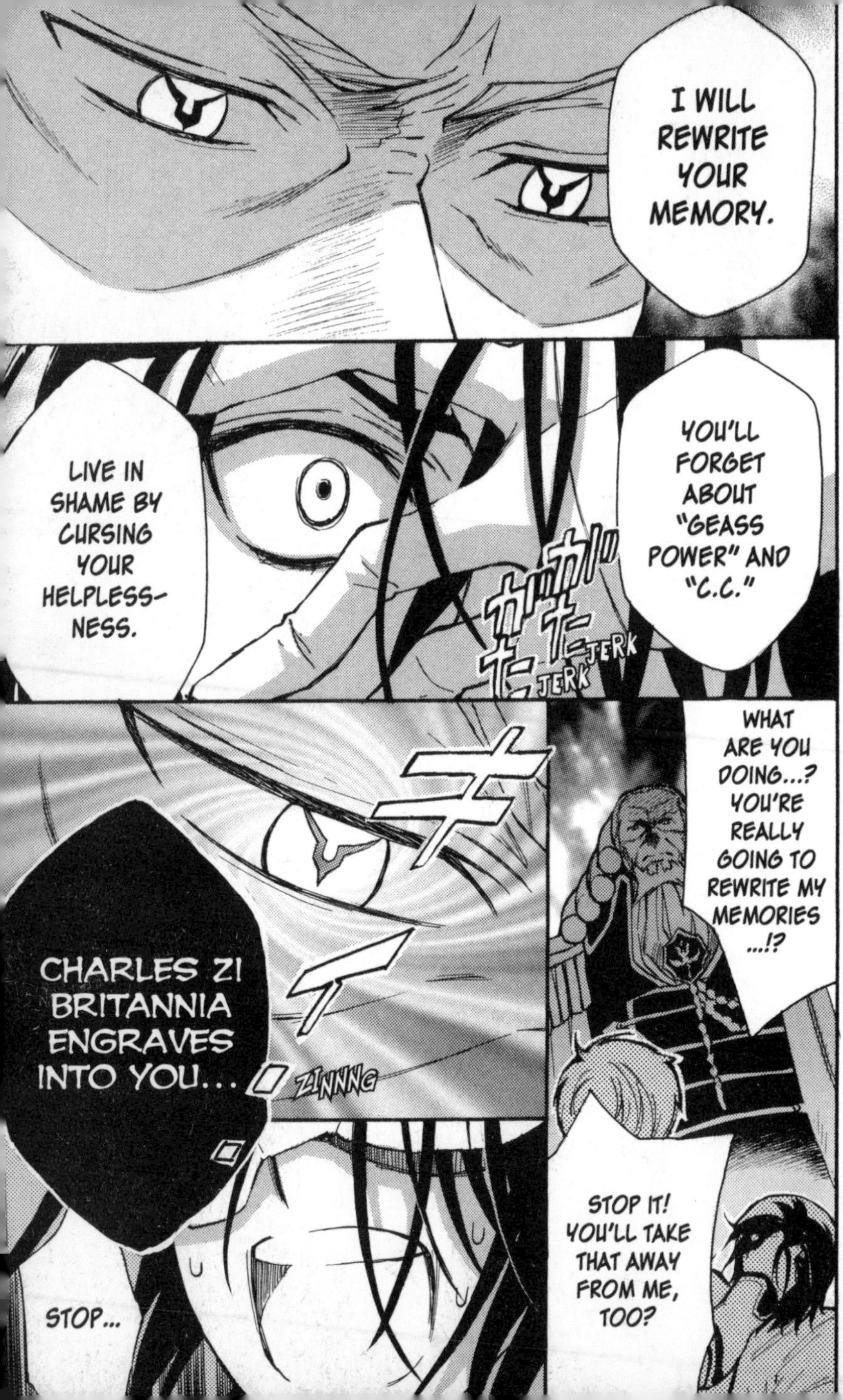
I WILL REWRITE YOUR MEMORY.
YOU'LL FORGET ABOUT "GEASS POWER" AND "C.C."
JERK JERK
LIVE IN SHAME BY CURSING YOUR HELPLESSNESS.
WHAT ARE YOU DOING...? YOU'RE REALLY GOING TO REWRITE MY MEMORIES ...!?
STOP IT! YOU'LL TAKE THAT AWAY FROM ME, TOO?
CHARLES ZI BRITANNIA ENGRAVES INTO YOU...
ZINNNG
STOP...

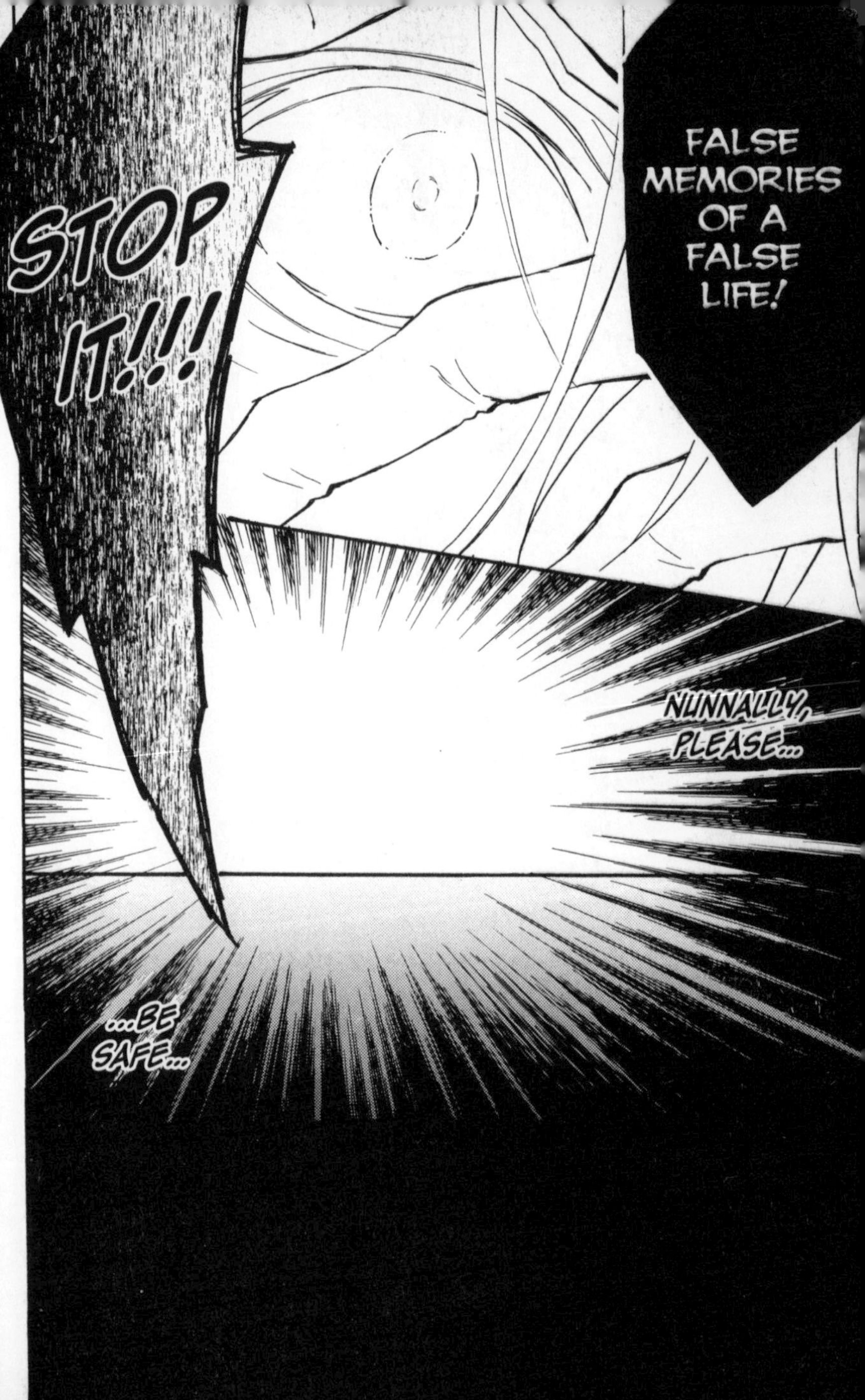
FALSE MEMORIES OF A FALSE LIFE!
STOP IT!!!
NUNNALLY, PLEASE...
...BE SAFE...

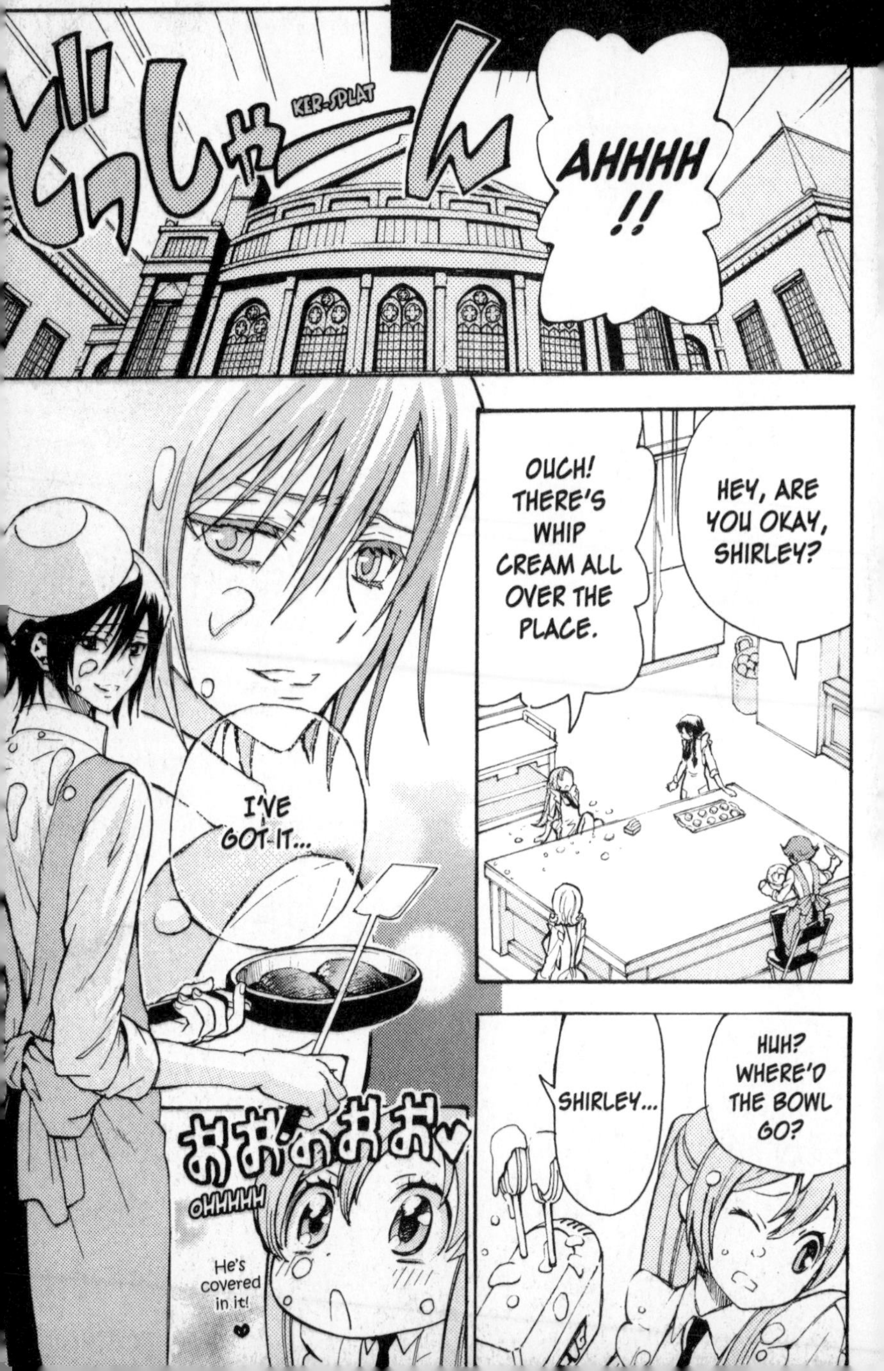
AHHHH!!
どっしゃーん
KER-SPLAT
HEY, ARE YOU OKAY, SHIRLEY?
OUCH! THERE'S WHIP CREAM ALL OVER THE PLACE.
HUH? WHERE'D THE BOWL GO?
SHIRLEY...
I'VE GOT IT...
おおのおお♥
OHHHHH
He's covered in it!

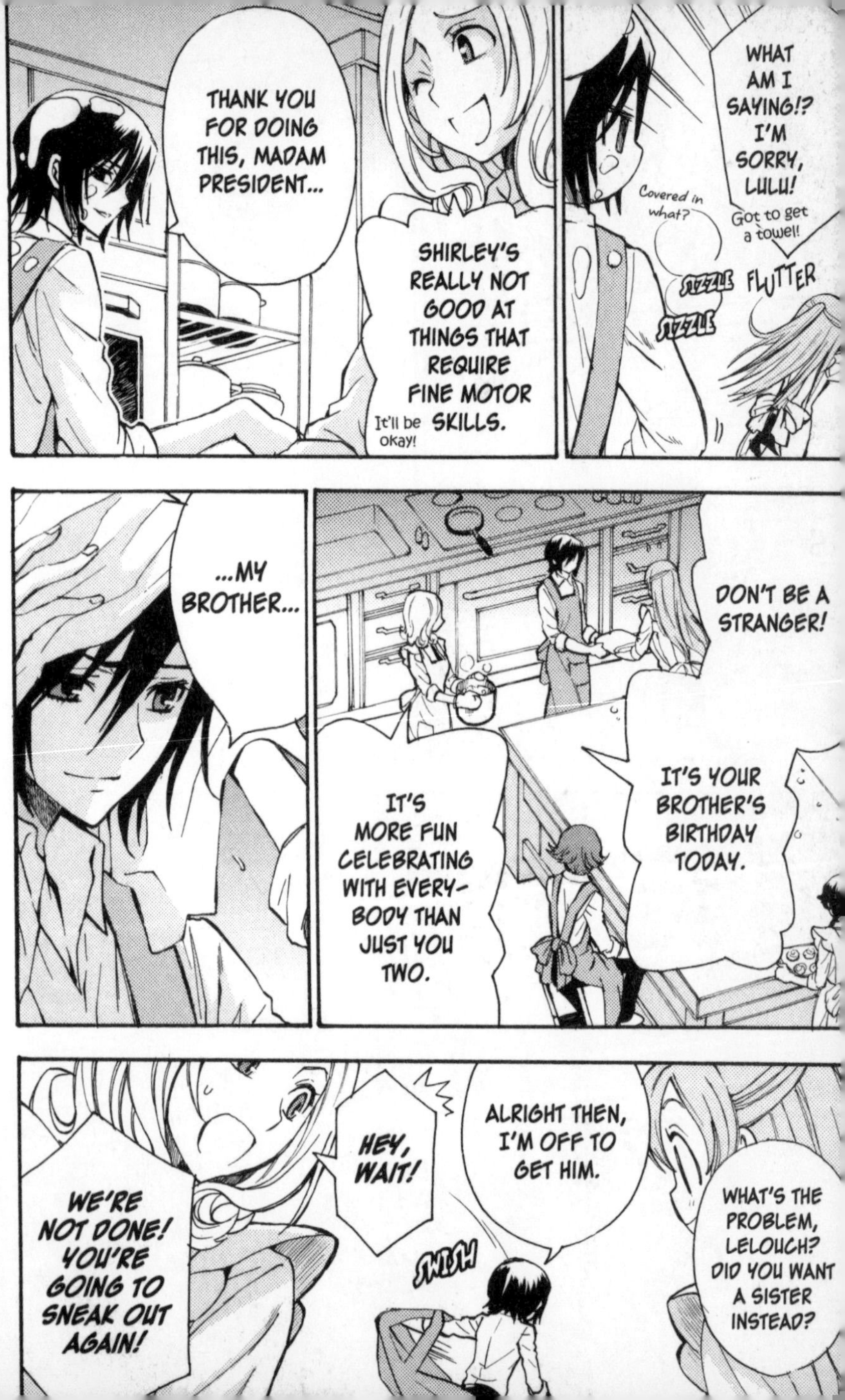
WHAT AM I SAYING!? I'M SORRY, LULU!
Got to get a towel!
Covered in what?
SIZZLE
SIZZLE
FLUTTER
SHIRLEY'S REALLY NOT GOOD AT THINGS THAT REQUIRE FINE MOTOR SKILLS.
It'll be okay!
THANK YOU FOR DOING THIS, MADAM PRESIDENT...
DON'T BE A STRANGER!
IT'S YOUR BROTHER'S BIRTHDAY TODAY.
IT'S MORE FUN CELEBRATING WITH EVERY-BODY THAN JUST YOU TWO.
...MY BROTHER...
WHAT'S THE PROBLEM, LELOUCH? DID YOU WANT A SISTER INSTEAD?
ALRIGHT THEN, I'M OFF TO GET HIM.
SWISH
HEY, WAIT!
WE'RE NOT DONE! YOU'RE GOING TO SNEAK OUT AGAIN!

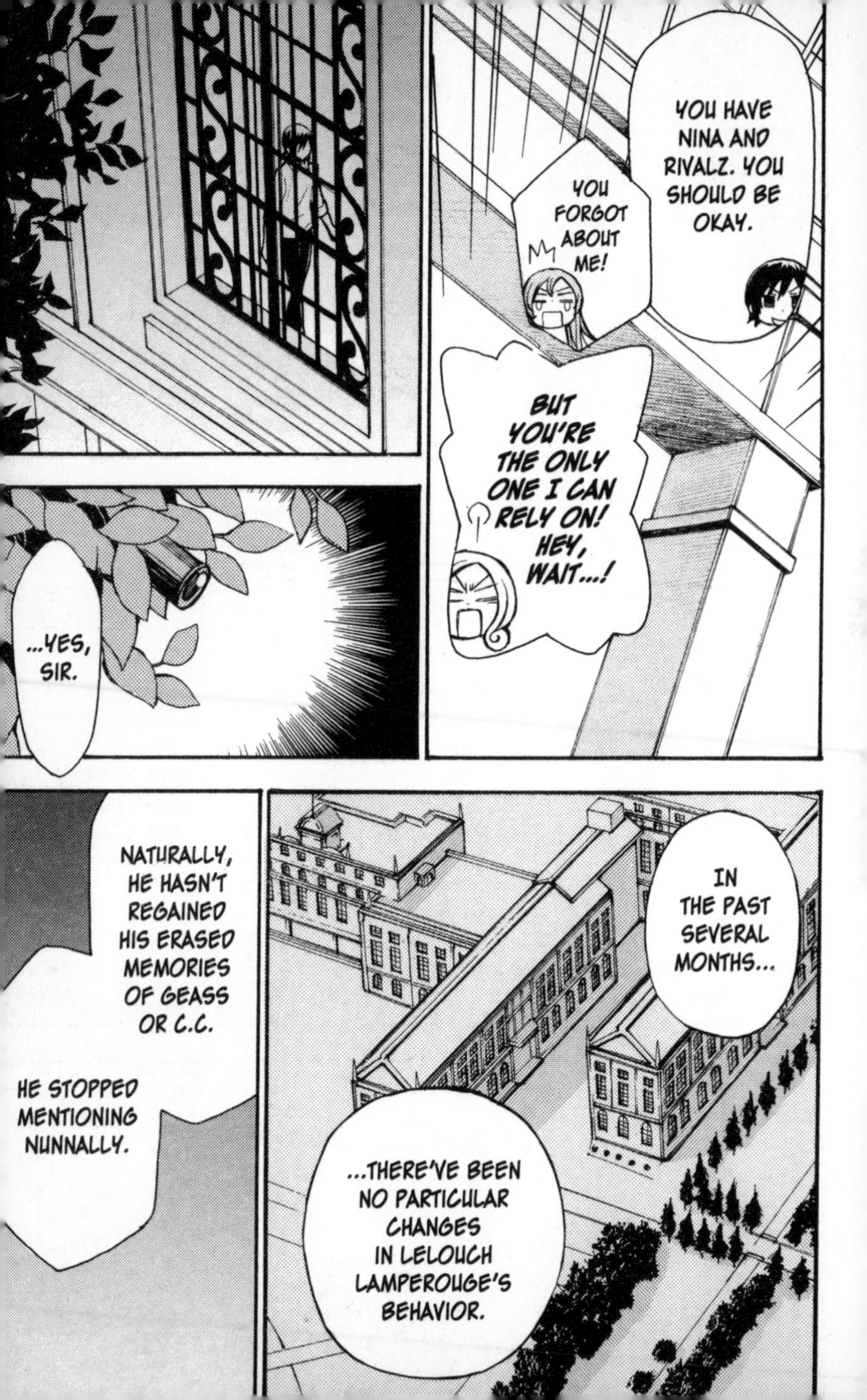
YOU HAVE NINA AND RIVALZ. YOU SHOULD BE OKAY.
YOU FORGOT ABOUT ME!
BUT YOU'RE THE ONLY ONE I CAN RELY ON! HEY, WAIT...!
...YES, SIR.
IN THE PAST SEVERAL MONTHS...
...THERE'VE BEEN NO PARTICULAR CHANGES IN LELOUCH LAMPEROUGE'S BEHAVIOR.
NATURALLY, HE HASN'T REGAINED HIS ERASED MEMORIES OF GEASS OR C.C.
HE STOPPED MENTIONING NUNNALLY.

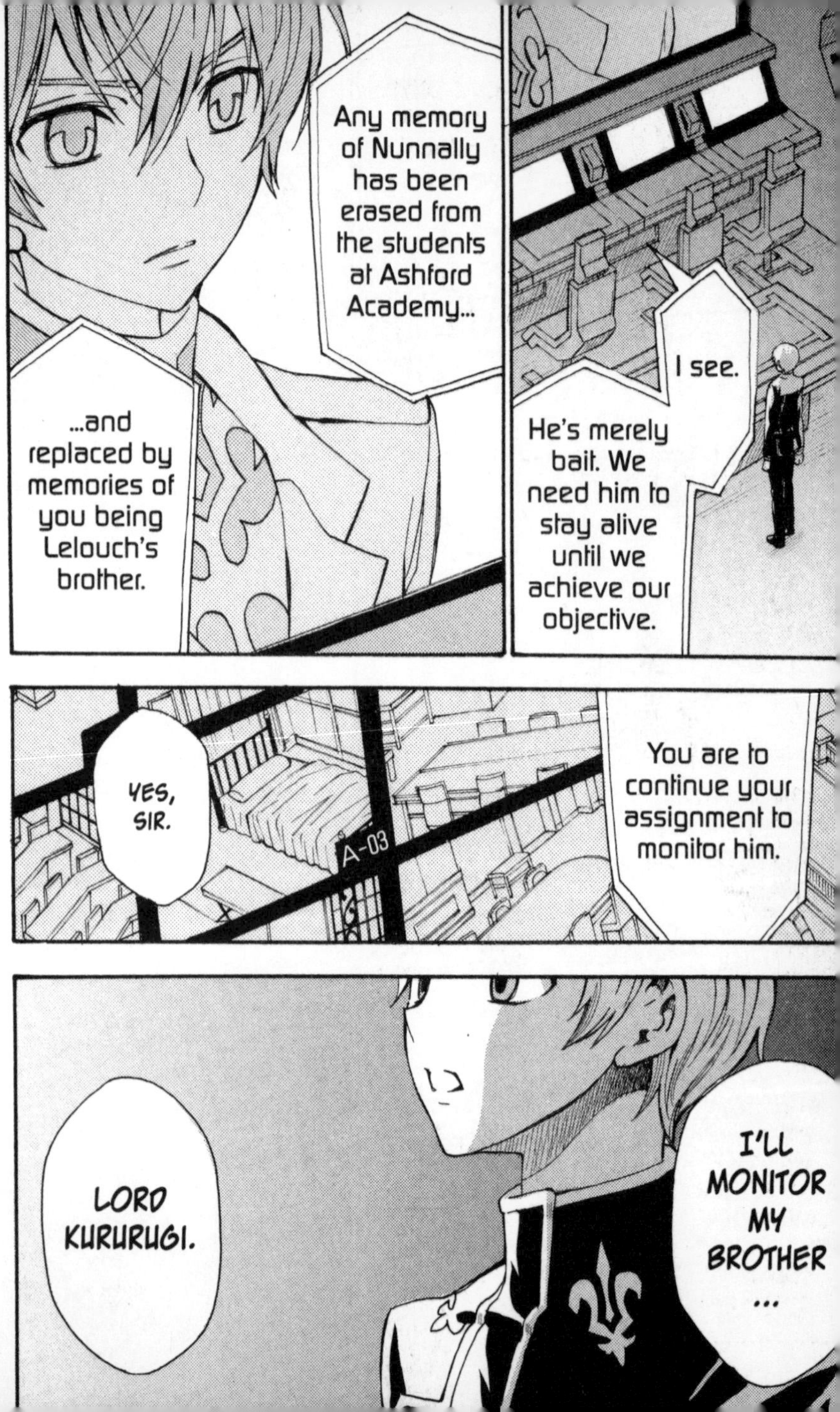
I see.
He's merely bait. We need him to stay alive until we achieve our objective.
Any memory of Nunnally has been erased from the students at Ashford Academy...
...and replaced by memories of you being Lelouch's brother.
You are to continue your assignment to monitor him.
A-03
YES, SIR.
I'LL MONITOR MY BROTHER ...
LORD KURURUGI.

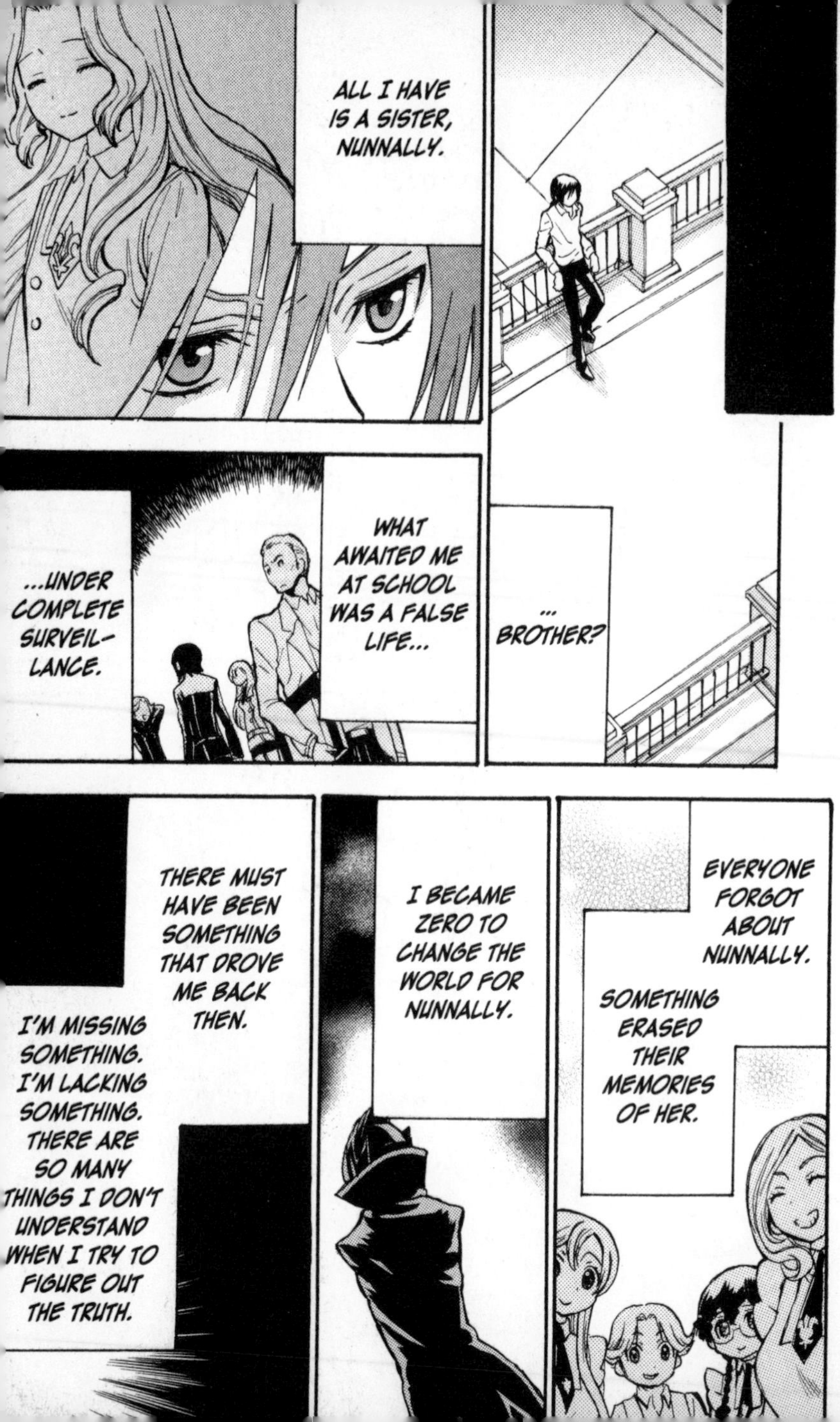
ALL I HAVE IS A SISTER, NUNNALLY.
... BROTHER?
WHAT AWAITED ME AT SCHOOL WAS A FALSE LIFE...
...UNDER COMPLETE SURVEIL-LANCE.
EVERYONE FORGOT ABOUT NUNNALLY.
SOMETHING ERASED THEIR MEMORIES OF HER.
I BECAME ZERO TO CHANGE THE WORLD FOR NUNNALLY.
THERE MUST HAVE BEEN SOMETHING THAT DROVE ME BACK THEN.
I'M MISSING SOMETHING. I'M LACKING SOMETHING. THERE ARE SO MANY THINGS I DON'T UNDERSTAND WHEN I TRY TO FIGURE OUT THE TRUTH.

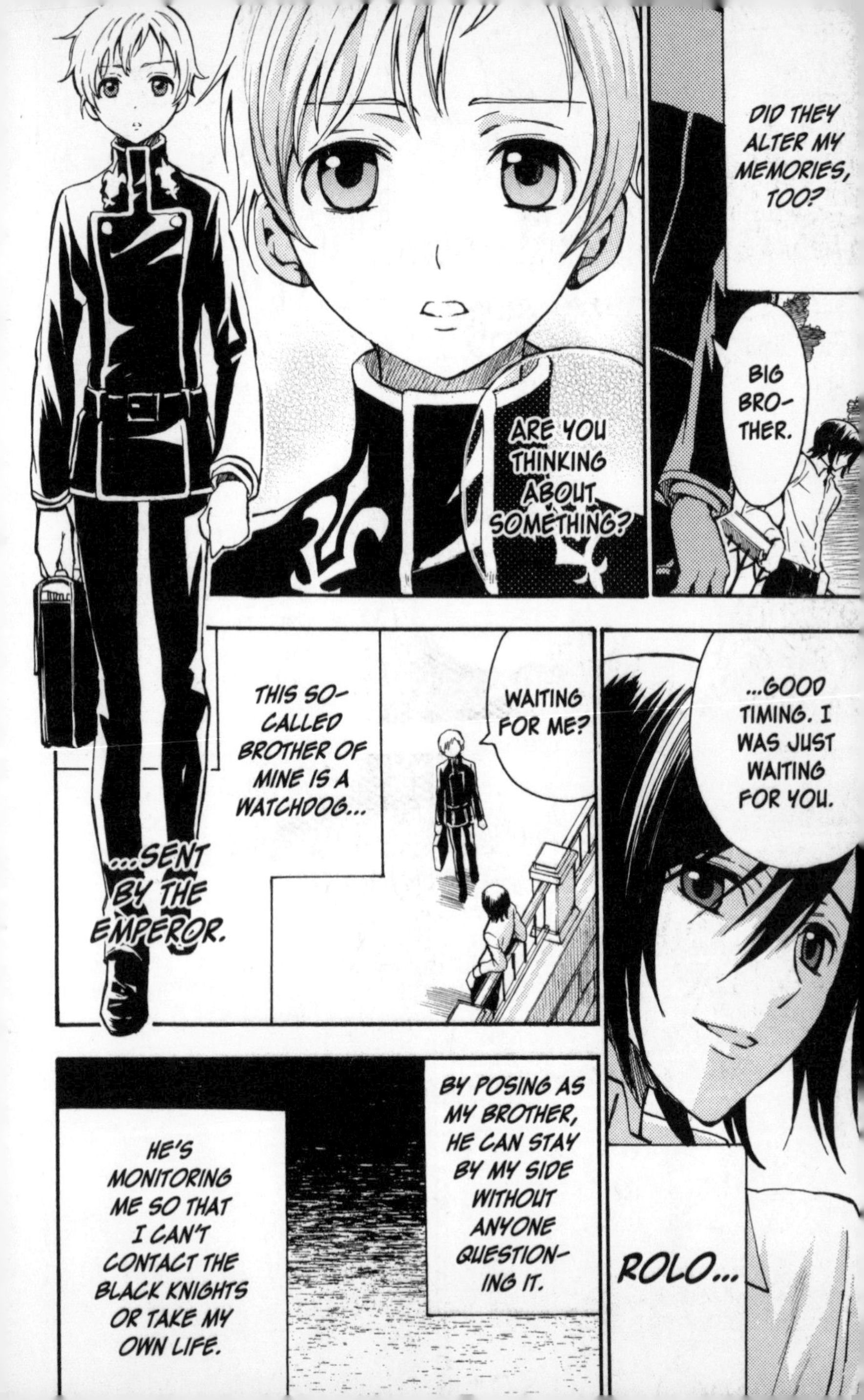
DID THEY ALTER MY MEMORIES, TOO?
BIG BROTHER.
ARE YOU THINKING ABOUT SOMETHING?
...GOOD TIMING. I WAS JUST WAITING FOR YOU.
WAITING FOR ME?
THIS SO-CALLED BROTHER OF MINE IS A WATCHDOG...
...SENT BY THE EMPEROR.
ROLO...
BY POSING AS MY BROTHER, HE CAN STAY BY MY SIDE WITHOUT ANYONE QUESTIONING IT.
HE'S MONITORING ME SO THAT I CAN'T CONTACT THE BLACK KNIGHTS OR TAKE MY OWN LIFE.

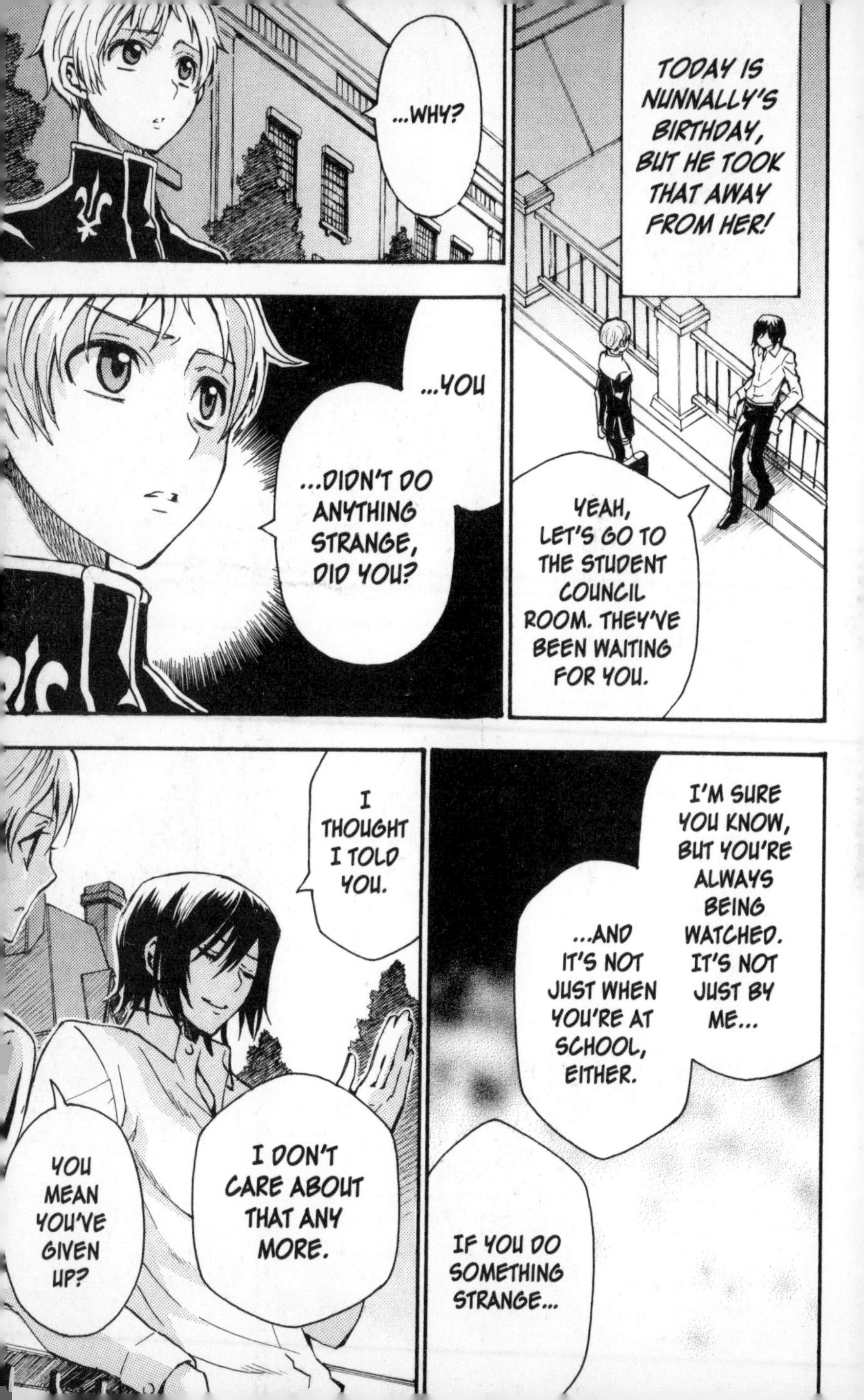
TODAY IS NUNNALLY'S BIRTHDAY, BUT HE TOOK THAT AWAY FROM HER!
YEAH, LET'S GO TO THE STUDENT COUNCIL ROOM. THEY'VE BEEN WAITING FOR YOU.
...WHY?
...YOU
...DIDN'T DO ANYTHING STRANGE, DID YOU?
I'M SURE YOU KNOW, BUT YOU'RE ALWAYS BEING WATCHED. IT'S NOT JUST BY ME...
...AND IT'S NOT JUST WHEN YOU'RE AT SCHOOL, EITHER.
IF YOU DO SOMETHING STRANGE...
I THOUGHT I TOLD YOU.
I DON'T CARE ABOUT THAT ANY MORE.
YOU MEAN YOU'VE GIVEN UP?

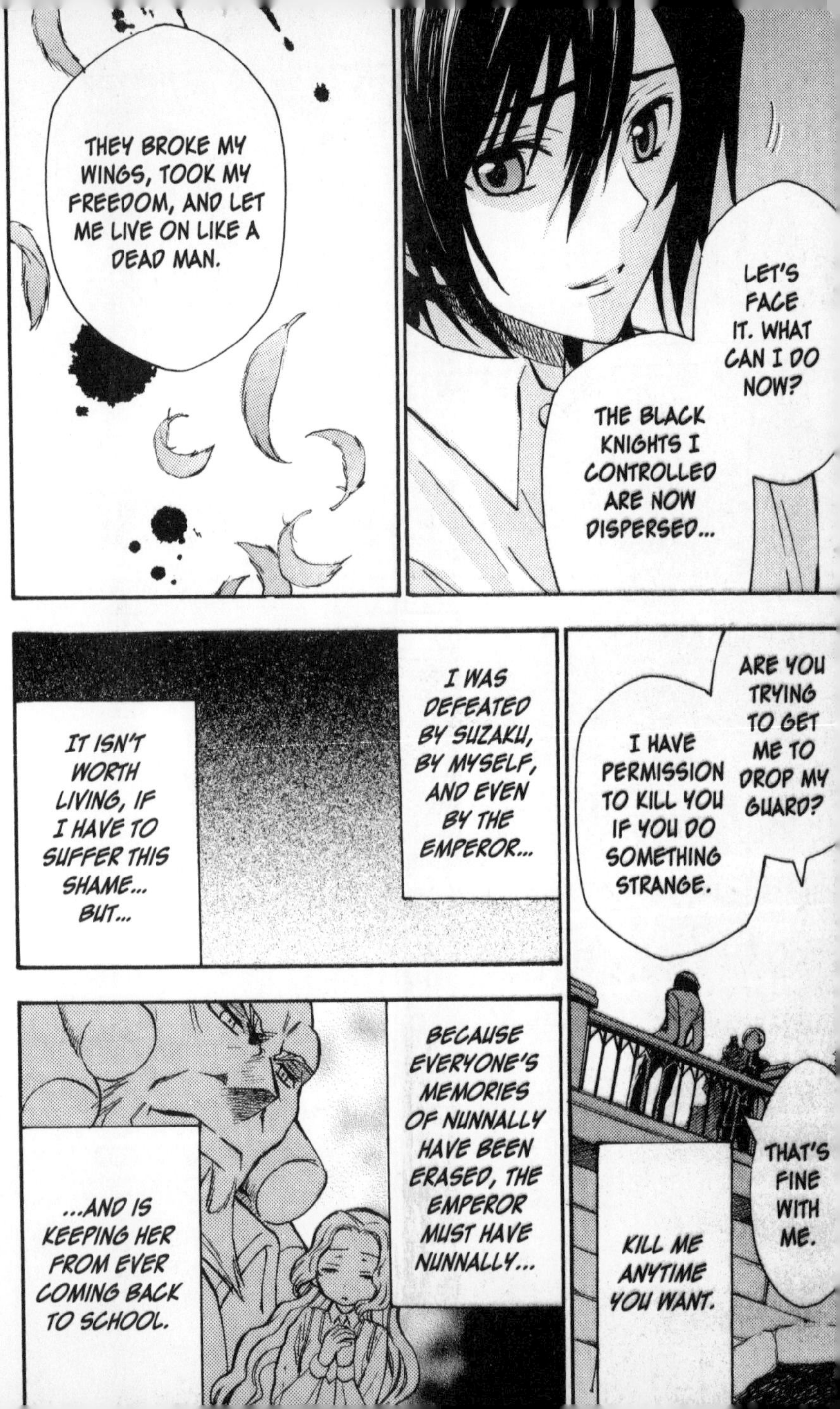
LET'S FACE IT. WHAT CAN I DO NOW?
THE BLACK KNIGHTS I CONTROLLED ARE NOW DISPERSED...
THEY BROKE MY WINGS, TOOK MY FREEDOM, AND LET ME LIVE ON LIKE A DEAD MAN.
ARE YOU TRYING TO GET ME TO DROP MY GUARD?
I HAVE PERMISSION TO KILL YOU IF YOU DO SOMETHING STRANGE.
THAT'S FINE WITH ME.
KILL ME ANYTIME YOU WANT.
I WAS DEFEATED BY SUZAKU, BY MYSELF, AND EVEN BY THE EMPEROR...
IT ISN'T WORTH LIVING, IF I HAVE TO SUFFER THIS SHAME... BUT...
BECAUSE EVERYONE'S MEMORIES OF NUNNALLY HAVE BEEN ERASED, THE EMPEROR MUST HAVE NUNNALLY...
...AND IS KEEPING HER FROM EVER COMING BACK TO SCHOOL.

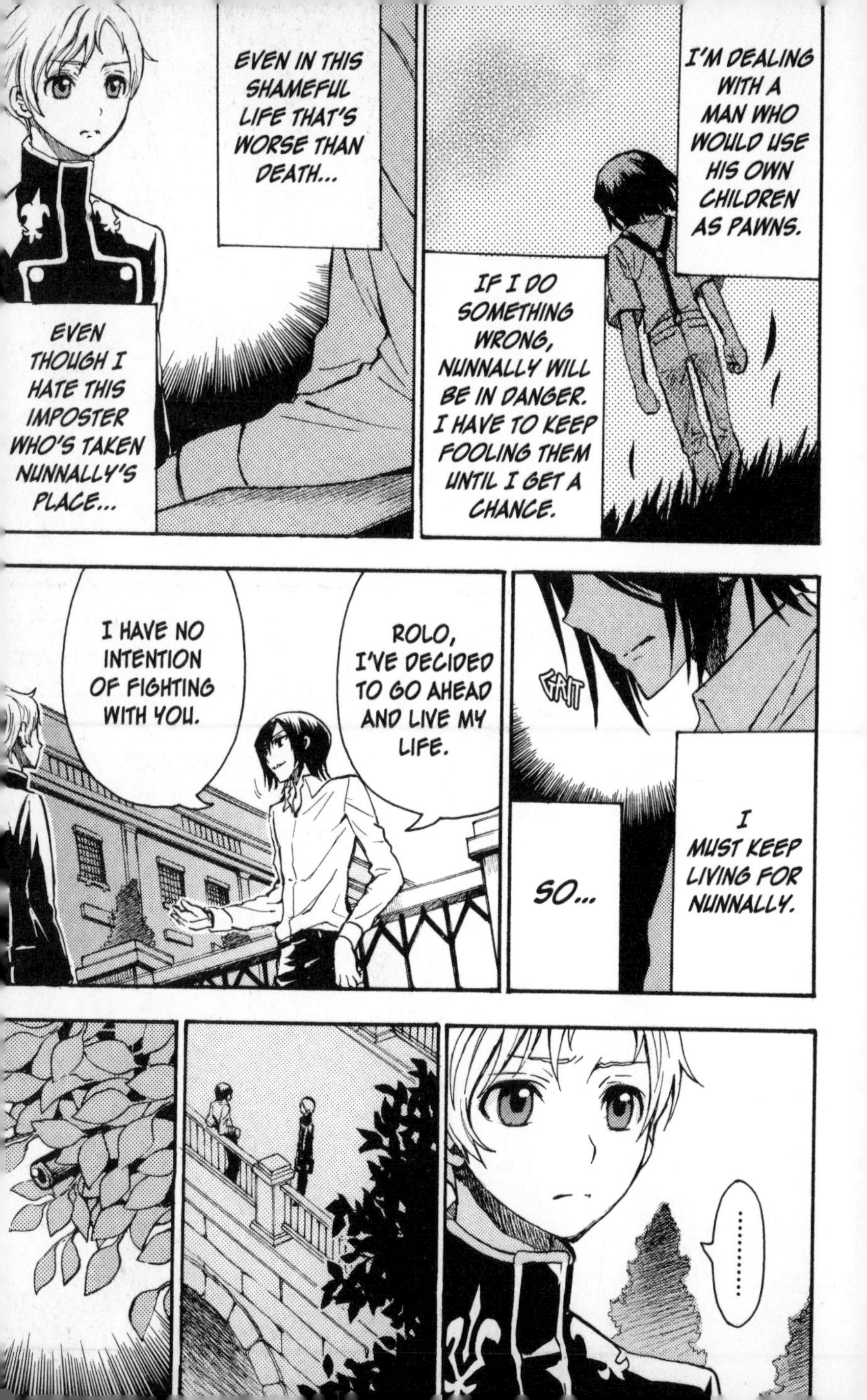
I'M DEALING WITH A MAN WHO WOULD USE HIS OWN CHILDREN AS PAWNS.
IF I DO SOMETHING WRONG, NUNNALLY WILL BE IN DANGER. I HAVE TO KEEP FOOLING THEM UNTIL I GET A CHANCE.
EVEN IN THIS SHAMEFUL LIFE THAT'S WORSE THAN DEATH...
EVEN THOUGH I HATE THIS IMPOSTER WHO'S TAKEN NUNNALLY'S PLACE...
GRIT
I MUST KEEP LIVING FOR NUNNALLY.
SO...
ROLO, I'VE DECIDED TO GO AHEAD AND LIVE MY LIFE.
I HAVE NO INTENTION OF FIGHTING WITH YOU.
....

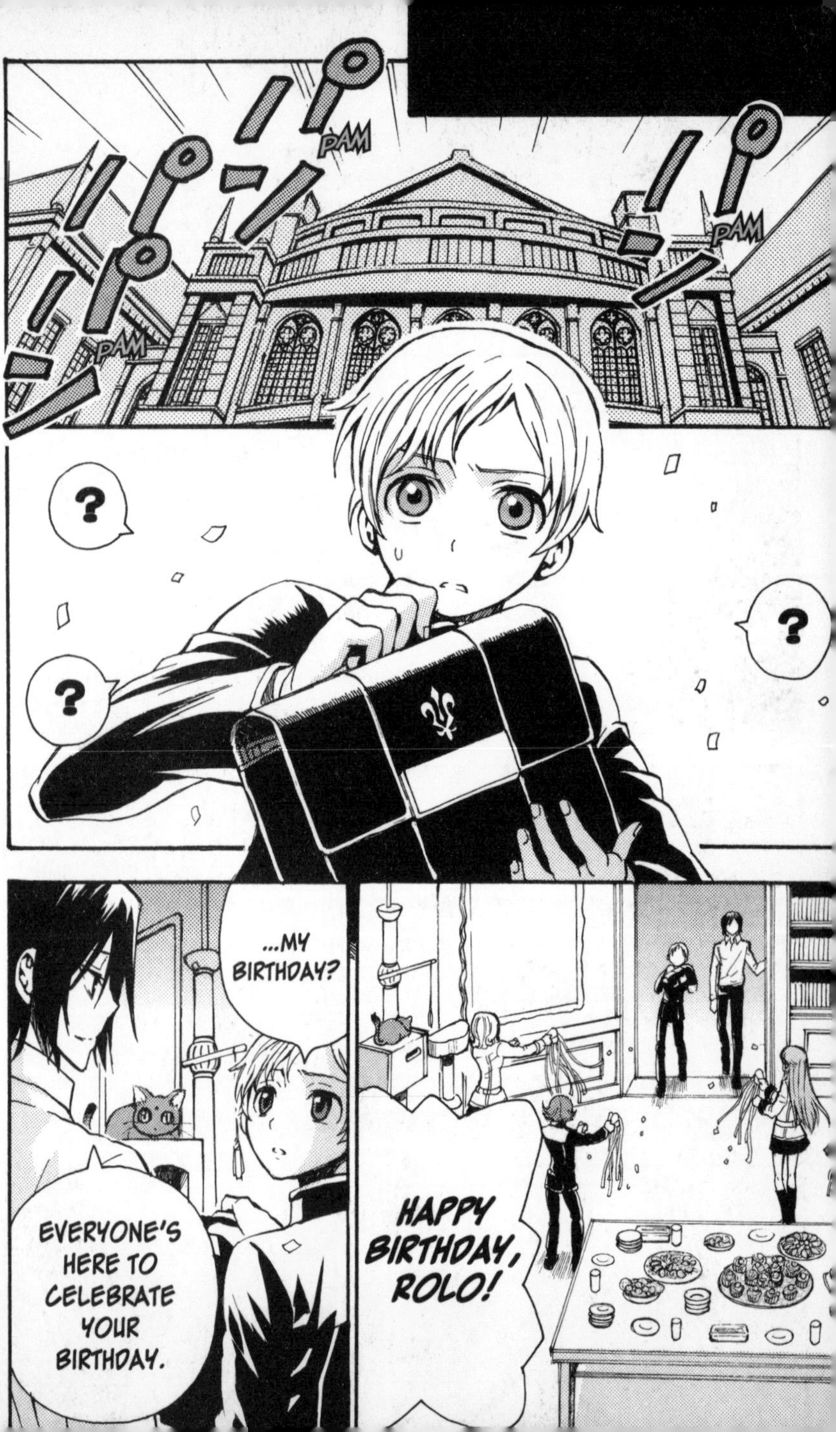
PAM
PAM
PAM
?
?
?
HAPPY BIRTHDAY, ROLO!
...MY BIRTHDAY?
EVERYONE'S HERE TO CELEBRATE YOUR BIRTHDAY.

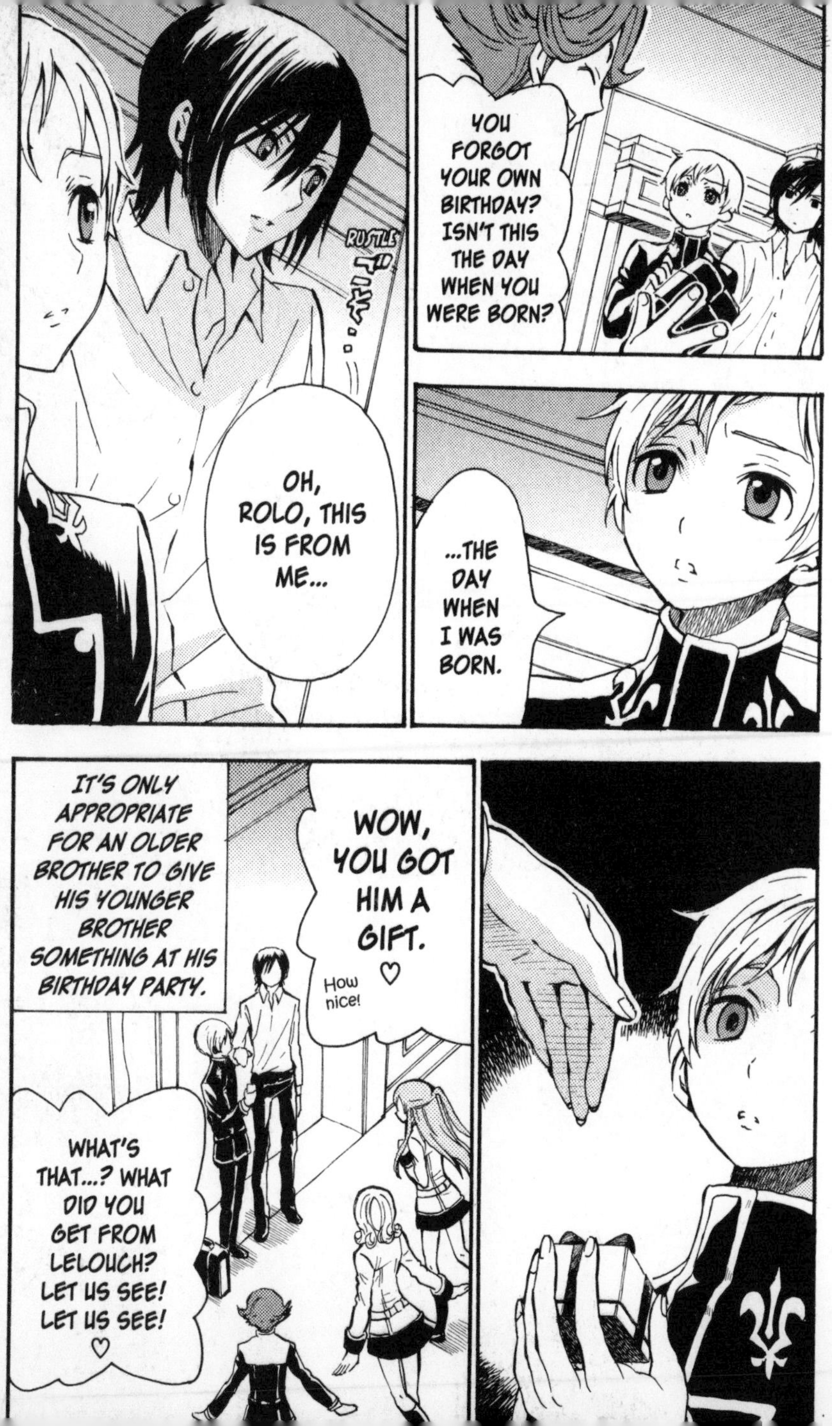
YOU FORGOT YOUR OWN BIRTHDAY? ISN'T THIS THE DAY WHEN YOU WERE BORN?
...THE DAY WHEN I WAS BORN.
RUSTLE
OH, ROLO, THIS IS FROM ME...
WOW, YOU GOT HIM A GIFT. ♡
How nice!
IT'S ONLY APPROPRIATE FOR AN OLDER BROTHER TO GIVE HIS YOUNGER BROTHER SOMETHING AT HIS BIRTHDAY PARTY.
WHAT'S THAT...? WHAT DID YOU GET FROM LELOUCH? LET US SEE! LET US SEE! ♡

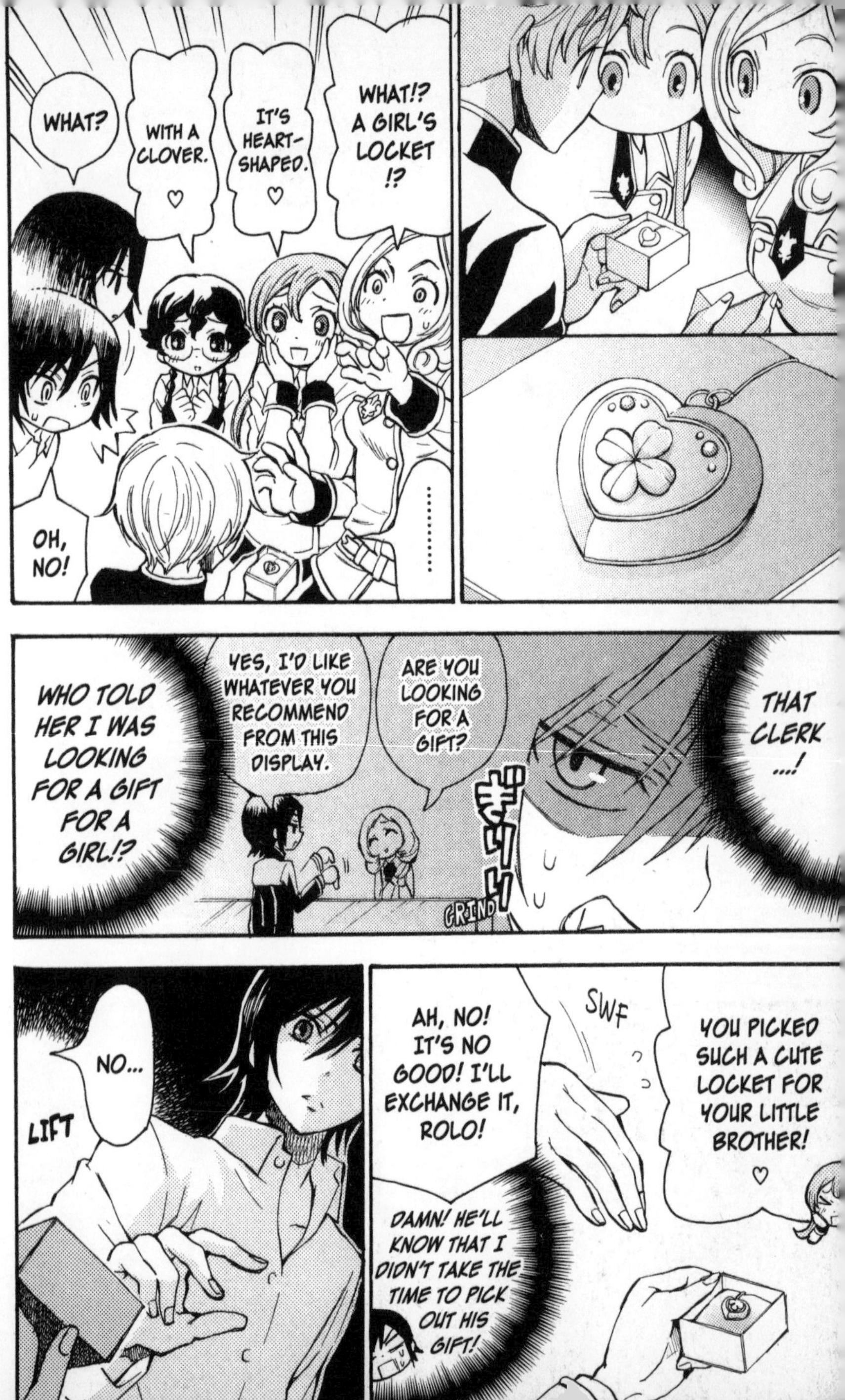
WHAT!? A GIRL'S LOCKET !?
IT'S HEART-SHAPED. ♡
WITH A CLOVER. ♡
WHAT?
OH, NO!
......
THAT CLERK ...!
GRIND
ARE YOU LOOKING FOR A GIFT?
YES, I'D LIKE WHATEVER YOU RECOMMEND FROM THIS DISPLAY.
WHO TOLD HER I WAS LOOKING FOR A GIFT FOR A GIRL!?
YOU PICKED SUCH A CUTE LOCKET FOR YOUR LITTLE BROTHER! ♡
SWF
AH, NO! IT'S NO GOOD! I'LL EXCHANGE IT, ROLO!
DAMN! HE'LL KNOW THAT I DIDN'T TAKE THE TIME TO PICK OUT HIS GIFT!
NO...
LIFT

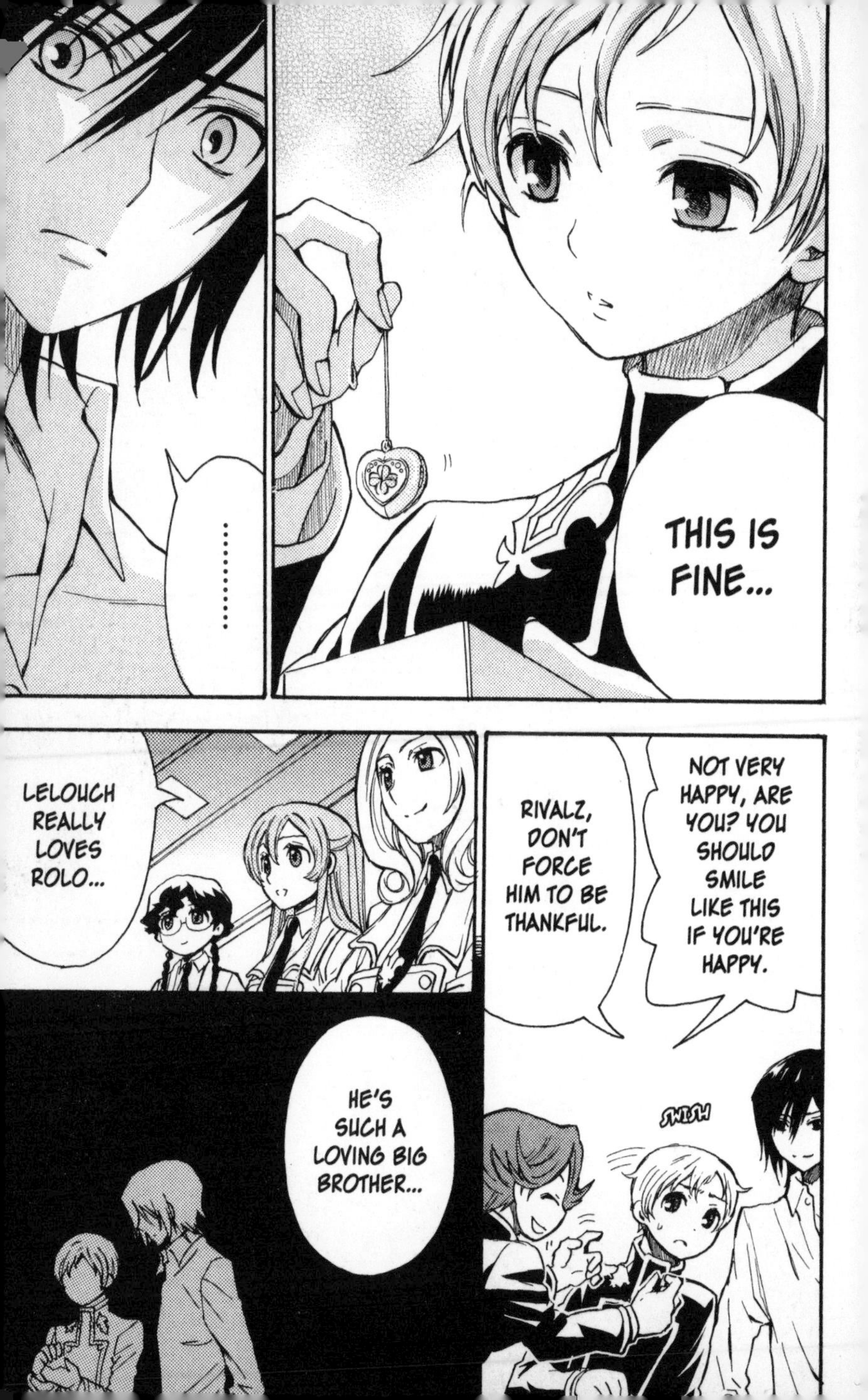
THIS IS FINE...
....
NOT VERY HAPPY, ARE YOU? YOU SHOULD SMILE LIKE THIS IF YOU'RE HAPPY.
RIVALZ, DON'T FORCE HIM TO BE THANKFUL.
SWISH
LELOUCH REALLY LOVES ROLO...
HE'S SUCH A LOVING BIG BROTHER...

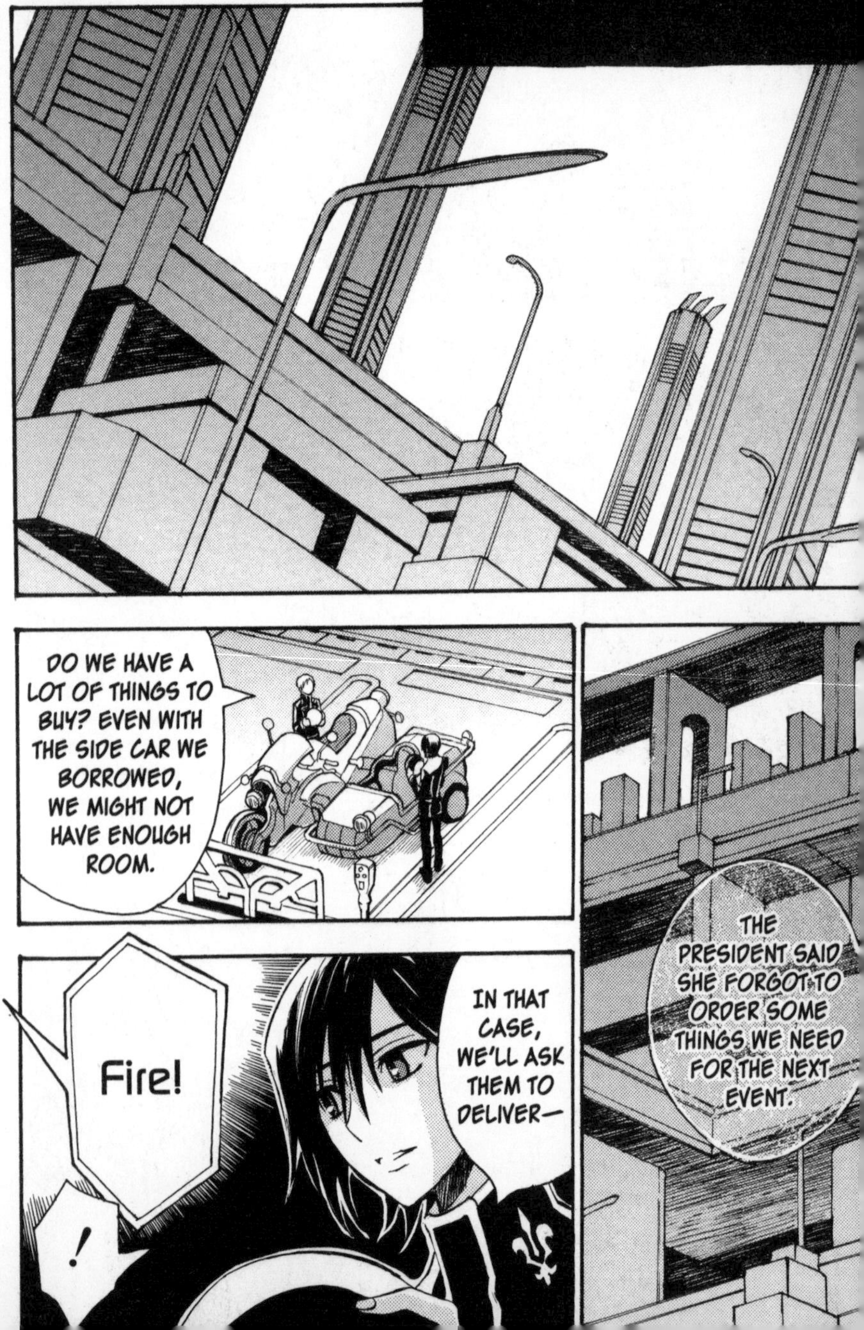
THE PRESIDENT SAID SHE FORGOT TO ORDER SOME THINGS WE NEED FOR THE NEXT EVENT.
DO WE HAVE A LOT OF THINGS TO BUY? EVEN WITH THE SIDE CAR WE BORROWED, WE MIGHT NOT HAVE ENOUGH ROOM.
IN THAT CASE, WE'LL ASK THEM TO DELIVER—
Fire!
!

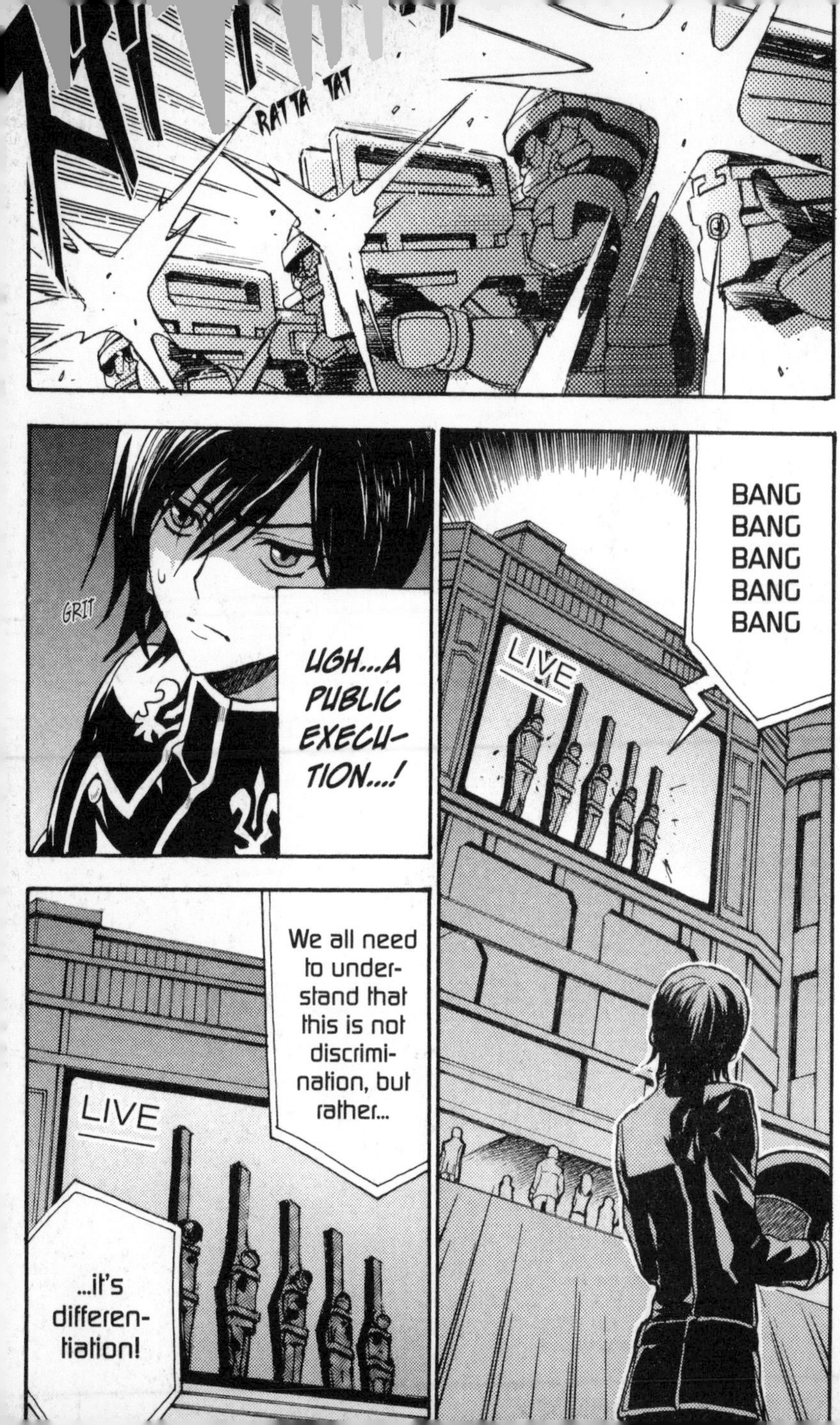
RATTA TAT
BANG BANG BANG BANG BANG
LIVE
GRIT
UGH...A PUBLIC EXECUTION...!
LIVE
We all need to understand that this is not discrimination, but rather...
...it's differentiation!

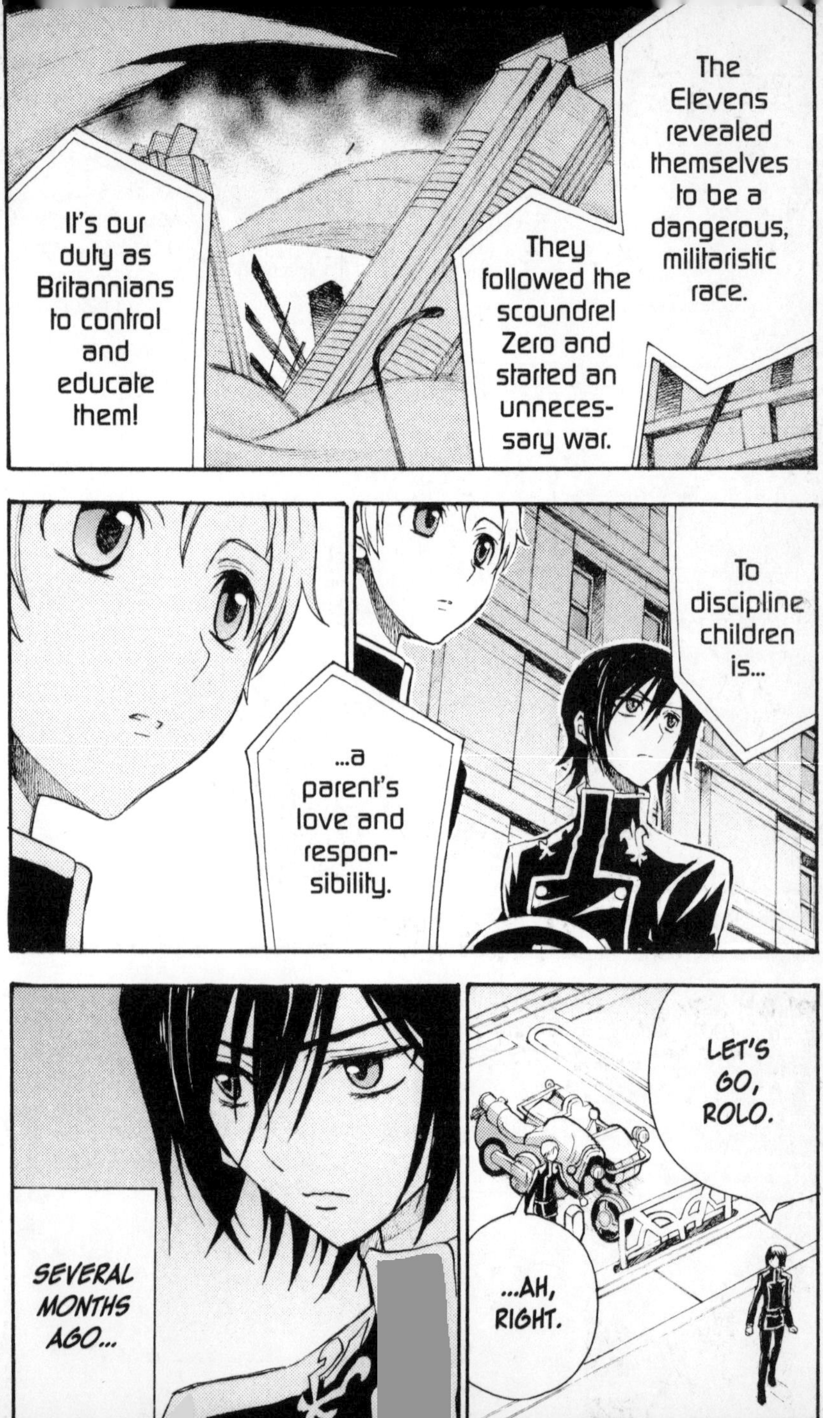
The Elevens revealed themselves to be a dangerous, militaristic race.
They followed the scoundrel Zero and started an unneces-sary war.
It's our duty as Britannians to control and educate them!
To discipline children is...
...a parent's love and respon-sibility.
LET'S GO, ROLO.
...AH, RIGHT.
SEVERAL MONTHS AGO...

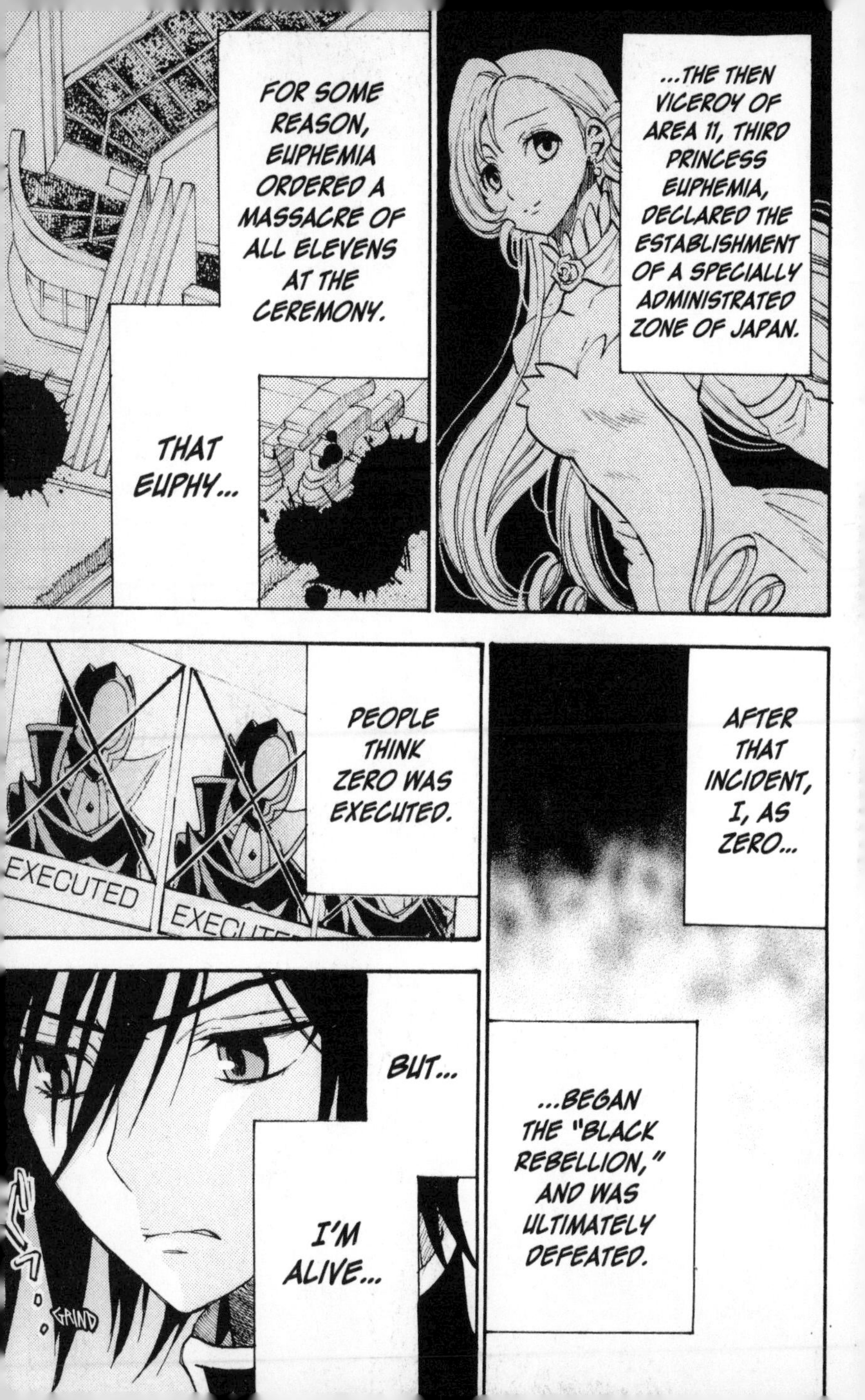
...THE THEN VICEROY OF AREA 11, THIRD PRINCESS EUPHEMIA, DECLARED THE ESTABLISHMENT OF A SPECIALLY ADMINISTRATED ZONE OF JAPAN.
FOR SOME REASON, EUPHEMIA ORDERED A MASSACRE OF ALL ELEVENS AT THE CEREMONY.
THAT EUPHY...
AFTER THAT INCIDENT, I, AS ZERO...
...BEGAN THE "BLACK REBELLION," AND WAS ULTIMATELY DEFEATED.
PEOPLE THINK ZERO WAS EXECUTED.
EXECUTED
BUT...
I'M ALIVE...
GRIND

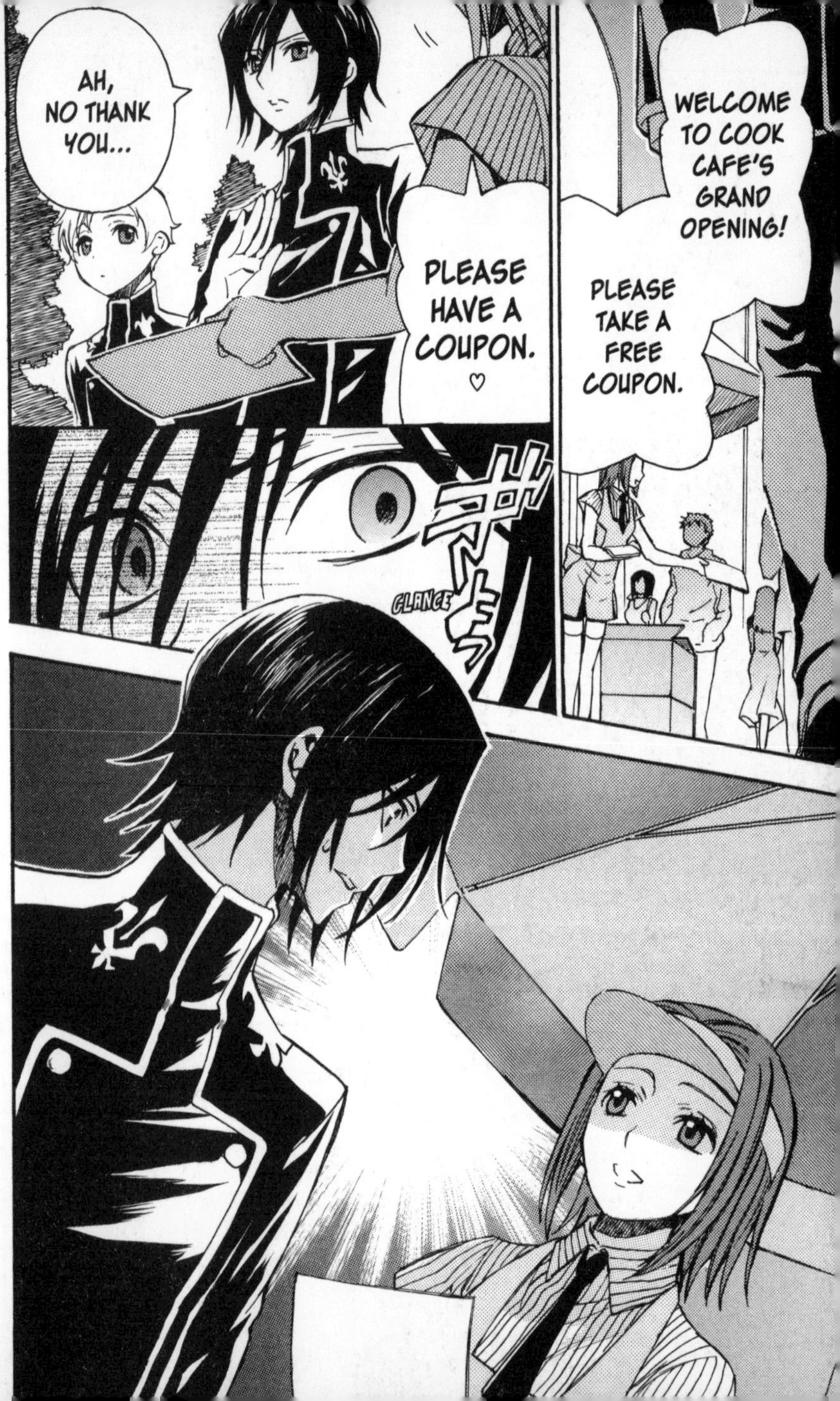
WELCOME TO COOK CAFE'S GRAND OPENING!
PLEASE TAKE A FREE COUPON.
PLEASE HAVE A COUPON. ♡
AH, NO THANK YOU...
GLANCE

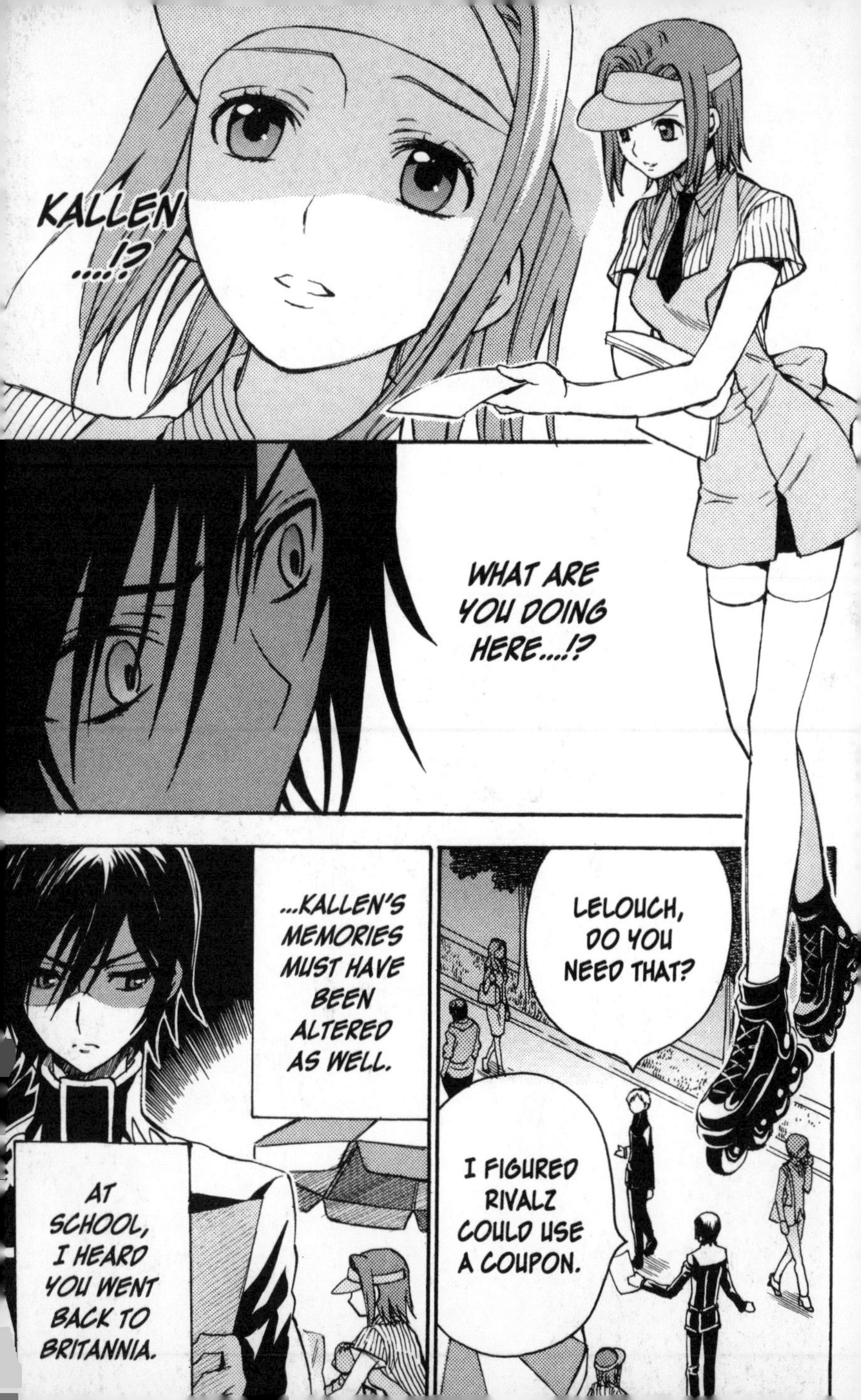
KALLEN ...!?
WHAT ARE YOU DOING HERE...!?
LELOUCH, DO YOU NEED THAT?
I FIGURED RIVALZ COULD USE A COUPON.
...KALLEN'S MEMORIES MUST HAVE BEEN ALTERED AS WELL.
AT SCHOOL, I HEARD YOU WENT BACK TO BRITANNIA.

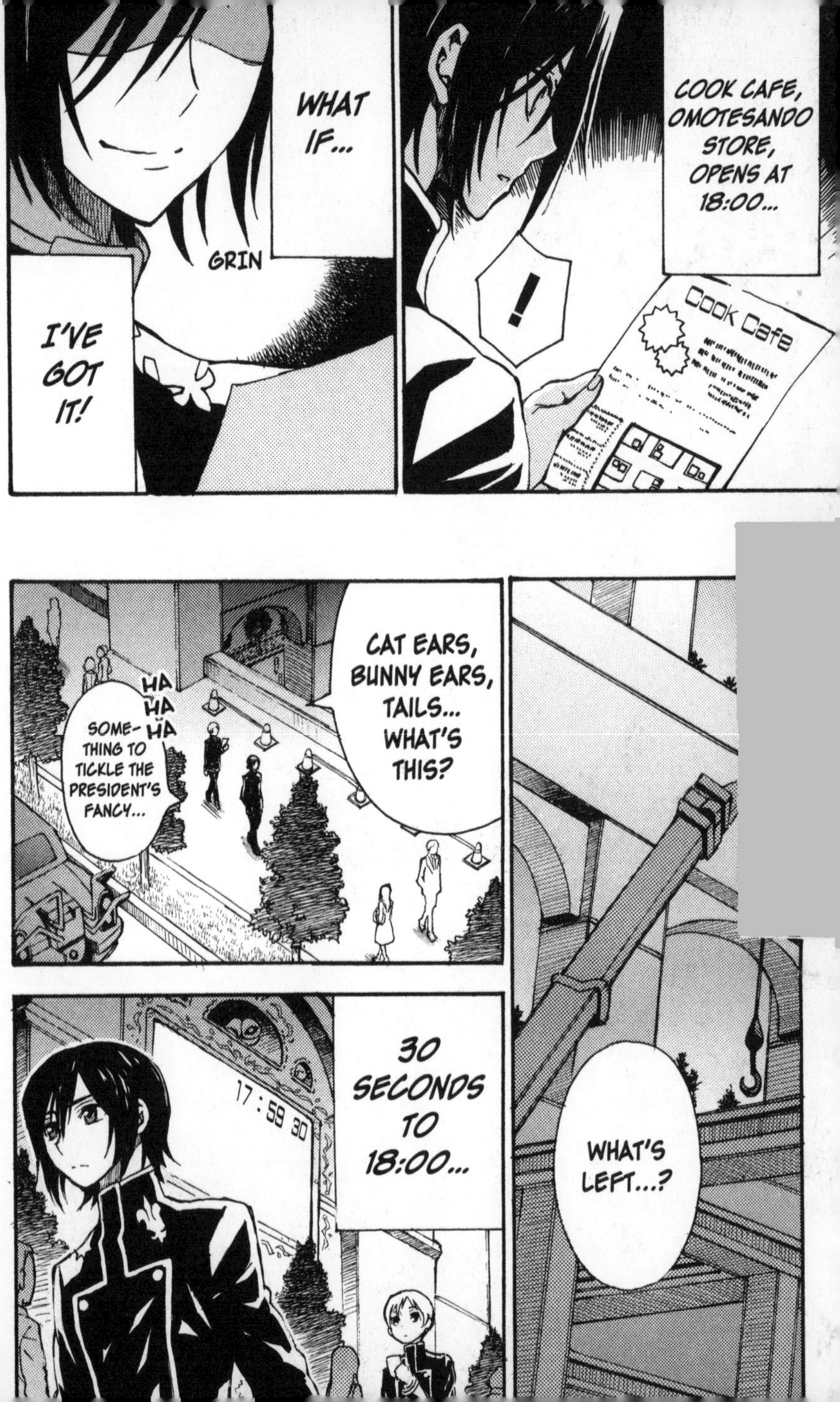
COOK CAFE, OMOTESANDO STORE, OPENS AT 18:00...
!
Cook Cafe
WHAT IF...
GRIN
I'VE GOT IT!
WHAT'S LEFT...?
CAT EARS, BUNNY EARS, TAILS... WHAT'S THIS?
HA HA HA
SOME-THING TO TICKLE THE PRESIDENT'S FANCY...
30 SECONDS TO 18:00...
17:59 30

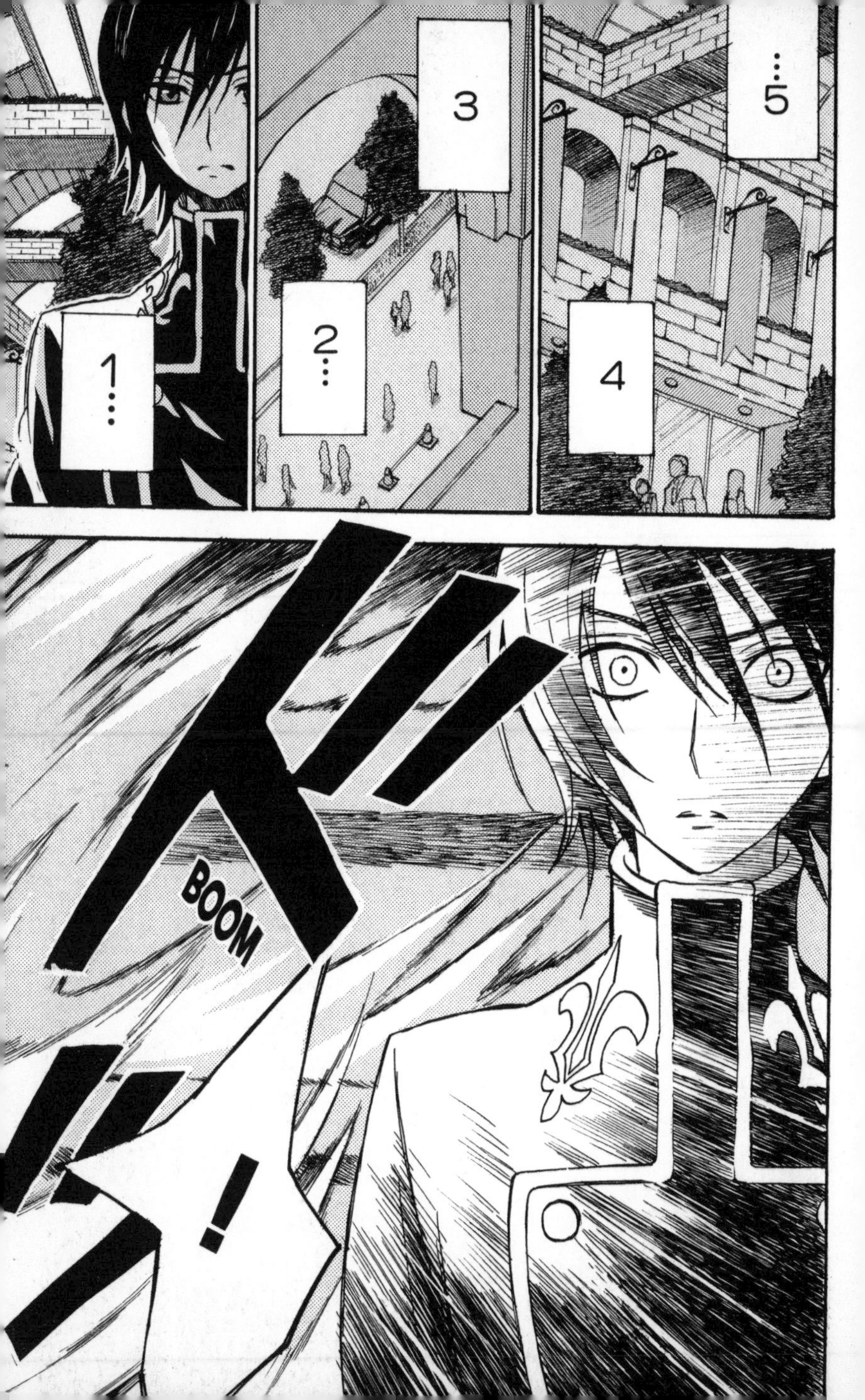
1...
2...
3
4
...5
BOOM
!

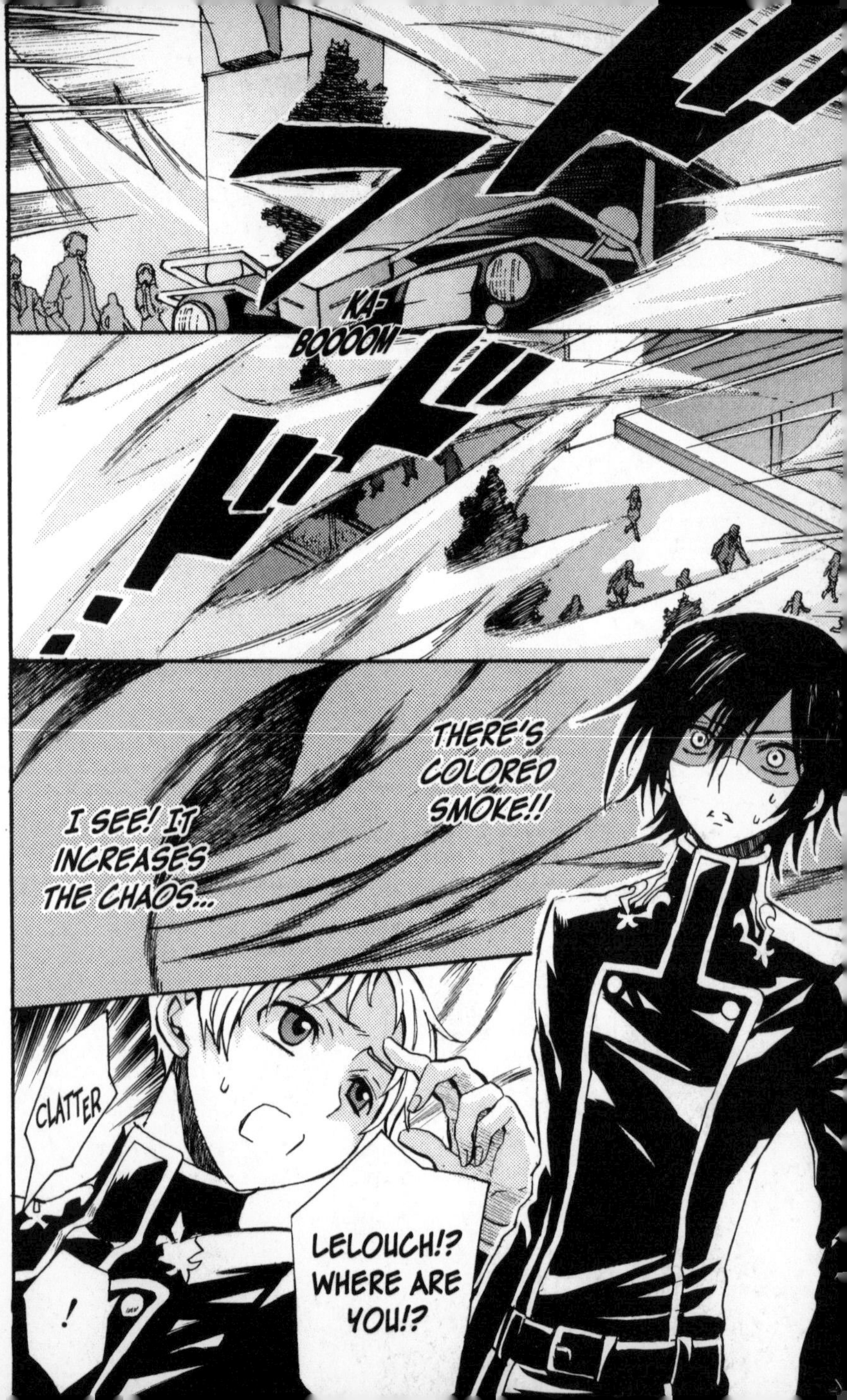
KA-BOOOOM
THERE'S COLORED SMOKE!!
I SEE! IT INCREASES THE CHAOS...
LELOUCH!? WHERE ARE YOU!?
CLATTER
!

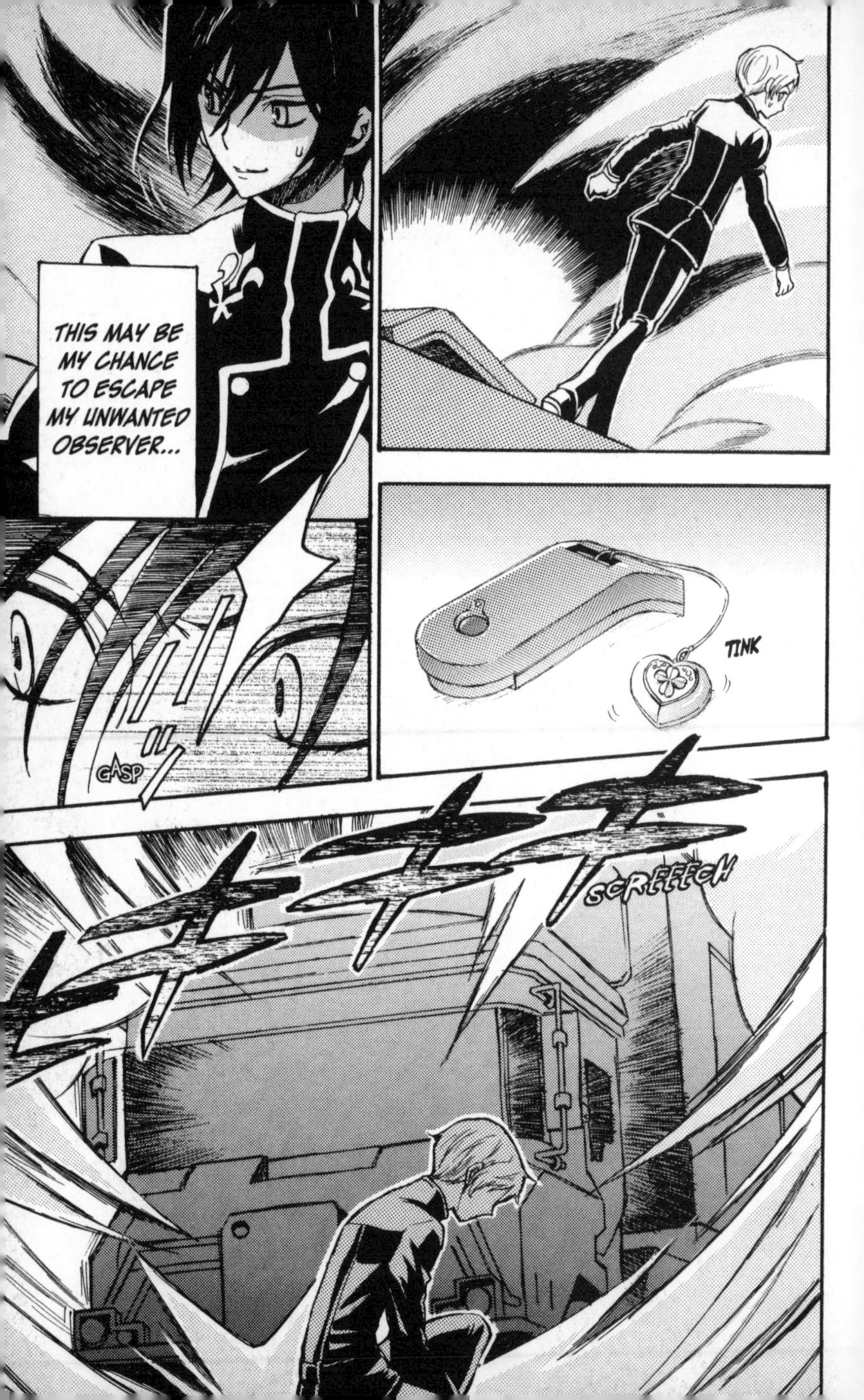
THIS MAY BE MY CHANCE TO ESCAPE MY UNWANTED OBSERVER...
TINK
GASP
SCREEECH

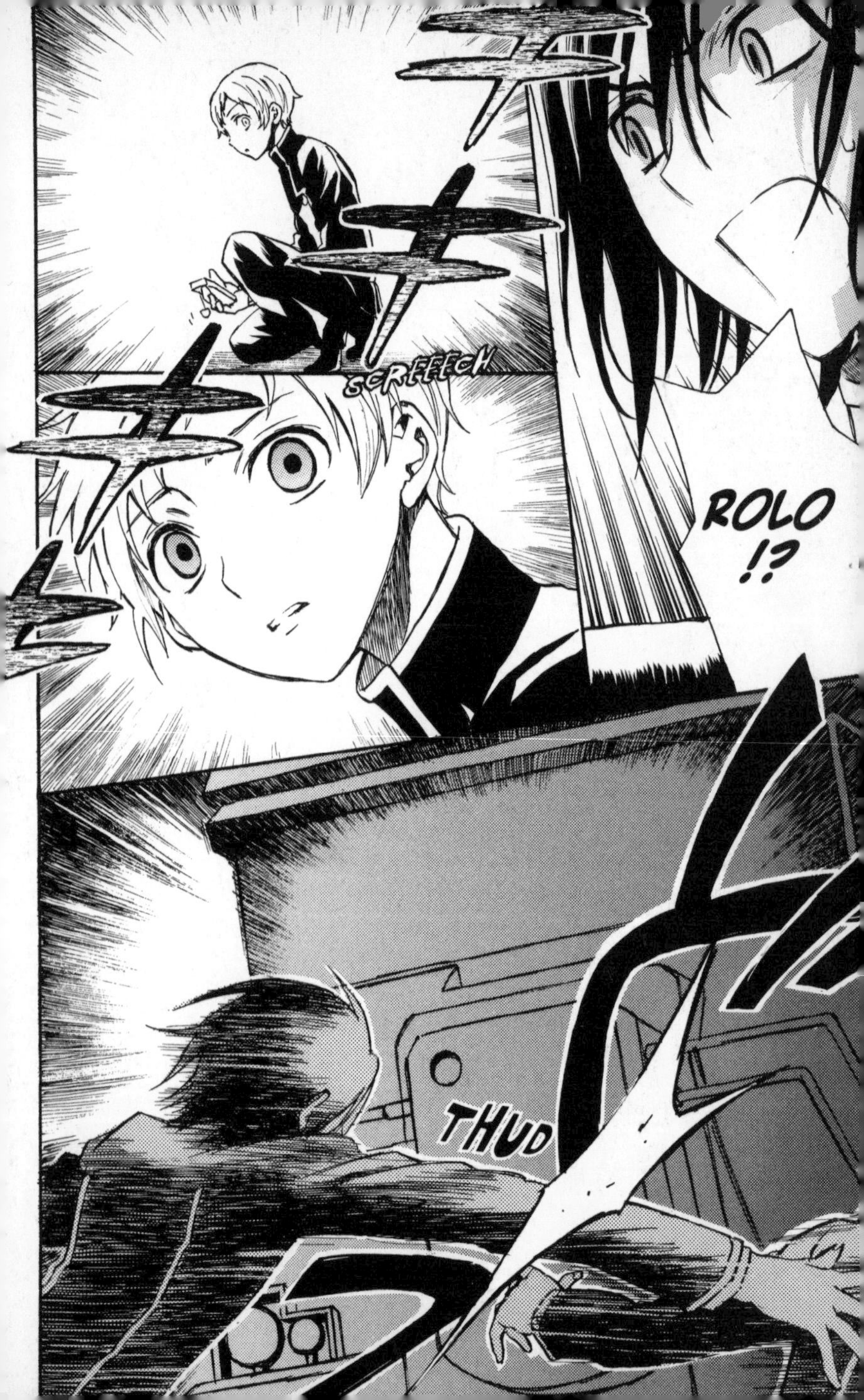
SCREEECH
ROLO !?
THUD

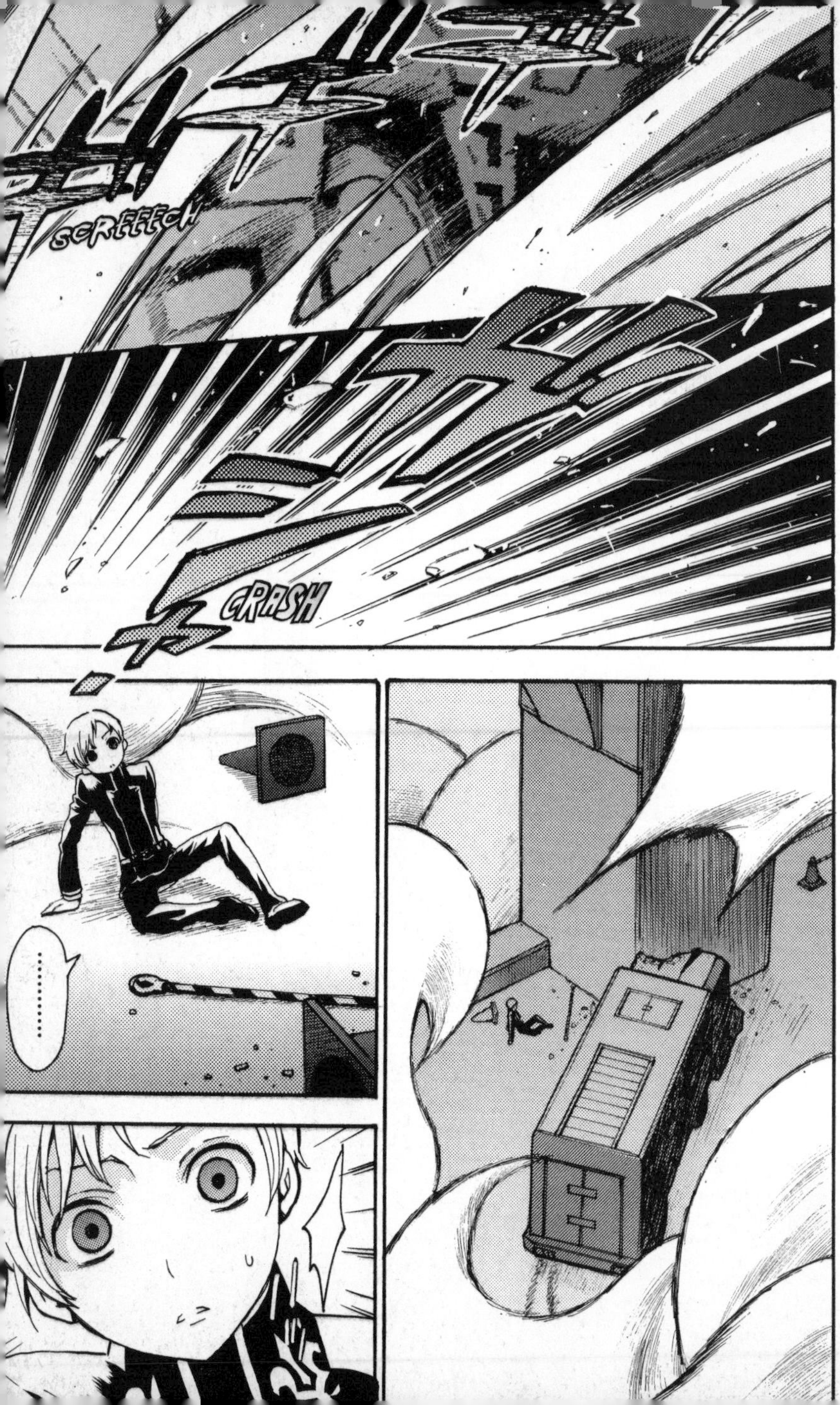
SCREEECH
CRASH
......

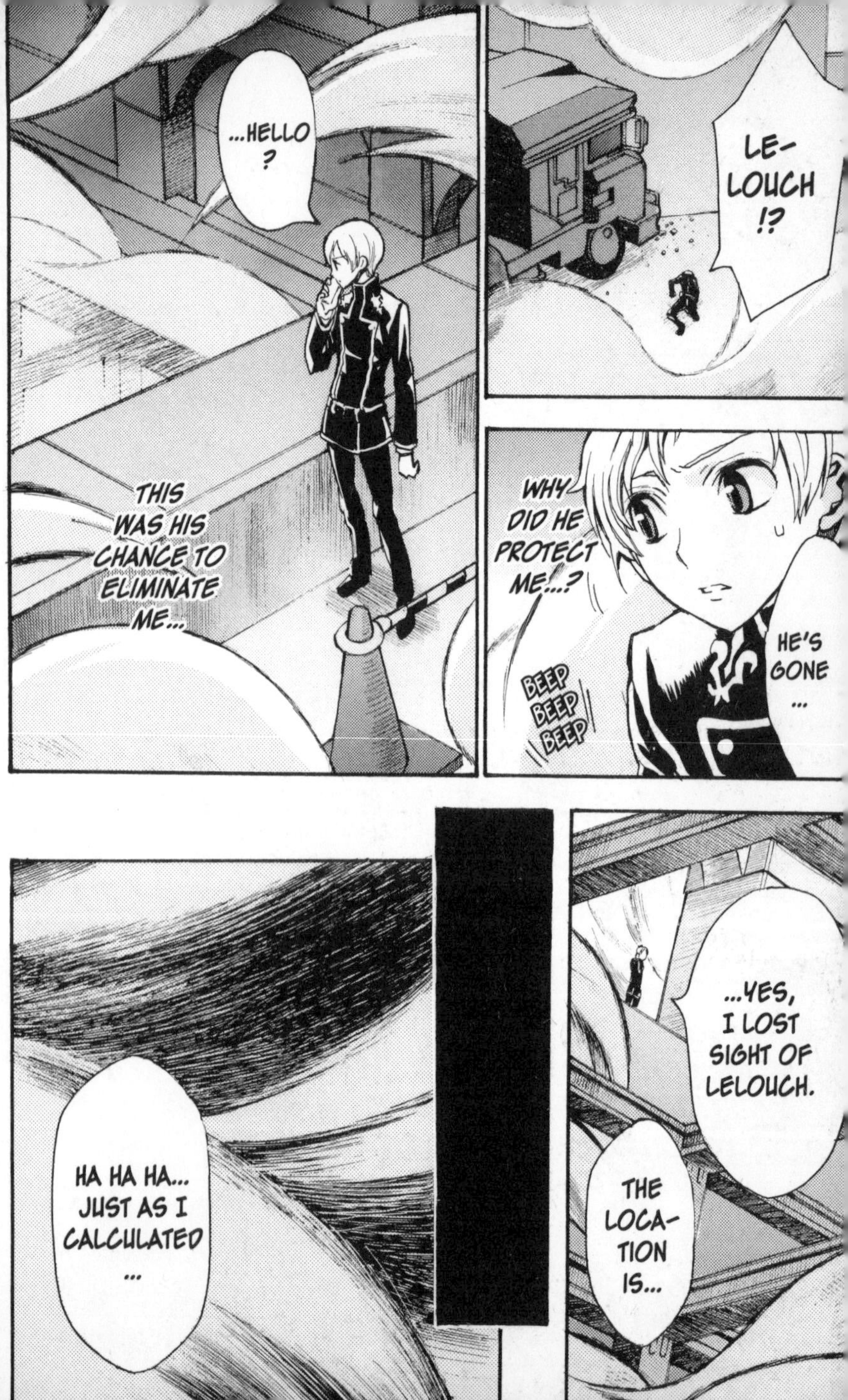
LE-LOUCH!?
WHY DID HE PROTECT ME...?
HE'S GONE...
BEEP BEEP BEEP
...HELLO?
THIS WAS HIS CHANCE TO ELIMINATE ME...
...YES, I LOST SIGHT OF LELOUCH.
THE LOCA-TION IS...
HA HA HA... JUST AS I CALCULATED...

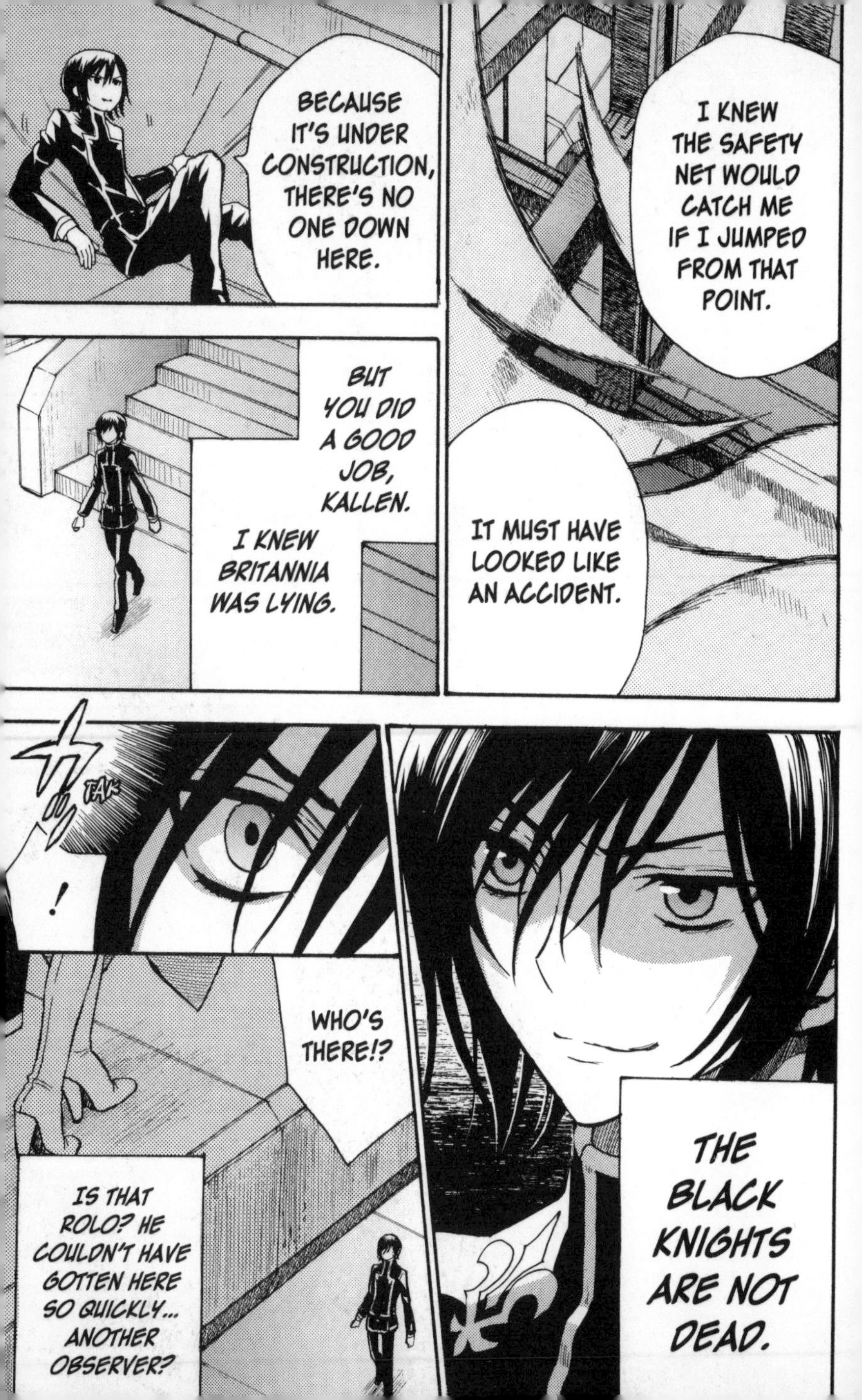
I KNEW THE SAFETY NET WOULD CATCH ME IF I JUMPED FROM THAT POINT.
IT MUST HAVE LOOKED LIKE AN ACCIDENT.
BECAUSE IT'S UNDER CONSTRUCTION, THERE'S NO ONE DOWN HERE.
BUT YOU DID A GOOD JOB, KALLEN.
I KNEW BRITANNIA WAS LYING.
THE BLACK KNIGHTS ARE NOT DEAD.
TAK
!
WHO'S THERE!?
IS THAT ROLO? HE COULDN'T HAVE GOTTEN HERE SO QUICKLY... ANOTHER OBSERVER?

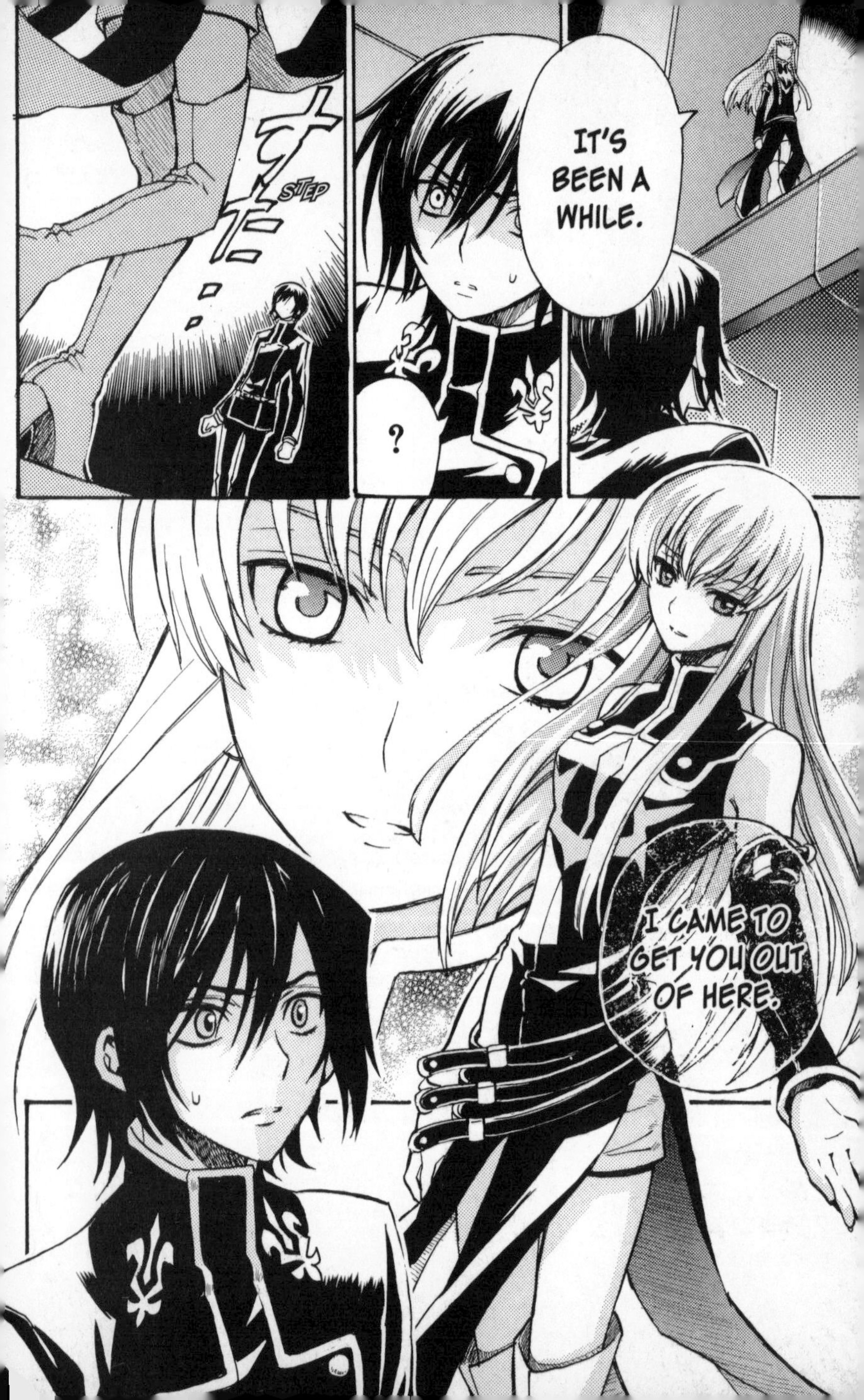
IT'S BEEN A WHILE.
?
STEP
I CAME TO GET YOU OUT OF HERE.

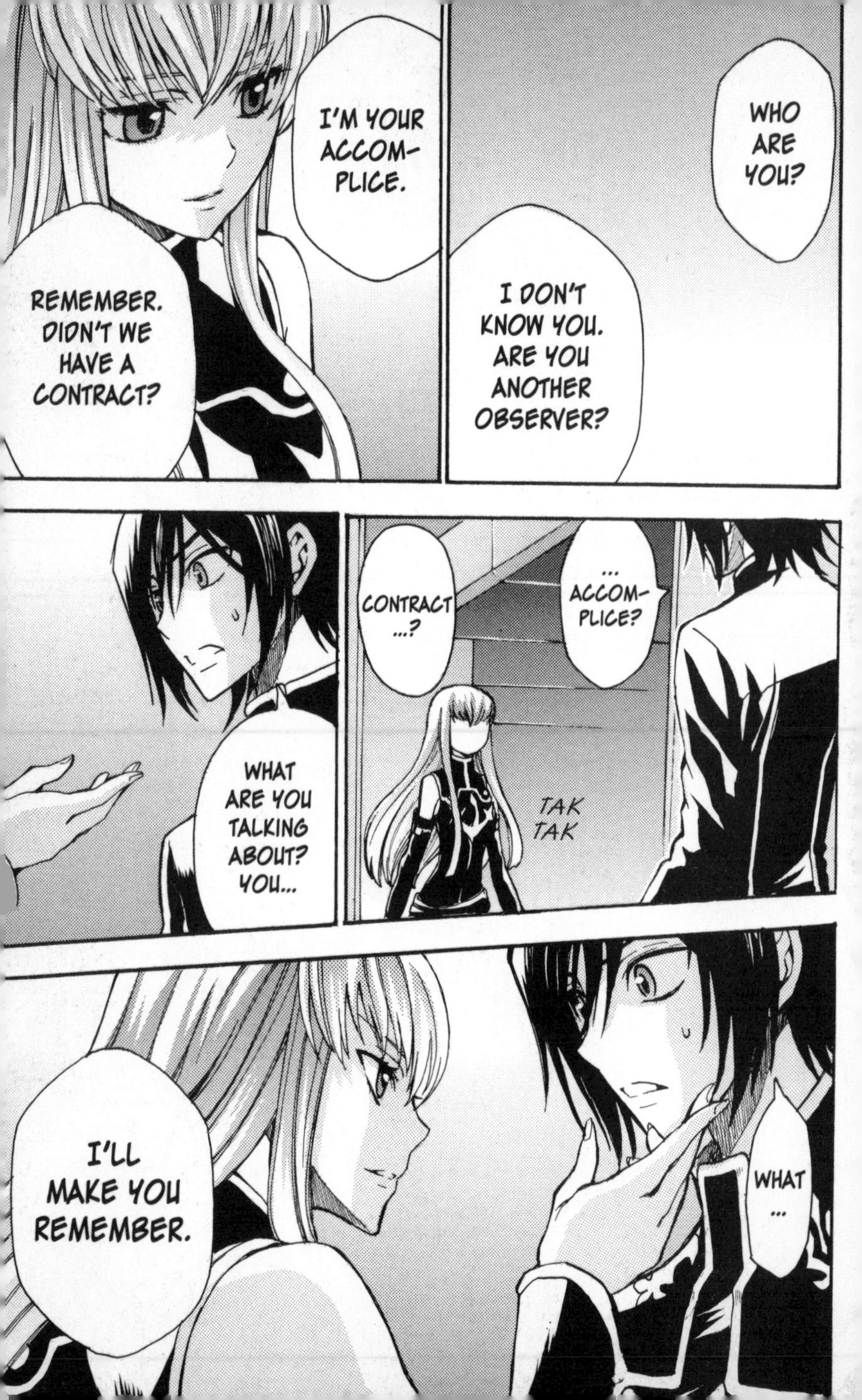
WHO ARE YOU?
I DON'T KNOW YOU. ARE YOU ANOTHER OBSERVER?
I'M YOUR ACCOMPLICE.
REMEMBER. DIDN'T WE HAVE A CONTRACT?
... ACCOMPLICE?
CONTRACT ...?
TAK TAK
WHAT ARE YOU TALKING ABOUT? YOU...
WHAT ...
I'LL MAKE YOU REMEMBER.

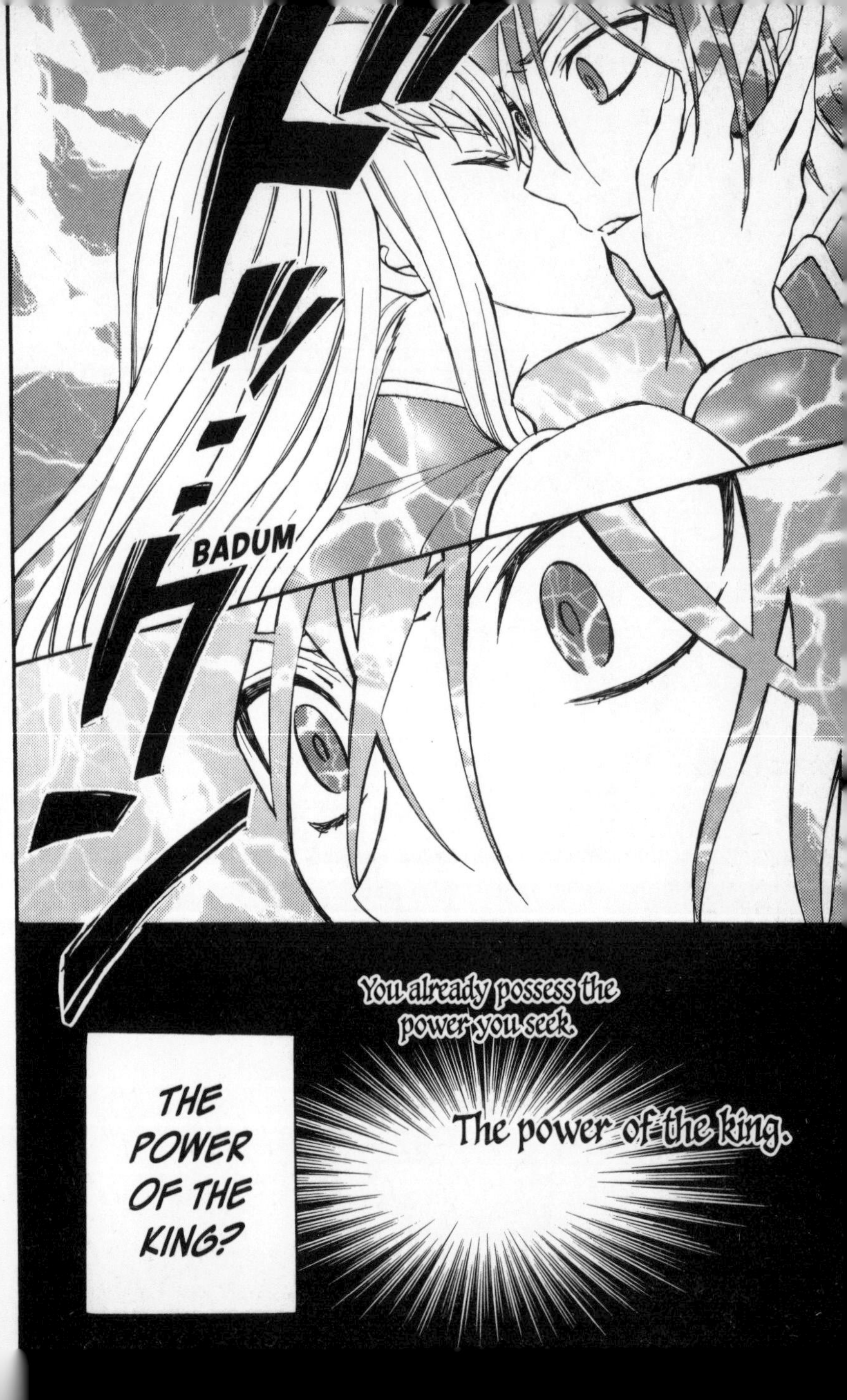
BADUM
You already possess the power you seek.
The power of the king.
THE POWER OF THE KING?

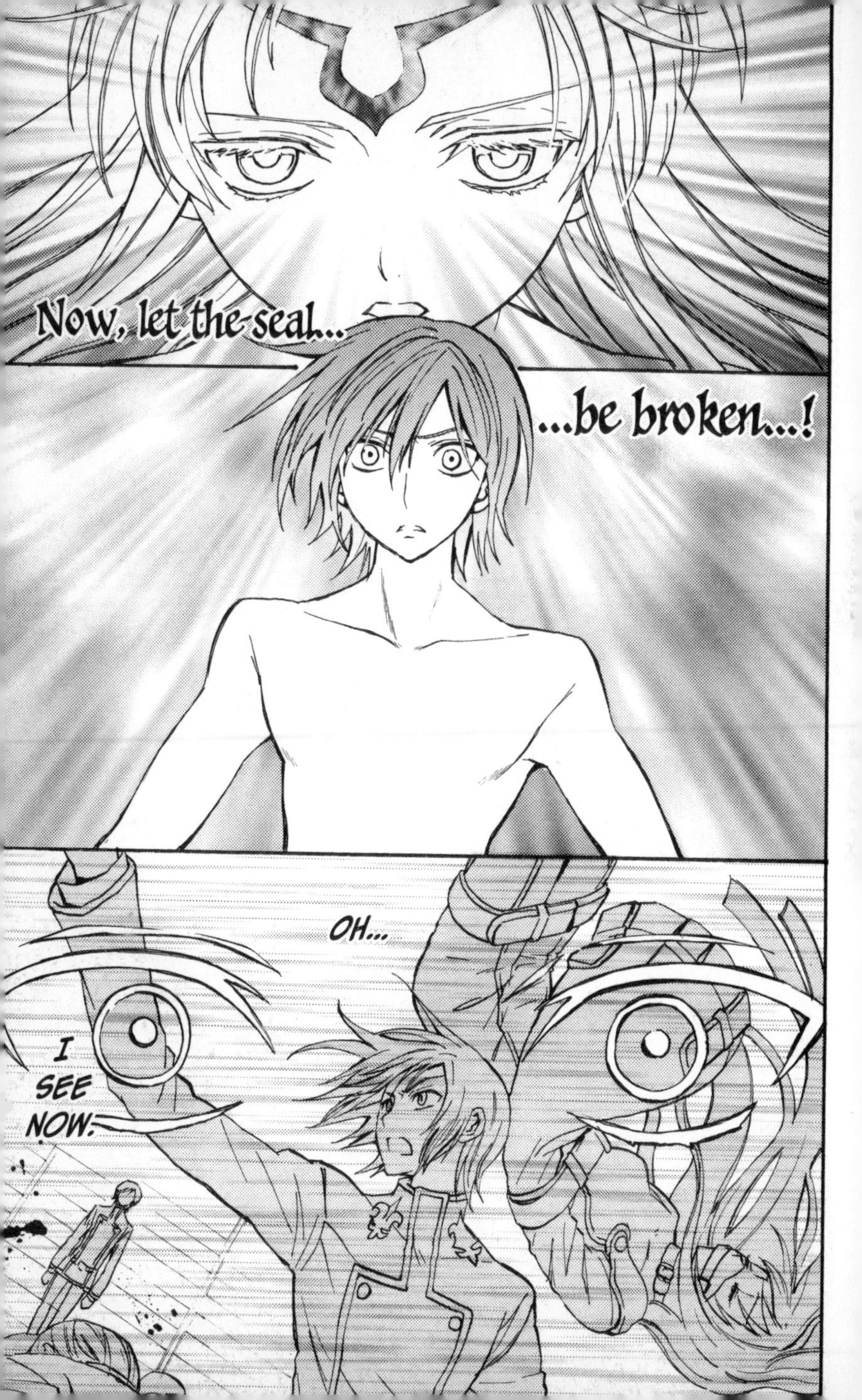
Now, let the seal...
...be broken...!
OH...
I SEE NOW.

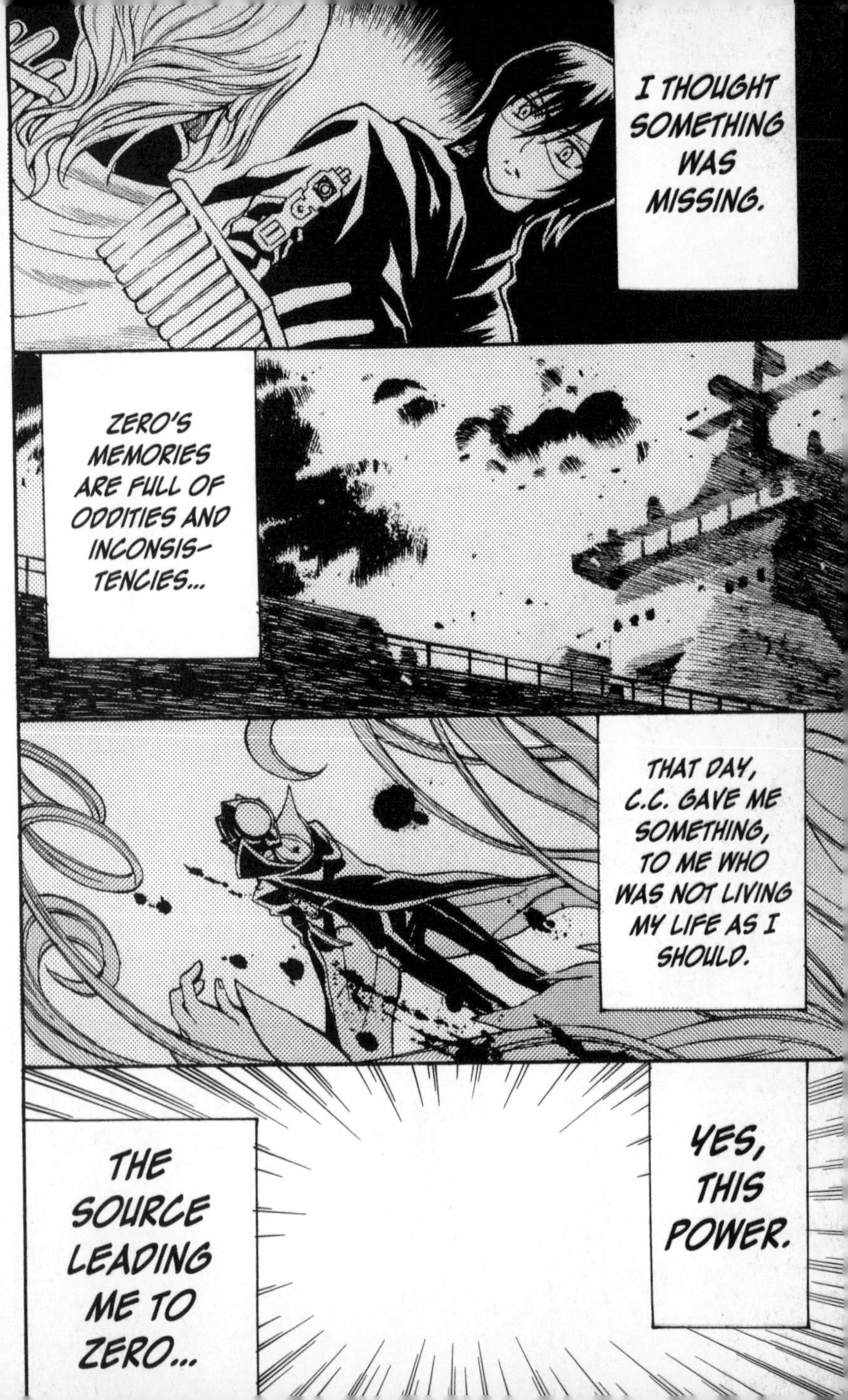
I THOUGHT SOMETHING WAS MISSING.
ZERO'S MEMORIES ARE FULL OF ODDITIES AND INCONSIS-TENCIES...
THAT DAY, C.C. GAVE ME SOMETHING, TO ME WHO WAS NOT LIVING MY LIFE AS I SHOULD.
YES, THIS POWER.
THE SOURCE LEADING ME TO ZERO...

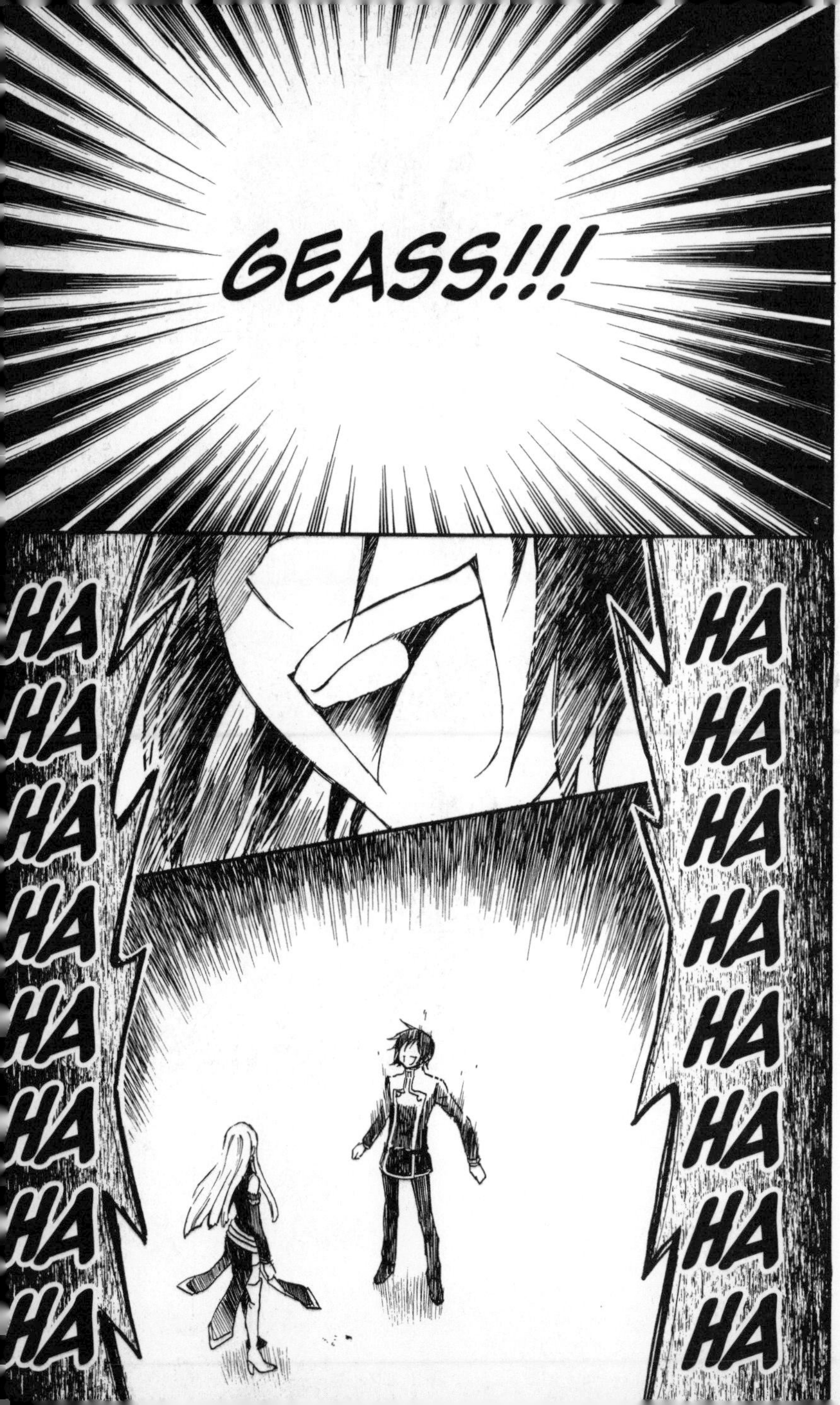
GEASS!!!
HA HA HA HA HA HA HA HA
HA HA HA HA HA HA HA HA

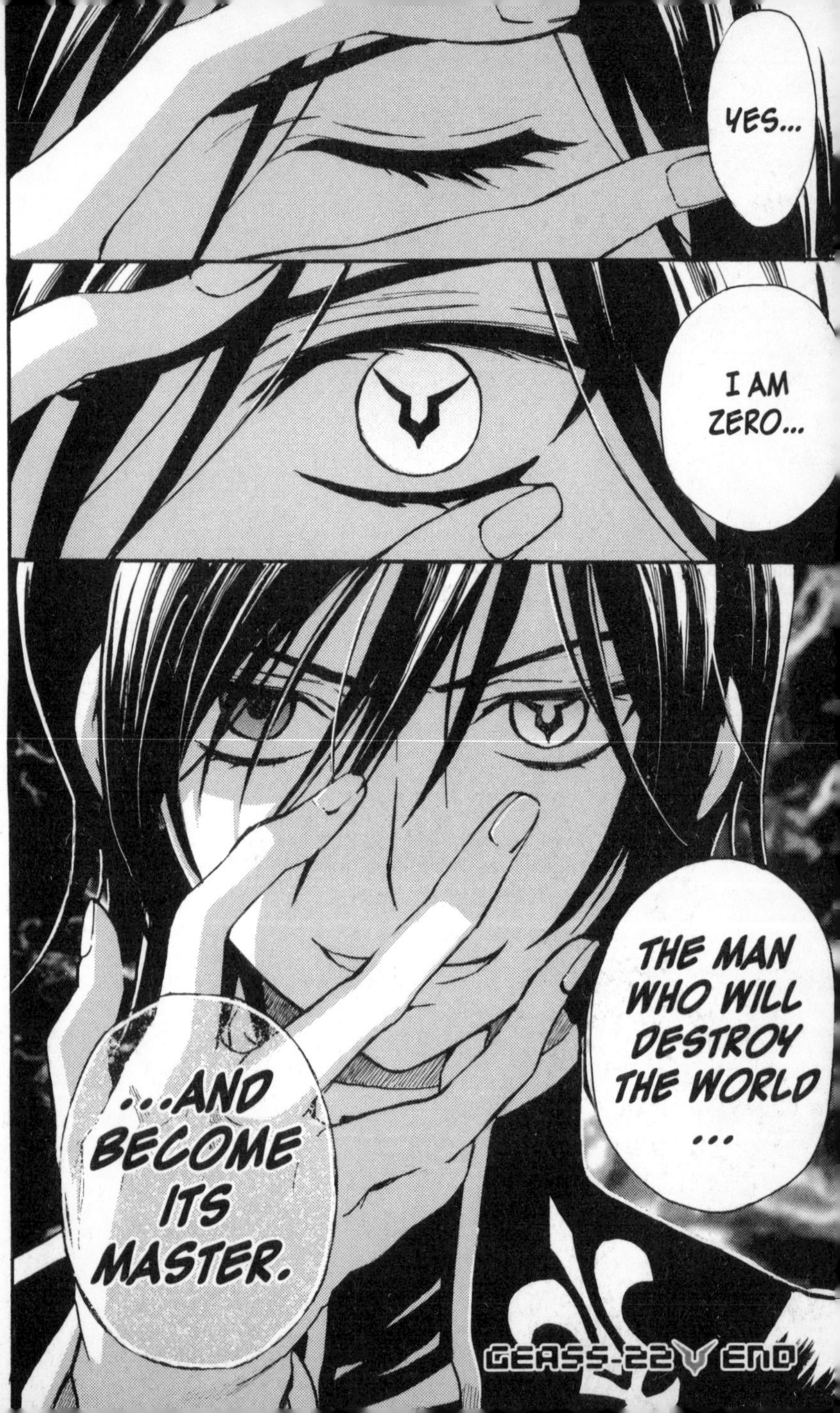
YES...
I AM ZERO...
THE MAN WHO WILL DESTROY THE WORLD ...
...AND BECOME ITS MASTER.
GEASS-22 END

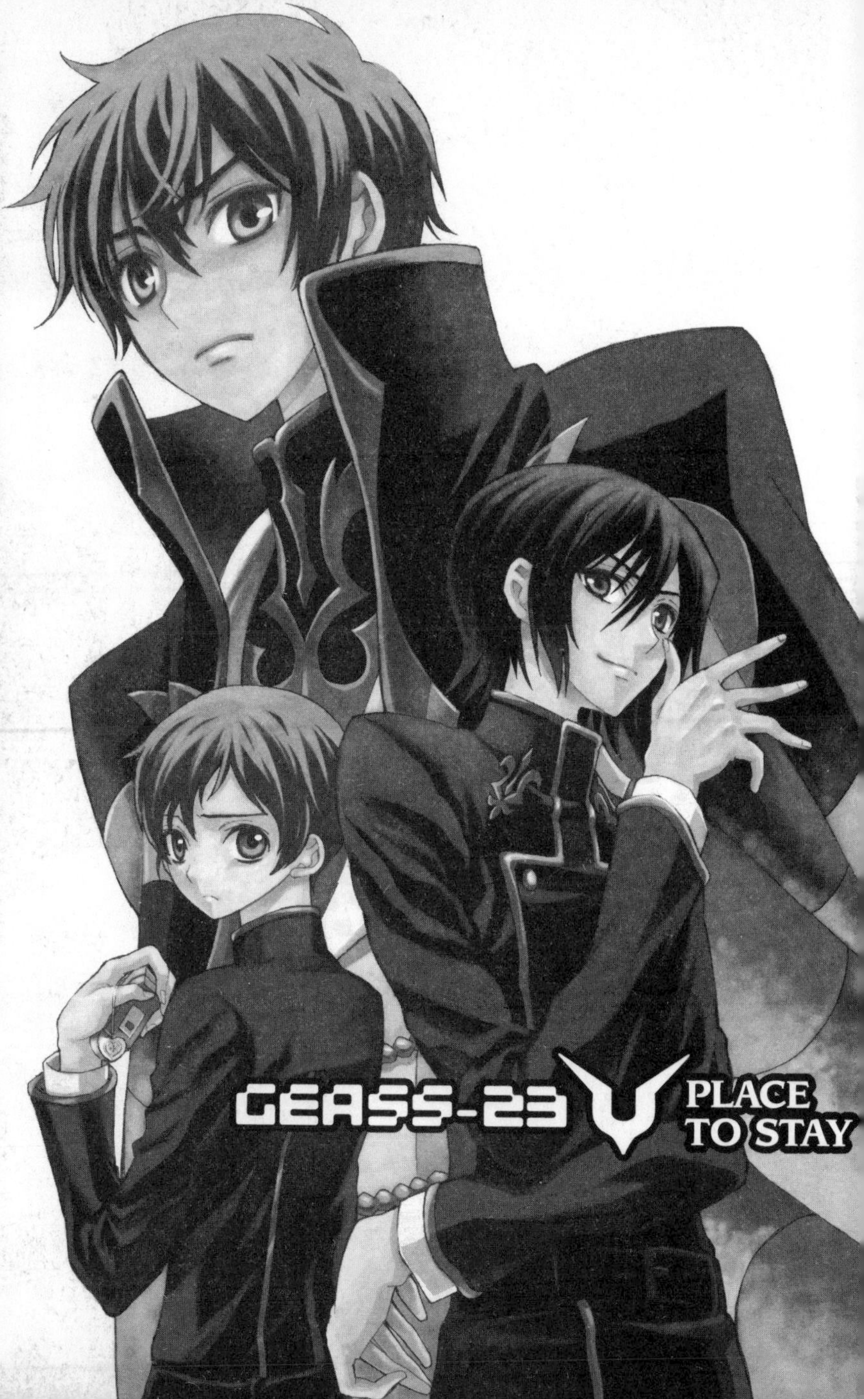
GEASS-23
PLACE TO STAY

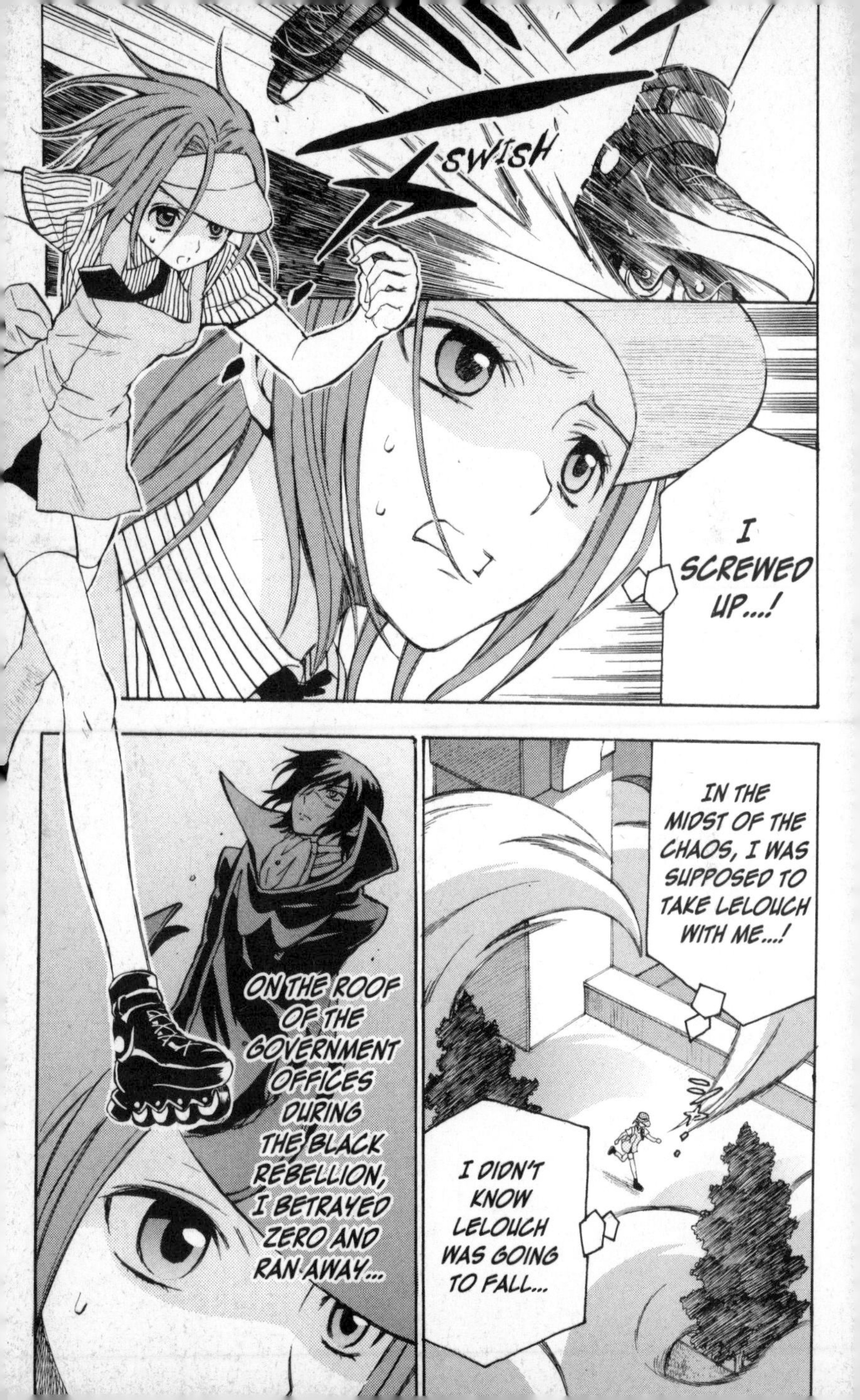
SWISH
I SCREWED UP...!
IN THE MIDST OF THE CHAOS, I WAS SUPPOSED TO TAKE LELOUCH WITH ME...!
I DIDN'T KNOW LELOUCH WAS GOING TO FALL...
ON THE ROOF OF THE GOVERNMENT OFFICES DURING THE BLACK REBELLION, I BETRAYED ZERO AND RAN AWAY...

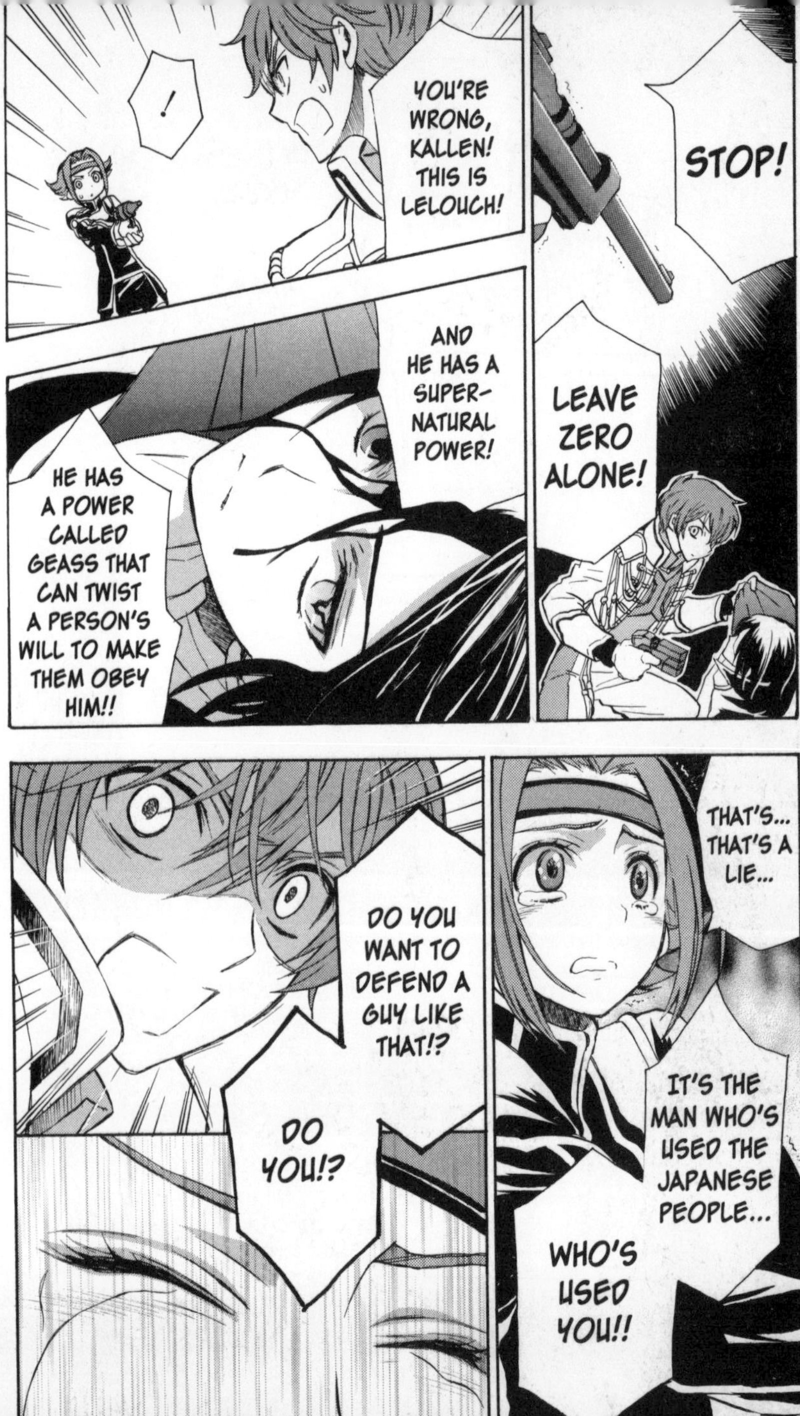
STOP!
LEAVE ZERO ALONE!
!
YOU'RE WRONG, KALLEN! THIS IS LELOUCH!
AND HE HAS A SUPER-NATURAL POWER!
HE HAS A POWER CALLED GEASS THAT CAN TWIST A PERSON'S WILL TO MAKE THEM OBEY HIM!!
THAT'S... THAT'S A LIE...
IT'S THE MAN WHO'S USED THE JAPANESE PEOPLE...
WHO'S USED YOU!!
DO YOU WANT TO DEFEND A GUY LIKE THAT!?
DO YOU!?

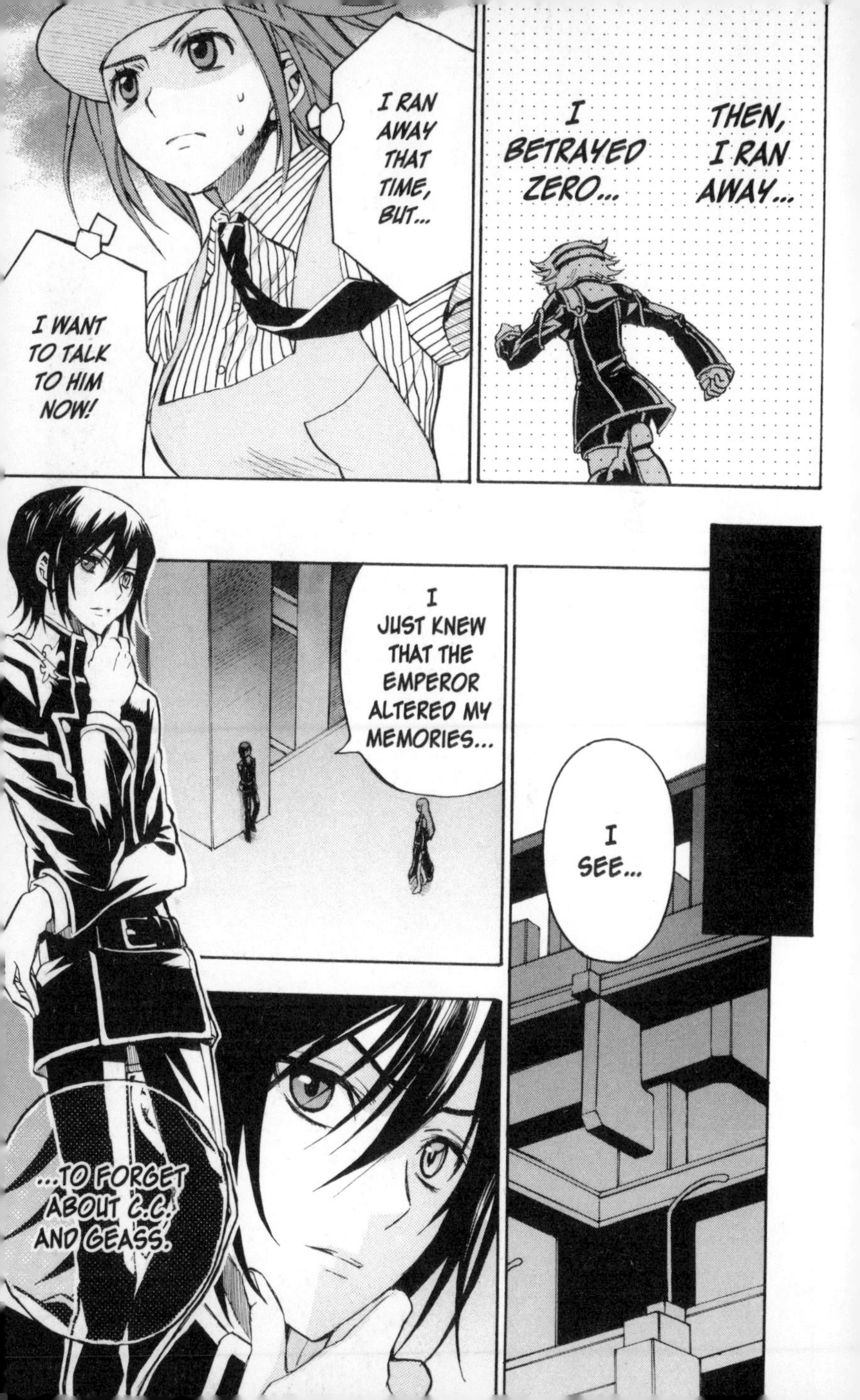
THEN, I RAN AWAY...
I BETRAYED ZERO...
I RAN AWAY THAT TIME, BUT...
I WANT TO TALK TO HIM NOW!
I SEE...
I JUST KNEW THAT THE EMPEROR ALTERED MY MEMORIES...
...TO FORGET ABOUT C.C. AND GEASS.

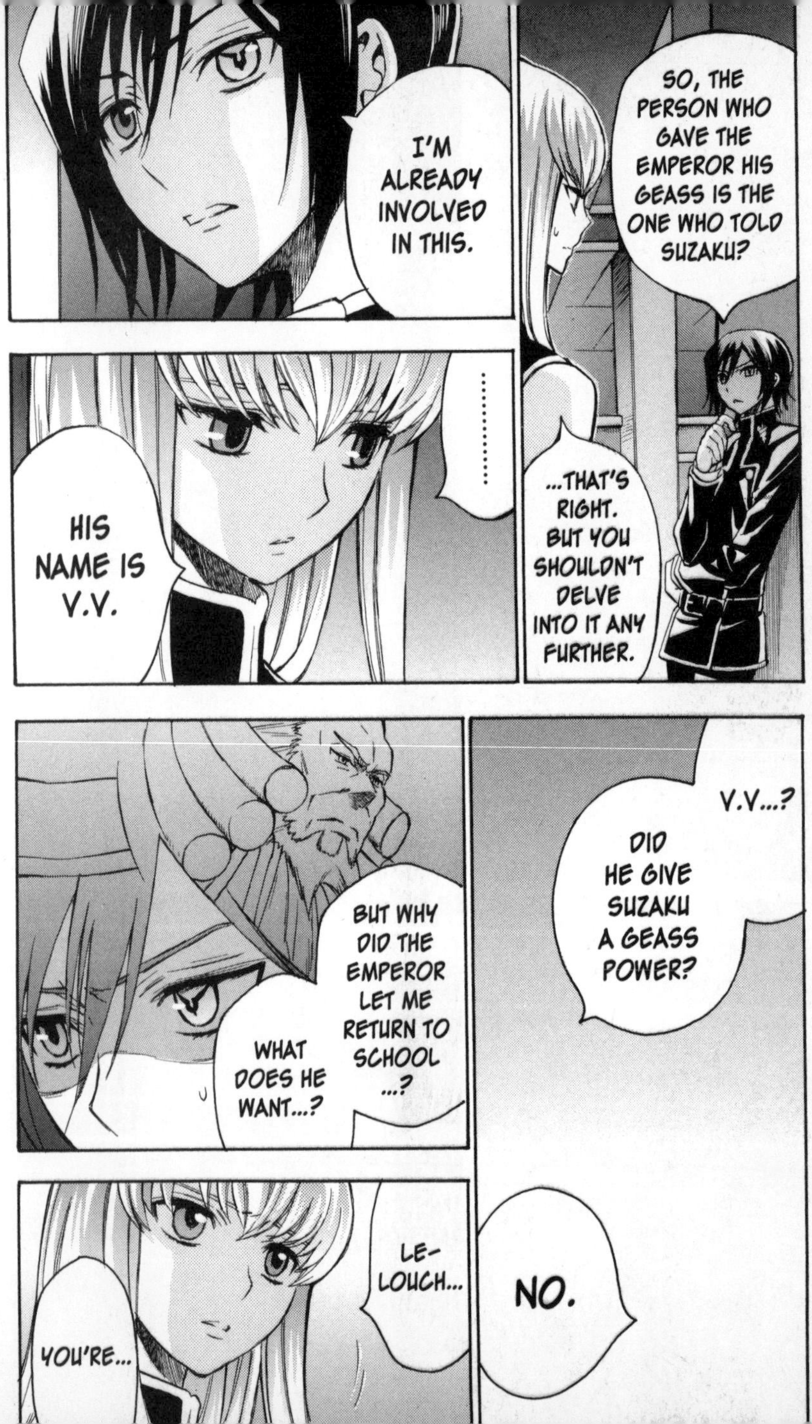
SO, THE PERSON WHO GAVE THE EMPEROR HIS GEASS IS THE ONE WHO TOLD SUZAKU?
...THAT'S RIGHT. BUT YOU SHOULDN'T DELVE INTO IT ANY FURTHER.
I'M ALREADY INVOLVED IN THIS.
......
HIS NAME IS V.V.
V.V...?
DID HE GIVE SUZAKU A GEASS POWER?
NO.
BUT WHY DID THE EMPEROR LET ME RETURN TO SCHOOL ...?
WHAT DOES HE WANT...?
LE-LOUCH...
YOU'RE...

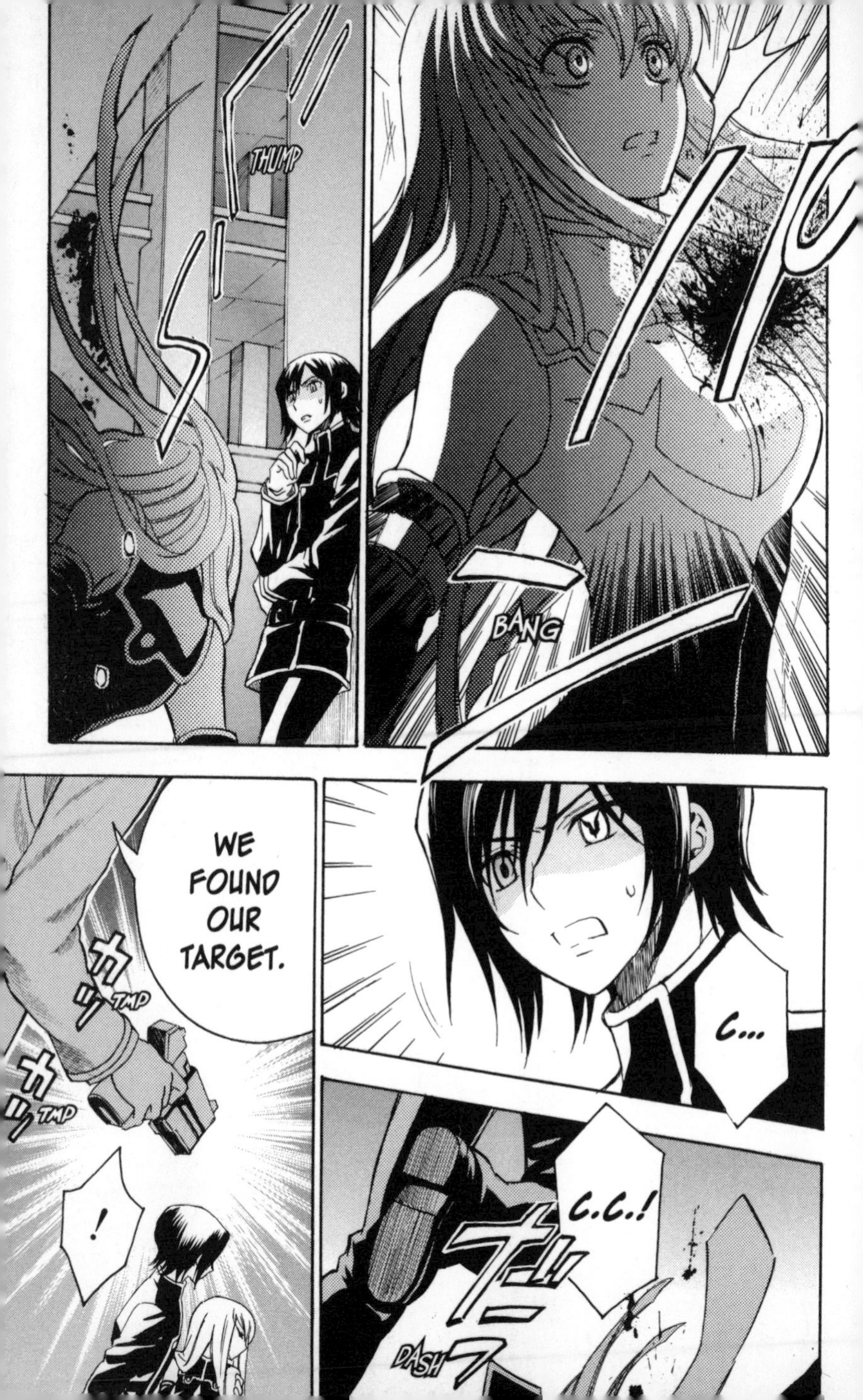
BANG
THUMP
C...
C.C.!
DASH
WE FOUND OUR TARGET.
TMP
TMP
!

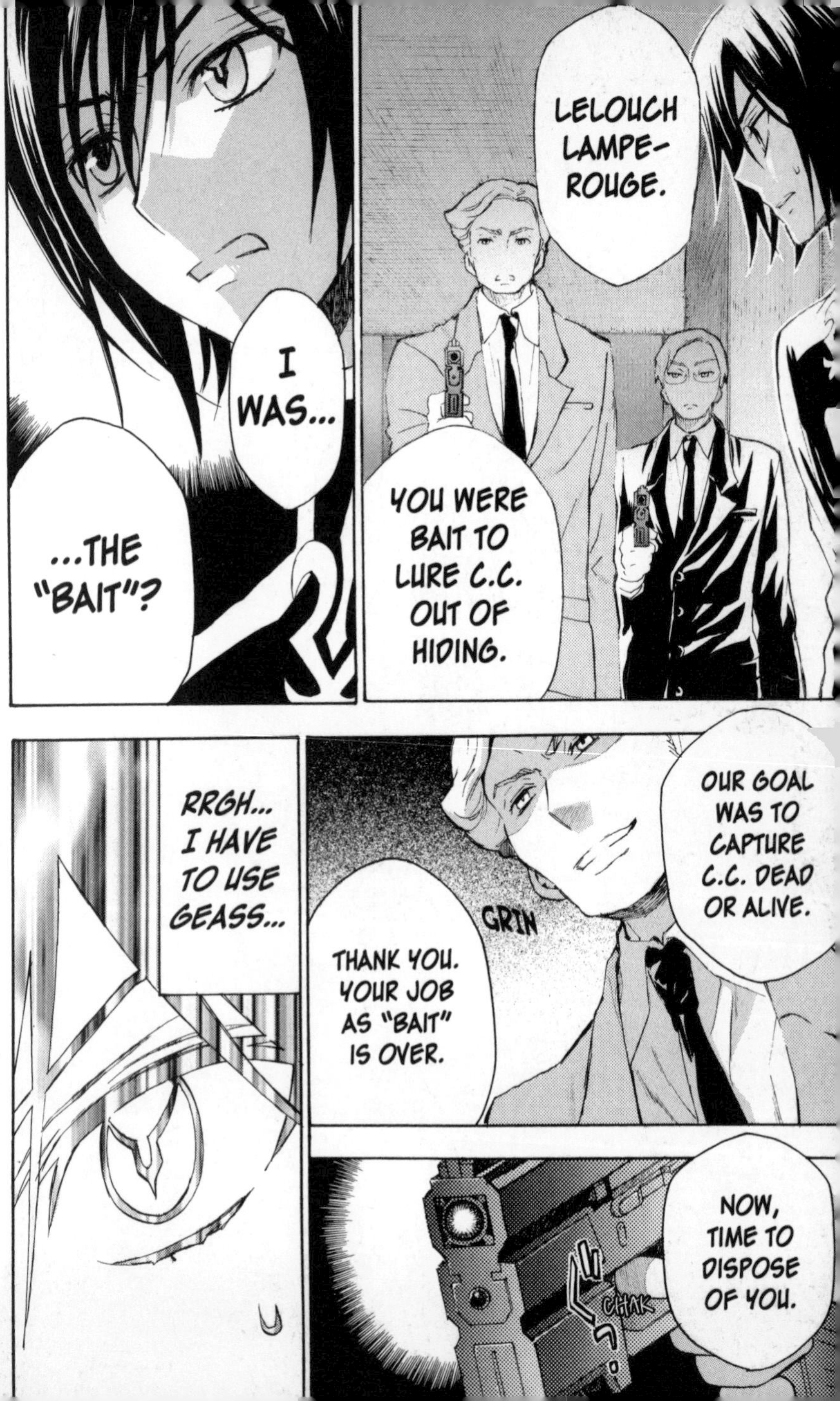
LELOUCH LAMPE-ROUGE.
YOU WERE BAIT TO LURE C.C. OUT OF HIDING.
I WAS...
...THE "BAIT"?
OUR GOAL WAS TO CAPTURE C.C. DEAD OR ALIVE.
GRIN
THANK YOU. YOUR JOB AS "BAIT" IS OVER.
NOW, TIME TO DISPOSE OF YOU.
CHAK
RRGH... I HAVE TO USE GEASS...

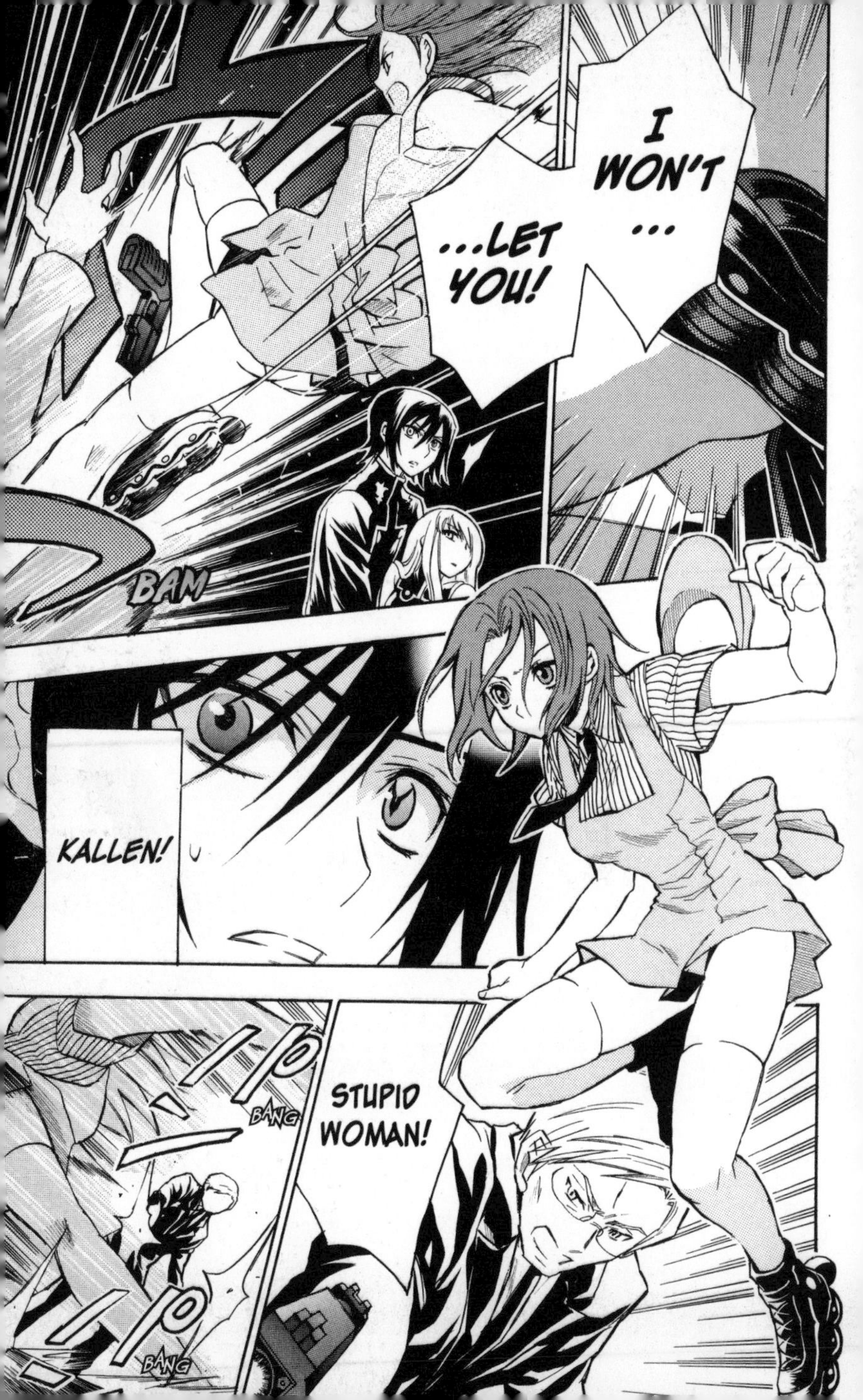
I WON'T ...
...LET YOU!
BAM
KALLEN!
STUPID WOMAN!
BANG
BANG

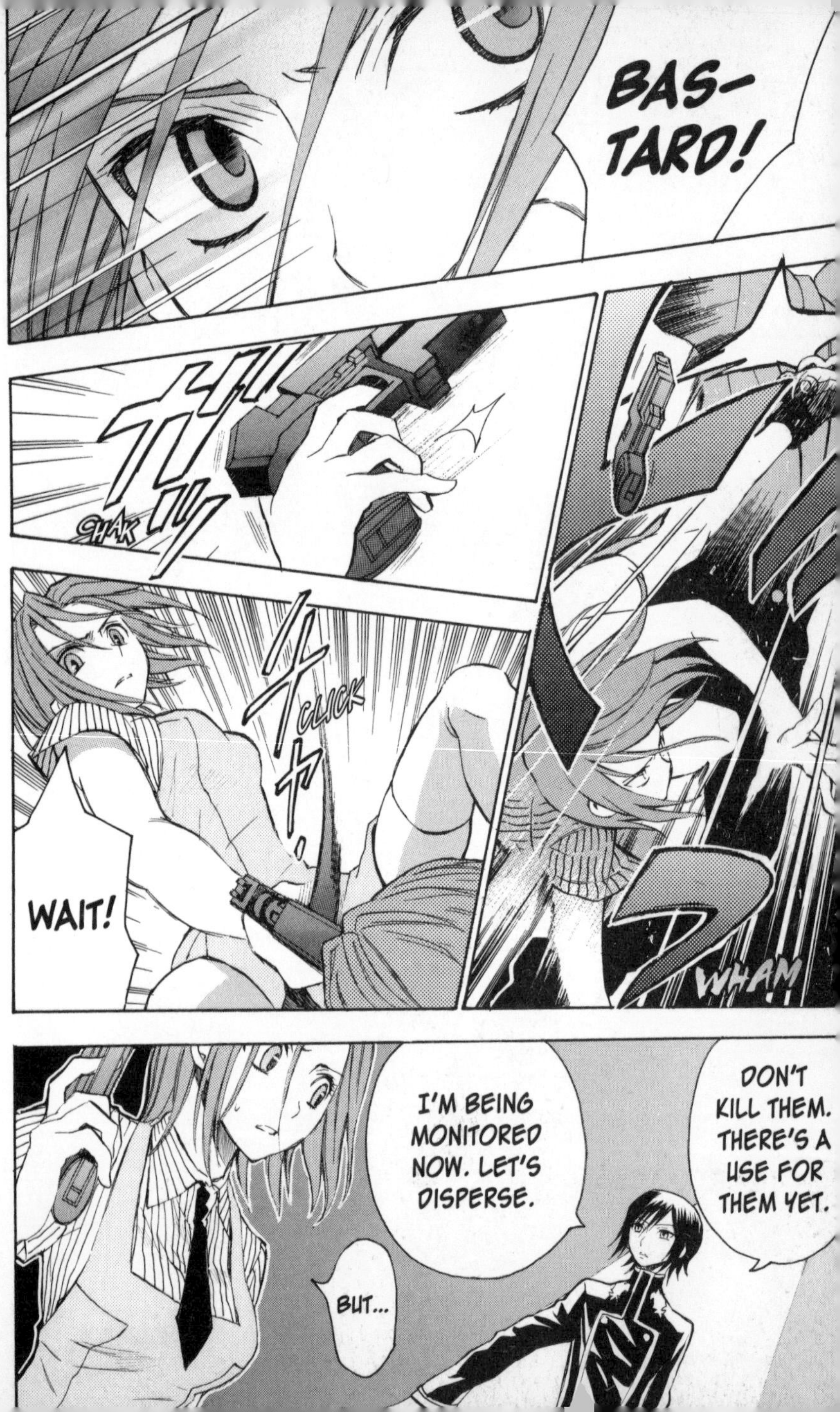
BAS-TARD!
WHAM
CHAK
CLICK
WAIT!
DON'T KILL THEM. THERE'S A USE FOR THEM YET.
I'M BEING MONITORED NOW. LET'S DISPERSE.
BUT...

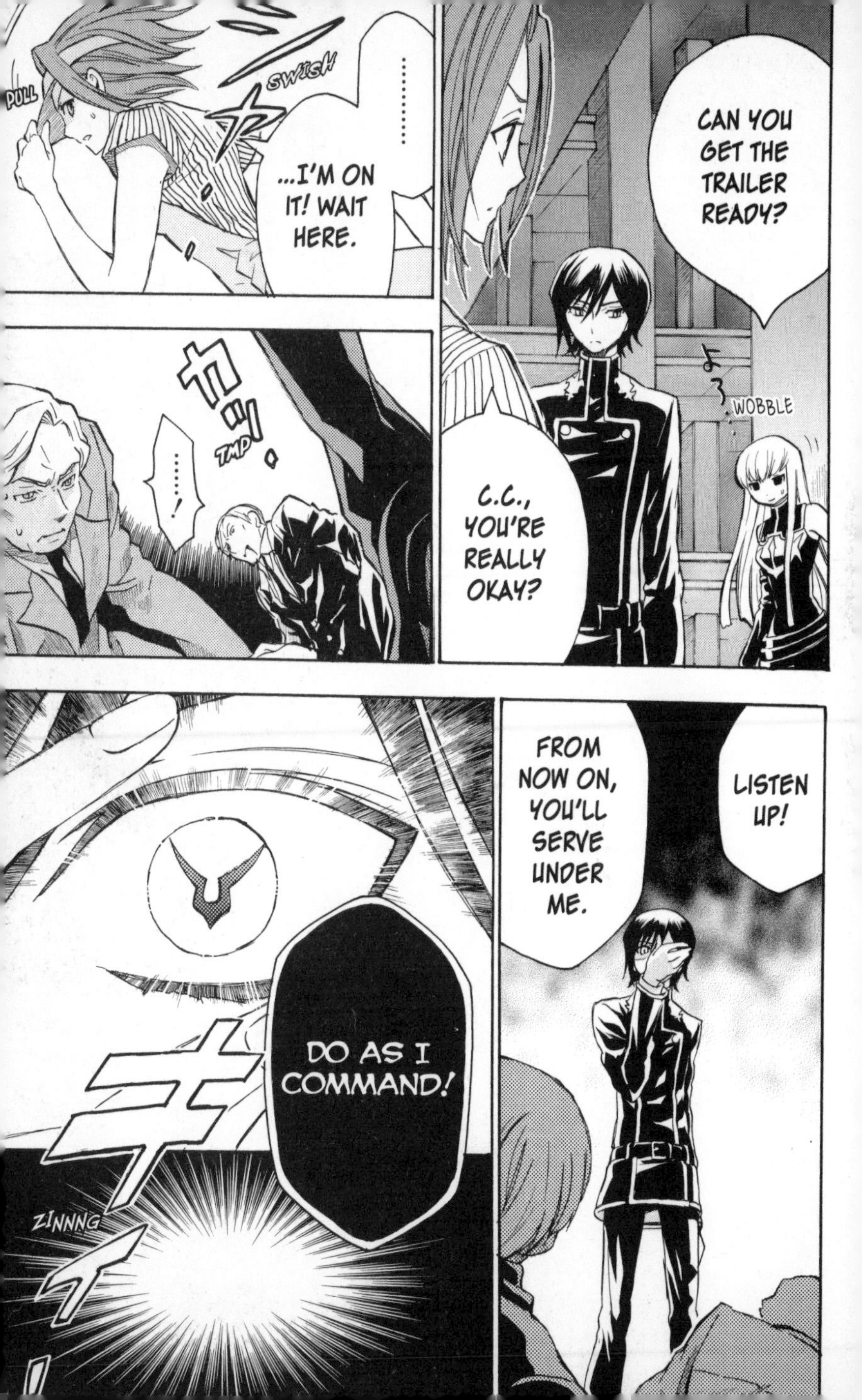
CAN YOU GET THE TRAILER READY?
WOBBLE
C.C., YOU'RE REALLY OKAY?
......
SWISH
...I'M ON IT! WAIT HERE.
PULL
TMP
......!
LISTEN UP!
FROM NOW ON, YOU'LL SERVE UNDER ME.
DO AS I COMMAND!
ZINNNG

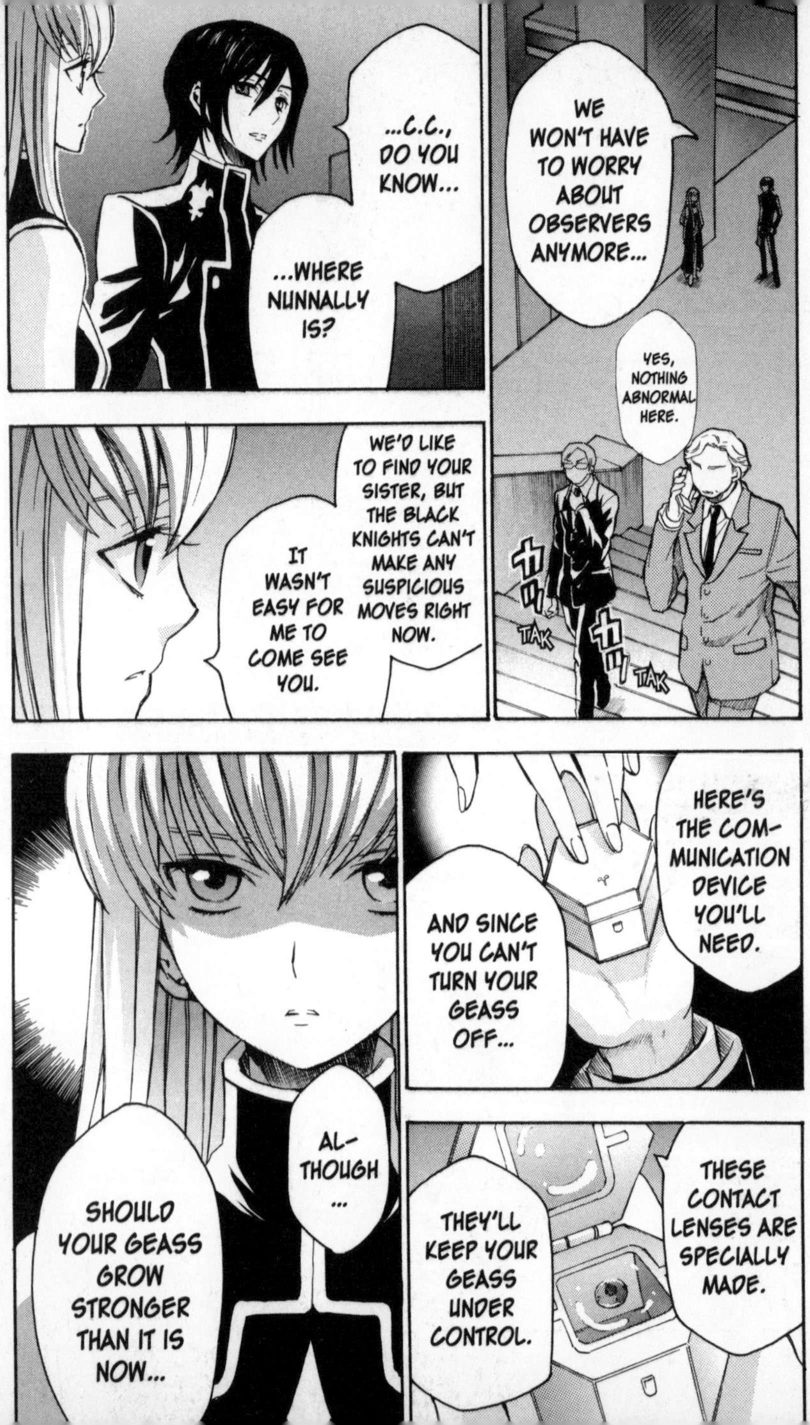
WE WON'T HAVE TO WORRY ABOUT OBSERVERS ANYMORE...
YES, NOTHING ABNORMAL HERE.
TAK
TAK
...C.C., DO YOU KNOW...
...WHERE NUNNALLY IS?
WE'D LIKE TO FIND YOUR SISTER, BUT THE BLACK KNIGHTS CAN'T MAKE ANY SUSPICIOUS MOVES RIGHT NOW.
IT WASN'T EASY FOR ME TO COME SEE YOU.
HERE'S THE COM-MUNICATION DEVICE YOU'LL NEED.
AND SINCE YOU CAN'T TURN YOUR GEASS OFF...
THESE CONTACT LENSES ARE SPECIALLY MADE.
THEY'LL KEEP YOUR GEASS UNDER CONTROL.
AL-THOUGH...
SHOULD YOUR GEASS GROW STRONGER THAN IT IS NOW...

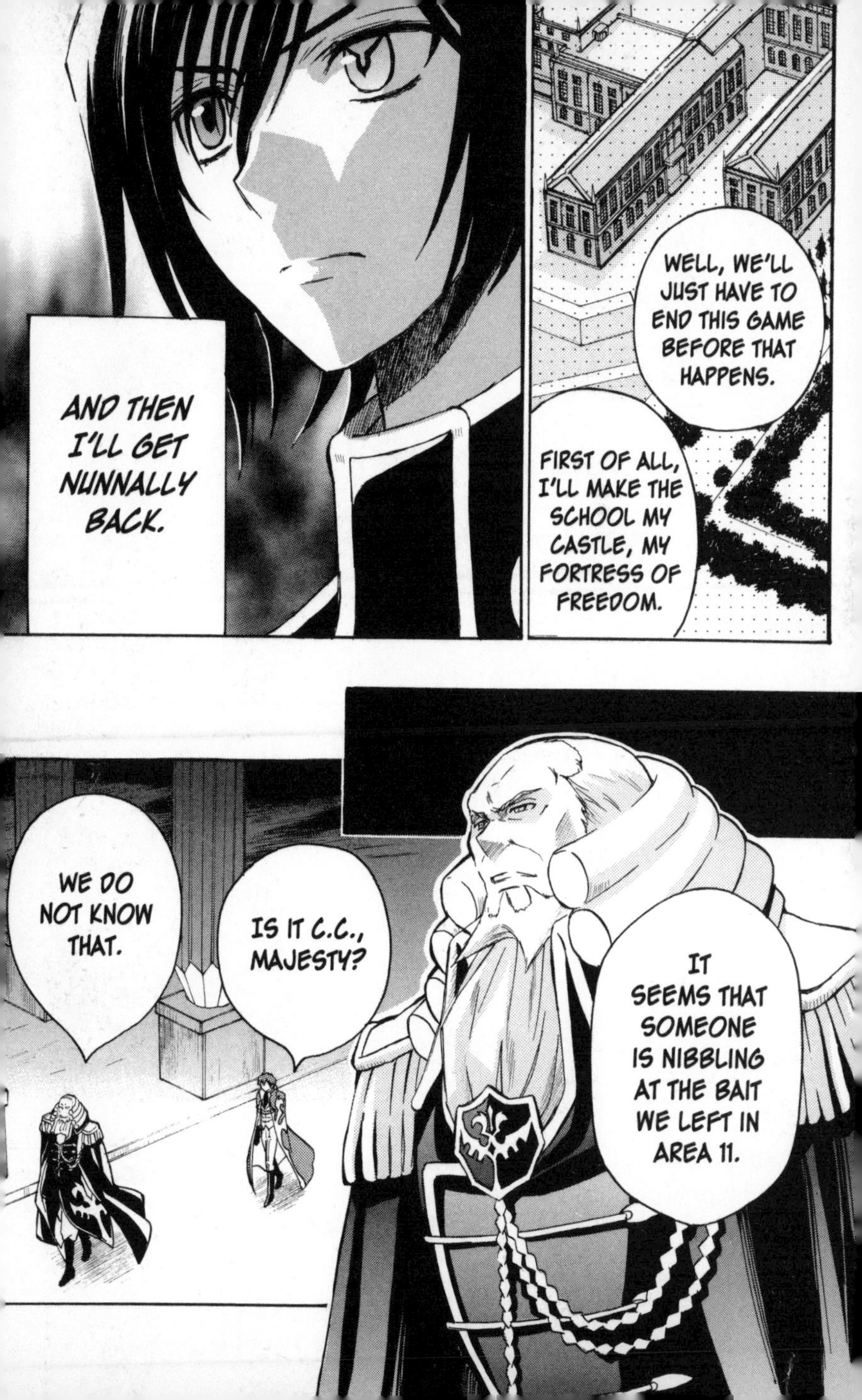
WELL, WE'LL JUST HAVE TO END THIS GAME BEFORE THAT HAPPENS.
FIRST OF ALL, I'LL MAKE THE SCHOOL MY CASTLE, MY FORTRESS OF FREEDOM.
AND THEN I'LL GET NUNNALLY BACK.
IT SEEMS THAT SOMEONE IS NIBBLING AT THE BAIT WE LEFT IN AREA 11.
IS IT C.C., MAJESTY?
WE DO NOT KNOW THAT.

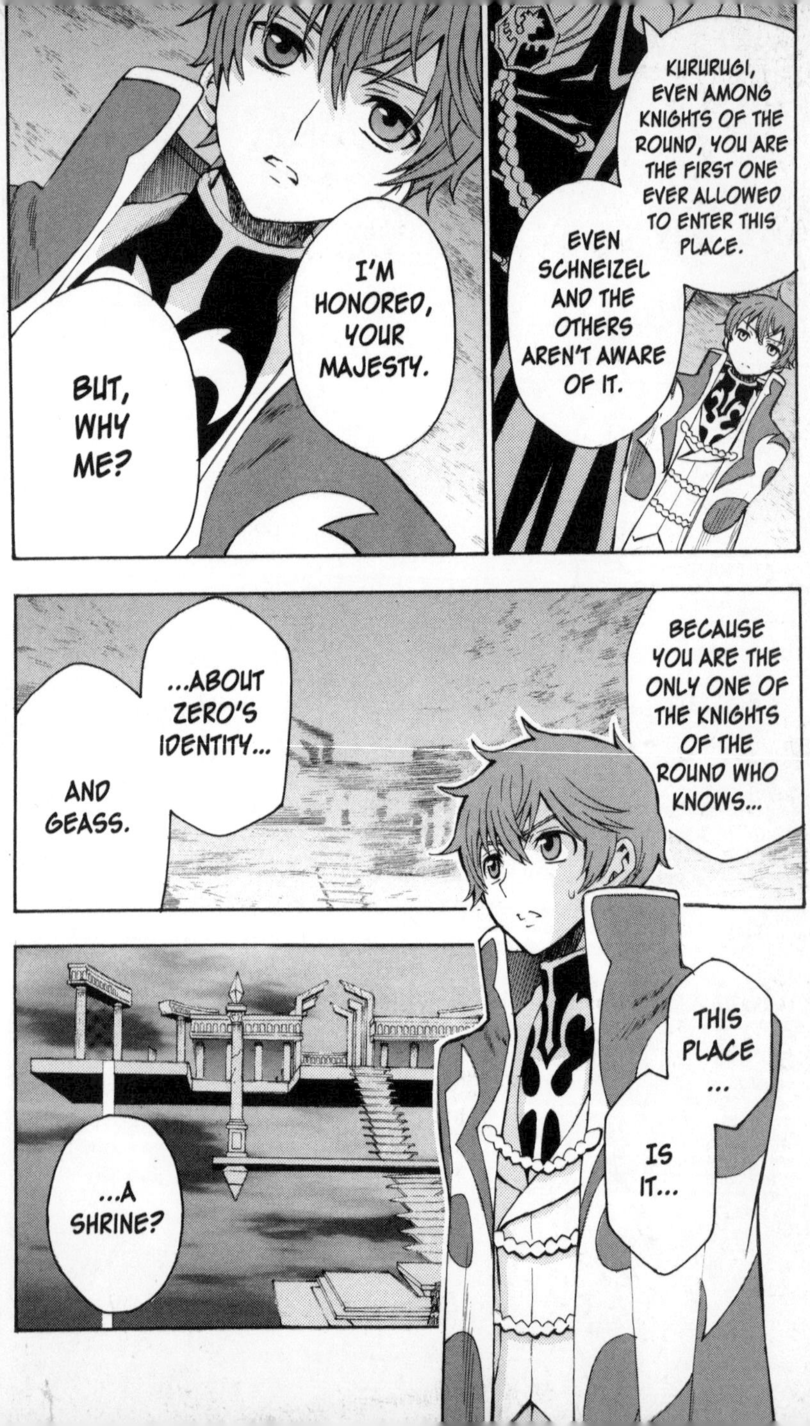
KURURUGI, EVEN AMONG KNIGHTS OF THE ROUND, YOU ARE THE FIRST ONE EVER ALLOWED TO ENTER THIS PLACE.
EVEN SCHNEIZEL AND THE OTHERS AREN'T AWARE OF IT.
I'M HONORED, YOUR MAJESTY.
BUT, WHY ME?
BECAUSE YOU ARE THE ONLY ONE OF THE KNIGHTS OF THE ROUND WHO KNOWS...
...ABOUT ZERO'S IDENTITY...
AND GEASS.
THIS PLACE ...
IS IT...
...A SHRINE?

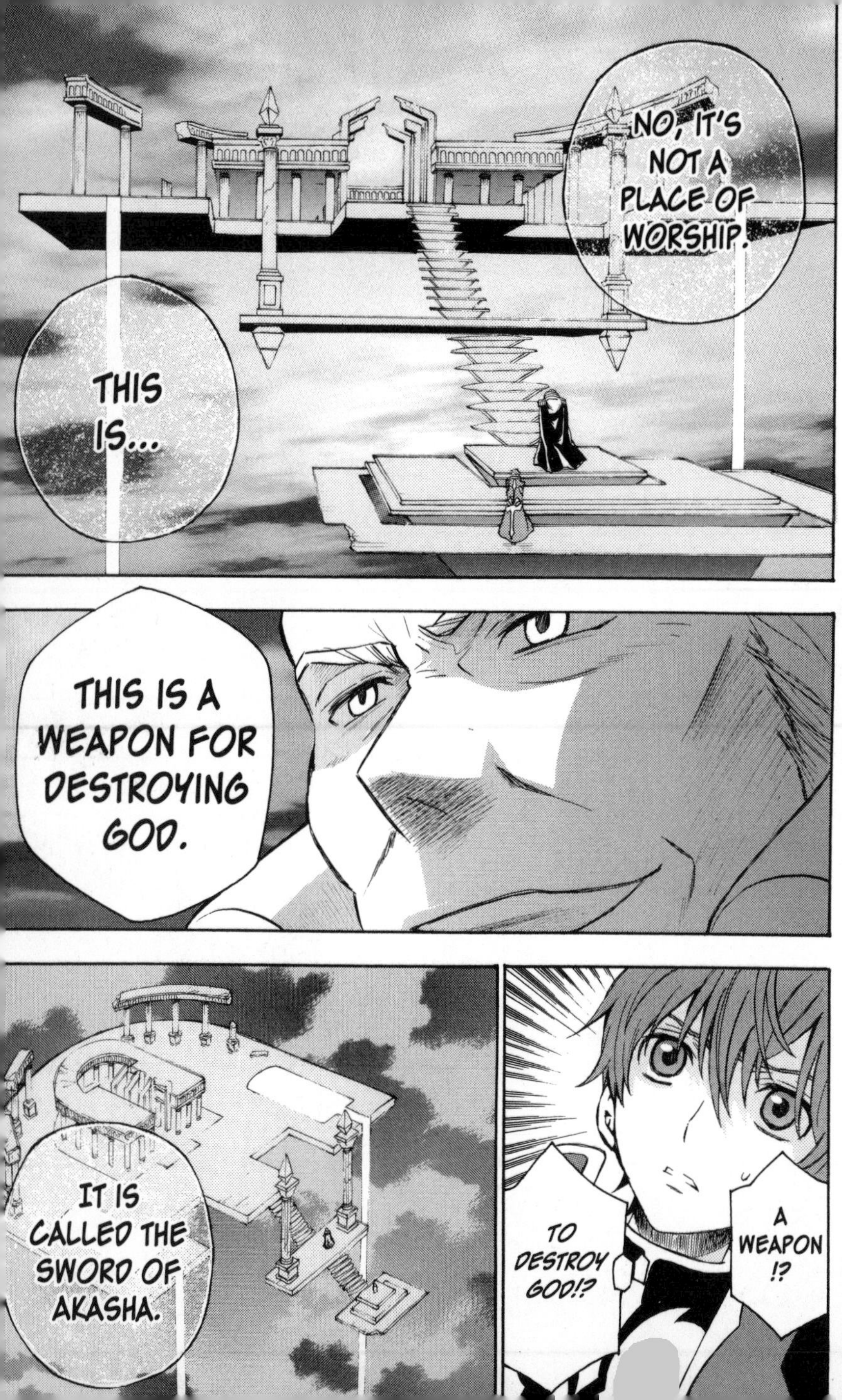
NO, IT'S NOT A PLACE OF WORSHIP.
THIS IS...
THIS IS A WEAPON FOR DESTROYING GOD.
A WEAPON!?
TO DESTROY GOD!?
IT IS CALLED THE SWORD OF AKASHA.

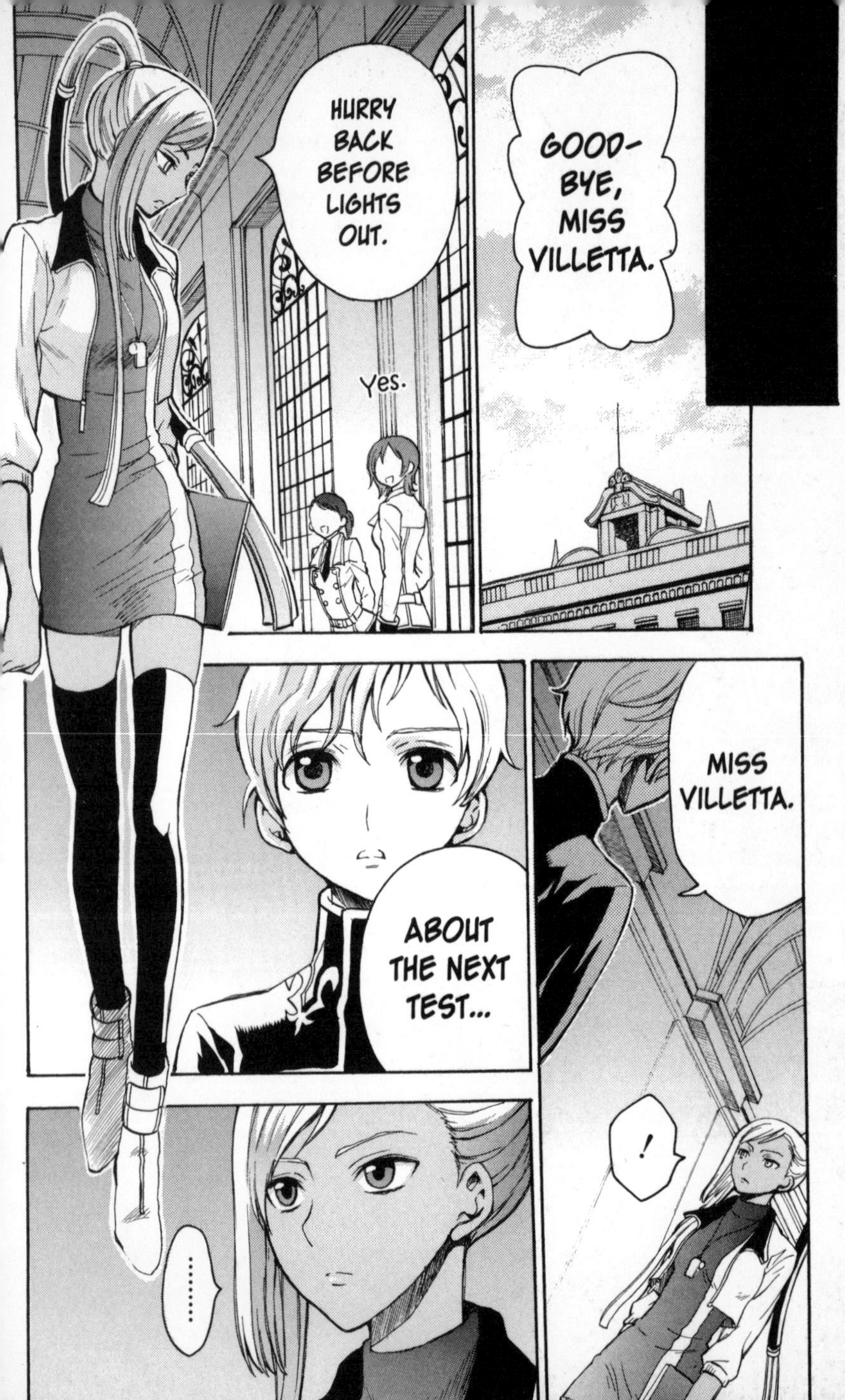
GOOD-BYE, MISS VILLETTA.
HURRY BACK BEFORE LIGHTS OUT.
Yes.
MISS VILLETTA.
ABOUT THE NEXT TEST...
!
....

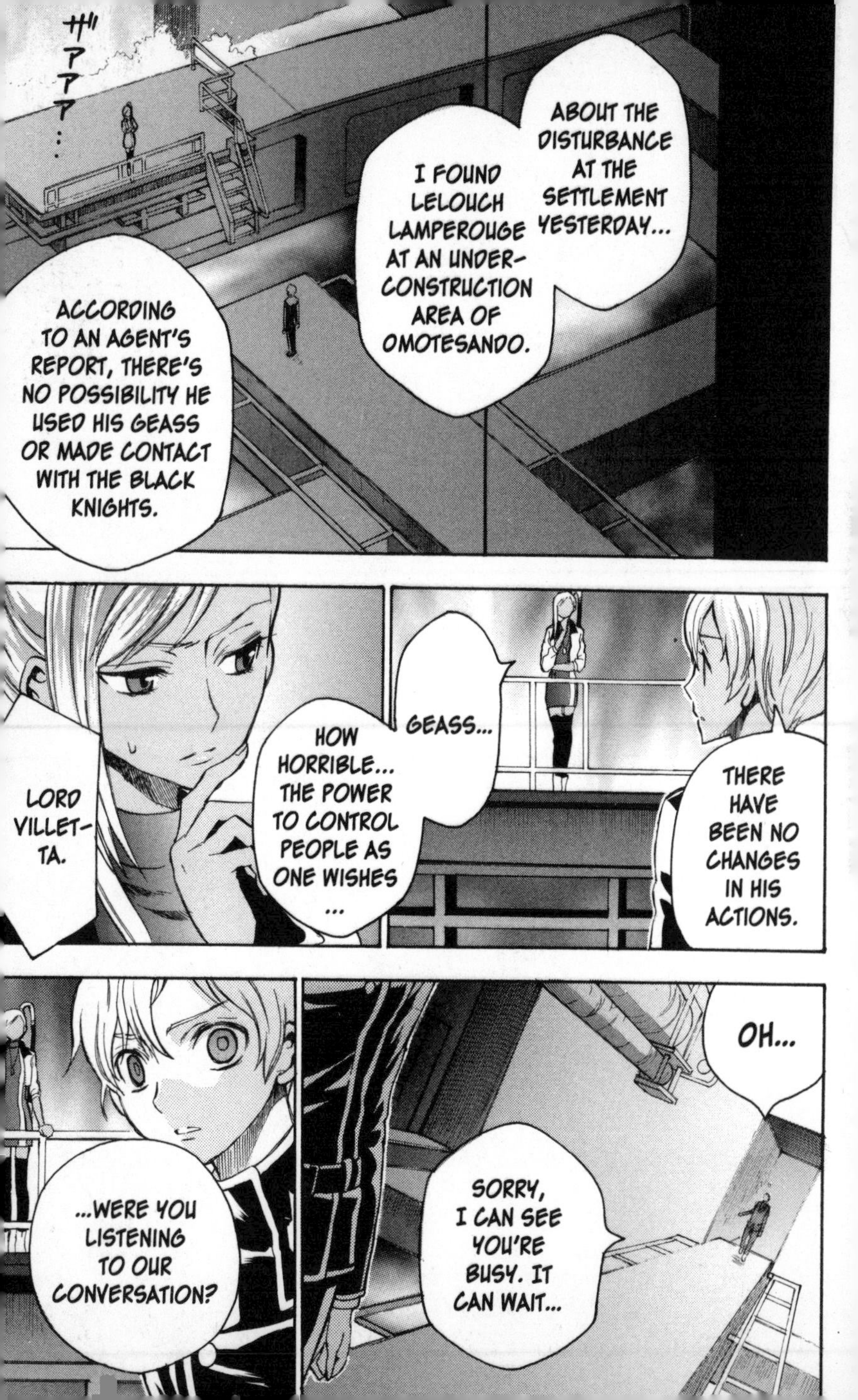

ABOUT THE DISTURBANCE AT THE SETTLEMENT YESTERDAY...
I FOUND LELOUCH LAMPEROUGE AT AN UNDER-CONSTRUCTION AREA OF OMOTESANDO.
ザァァァ...
ACCORDING TO AN AGENT'S REPORT, THERE'S NO POSSIBILITY HE USED HIS GEASS OR MADE CONTACT WITH THE BLACK KNIGHTS.
THERE HAVE BEEN NO CHANGES IN HIS ACTIONS.
GEASS...
HOW HORRIBLE... THE POWER TO CONTROL PEOPLE AS ONE WISHES...
LORD VILLETTA.
OH...
SORRY, I CAN SEE YOU'RE BUSY. IT CAN WAIT...
...WERE YOU LISTENING TO OUR CONVERSATION?

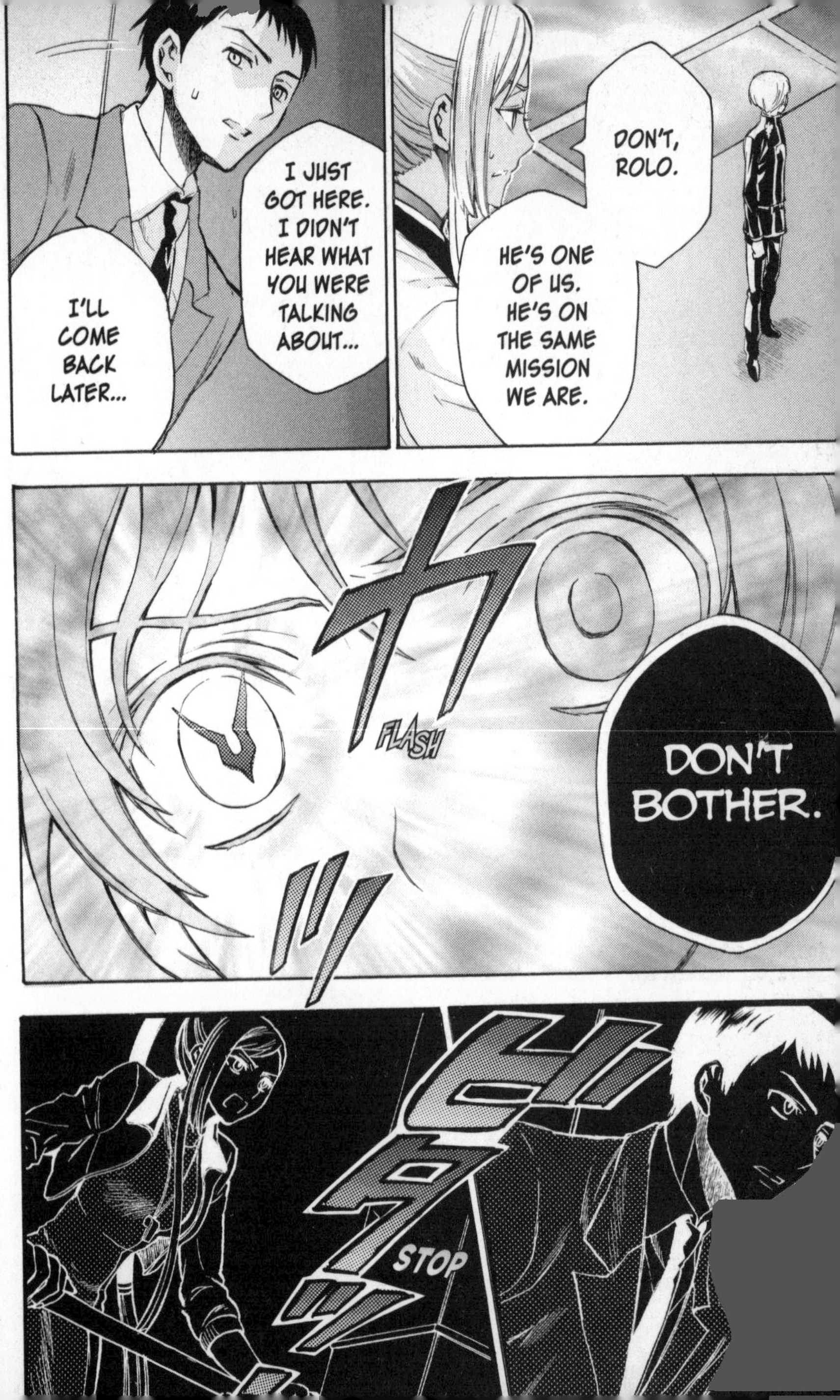
DON'T, ROLO.
HE'S ONE OF US. HE'S ON THE SAME MISSION WE ARE.
I JUST GOT HERE. I DIDN'T HEAR WHAT YOU WERE TALKING ABOUT...
I'LL COME BACK LATER...
DON'T BOTHER.
FLASH
STOP

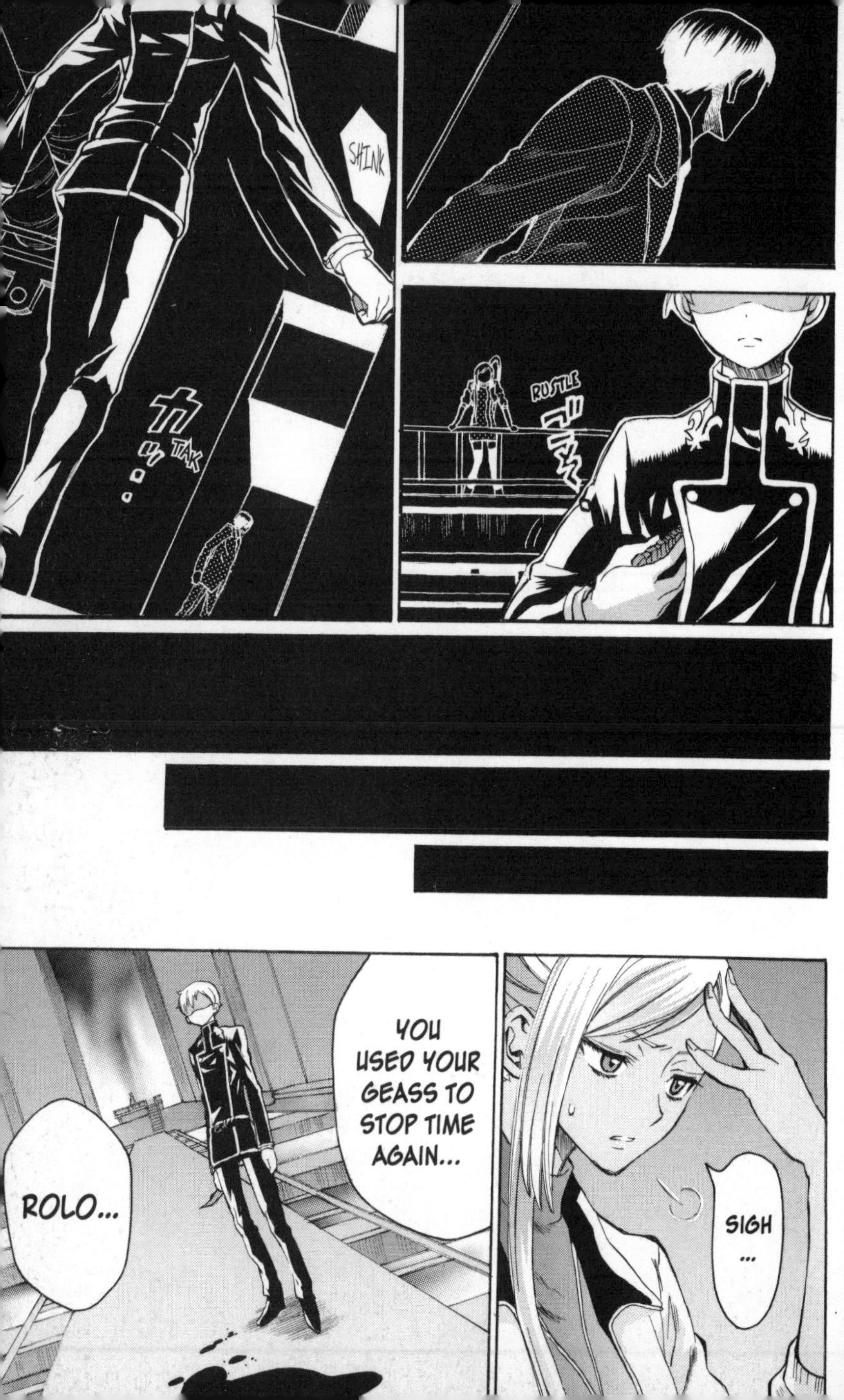
RUSTLE
SHINK
TAK
SIGH...
YOU USED YOUR GEASS TO STOP TIME AGAIN...
ROLO...

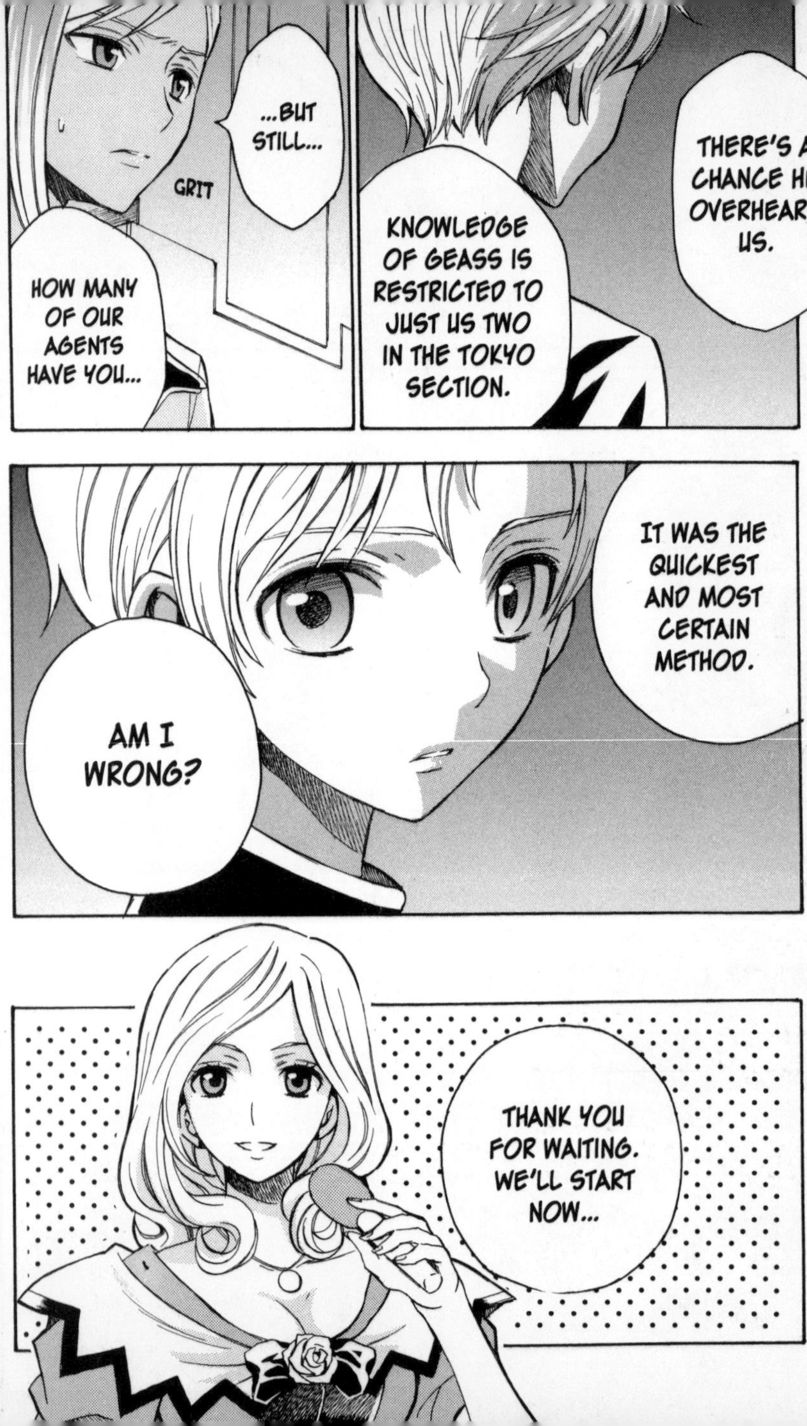
THERE'S A CHANCE HE OVERHEARD US.
KNOWLEDGE OF GEASS IS RESTRICTED TO JUST US TWO IN THE TOKYO SECTION.
...BUT STILL...
GRIT
HOW MANY OF OUR AGENTS HAVE YOU...
IT WAS THE QUICKEST AND MOST CERTAIN METHOD.
AM I WRONG?
THANK YOU FOR WAITING. WE'LL START NOW...

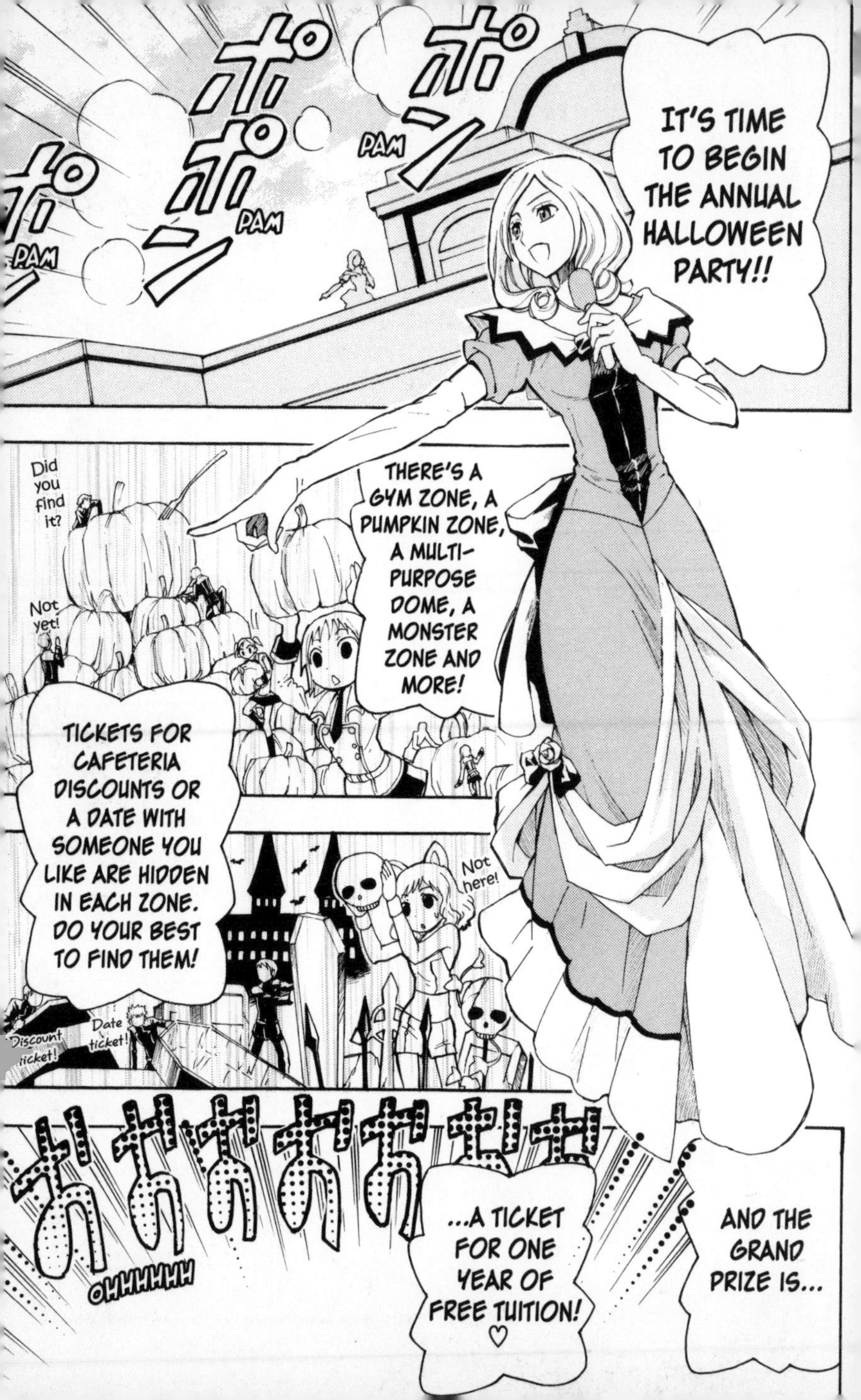

IT'S TIME TO BEGIN THE ANNUAL HALLOWEEN PARTY!!
PAM
PAM
PAM
THERE'S A GYM ZONE, A PUMPKIN ZONE, A MULTI-PURPOSE DOME, A MONSTER ZONE AND MORE!
Did you find it?
Not yet!
TICKETS FOR CAFETERIA DISCOUNTS OR A DATE WITH SOMEONE YOU LIKE ARE HIDDEN IN EACH ZONE. DO YOUR BEST TO FIND THEM!
Not here!
Date ticket!
Discount ticket!
AND THE GRAND PRIZE IS...
...A TICKET FOR ONE YEAR OF FREE TUITION! ♡
OHHHHHH

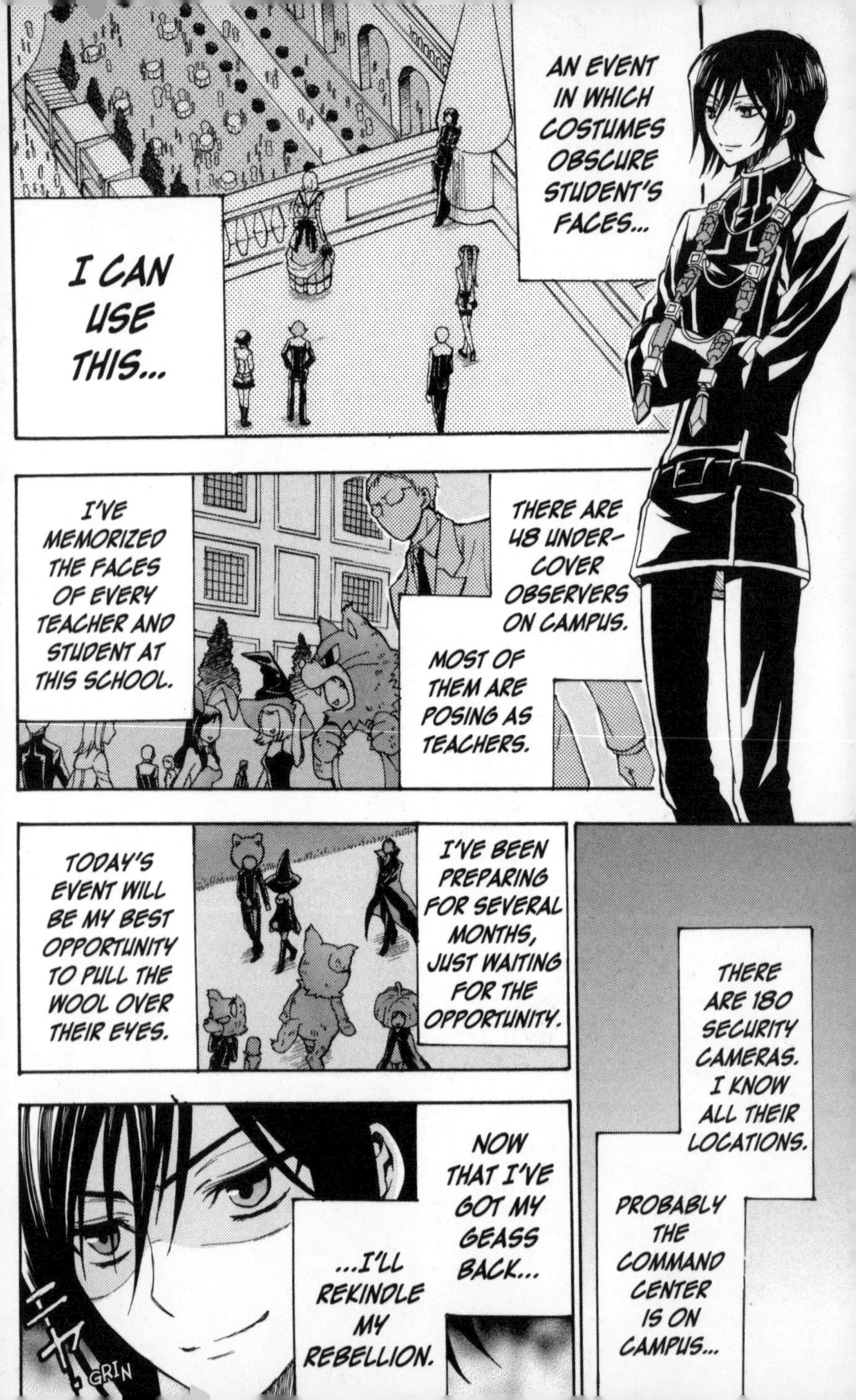
AN EVENT IN WHICH COSTUMES OBSCURE STUDENT'S FACES...
I CAN USE THIS...
THERE ARE 48 UNDER-COVER OBSERVERS ON CAMPUS.
MOST OF THEM ARE POSING AS TEACHERS.
I'VE MEMORIZED THE FACES OF EVERY TEACHER AND STUDENT AT THIS SCHOOL.
THERE ARE 180 SECURITY CAMERAS. I KNOW ALL THEIR LOCATIONS.
PROBABLY THE COMMAND CENTER IS ON CAMPUS...
I'VE BEEN PREPARING FOR SEVERAL MONTHS, JUST WAITING FOR THE OPPORTUNITY.
TODAY'S EVENT WILL BE MY BEST OPPORTUNITY TO PULL THE WOOL OVER THEIR EYES.
NOW THAT I'VE GOT MY GEASS BACK...
...I'LL REKINDLE MY REBELLION.
GRIN

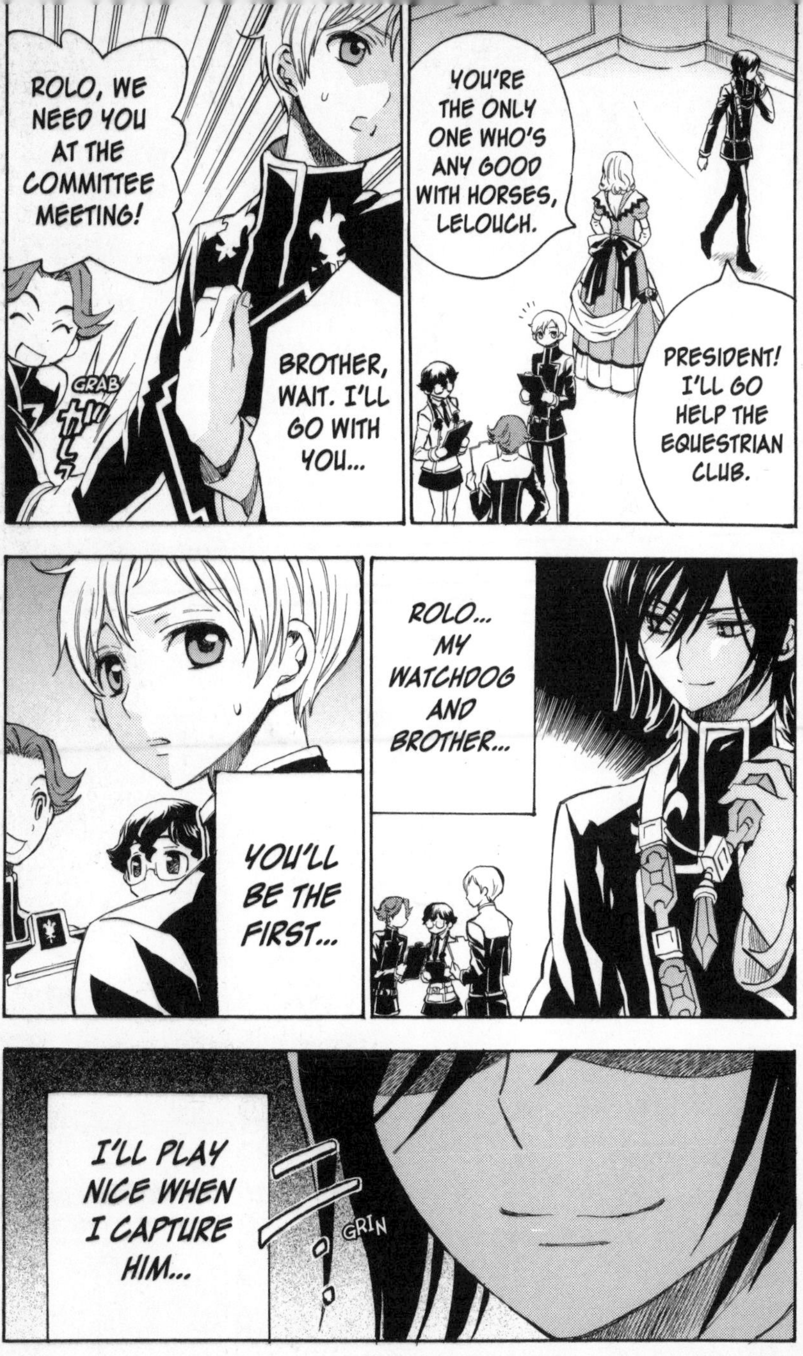
YOU'RE THE ONLY ONE WHO'S ANY GOOD WITH HORSES, LELOUCH.
PRESIDENT! I'LL GO HELP THE EQUESTRIAN CLUB.
BROTHER, WAIT. I'LL GO WITH YOU...
ROLO, WE NEED YOU AT THE COMMITTEE MEETING!
GRAB
ROLO... MY WATCHDOG AND BROTHER...
YOU'LL BE THE FIRST...
I'LL PLAY NICE WHEN I CAPTURE HIM...
GRIN

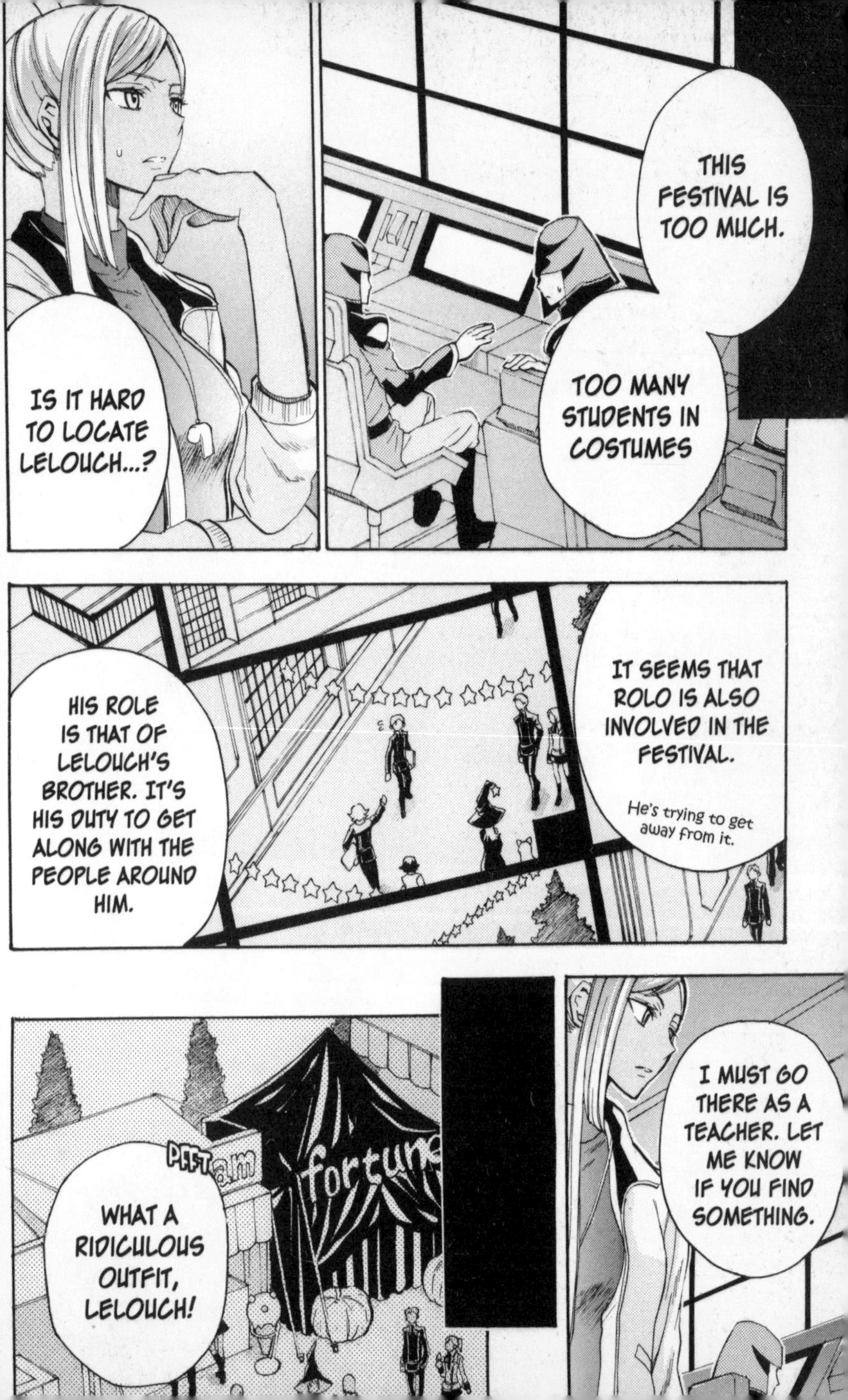
THIS FESTIVAL IS TOO MUCH.
TOO MANY STUDENTS IN COSTUMES
IS IT HARD TO LOCATE LELOUCH...?
IT SEEMS THAT ROLO IS ALSO INVOLVED IN THE FESTIVAL.
He's trying to get away from it.
HIS ROLE IS THAT OF LELOUCH'S BROTHER. IT'S HIS DUTY TO GET ALONG WITH THE PEOPLE AROUND HIM.
I MUST GO THERE AS A TEACHER. LET ME KNOW IF YOU FIND SOMETHING.
PFFT
WHAT A RIDICULOUS OUTFIT, LELOUCH!

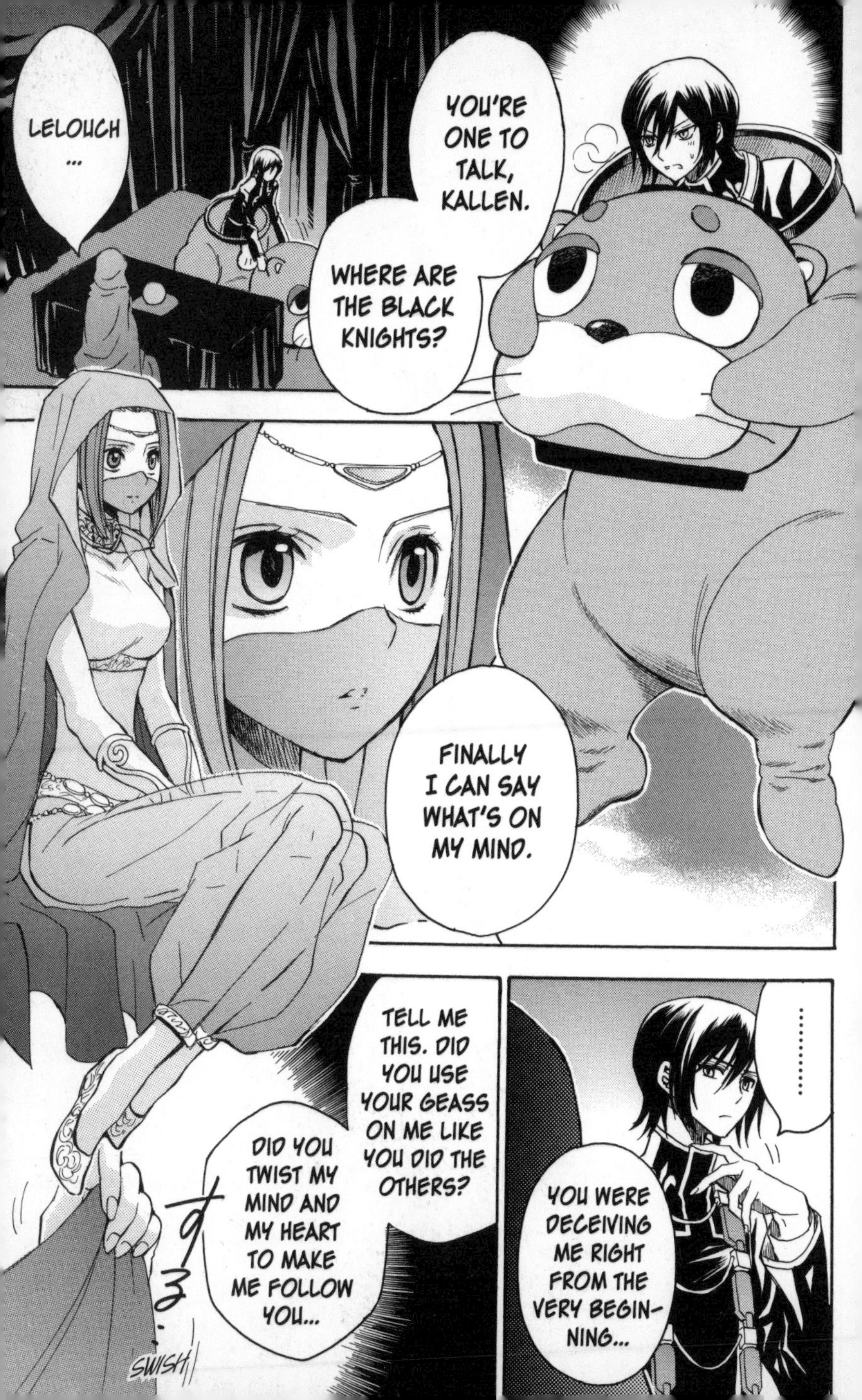
YOU'RE ONE TO TALK, KALLEN.
WHERE ARE THE BLACK KNIGHTS?
LELOUCH ...
FINALLY I CAN SAY WHAT'S ON MY MIND.
......
YOU WERE DECEIVING ME RIGHT FROM THE VERY BEGIN-NING...
TELL ME THIS. DID YOU USE YOUR GEASS ON ME LIKE YOU DID THE OTHERS?
DID YOU TWIST MY MIND AND MY HEART TO MAKE ME FOLLOW YOU...
SWISH

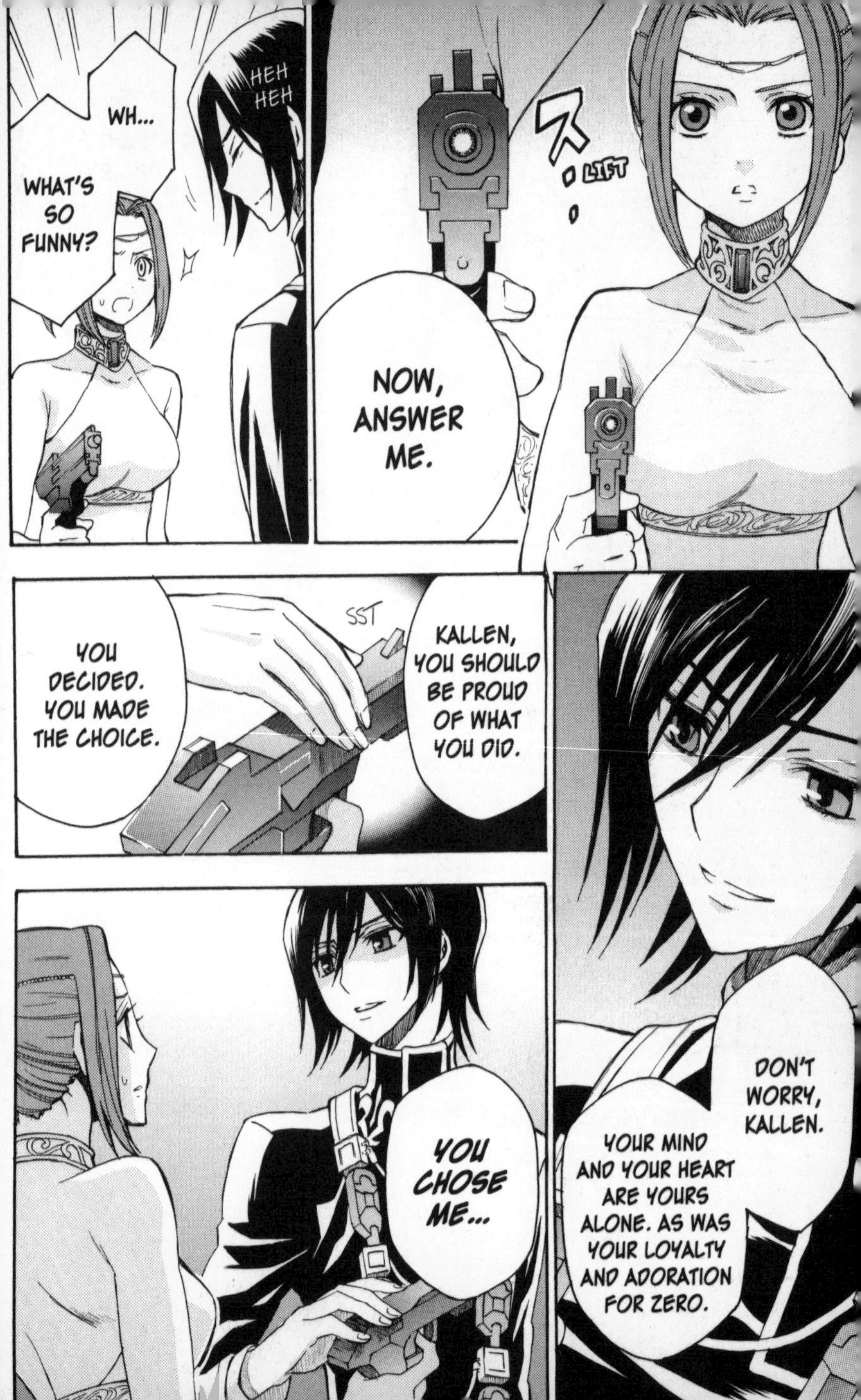
ス
LIFT
NOW, ANSWER ME.
HEH HEH
WH...
WHAT'S SO FUNNY?
DON'T WORRY, KALLEN.
YOUR MIND AND YOUR HEART ARE YOURS ALONE. AS WAS YOUR LOYALTY AND ADORATION FOR ZERO.
SST
KALLEN, YOU SHOULD BE PROUD OF WHAT YOU DID.
YOU DECIDED. YOU MADE THE CHOICE.
YOU CHOSE ME...

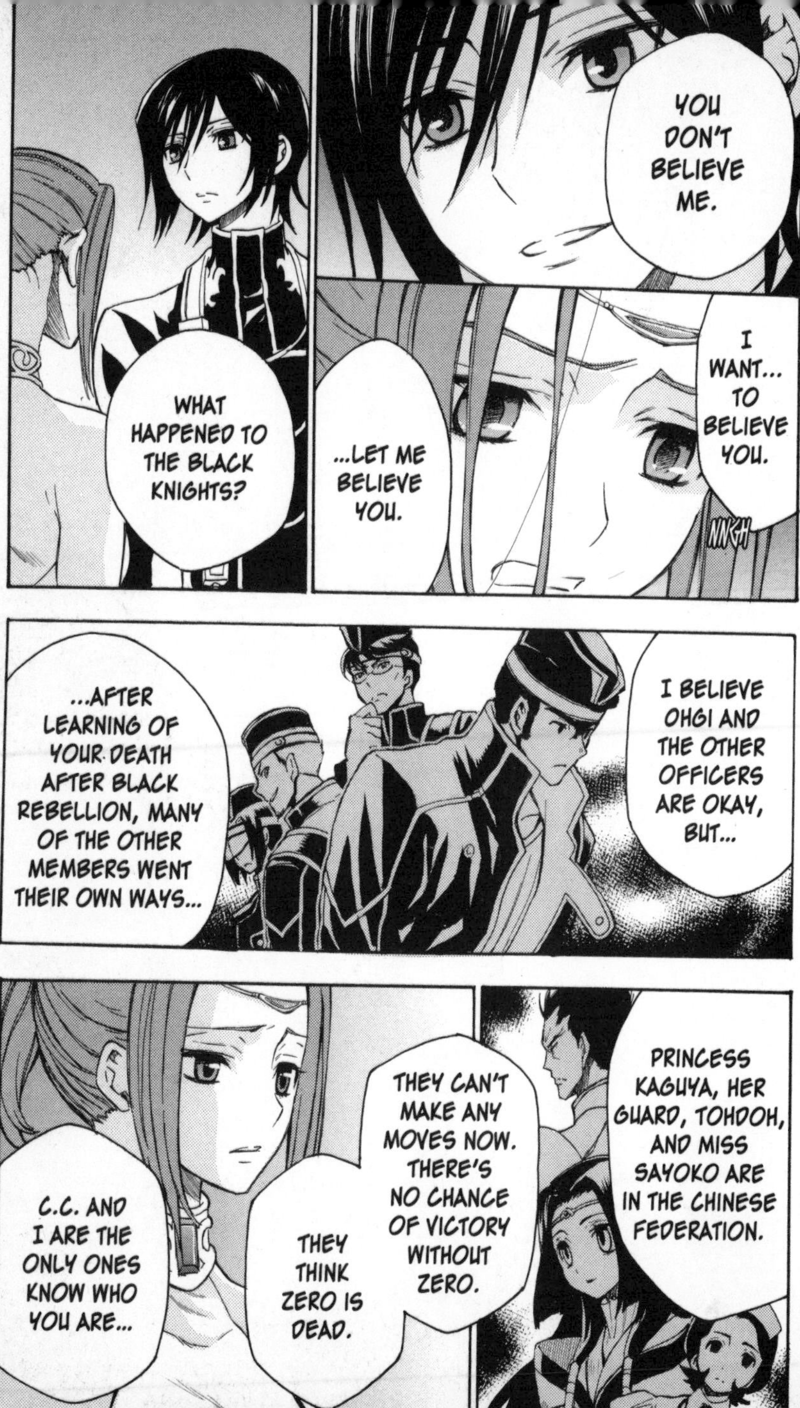
YOU DON'T BELIEVE ME.
I WANT... TO BELIEVE YOU.
NNGH
...LET ME BELIEVE YOU.
WHAT HAPPENED TO THE BLACK KNIGHTS?
I BELIEVE OHGI AND THE OTHER OFFICERS ARE OKAY, BUT...
...AFTER LEARNING OF YOUR DEATH AFTER BLACK REBELLION, MANY OF THE OTHER MEMBERS WENT THEIR OWN WAYS...
PRINCESS KAGUYA, HER GUARD, TOHDOH, AND MISS SAYOKO ARE IN THE CHINESE FEDERATION.
THEY CAN'T MAKE ANY MOVES NOW. THERE'S NO CHANCE OF VICTORY WITHOUT ZERO.
THEY THINK ZERO IS DEAD.
C.C. AND I ARE THE ONLY ONES KNOW WHO YOU ARE...

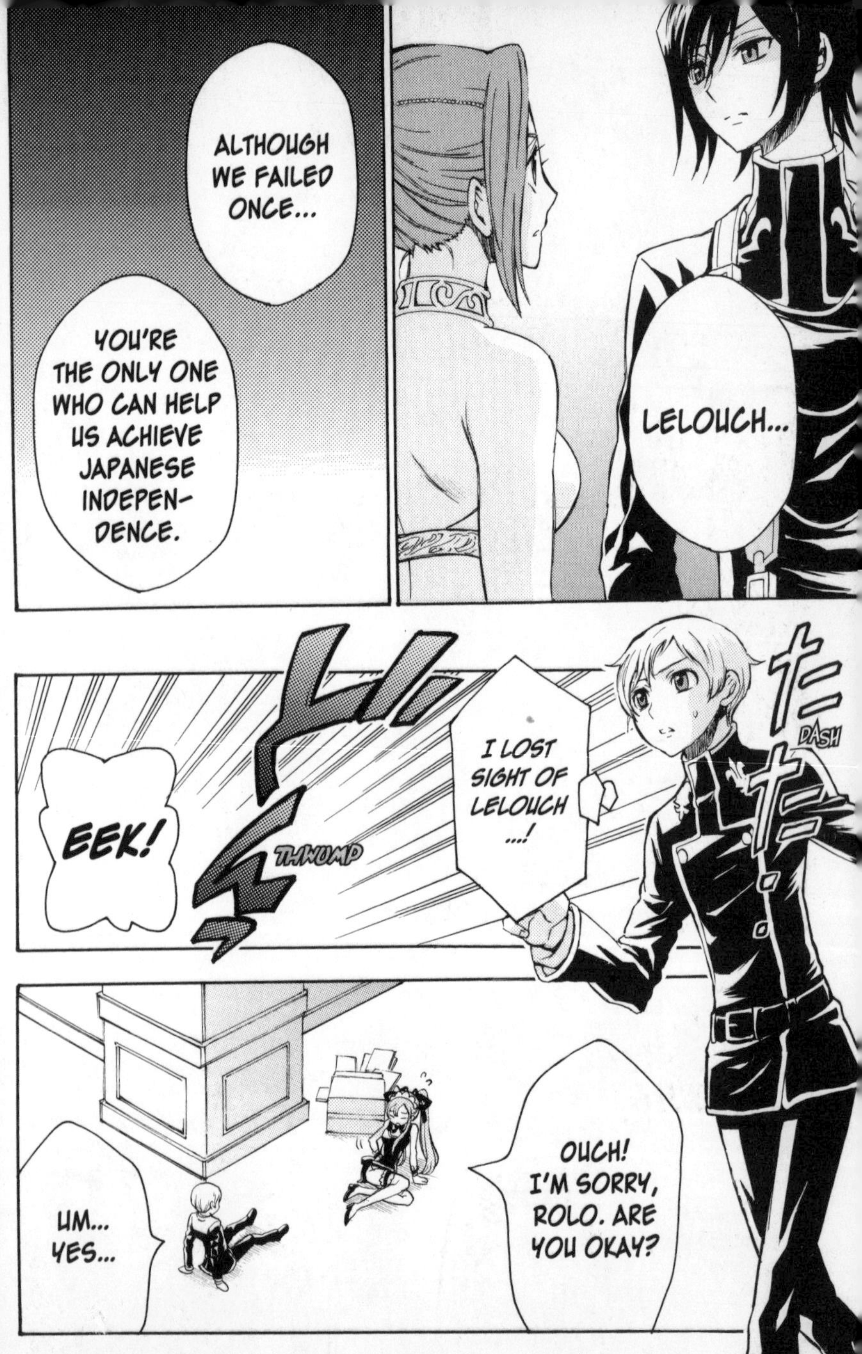
LELOUCH...
ALTHOUGH WE FAILED ONCE...
YOU'RE THE ONLY ONE WHO CAN HELP US ACHIEVE JAPANESE INDEPEN-DENCE.
DASH
I LOST SIGHT OF LELOUCH ...!
THWUMP
EEK!
OUCH! I'M SORRY, ROLO. ARE YOU OKAY?
UM... YES...

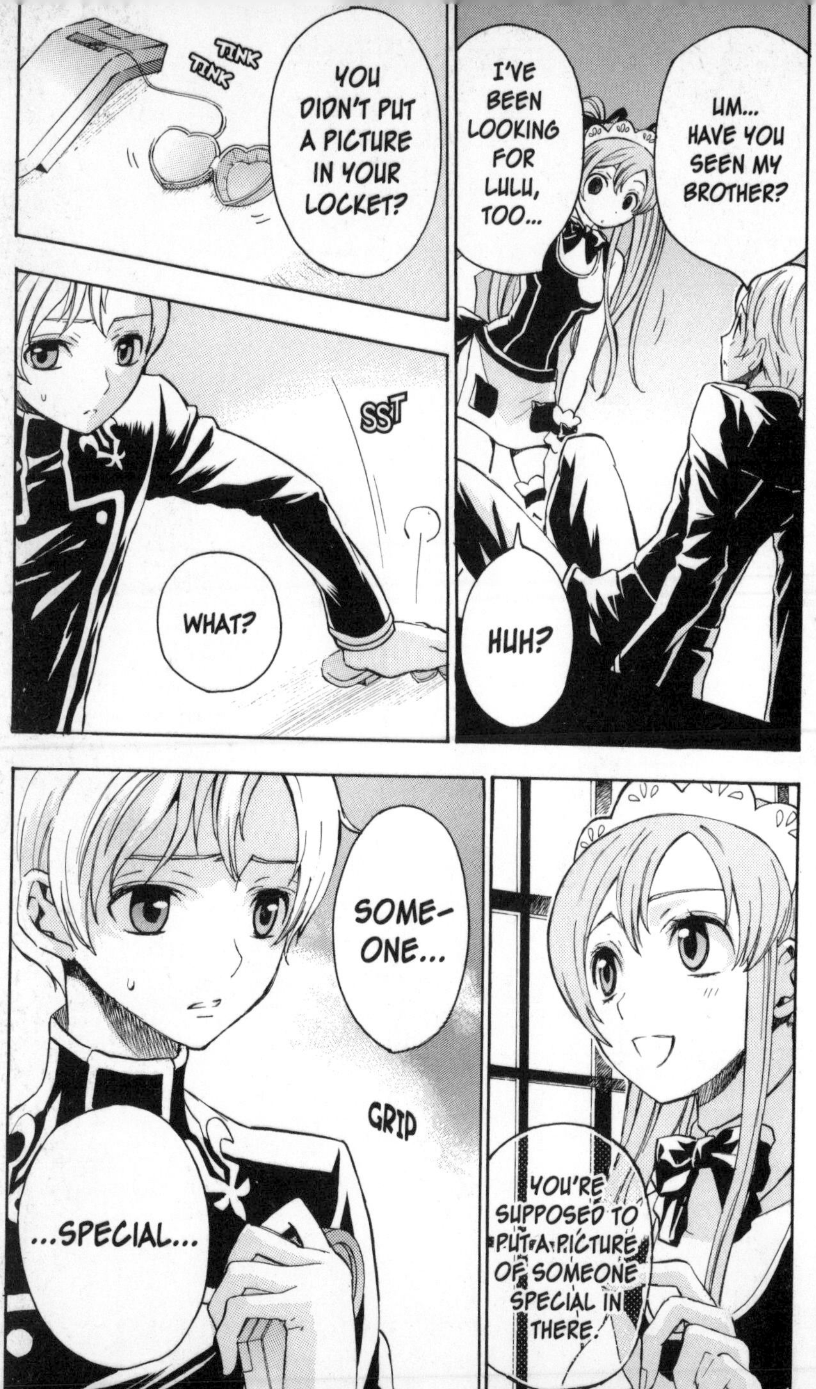
UM... HAVE YOU SEEN MY BROTHER?
I'VE BEEN LOOKING FOR LULU, TOO...
HUH?
TINK TINK
YOU DIDN'T PUT A PICTURE IN YOUR LOCKET?
SST
WHAT?
YOU'RE SUPPOSED TO PUT A PICTURE OF SOMEONE SPECIAL IN THERE.
SOME-ONE...
GRIP
...SPECIAL...

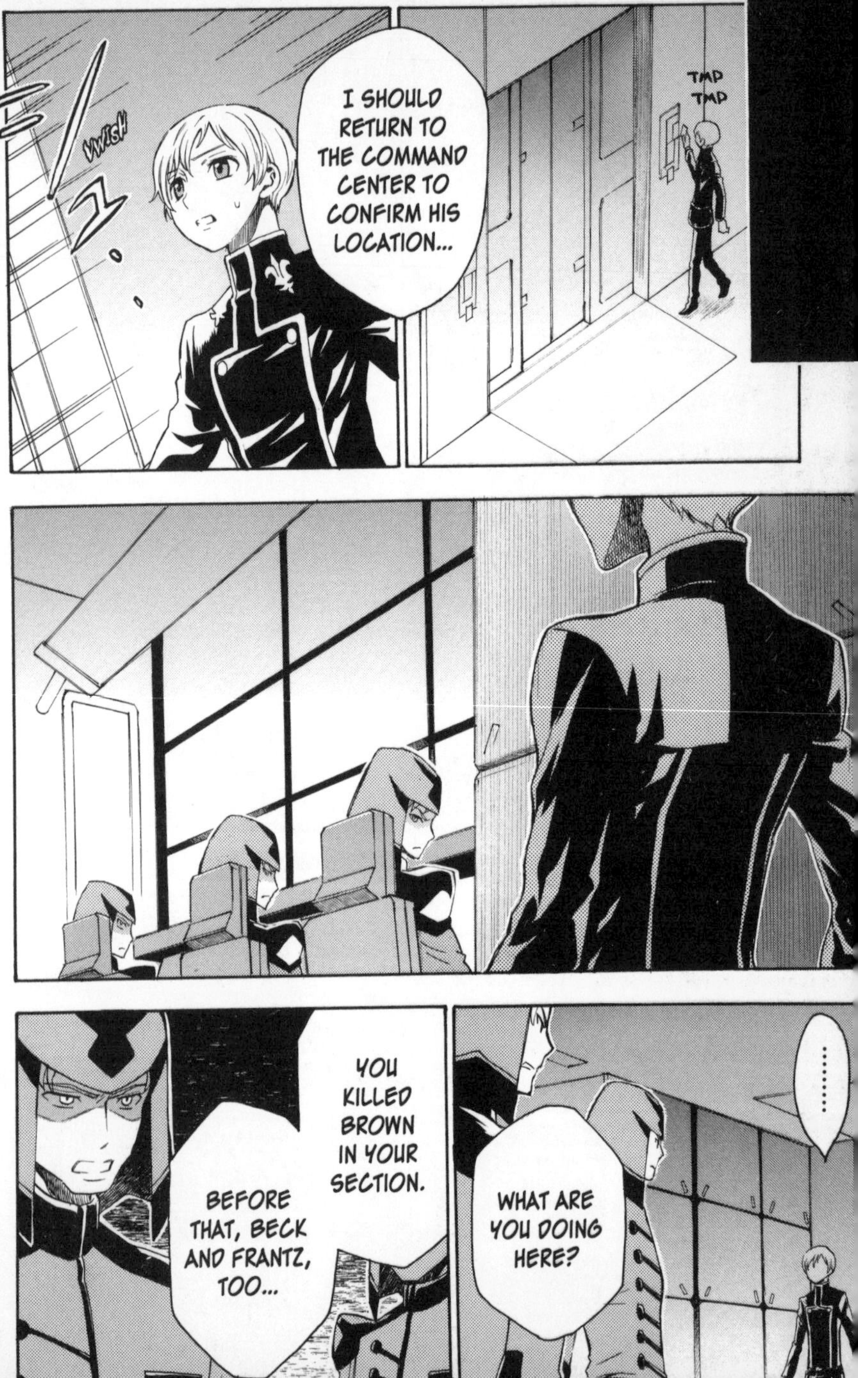
TMP
TMP
I SHOULD RETURN TO THE COMMAND CENTER TO CONFIRM HIS LOCATION...
VWISH
......
WHAT ARE YOU DOING HERE?
YOU KILLED BROWN IN YOUR SECTION.
BEFORE THAT, BECK AND FRANTZ, TOO...

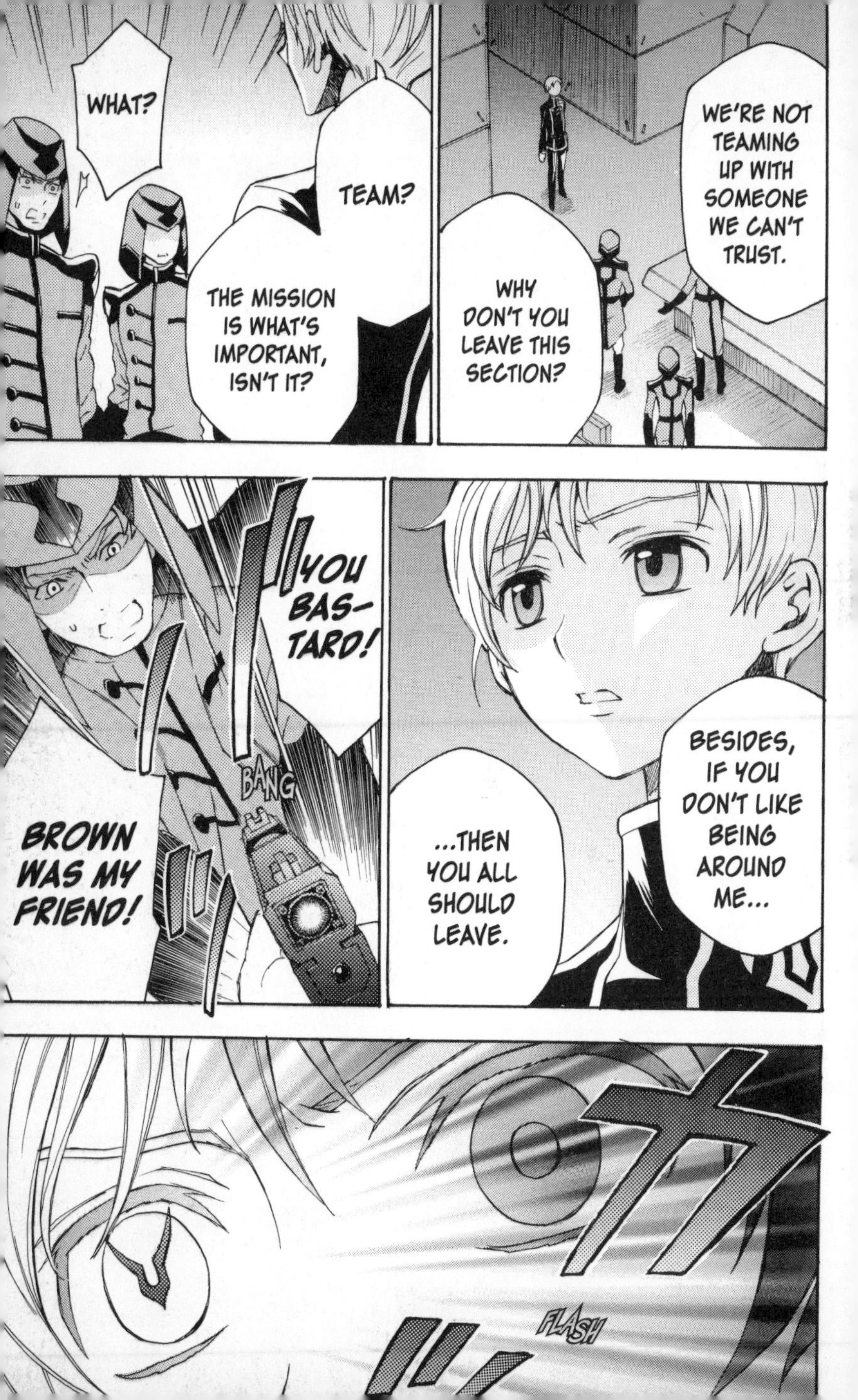
WE'RE NOT TEAMING UP WITH SOMEONE WE CAN'T TRUST.
WHY DON'T YOU LEAVE THIS SECTION?
WHAT?
TEAM?
THE MISSION IS WHAT'S IMPORTANT, ISN'T IT?
BESIDES, IF YOU DON'T LIKE BEING AROUND ME...
...THEN YOU ALL SHOULD LEAVE.
YOU BAS-TARD!
BANG
BROWN WAS MY FRIEND!
FLASH

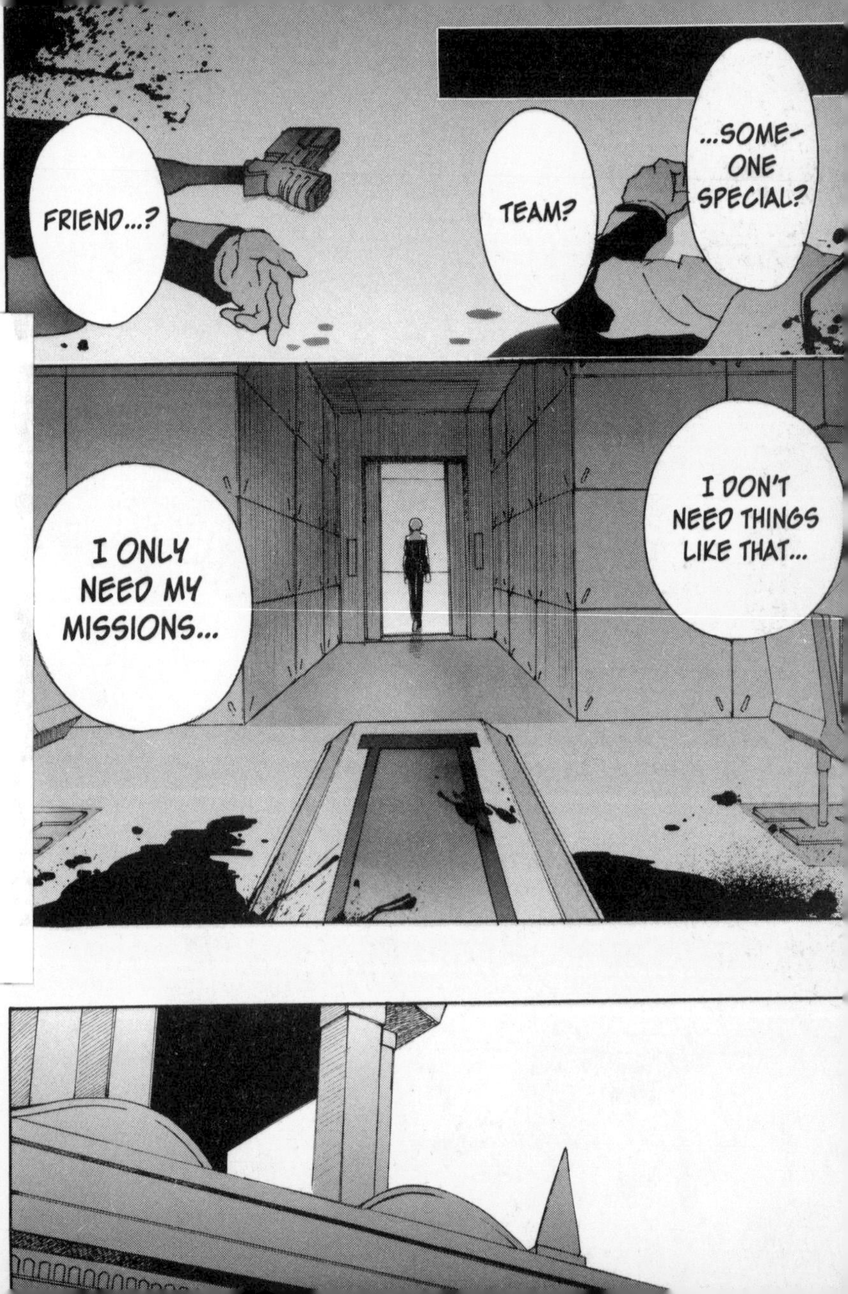
...SOME-ONE SPECIAL?
TEAM?
FRIEND...?
I DON'T NEED THINGS LIKE THAT...
I ONLY NEED MY MISSIONS...

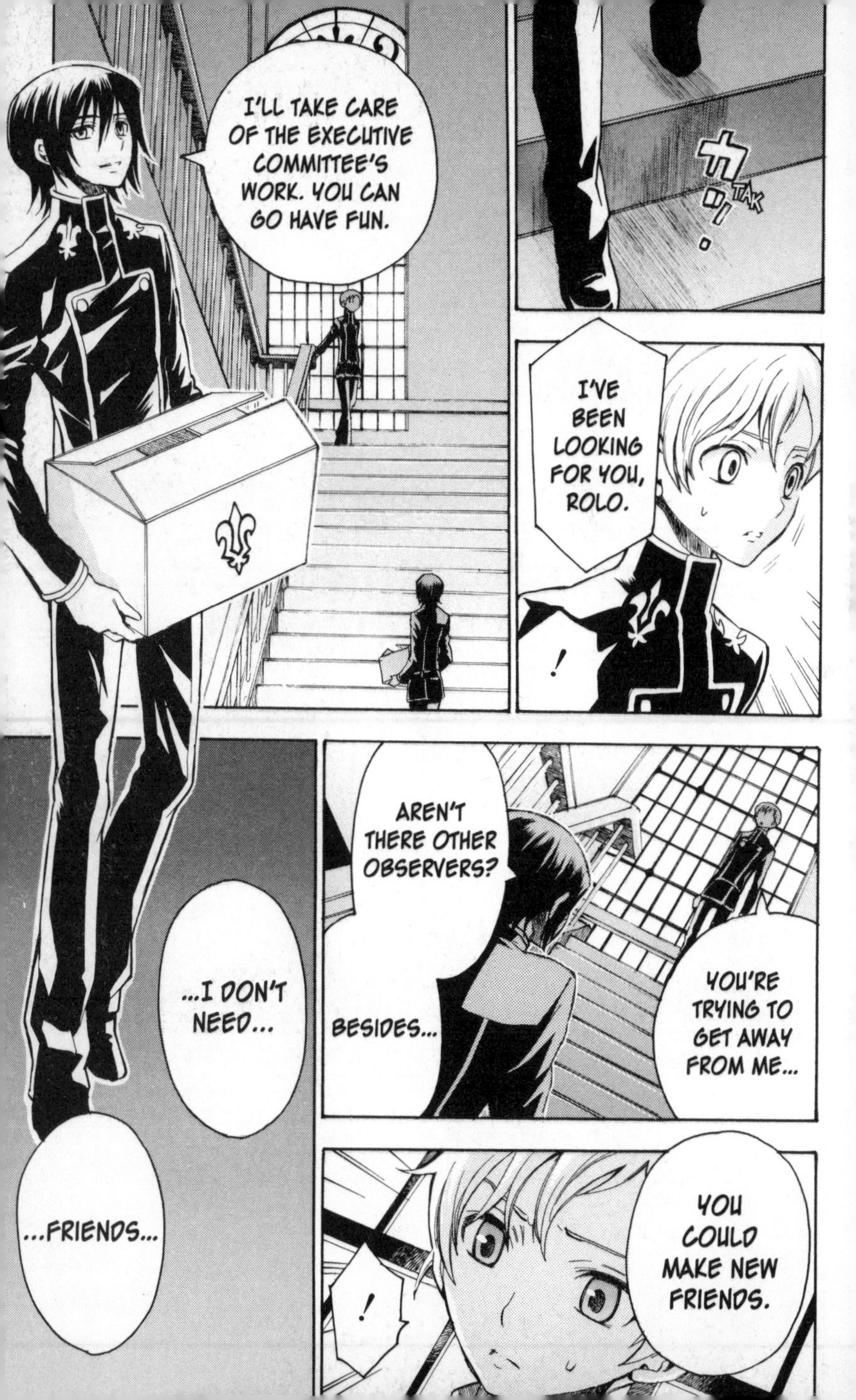
カツ
TAK
I'VE BEEN LOOKING FOR YOU, ROLO.
!
I'LL TAKE CARE OF THE EXECUTIVE COMMITTEE'S WORK. YOU CAN GO HAVE FUN.
AREN'T THERE OTHER OBSERVERS?
YOU'RE TRYING TO GET AWAY FROM ME...
BESIDES...
YOU COULD MAKE NEW FRIENDS.
!
...I DON'T NEED...
...FRIENDS...

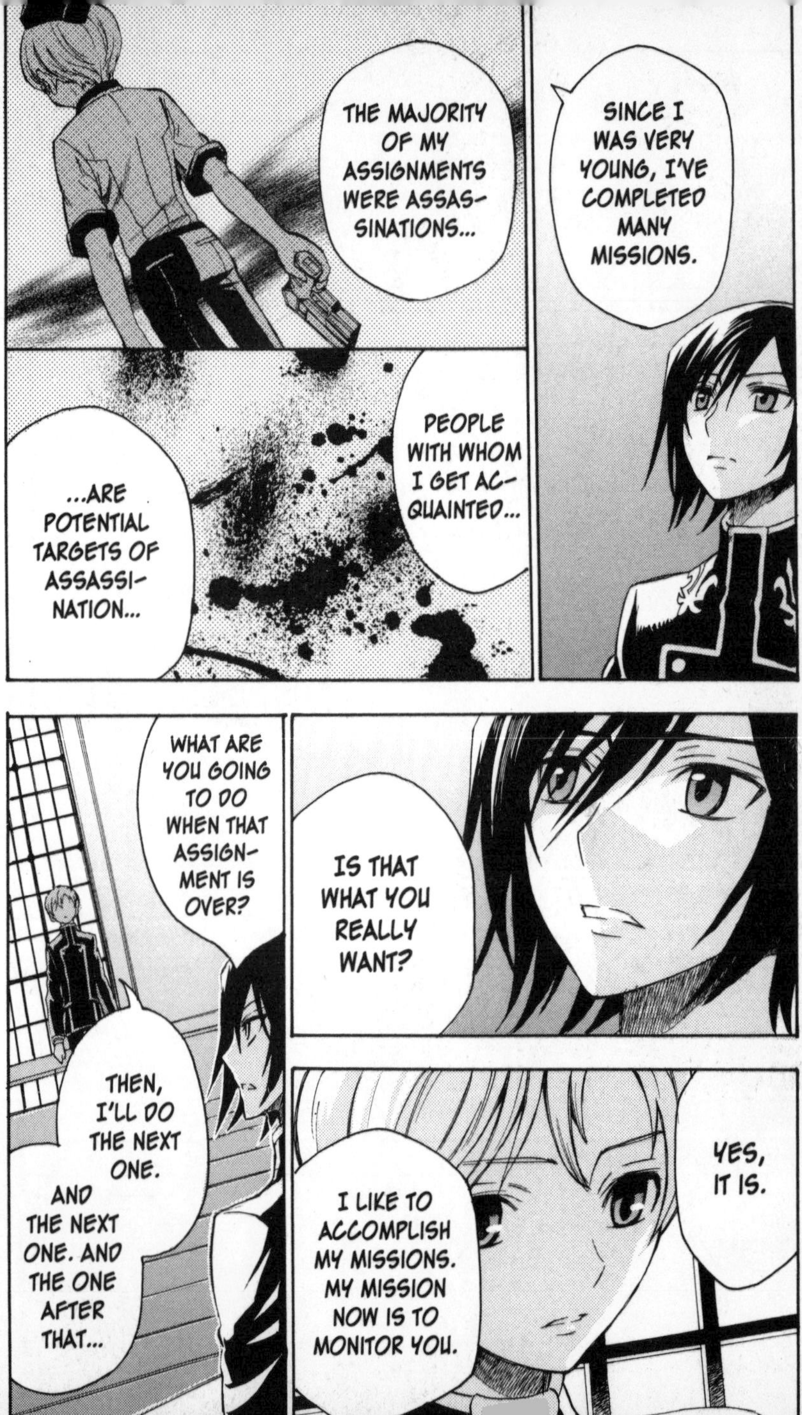
SINCE I WAS VERY YOUNG, I'VE COMPLETED MANY MISSIONS.
THE MAJORITY OF MY ASSIGNMENTS WERE ASSAS-SINATIONS...
PEOPLE WITH WHOM I GET AC-QUAINTED...
...ARE POTENTIAL TARGETS OF ASSASSI-NATION...
IS THAT WHAT YOU REALLY WANT?
YES, IT IS.
I LIKE TO ACCOMPLISH MY MISSIONS. MY MISSION NOW IS TO MONITOR YOU.
WHAT ARE YOU GOING TO DO WHEN THAT ASSIGN-MENT IS OVER?
THEN, I'LL DO THE NEXT ONE.
AND THE NEXT ONE. AND THE ONE AFTER THAT...

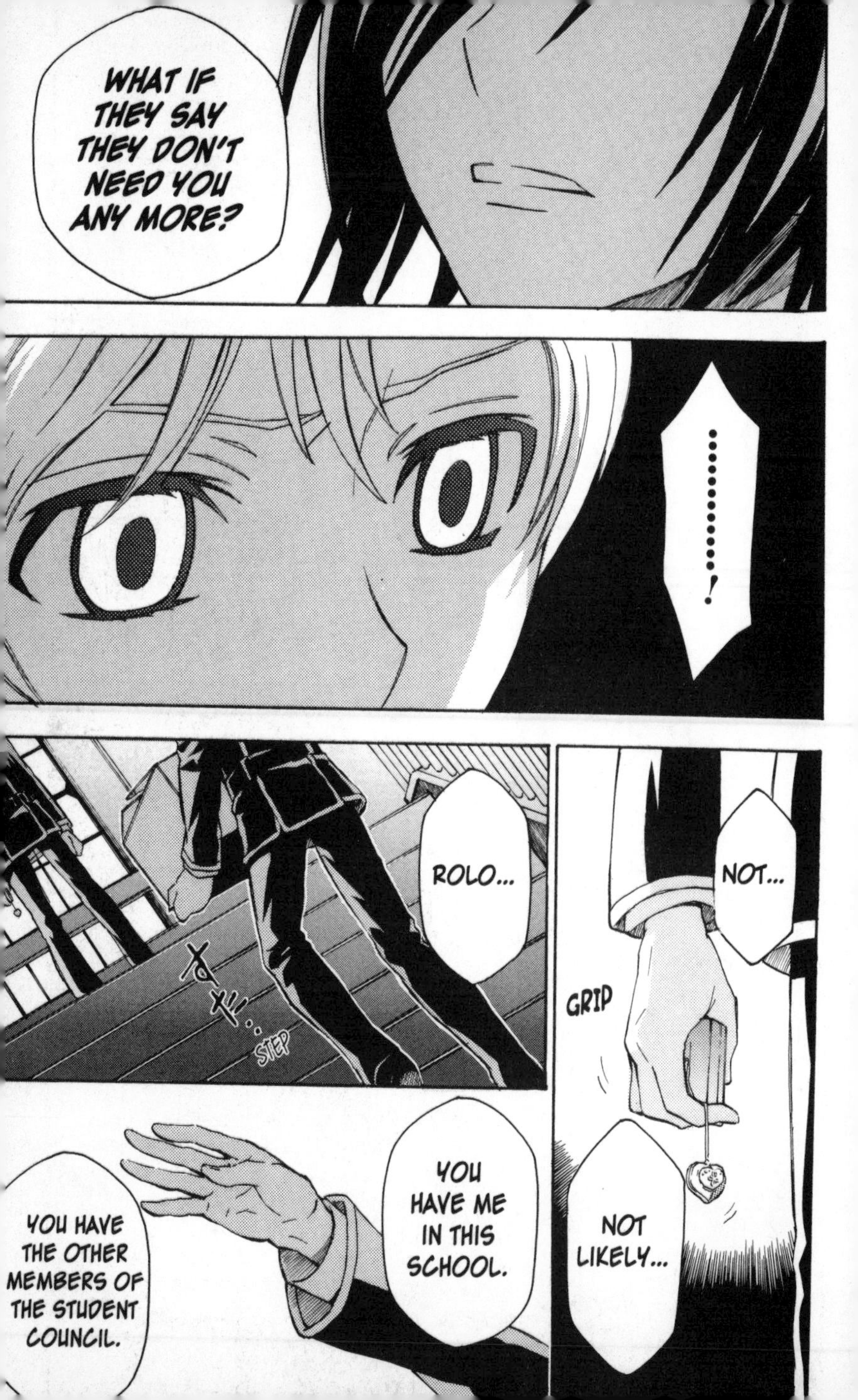
WHAT IF THEY SAY THEY DON'T NEED YOU ANY MORE?
......!
NOT...
GRIP
NOT LIKELY...
ROLO...
STEP
YOU HAVE ME IN THIS SCHOOL.
YOU HAVE THE OTHER MEMBERS OF THE STUDENT COUNCIL.

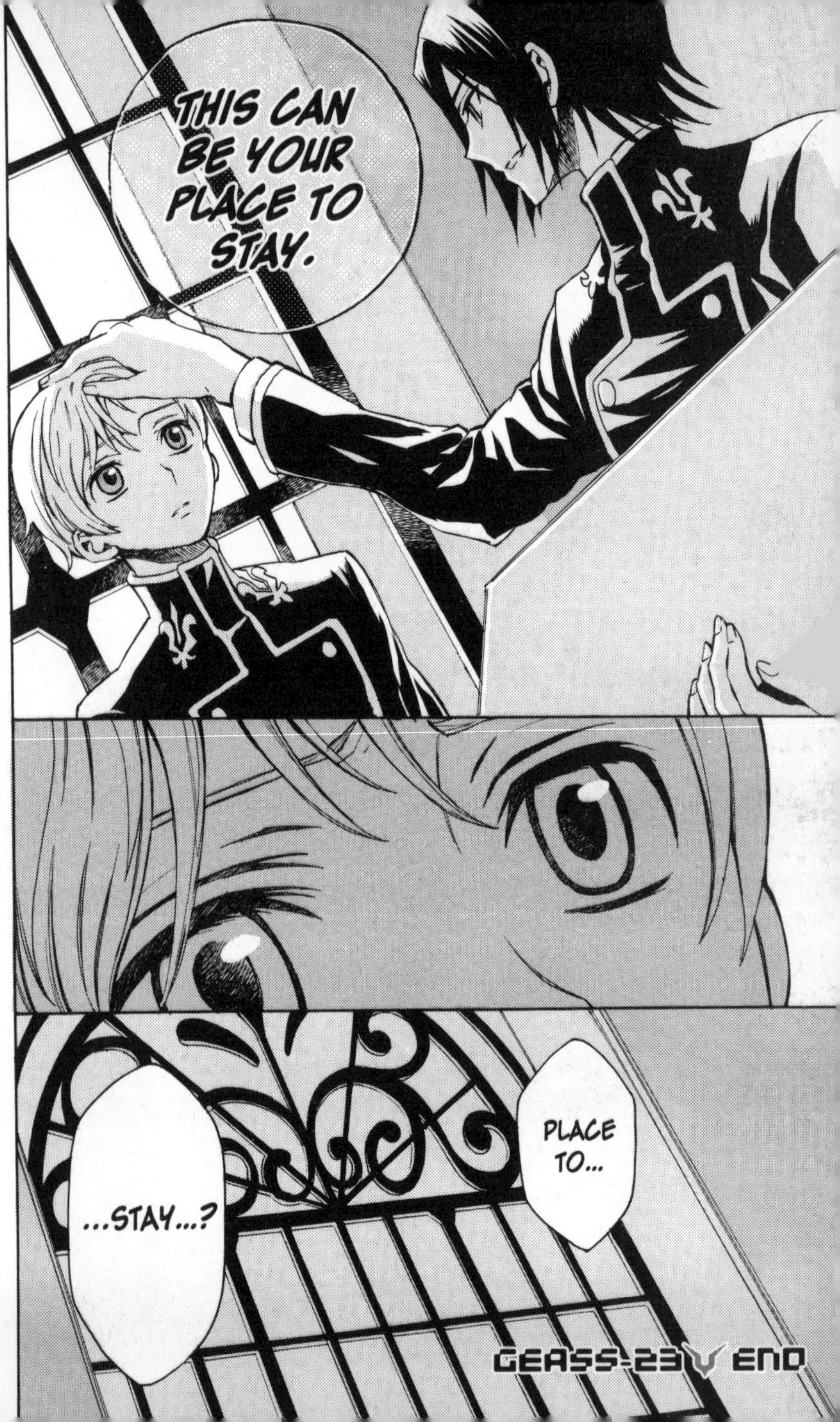
THIS CAN BE YOUR PLACE TO STAY.
PLACE TO...
...STAY...?
GEASS-23 END

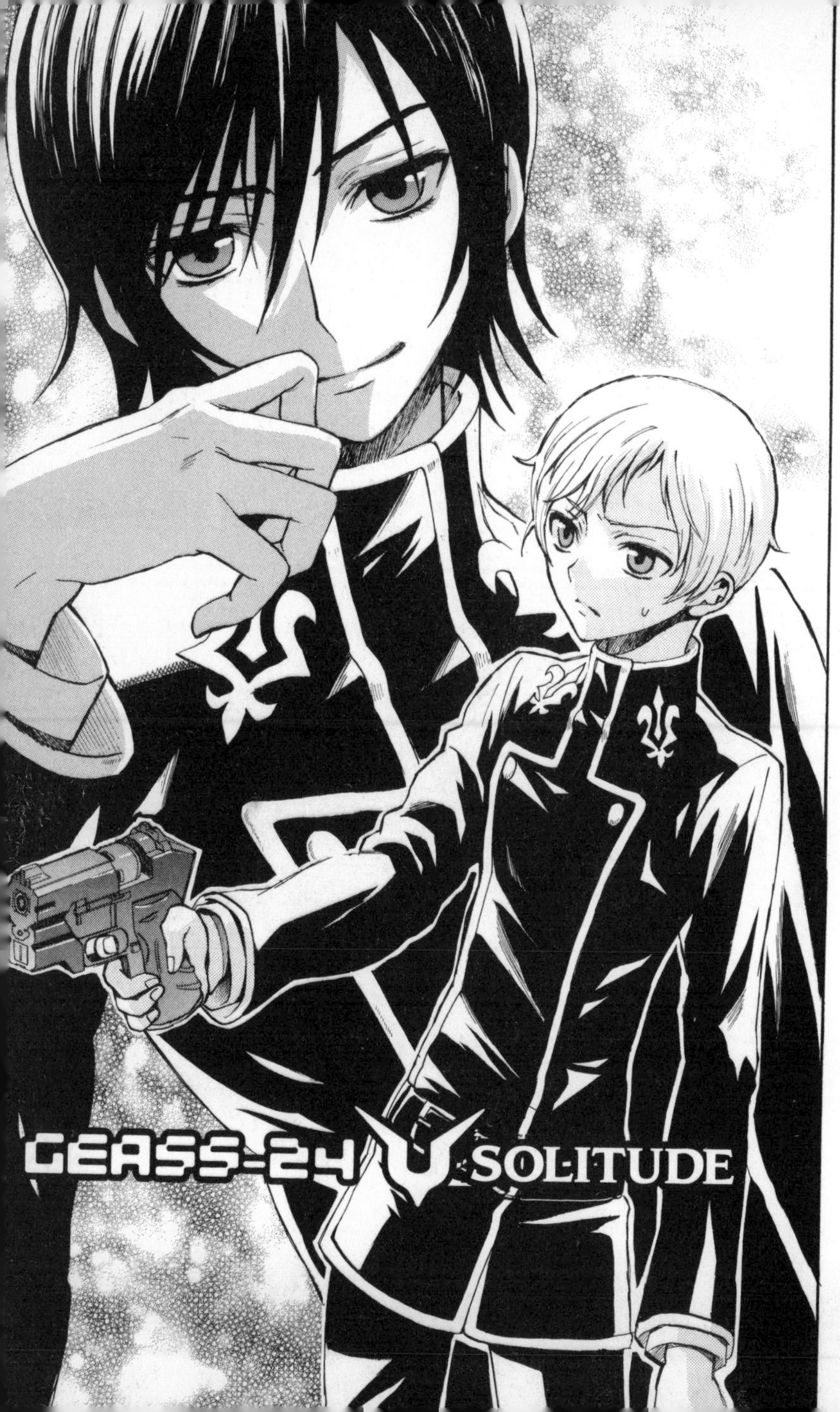
GEASS-24 SOLITUDE

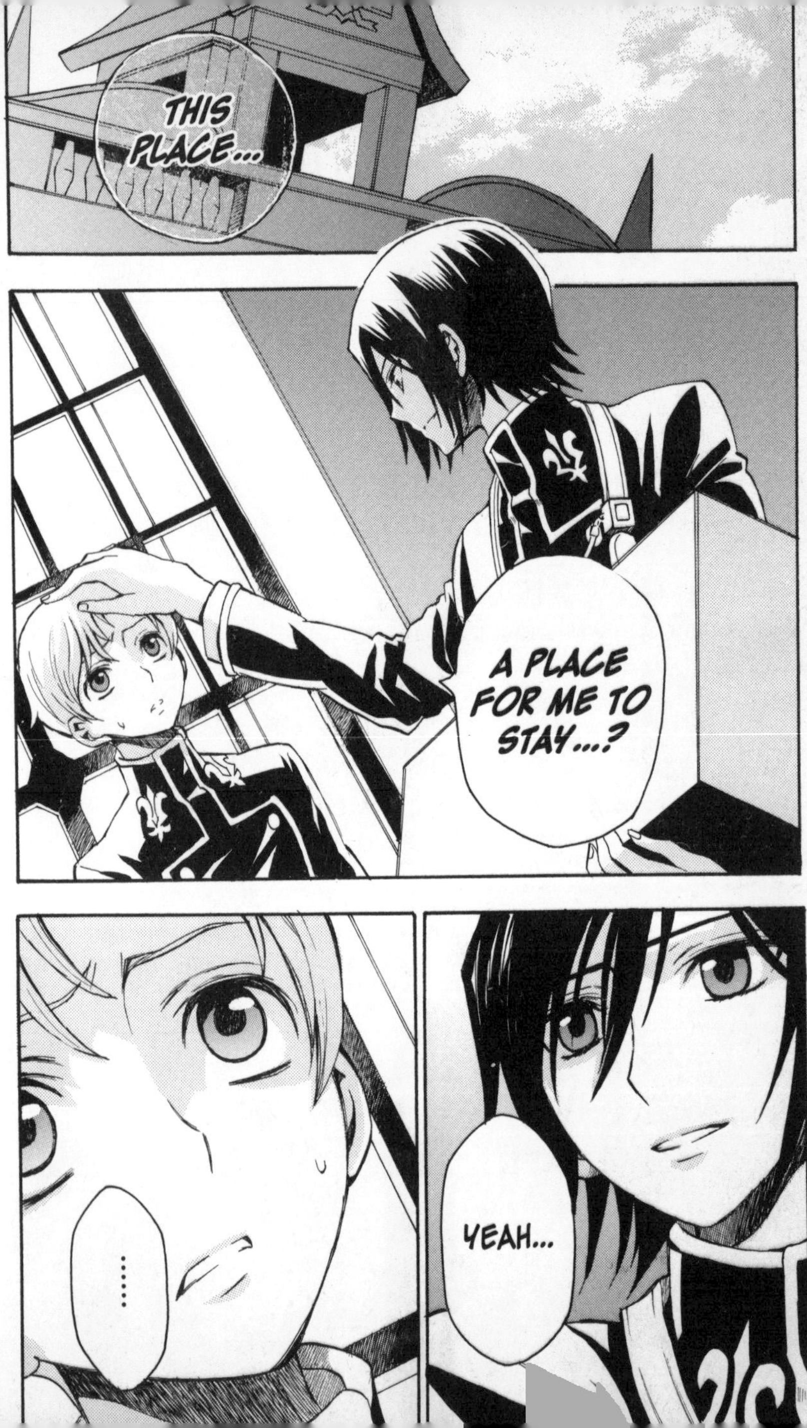
THIS PLACE...
A PLACE FOR ME TO STAY...?
YEAH...
......

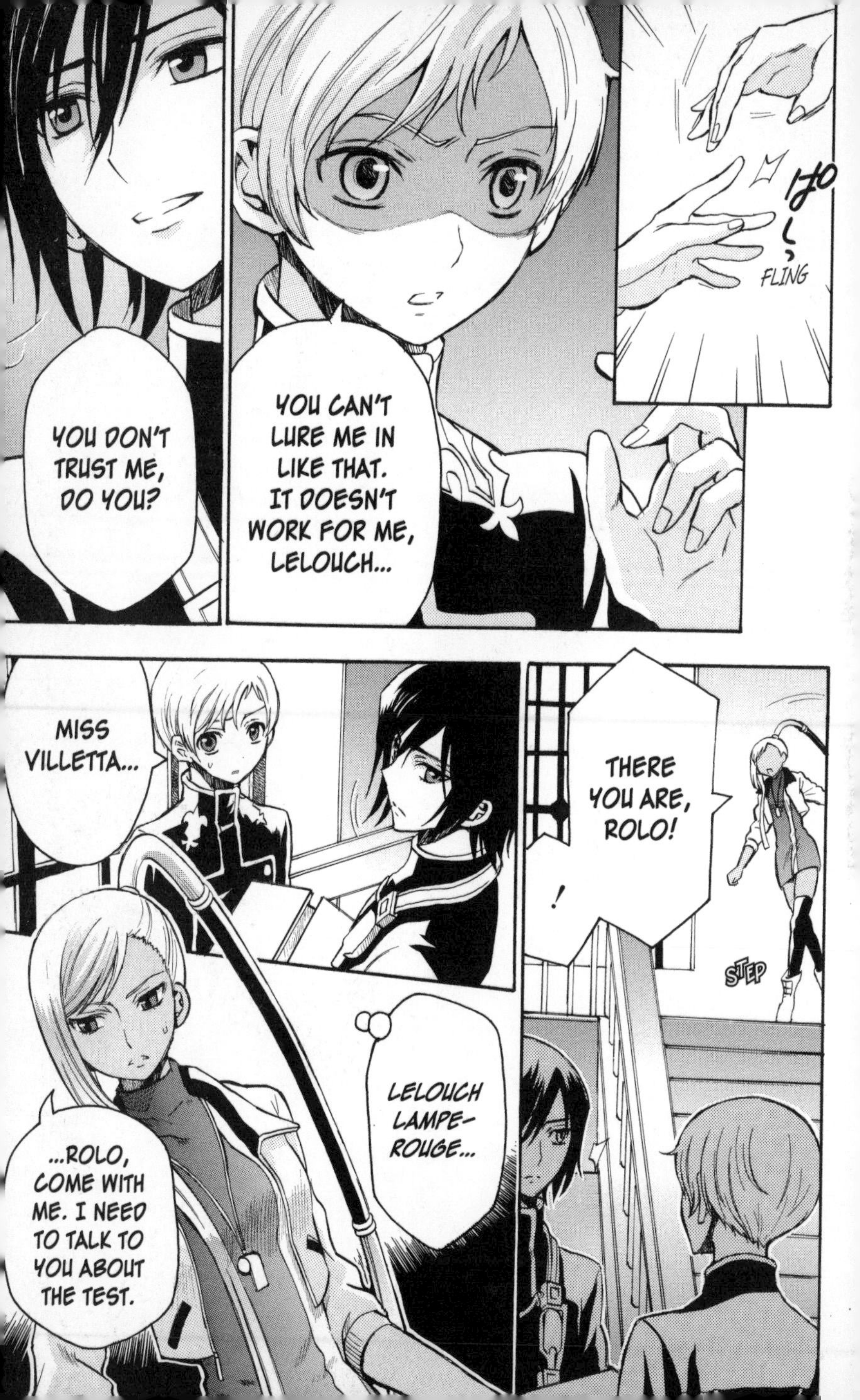
ぱしっ
FLING
YOU CAN'T LURE ME IN LIKE THAT. IT DOESN'T WORK FOR ME, LELOUCH...
YOU DON'T TRUST ME, DO YOU?
THERE YOU ARE, ROLO!
!
STEP
MISS VILLETTA...
LELOUCH LAMPE-ROUGE...
...ROLO, COME WITH ME. I NEED TO TALK TO YOU ABOUT THE TEST.

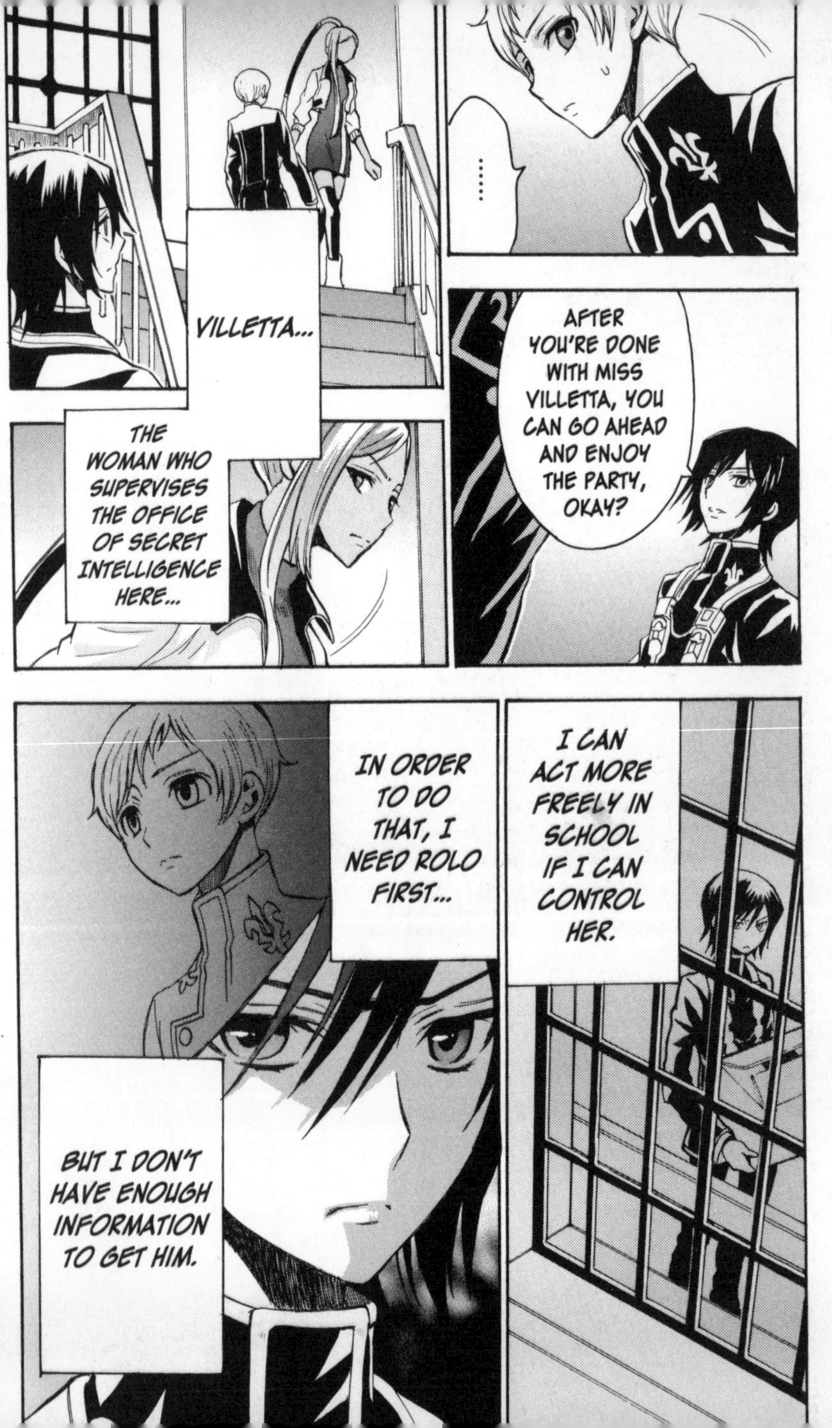
……
VILLETTA...
AFTER YOU'RE DONE WITH MISS VILLETTA, YOU CAN GO AHEAD AND ENJOY THE PARTY, OKAY?
THE WOMAN WHO SUPERVISES THE OFFICE OF SECRET INTELLIGENCE HERE...
I CAN ACT MORE FREELY IN SCHOOL IF I CAN CONTROL HER.
IN ORDER TO DO THAT, I NEED ROLO FIRST...
BUT I DON'T HAVE ENOUGH INFORMATION TO GET HIM.

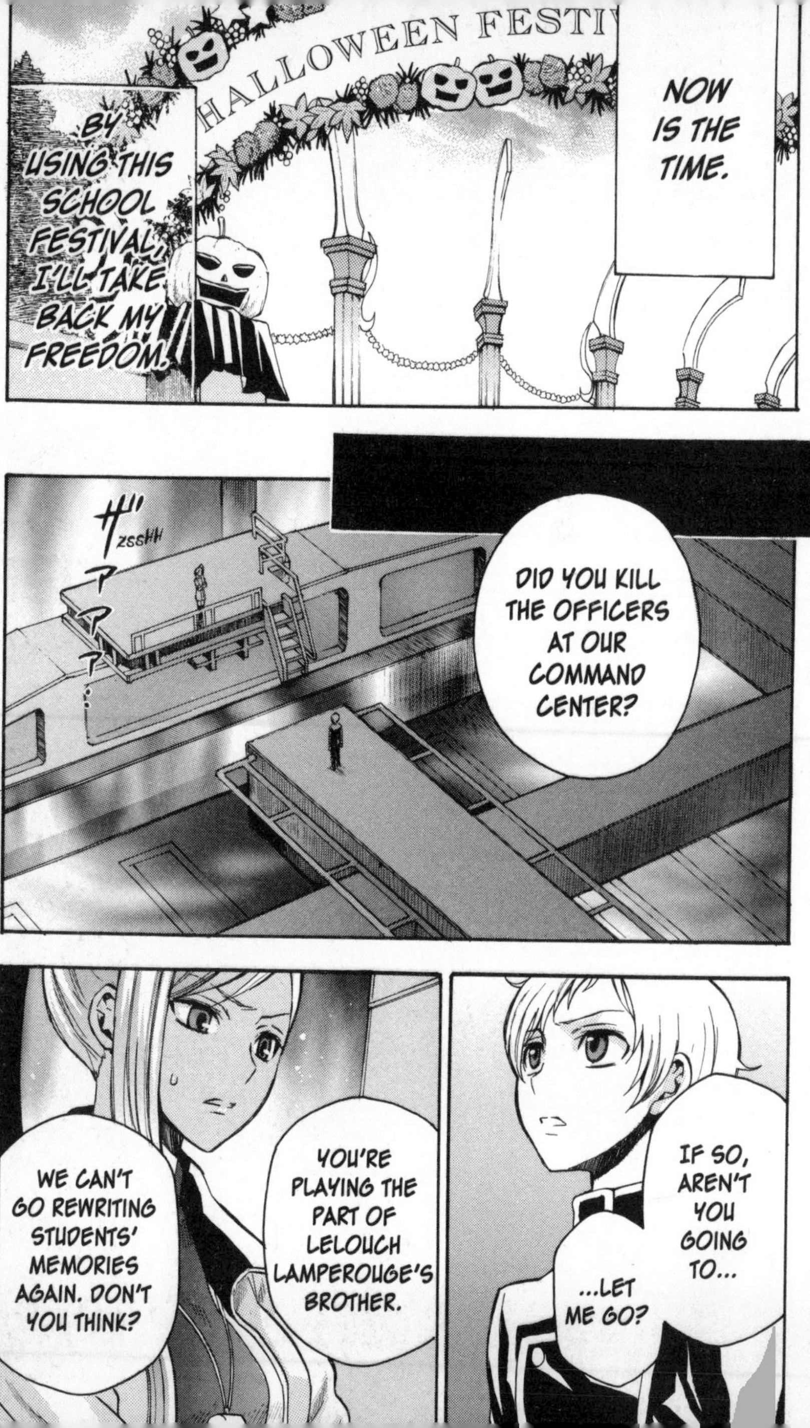
HALLOWEEN FESTIV
NOW IS THE TIME.
BY USING THIS SCHOOL FESTIVAL, I'LL TAKE BACK MY FREEDOM.
ザァァァ… ZSSHH
DID YOU KILL THE OFFICERS AT OUR COMMAND CENTER?
IF SO, AREN'T YOU GOING TO...
...LET ME GO?
YOU'RE PLAYING THE PART OF LELOUCH LAMPEROUGE'S BROTHER.
WE CAN'T GO REWRITING STUDENTS' MEMORIES AGAIN. DON'T YOU THINK?

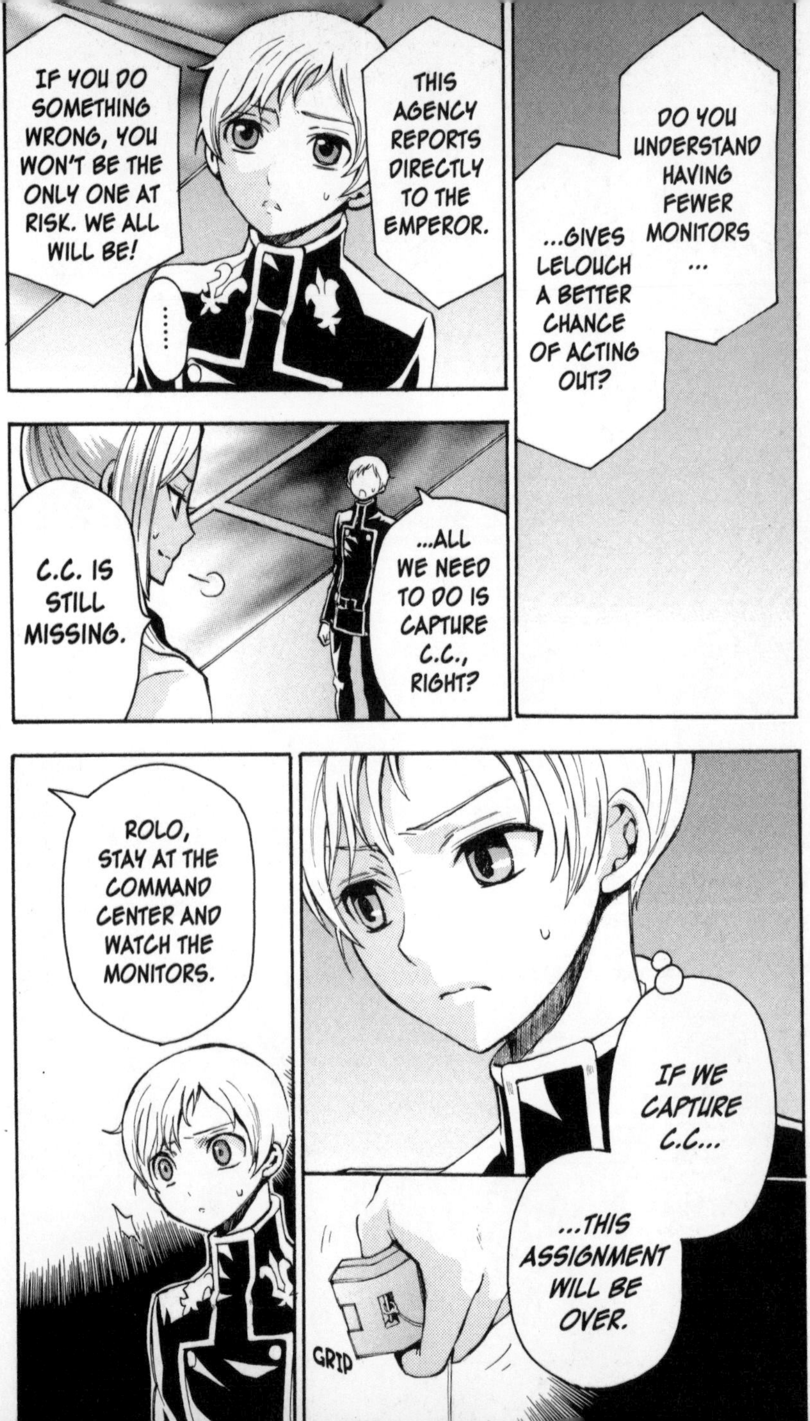
DO YOU UNDERSTAND HAVING FEWER MONITORS ...
...GIVES LELOUCH A BETTER CHANCE OF ACTING OUT?
THIS AGENCY REPORTS DIRECTLY TO THE EMPEROR.
IF YOU DO SOMETHING WRONG, YOU WON'T BE THE ONLY ONE AT RISK. WE ALL WILL BE!
......
...ALL WE NEED TO DO IS CAPTURE C.C., RIGHT?
C.C. IS STILL MISSING.
IF WE CAPTURE C.C...
...THIS ASSIGNMENT WILL BE OVER.
GRIP
ROLO, STAY AT THE COMMAND CENTER AND WATCH THE MONITORS.

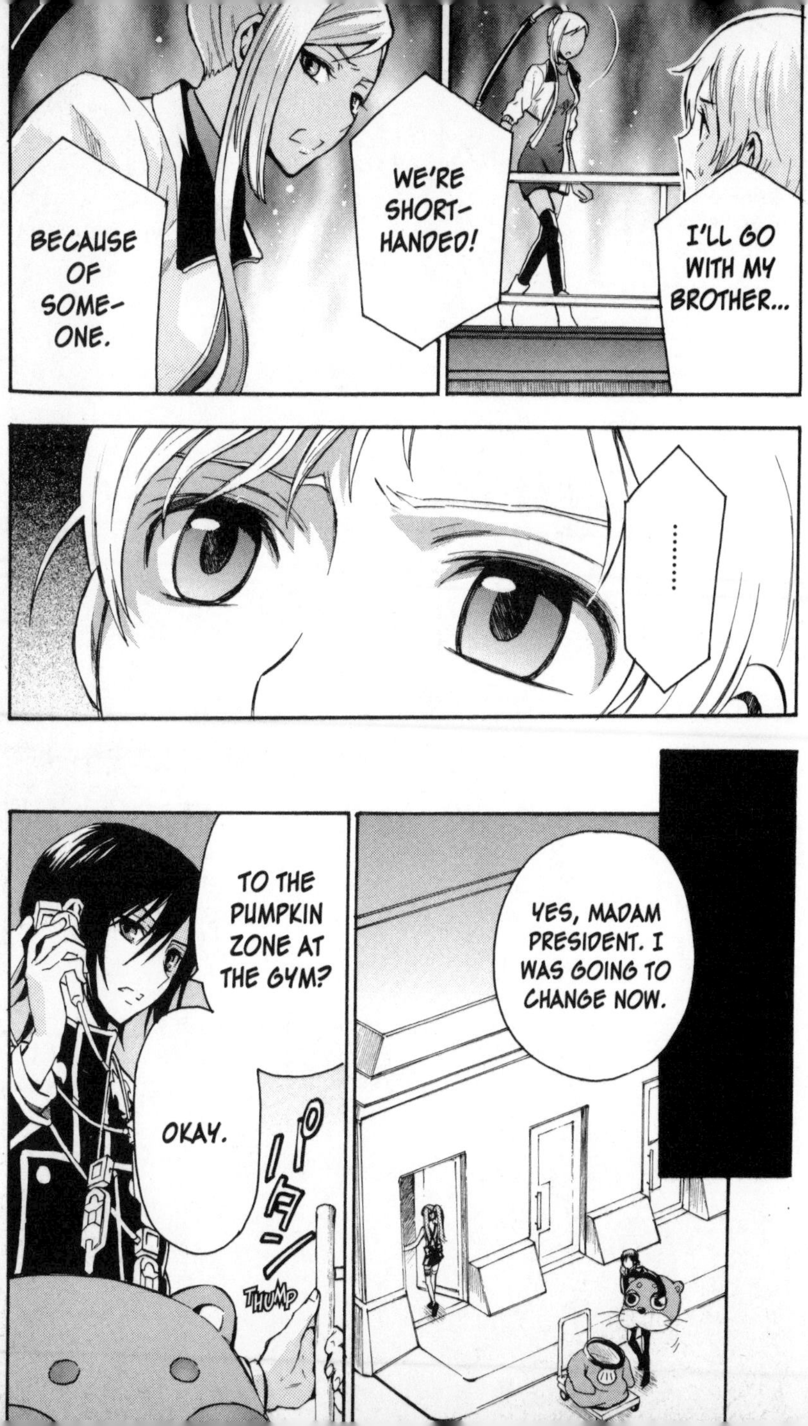
I'LL GO WITH MY BROTHER...
WE'RE SHORT-HANDED!
BECAUSE OF SOME-ONE.
....
YES, MADAM PRESIDENT. I WAS GOING TO CHANGE NOW.
TO THE PUMPKIN ZONE AT THE GYM?
OKAY.
THUMP

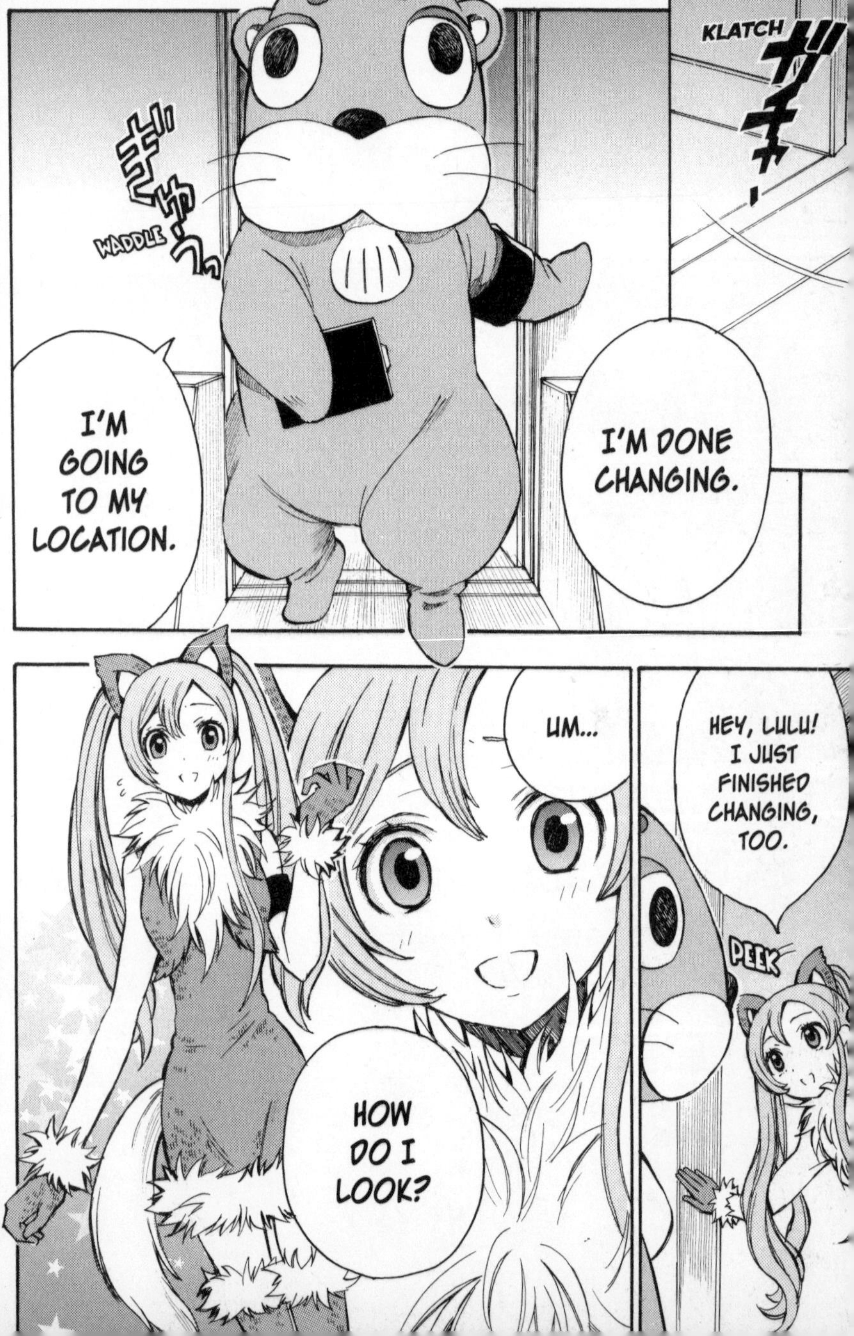
KLATCH
WADDLE
I'M DONE CHANGING.
I'M GOING TO MY LOCATION.
HEY, LULU! I JUST FINISHED CHANGING, TOO.
PEEK
UM...
HOW DO I LOOK?

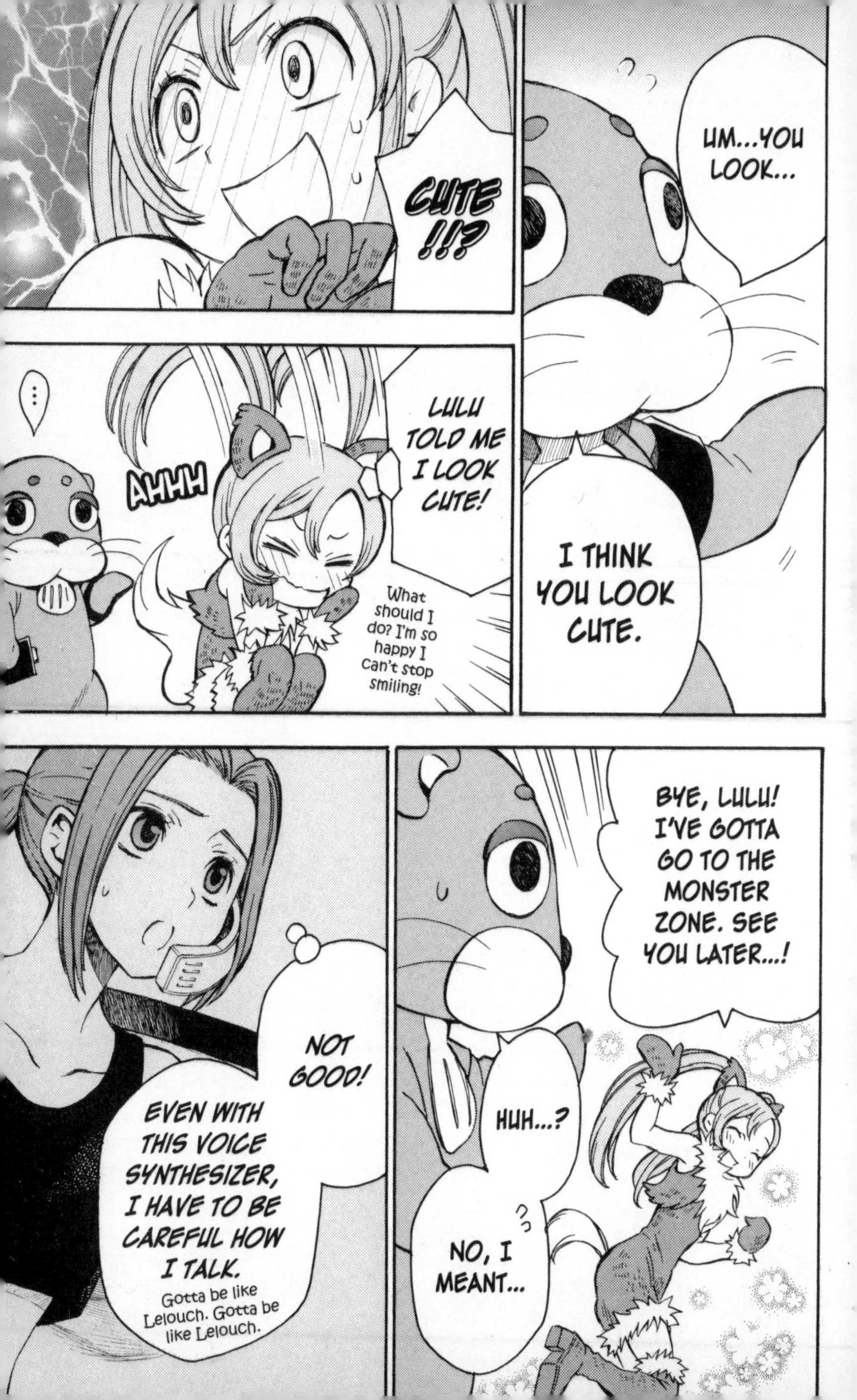
UM...YOU LOOK...
I THINK YOU LOOK CUTE.
CUTE!!?
LULU TOLD ME I LOOK CUTE!
AHHH
What should I do? I'm so happy I can't stop smiling!
...
BYE, LULU! I'VE GOTTA GO TO THE MONSTER ZONE. SEE YOU LATER...!
HUH...?
NO, I MEANT...
NOT GOOD!
EVEN WITH THIS VOICE SYNTHESIZER, I HAVE TO BE CAREFUL HOW I TALK.
Gotta be like Lelouch. Gotta be like Lelouch.

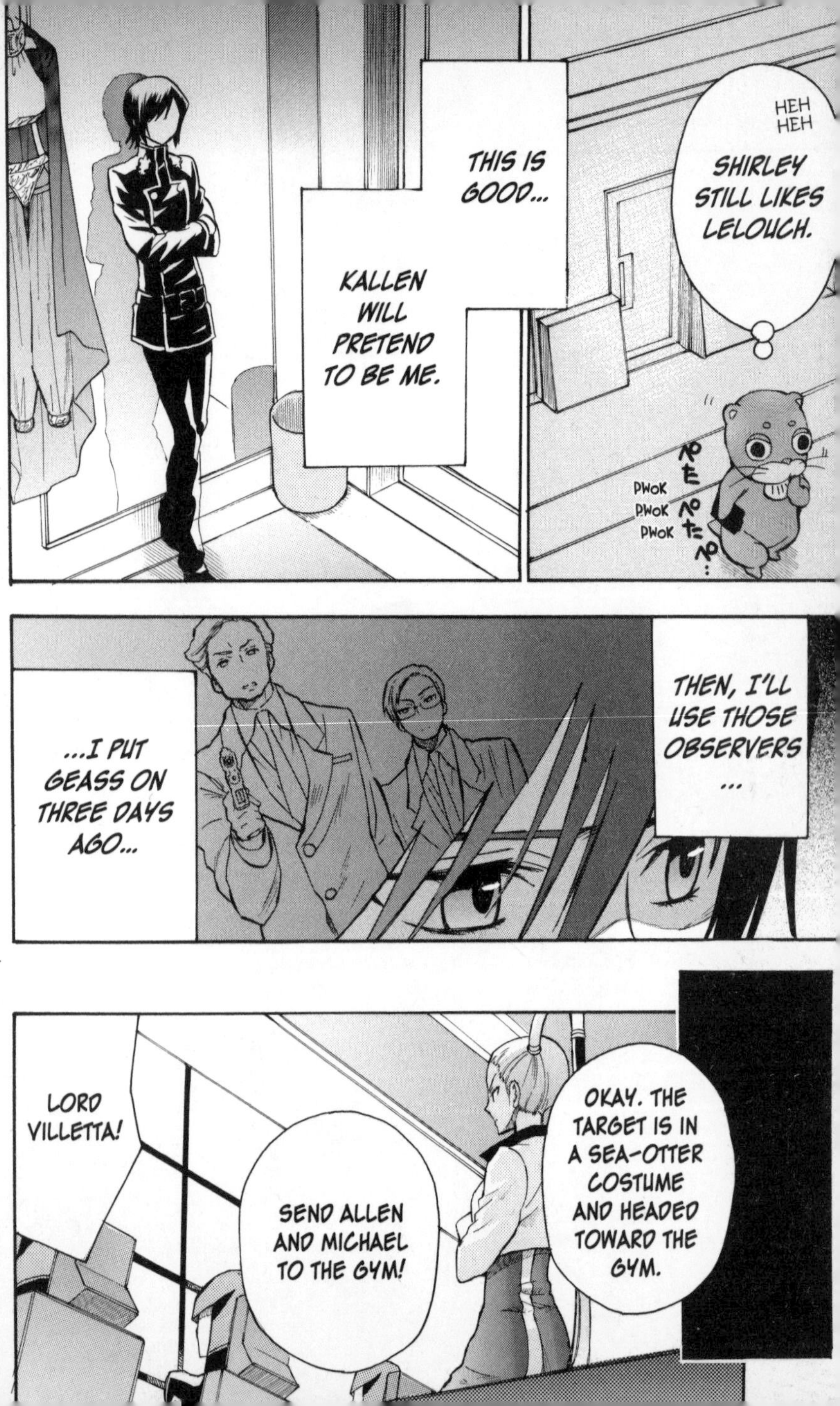
HEH HEH
SHIRLEY STILL LIKES LELOUCH.
PWOK PWOK PWOK
THIS IS GOOD...
KALLEN WILL PRETEND TO BE ME.
THEN, I'LL USE THOSE OBSERVERS ...
...I PUT GEASS ON THREE DAYS AGO...
OKAY. THE TARGET IS IN A SEA-OTTER COSTUME AND HEADED TOWARD THE GYM.
LORD VILLETTA!
SEND ALLEN AND MICHAEL TO THE GYM!

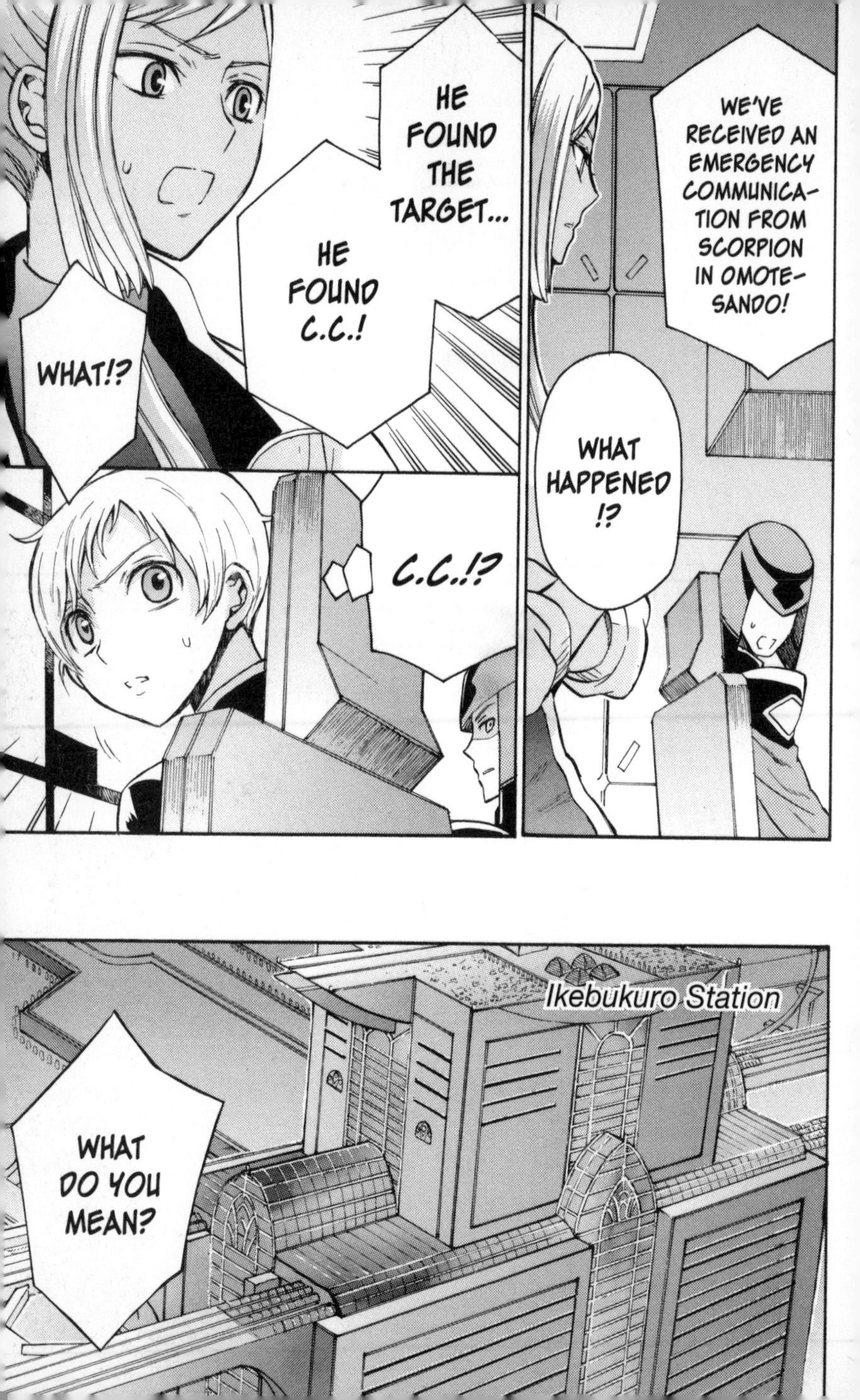
WE'VE RECEIVED AN EMERGENCY COMMUNICATION FROM SCORPION IN OMOTE-SANDO!
WHAT HAPPENED!?
HE FOUND THE TARGET...
HE FOUND C.C.!
WHAT!?
C.C..!?
Ikebukuro Station
WHAT DO YOU MEAN?

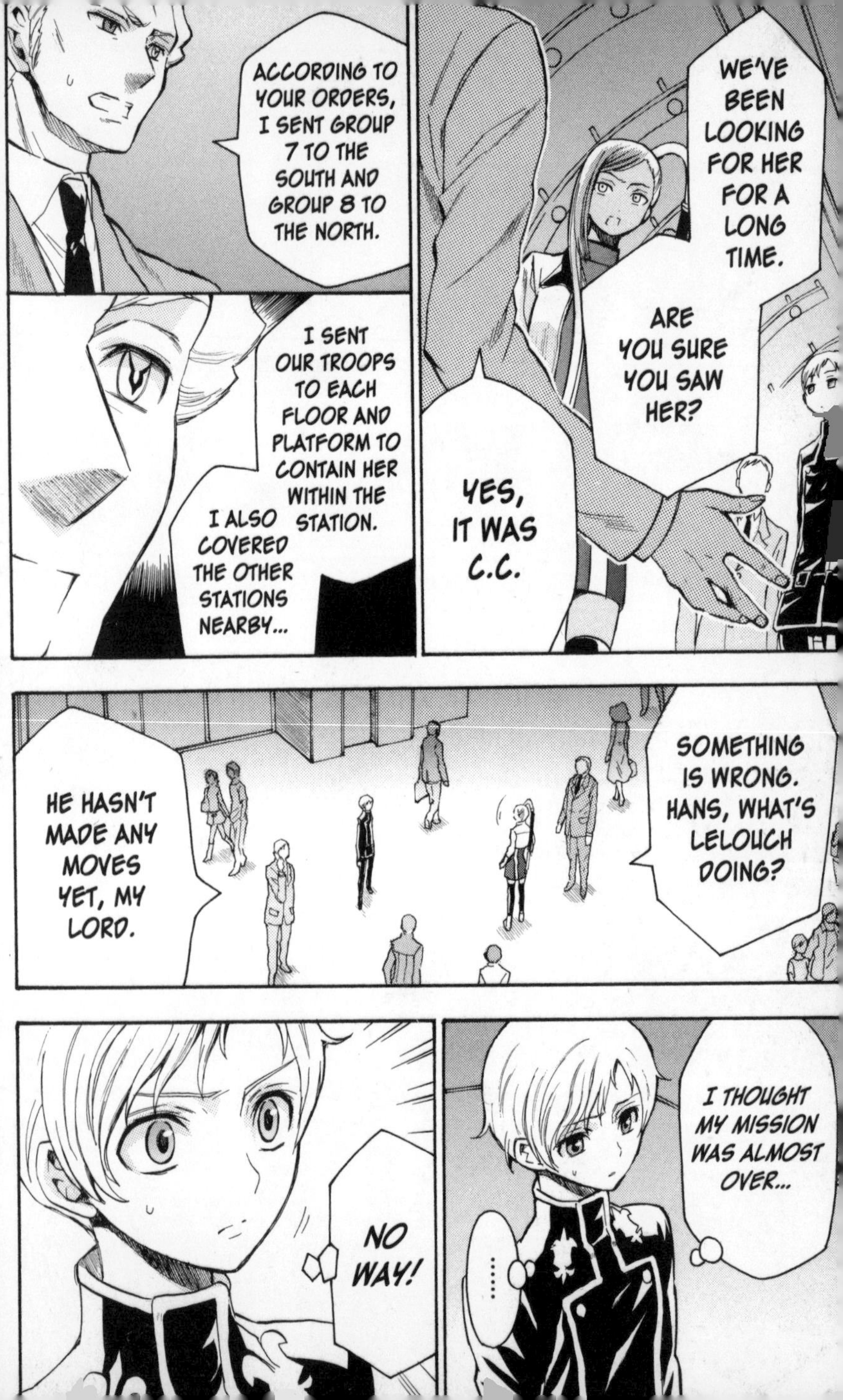
WE'VE BEEN LOOKING FOR HER FOR A LONG TIME.
ARE YOU SURE YOU SAW HER?
YES, IT WAS C.C.
ACCORDING TO YOUR ORDERS, I SENT GROUP 7 TO THE SOUTH AND GROUP 8 TO THE NORTH.
I SENT OUR TROOPS TO EACH FLOOR AND PLATFORM TO CONTAIN HER WITHIN THE STATION.
I ALSO COVERED THE OTHER STATIONS NEARBY...
SOMETHING IS WRONG. HANS, WHAT'S LELOUCH DOING?
HE HASN'T MADE ANY MOVES YET, MY LORD.
I THOUGHT MY MISSION WAS ALMOST OVER...
......
NO WAY!

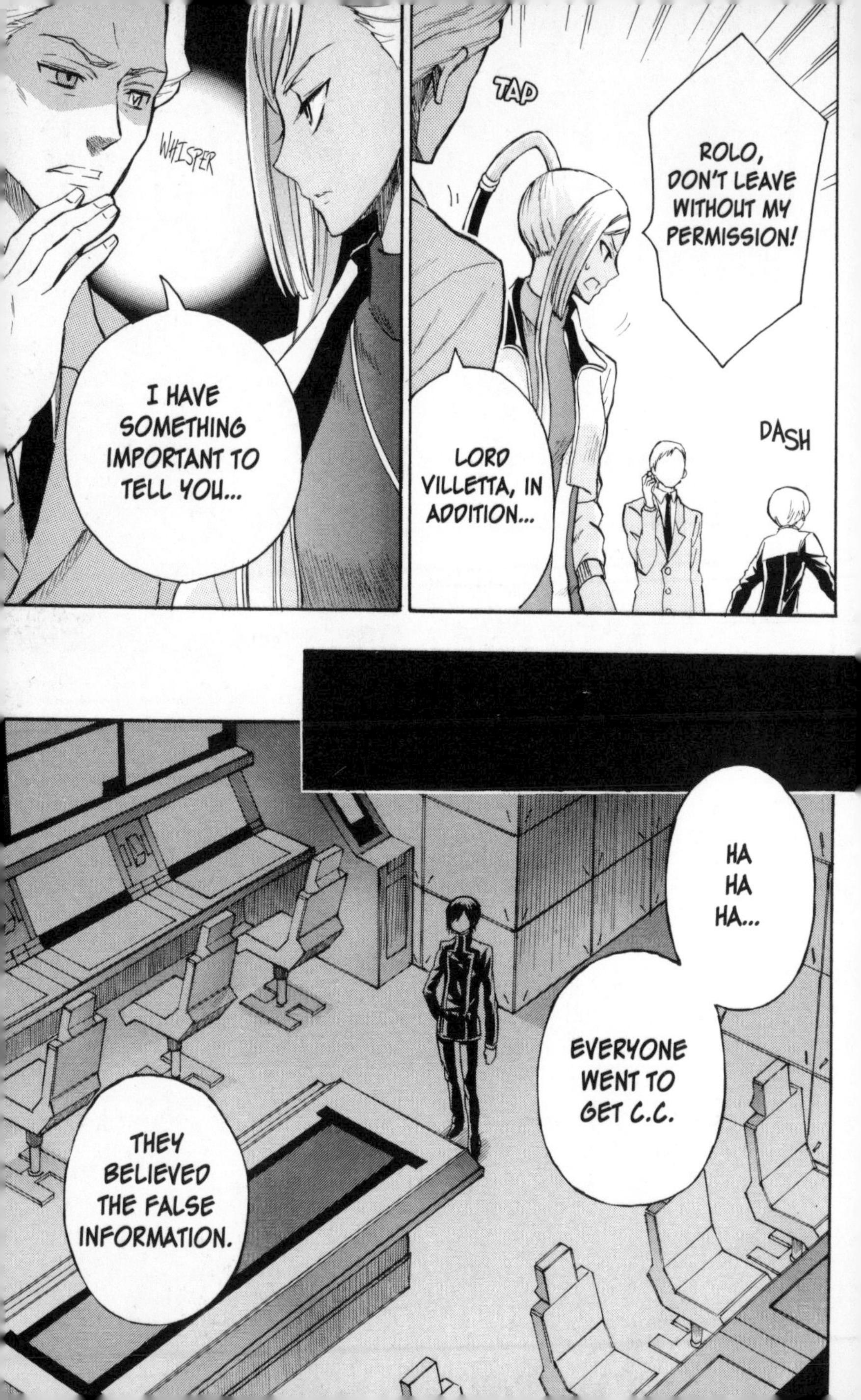
TAP
ROLO, DON'T LEAVE WITHOUT MY PERMISSION!
LORD VILLETTA, IN ADDITION...
DASH
WHISPER
I HAVE SOMETHING IMPORTANT TO TELL YOU...
HA HA HA...
EVERYONE WENT TO GET C.C.
THEY BELIEVED THE FALSE INFORMATION.

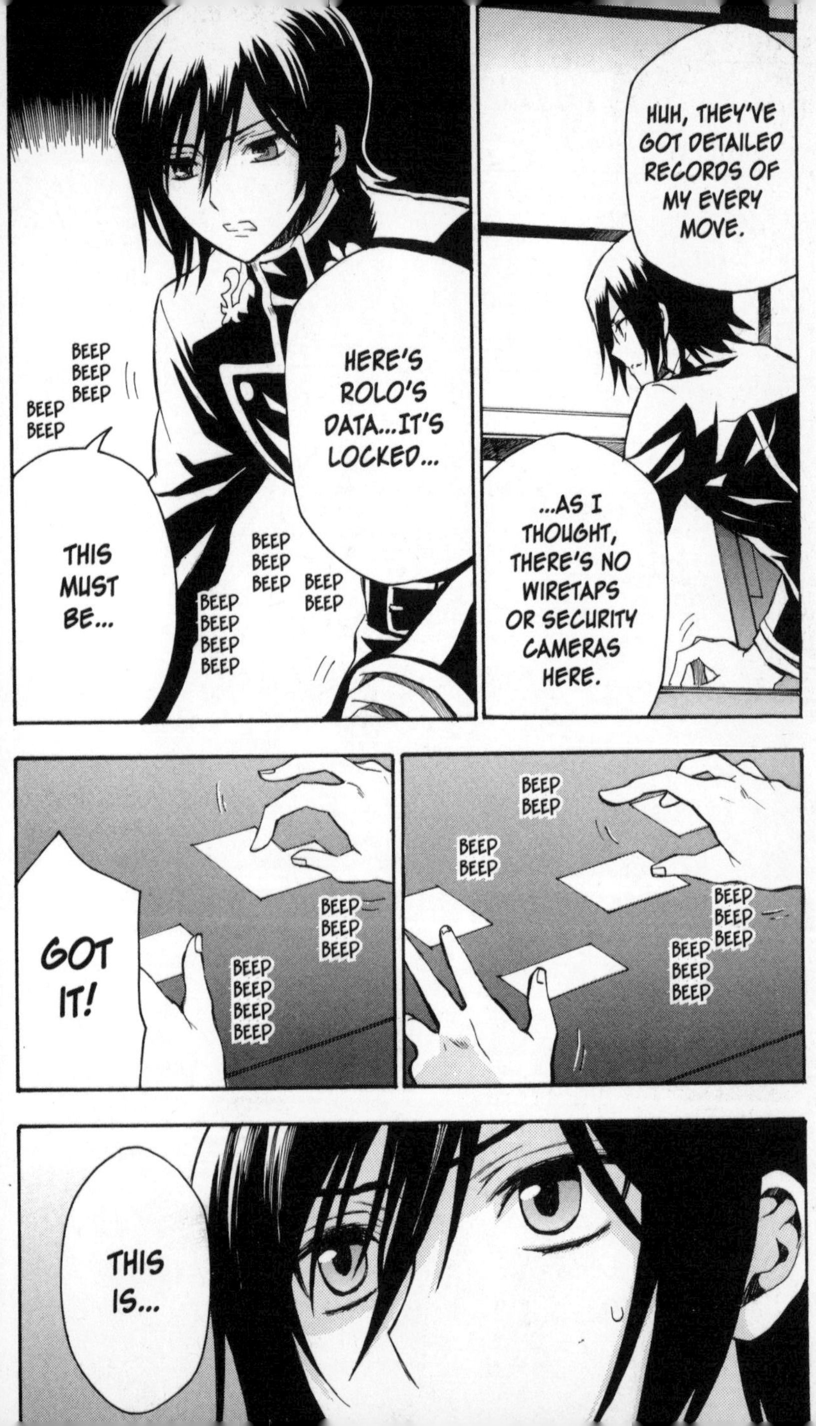
HUH, THEY'VE GOT DETAILED RECORDS OF MY EVERY MOVE.
...AS I THOUGHT, THERE'S NO WIRETAPS OR SECURITY CAMERAS HERE.
HERE'S ROLO'S DATA...IT'S LOCKED...
BEEP BEEP BEEP
BEEP BEEP
BEEP BEEP BEEP
BEEP BEEP
BEEP BEEP BEEP BEEP
THIS MUST BE...
BEEP BEEP
BEEP BEEP
BEEP BEEP BEEP
BEEP BEEP BEEP
BEEP BEEP BEEP
BEEP BEEP BEEP BEEP
GOT IT!
THIS IS...

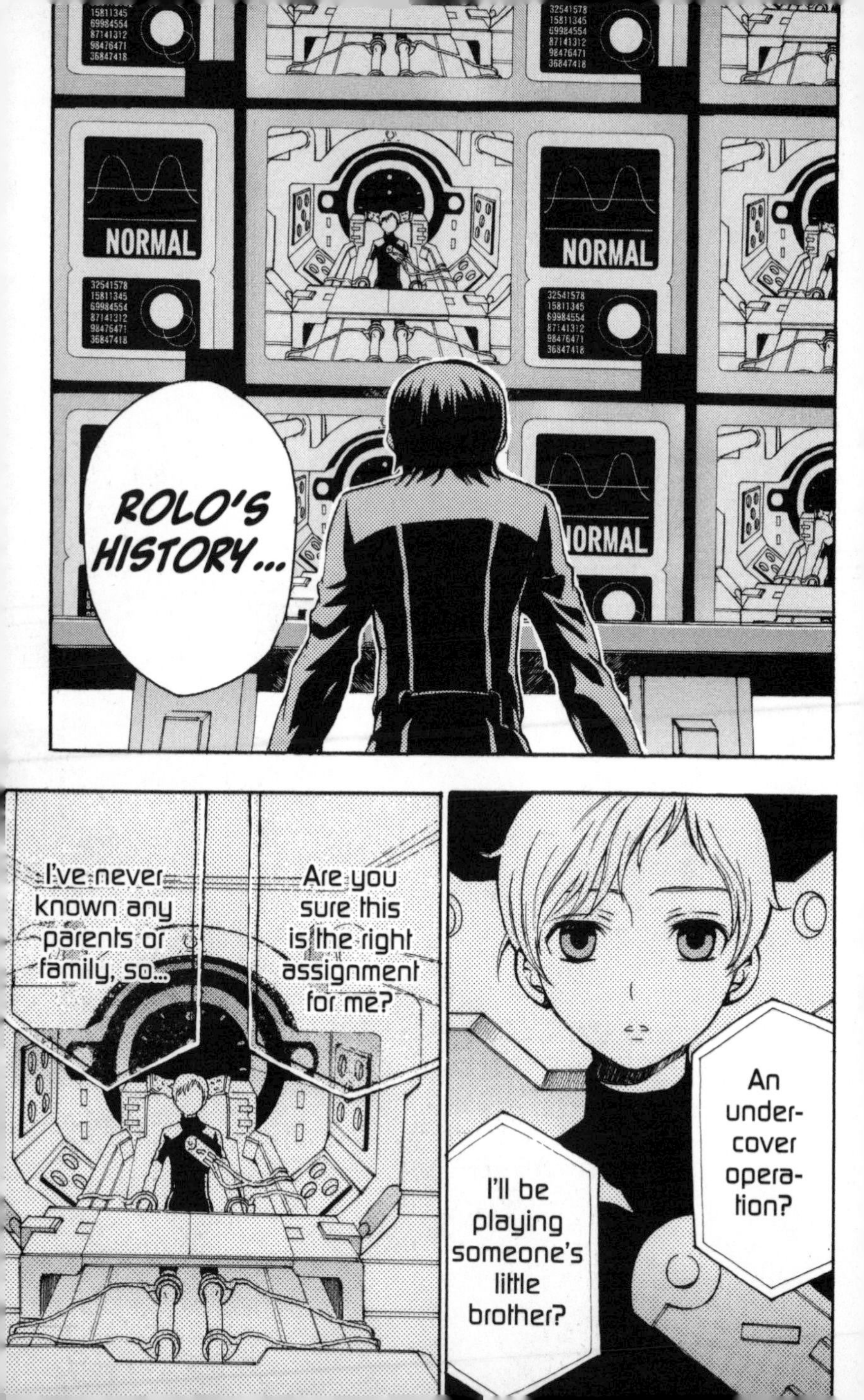
32541578 15811345 69984554 87141312 98476471 36847418
NORMAL
ROLO'S HISTORY...
An under-cover opera-tion?
I'll be playing someone's little brother?
Are you sure this is the right assignment for me?
I've never known any parents or family, so...

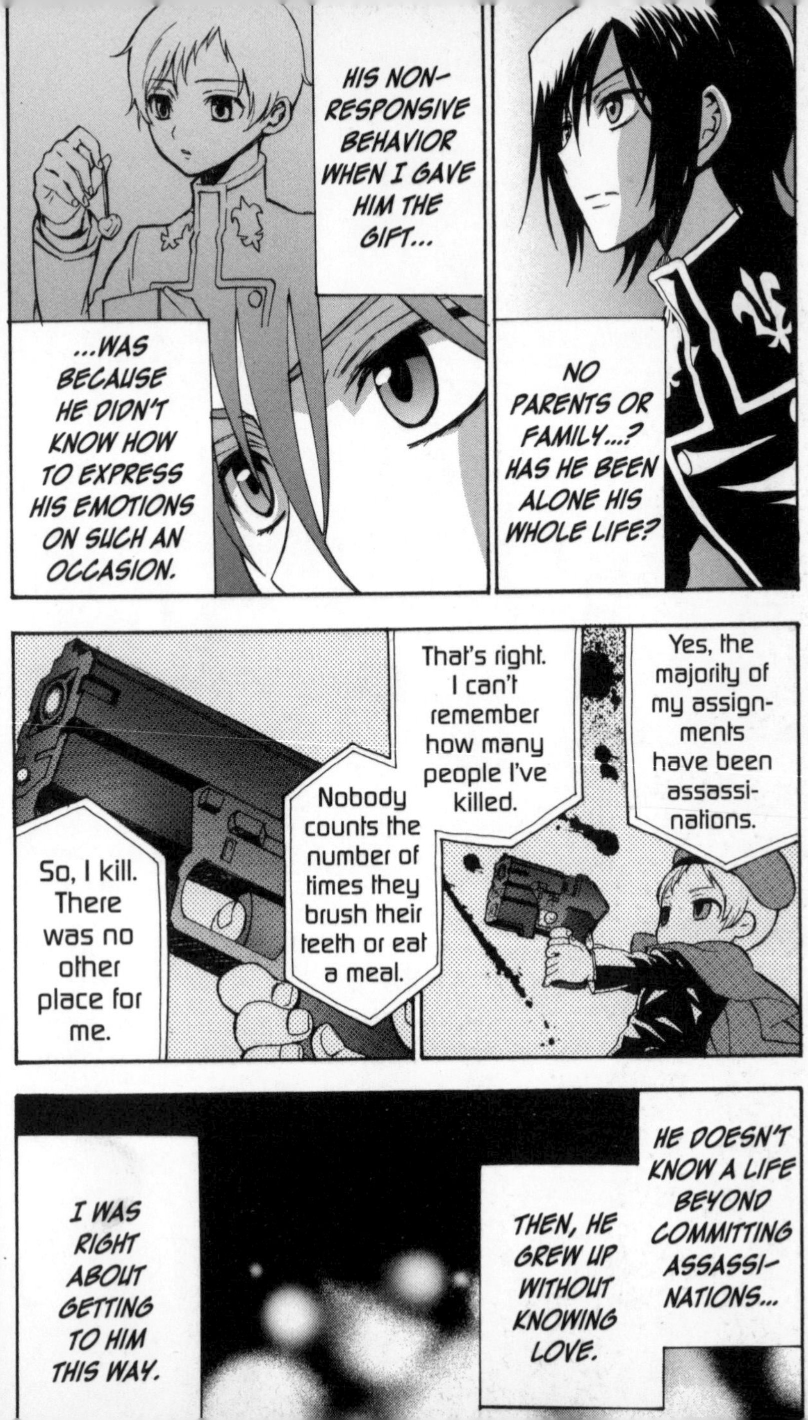
NO PARENTS OR FAMILY...? HAS HE BEEN ALONE HIS WHOLE LIFE?
HIS NON-RESPONSIVE BEHAVIOR WHEN I GAVE HIM THE GIFT...
...WAS BECAUSE HE DIDN'T KNOW HOW TO EXPRESS HIS EMOTIONS ON SUCH AN OCCASION.
Yes, the majority of my assignments have been assassinations.
That's right. I can't remember how many people I've killed.
Nobody counts the number of times they brush their teeth or eat a meal.
So, I kill. There was no other place for me.
HE DOESN'T KNOW A LIFE BEYOND COMMITTING ASSASSINATIONS...
THEN, HE GREW UP WITHOUT KNOWING LOVE.
I WAS RIGHT ABOUT GETTING TO HIM THIS WAY.

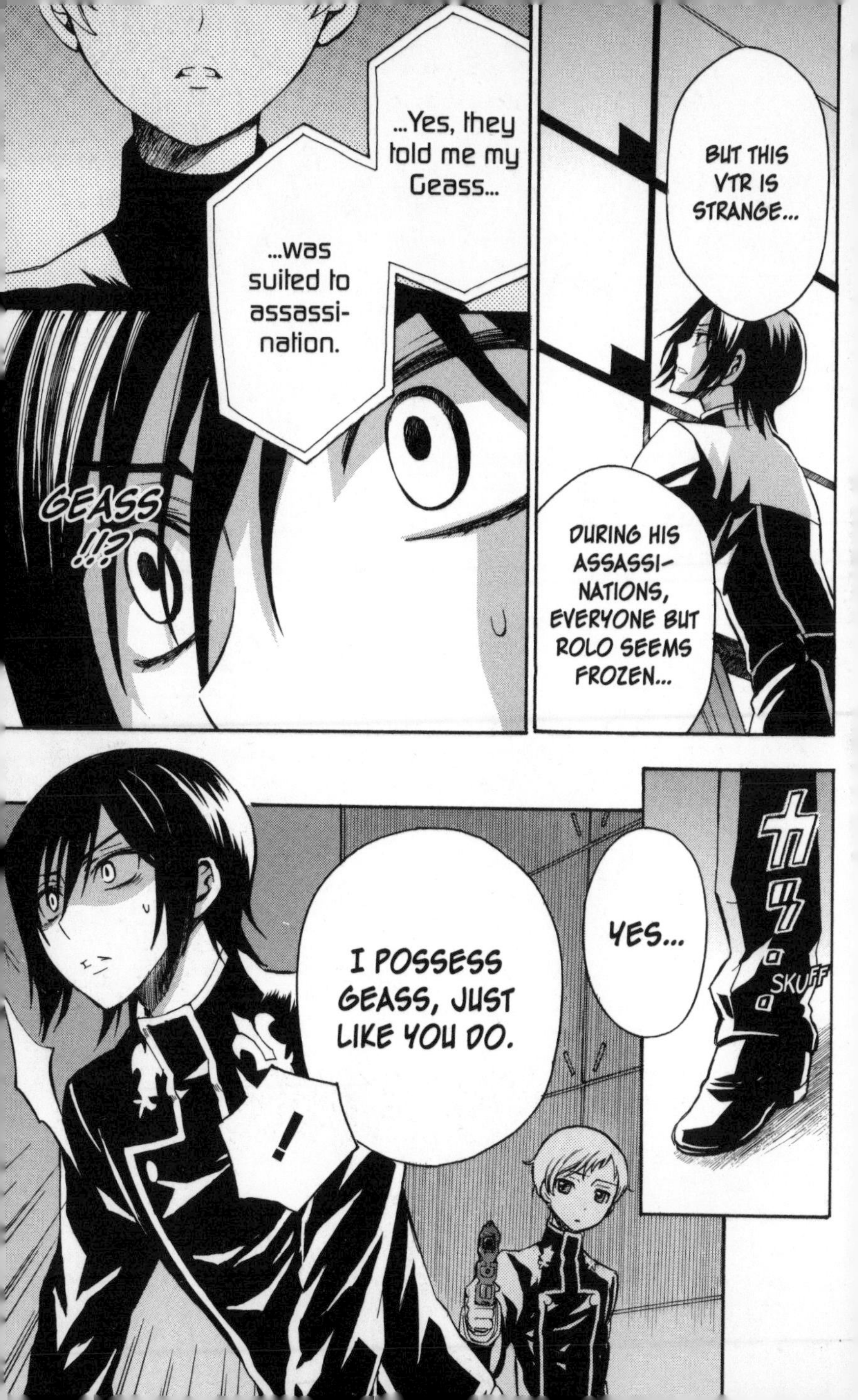
BUT THIS VTR IS STRANGE...
DURING HIS ASSASSI-NATIONS, EVERYONE BUT ROLO SEEMS FROZEN...
...Yes, they told me my Geass...
...was suited to assassi-nation.
GEASS !!?
SKUFF
YES...
I POSSESS GEASS, JUST LIKE YOU DO.
!

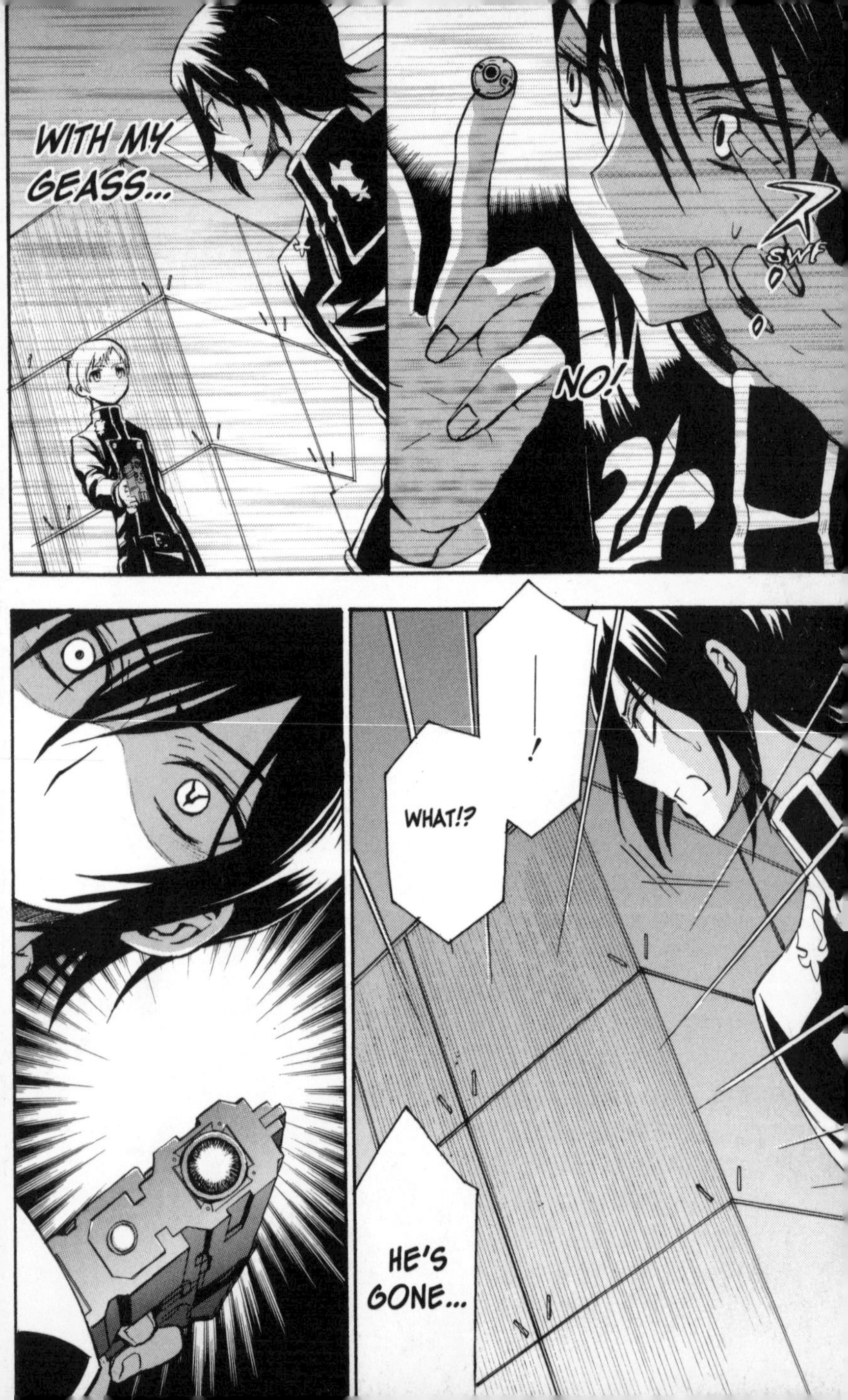
SWF
NO!
WITH MY GEASS...
!
WHAT!?
HE'S GONE...

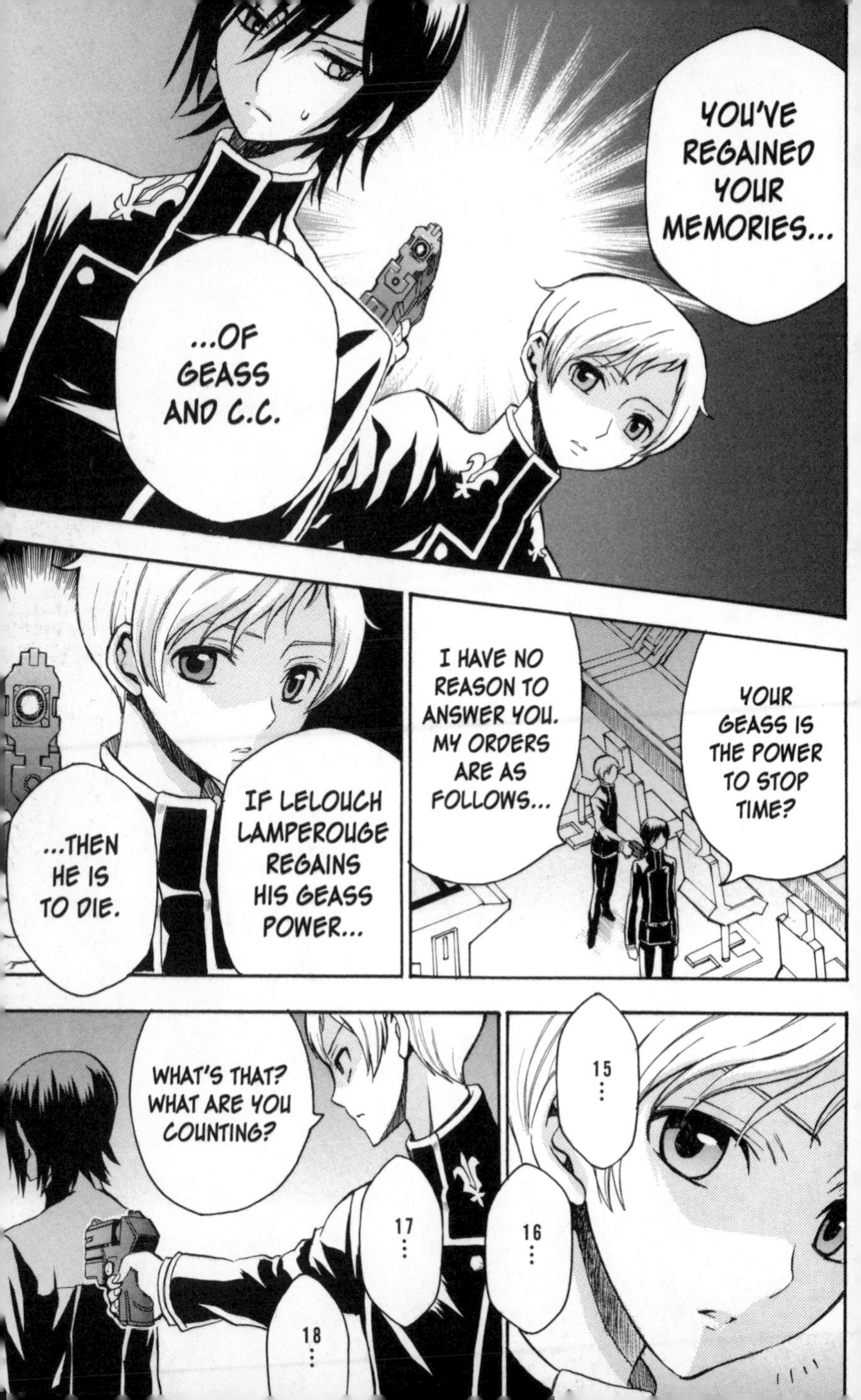
YOU'VE REGAINED YOUR MEMORIES...
...OF GEASS AND C.C.
YOUR GEASS IS THE POWER TO STOP TIME?
I HAVE NO REASON TO ANSWER YOU. MY ORDERS ARE AS FOLLOWS...
IF LELOUCH LAMPEROUGE REGAINS HIS GEASS POWER...
...THEN HE IS TO DIE.
15...
16...
WHAT'S THAT? WHAT ARE YOU COUNTING?
17...
18...

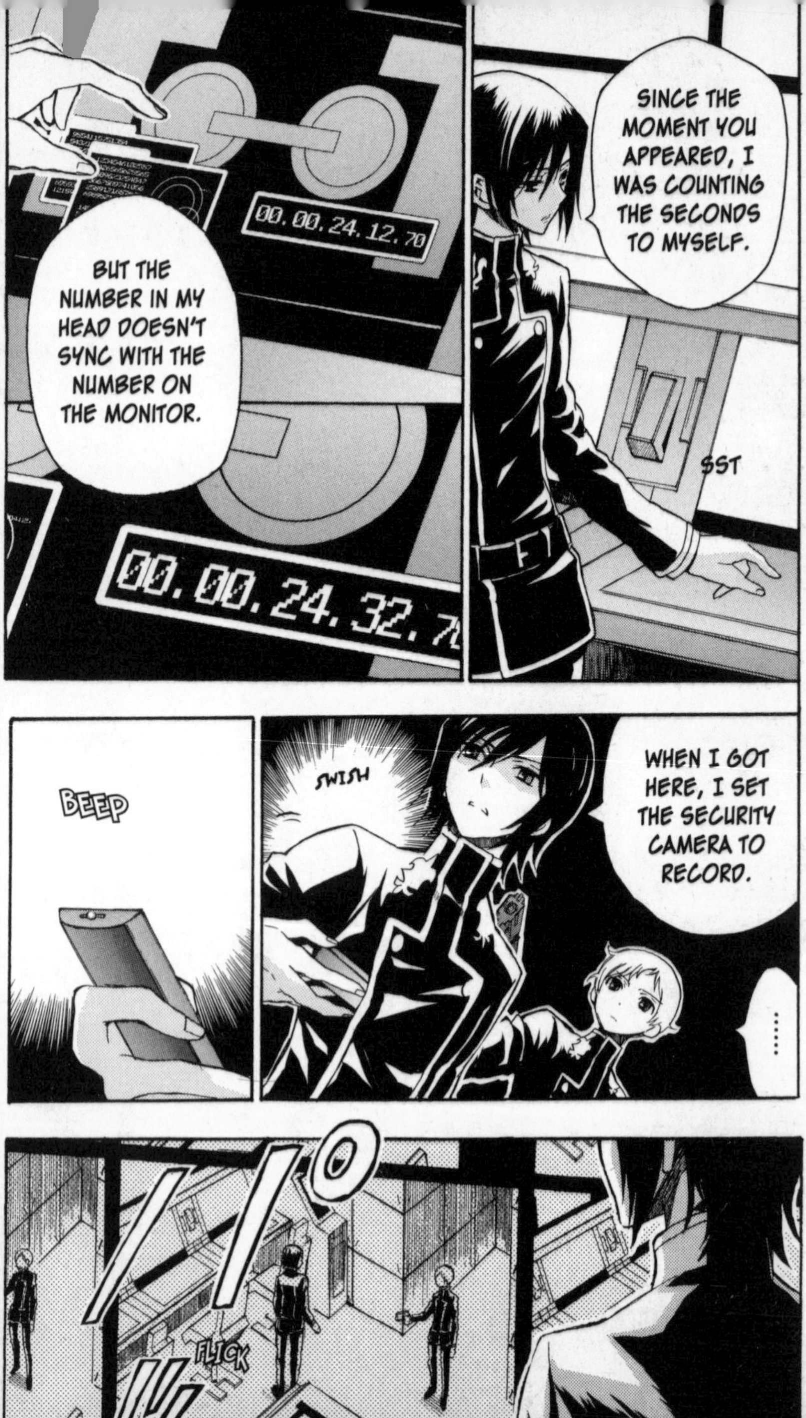
SINCE THE MOMENT YOU APPEARED, I WAS COUNTING THE SECONDS TO MYSELF.
SST
00.00.24.12.70
BUT THE NUMBER IN MY HEAD DOESN'T SYNC WITH THE NUMBER ON THE MONITOR.
00.00.24.32.7
WHEN I GOT HERE, I SET THE SECURITY CAMERA TO RECORD.
SWISH
......
BEEP
FLICK

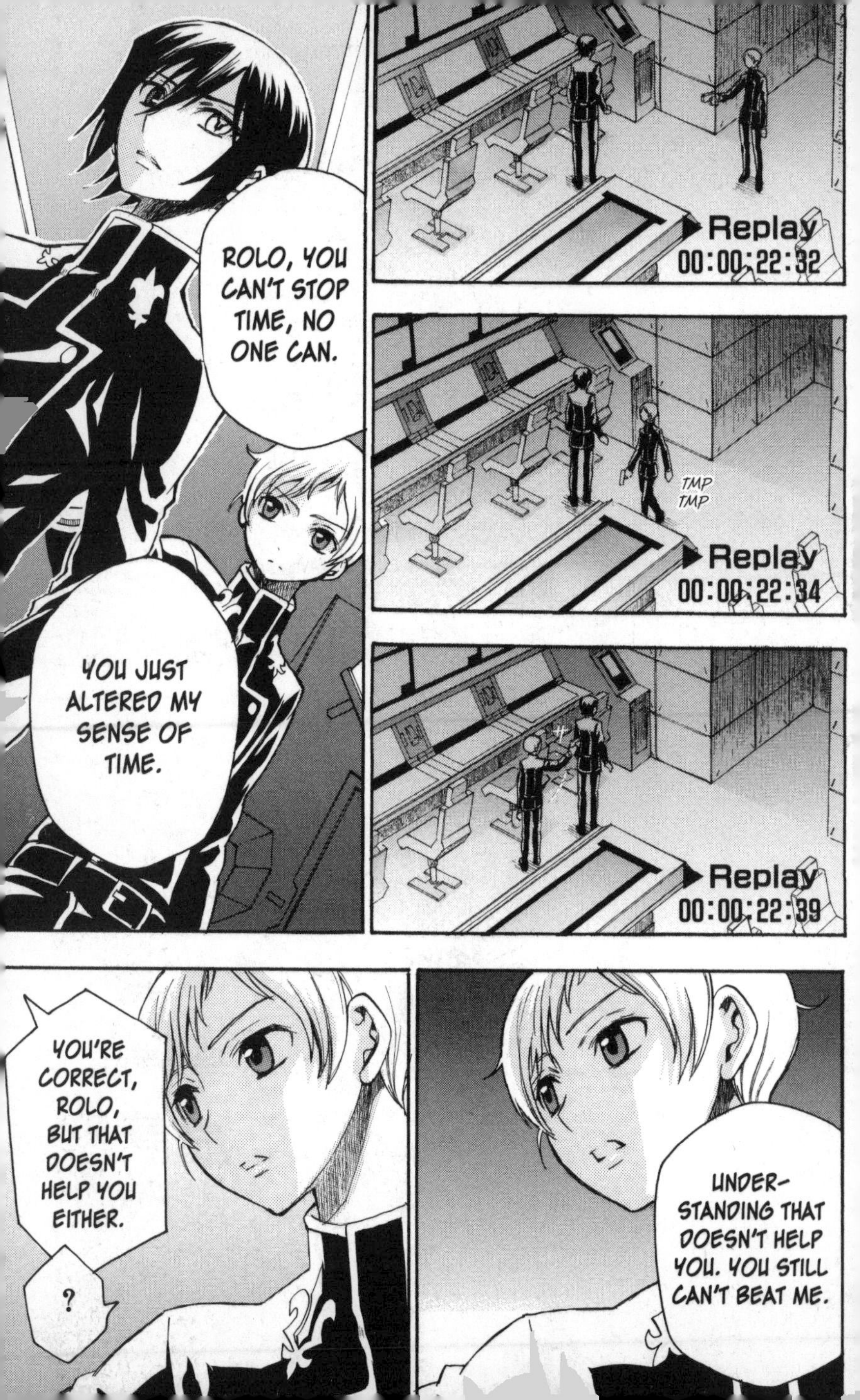
Replay
00:00:22:32
Replay
00:00:22:34
TMP TMP
Replay
00:00:22:39
ROLO, YOU CAN'T STOP TIME, NO ONE CAN.
YOU JUST ALTERED MY SENSE OF TIME.
UNDER-STANDING THAT DOESN'T HELP YOU. YOU STILL CAN'T BEAT ME.
YOU'RE CORRECT, ROLO, BUT THAT DOESN'T HELP YOU EITHER.
?

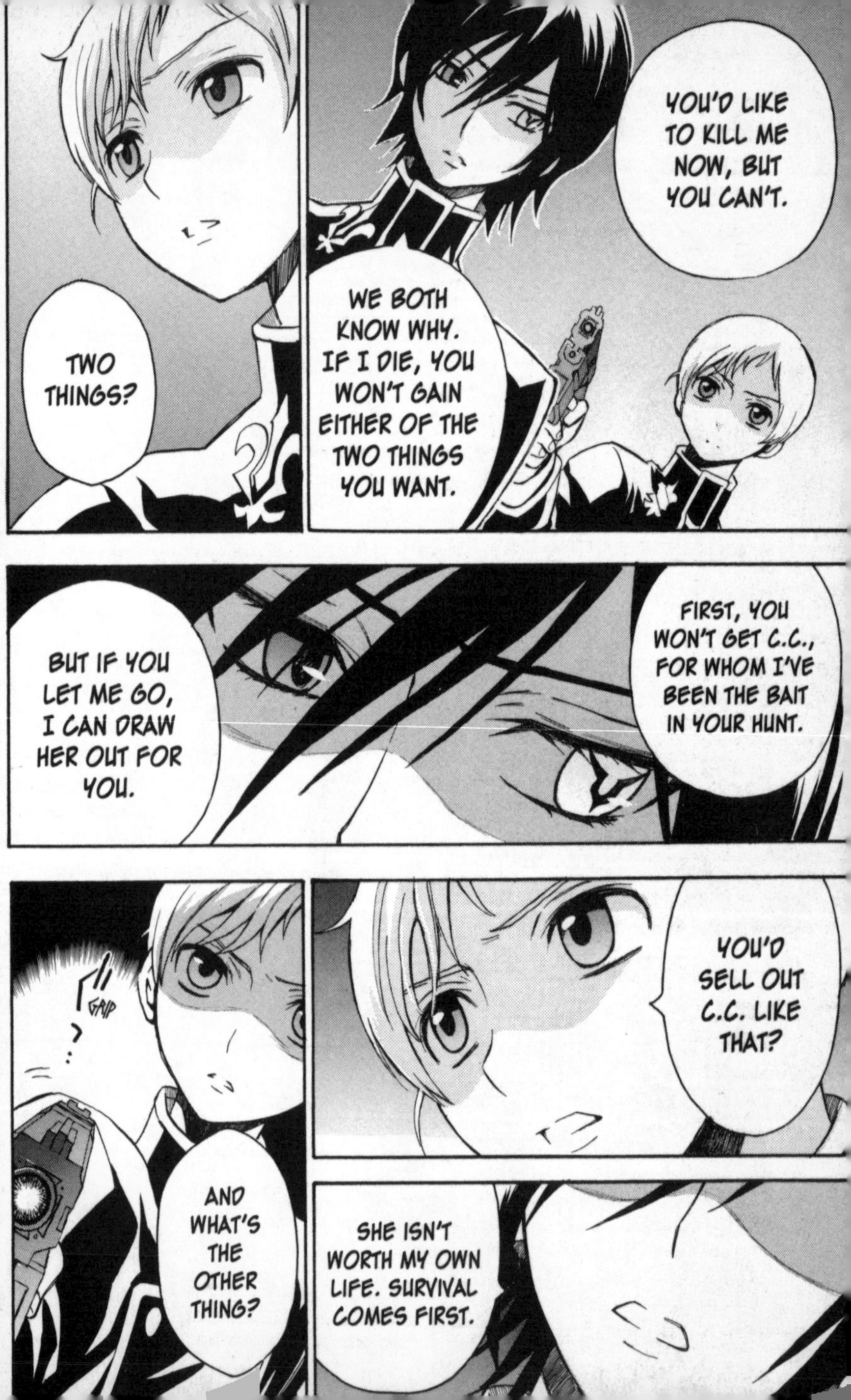
YOU'D LIKE TO KILL ME NOW, BUT YOU CAN'T.
WE BOTH KNOW WHY. IF I DIE, YOU WON'T GAIN EITHER OF THE TWO THINGS YOU WANT.
TWO THINGS?
FIRST, YOU WON'T GET C.C., FOR WHOM I'VE BEEN THE BAIT IN YOUR HUNT.
BUT IF YOU LET ME GO, I CAN DRAW HER OUT FOR YOU.
YOU'D SELL OUT C.C. LIKE THAT?
SHE ISN'T WORTH MY OWN LIFE. SURVIVAL COMES FIRST.
GRIP
AND WHAT'S THE OTHER THING?

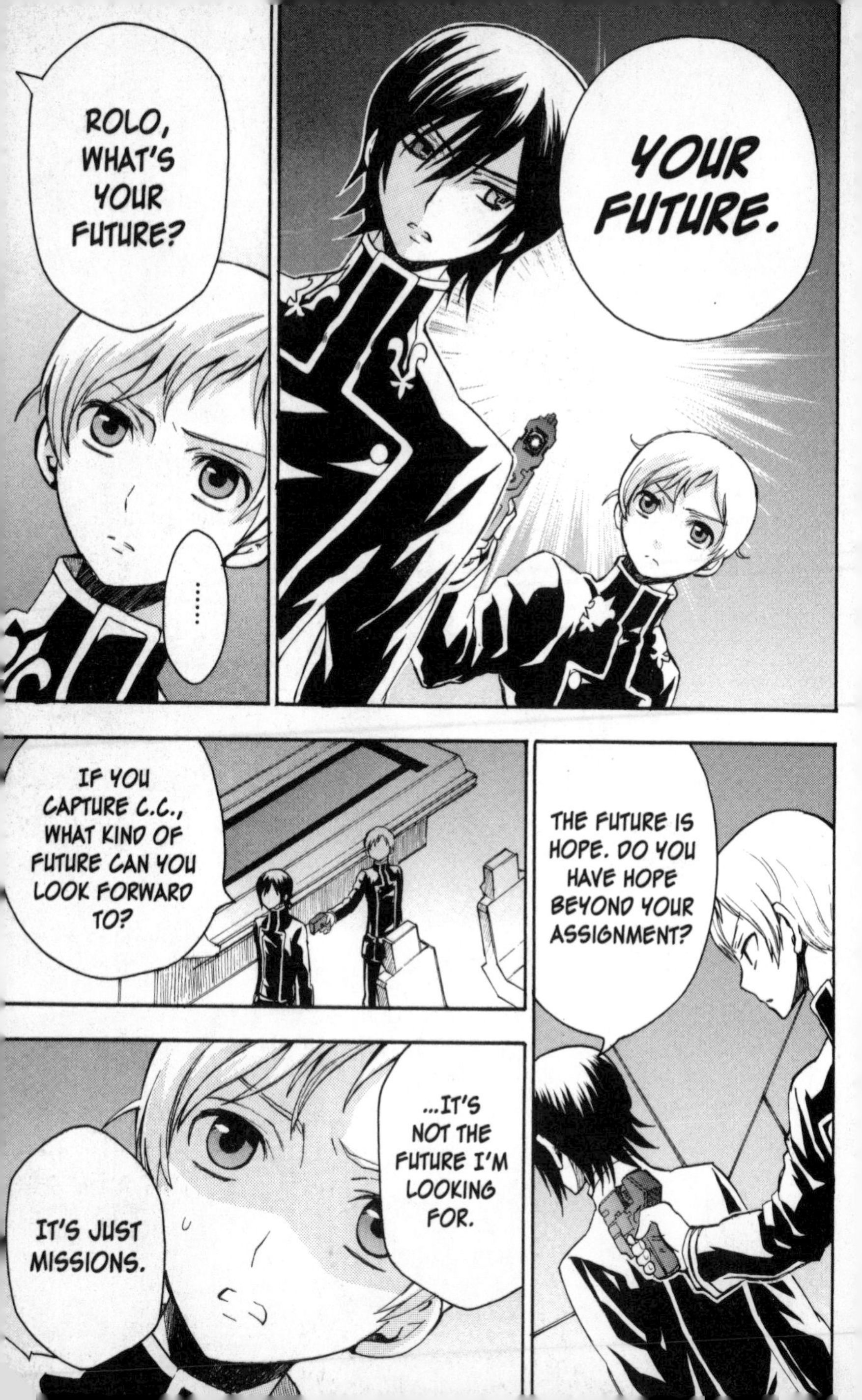
YOUR FUTURE.
ROLO, WHAT'S YOUR FUTURE?
......
THE FUTURE IS HOPE. DO YOU HAVE HOPE BEYOND YOUR ASSIGNMENT?
IF YOU CAPTURE C.C., WHAT KIND OF FUTURE CAN YOU LOOK FORWARD TO?
...IT'S NOT THE FUTURE I'M LOOKING FOR.
IT'S JUST MISSIONS.

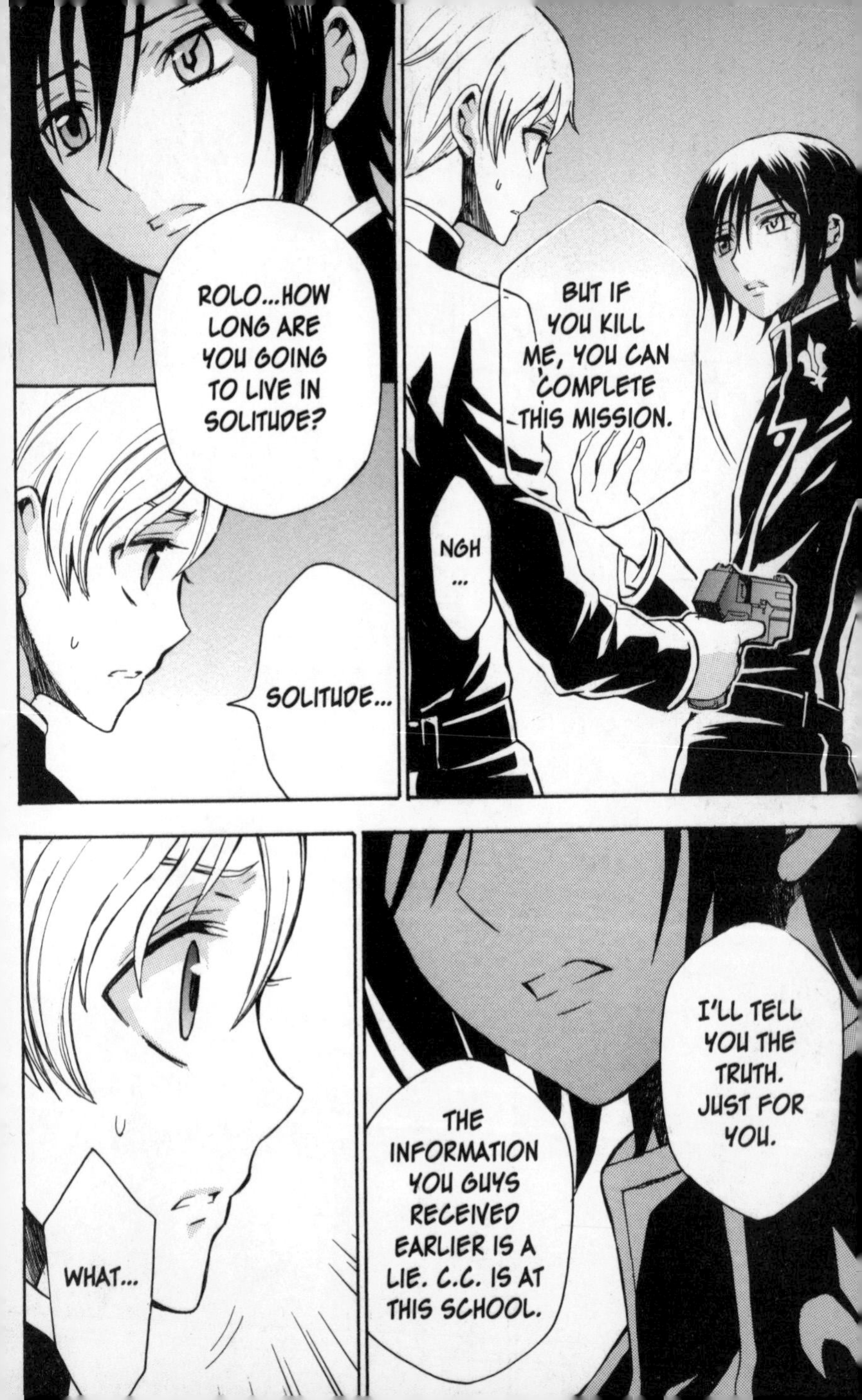
BUT IF YOU KILL ME, YOU CAN COMPLETE THIS MISSION.
NGH...
ROLO...HOW LONG ARE YOU GOING TO LIVE IN SOLITUDE?
SOLITUDE...
I'LL TELL YOU THE TRUTH. JUST FOR YOU.
THE INFORMATION YOU GUYS RECEIVED EARLIER IS A LIE. C.C. IS AT THIS SCHOOL.
WHAT...

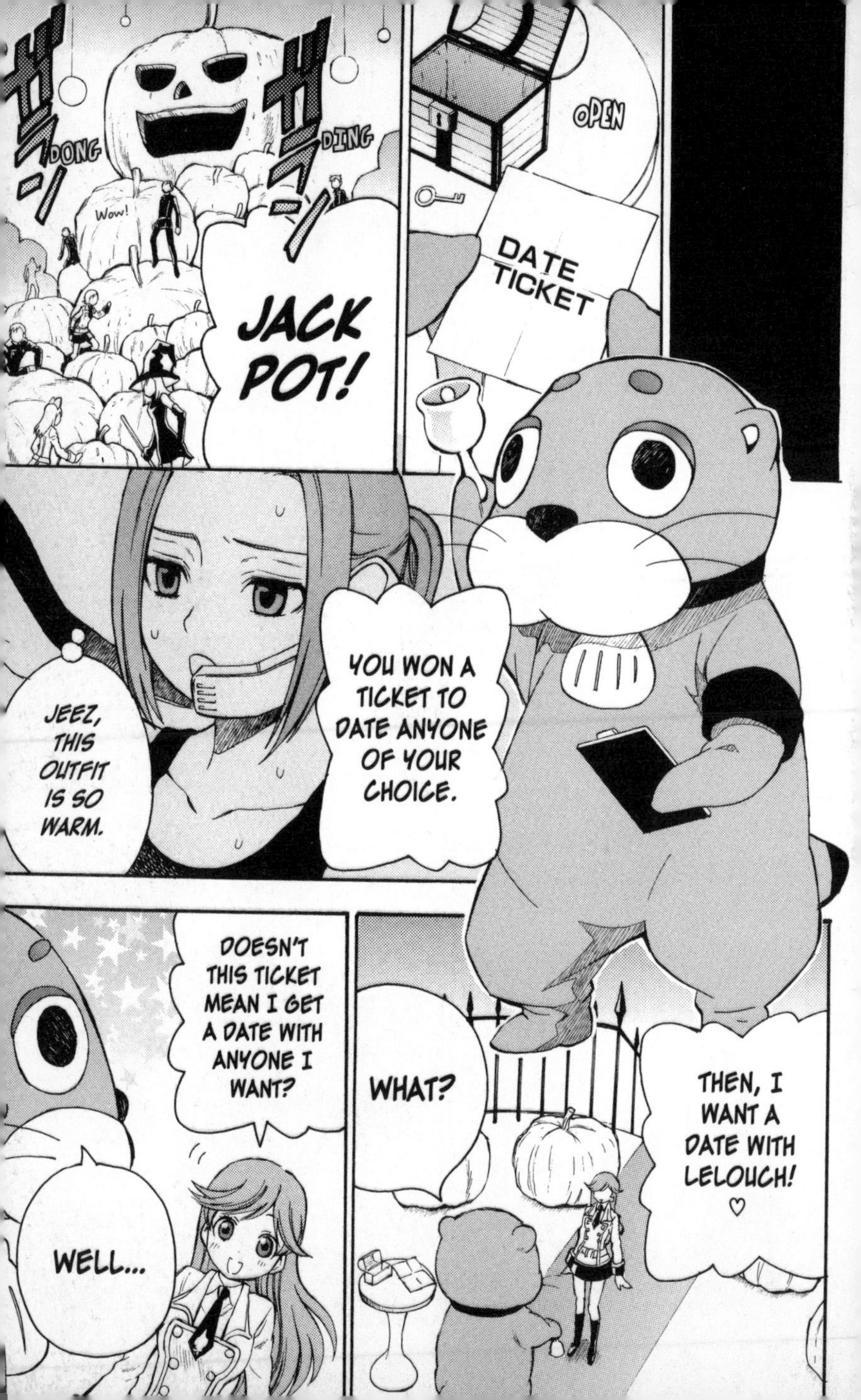
DONG
DING
Wow!
JACK POT!
OPEN
DATE TICKET
JEEZ, THIS OUTFIT IS SO WARM.
YOU WON A TICKET TO DATE ANYONE OF YOUR CHOICE.
DOESN'T THIS TICKET MEAN I GET A DATE WITH ANYONE I WANT?
WELL...
WHAT?
THEN, I WANT A DATE WITH LELOUCH! ♡

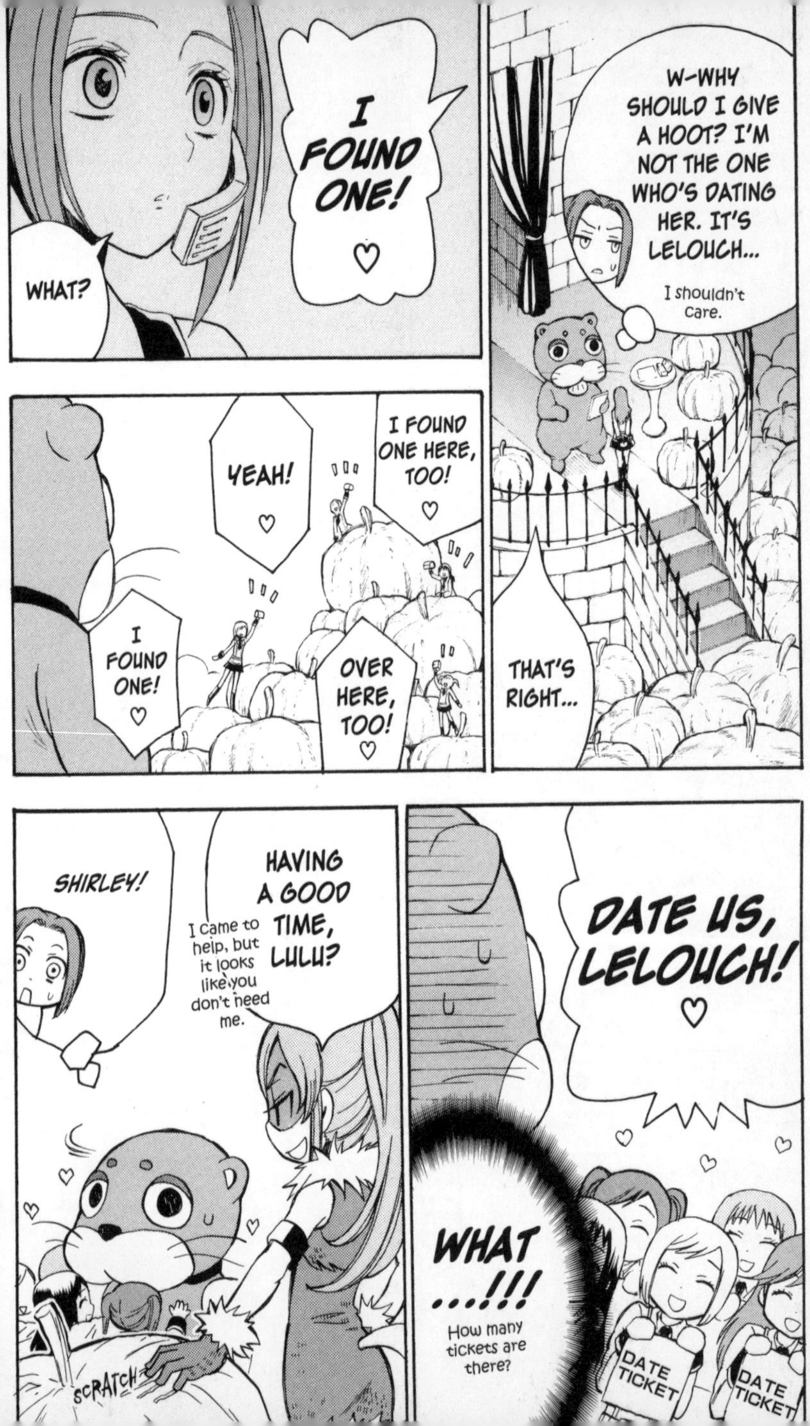
W-WHY SHOULD I GIVE A HOOT? I'M NOT THE ONE WHO'S DATING HER. IT'S LELOUCH...
I shouldn't care.
THAT'S RIGHT...
I FOUND ONE!
WHAT?
I FOUND ONE HERE, TOO!
YEAH!
OVER HERE, TOO!
I FOUND ONE!
DATE US, LELOUCH!
WHAT ...!!!
How many tickets are there?
DATE TICKET
DATE TICKET
HAVING A GOOD TIME, LULU?
I came to help, but it looks like you don't need me.
SHIRLEY!
SCRATCH

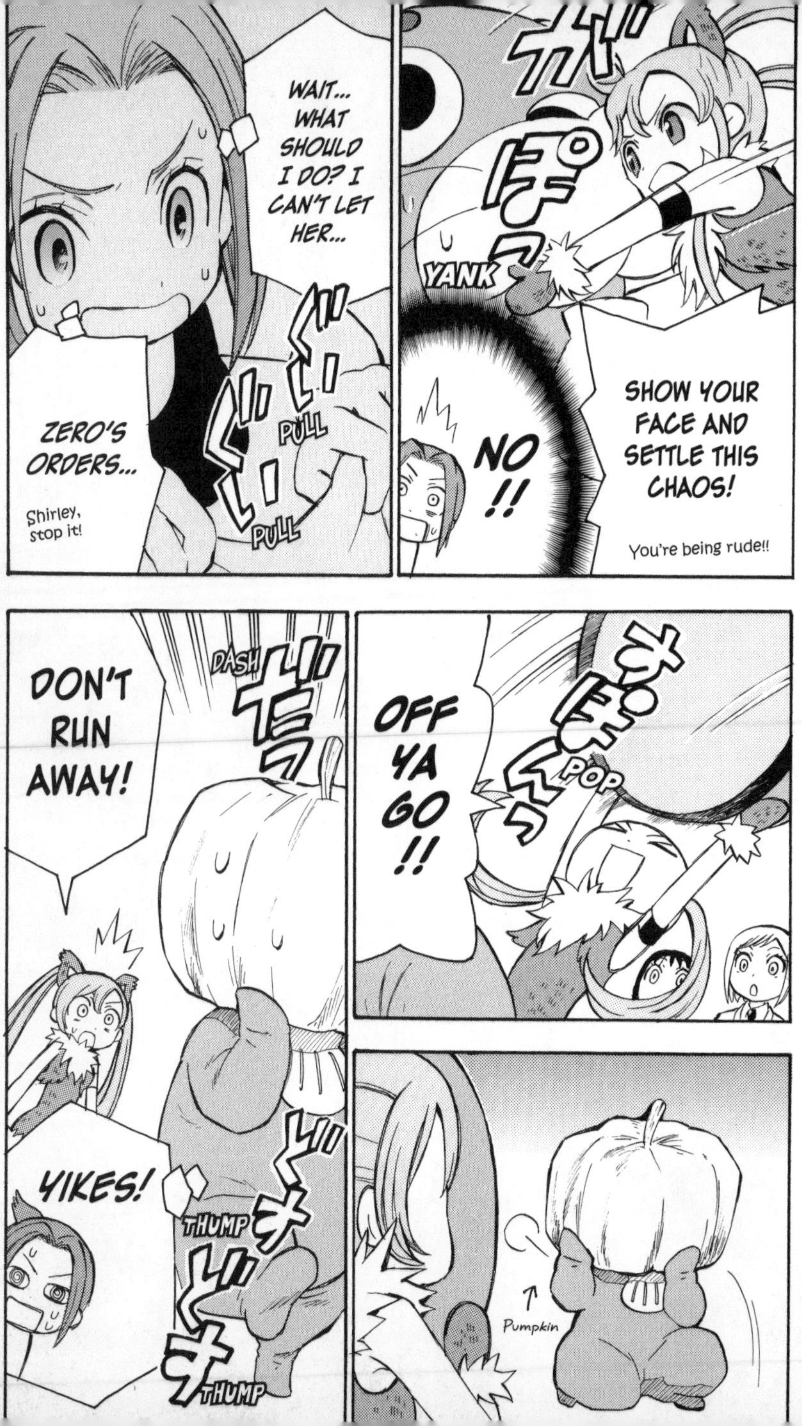
YANK
SHOW YOUR FACE AND SETTLE THIS CHAOS!
NO!!
You're being rude!!
WAIT... WHAT SHOULD I DO? I CAN'T LET HER...
PULL
PULL
ZERO'S ORDERS...
Shirley, stop it!
OFF YA GO!!
POP
Pumpkin
DASH
DON'T RUN AWAY!
YIKES!
THUMP
THUMP

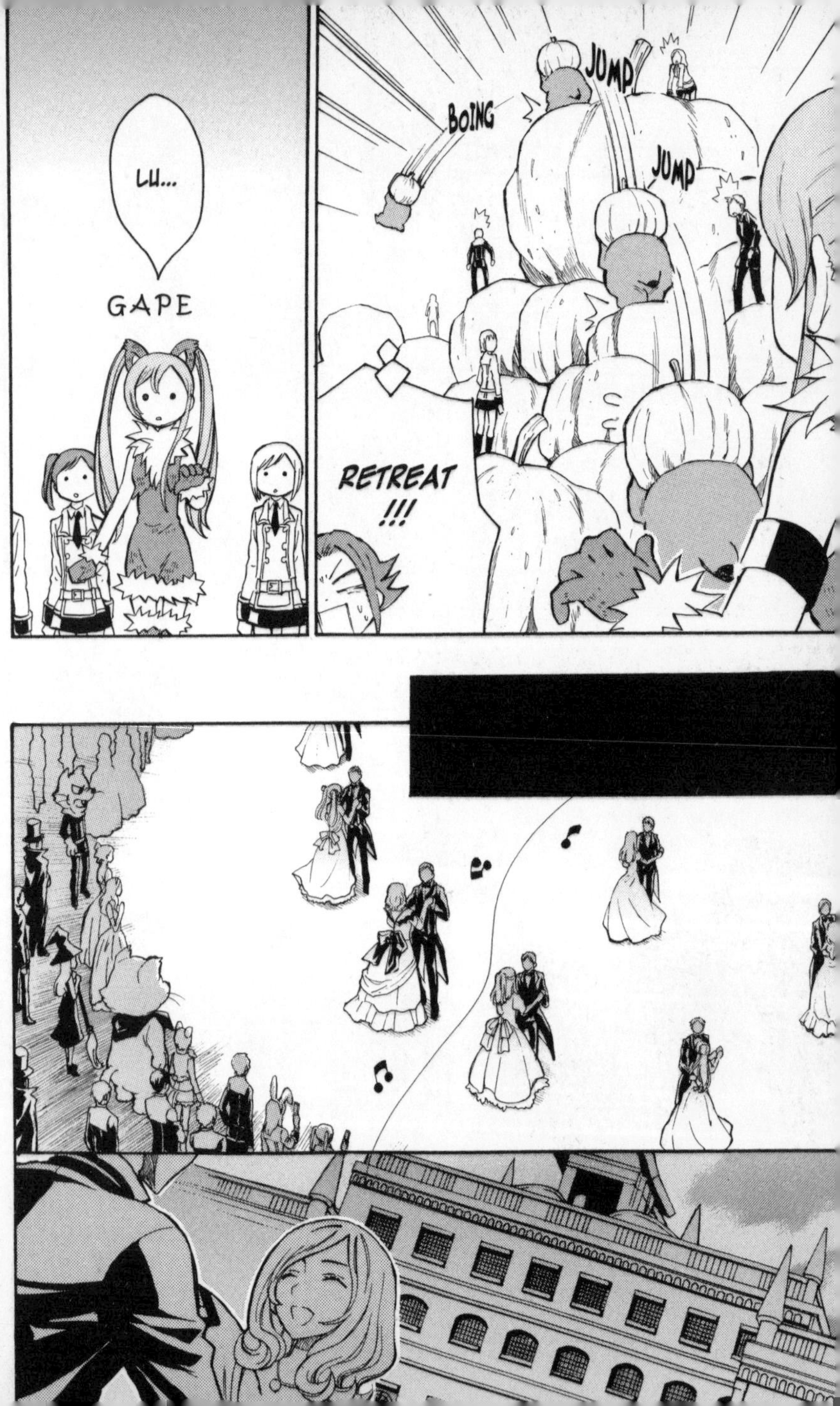
JUMP
BOING
JUMP
RETREAT !!!
LU...
GAPE
[redacted]

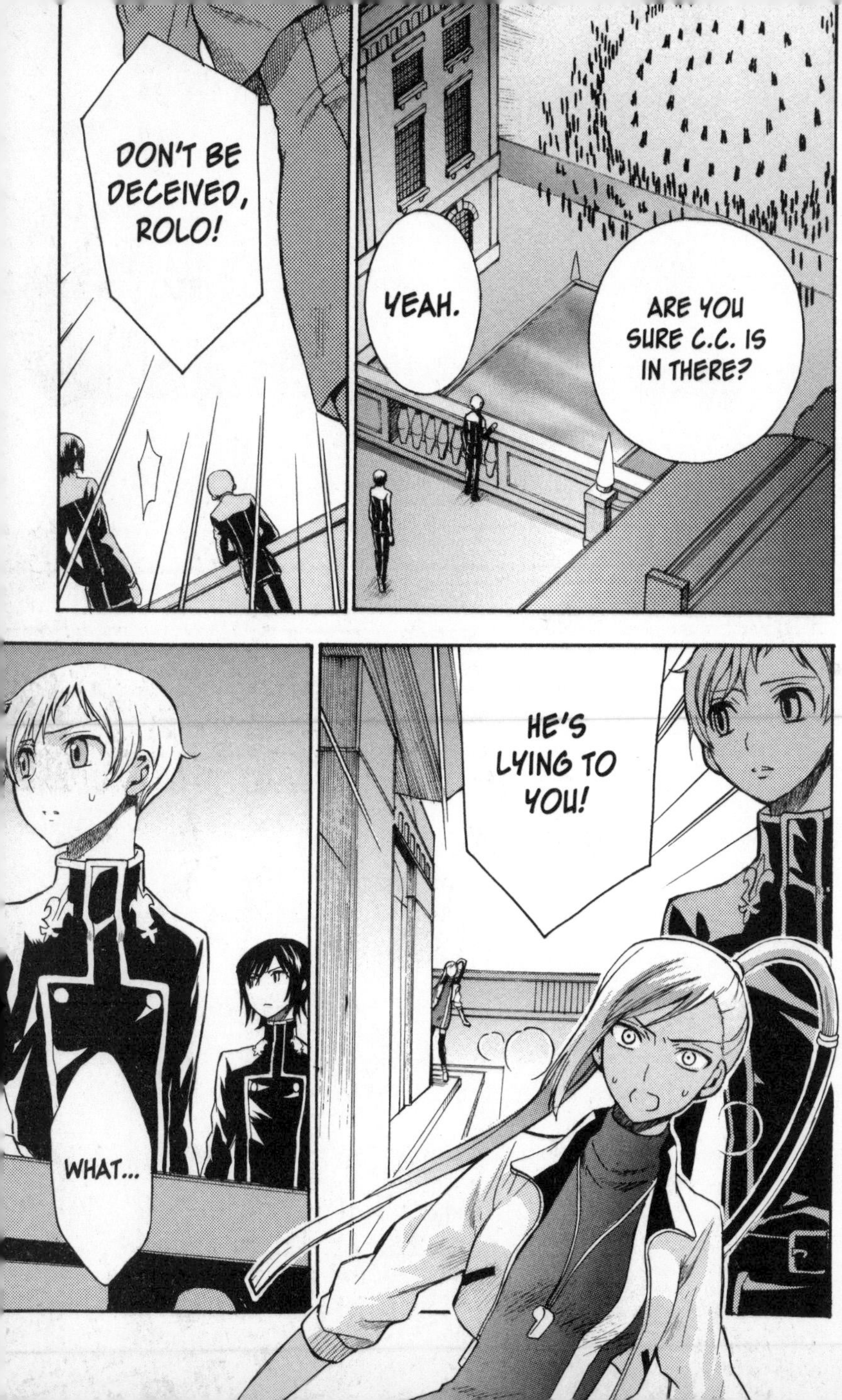
ARE YOU SURE C.C. IS IN THERE?
YEAH.
DON'T BE DECEIVED, ROLO!
HE'S LYING TO YOU!
WHAT...

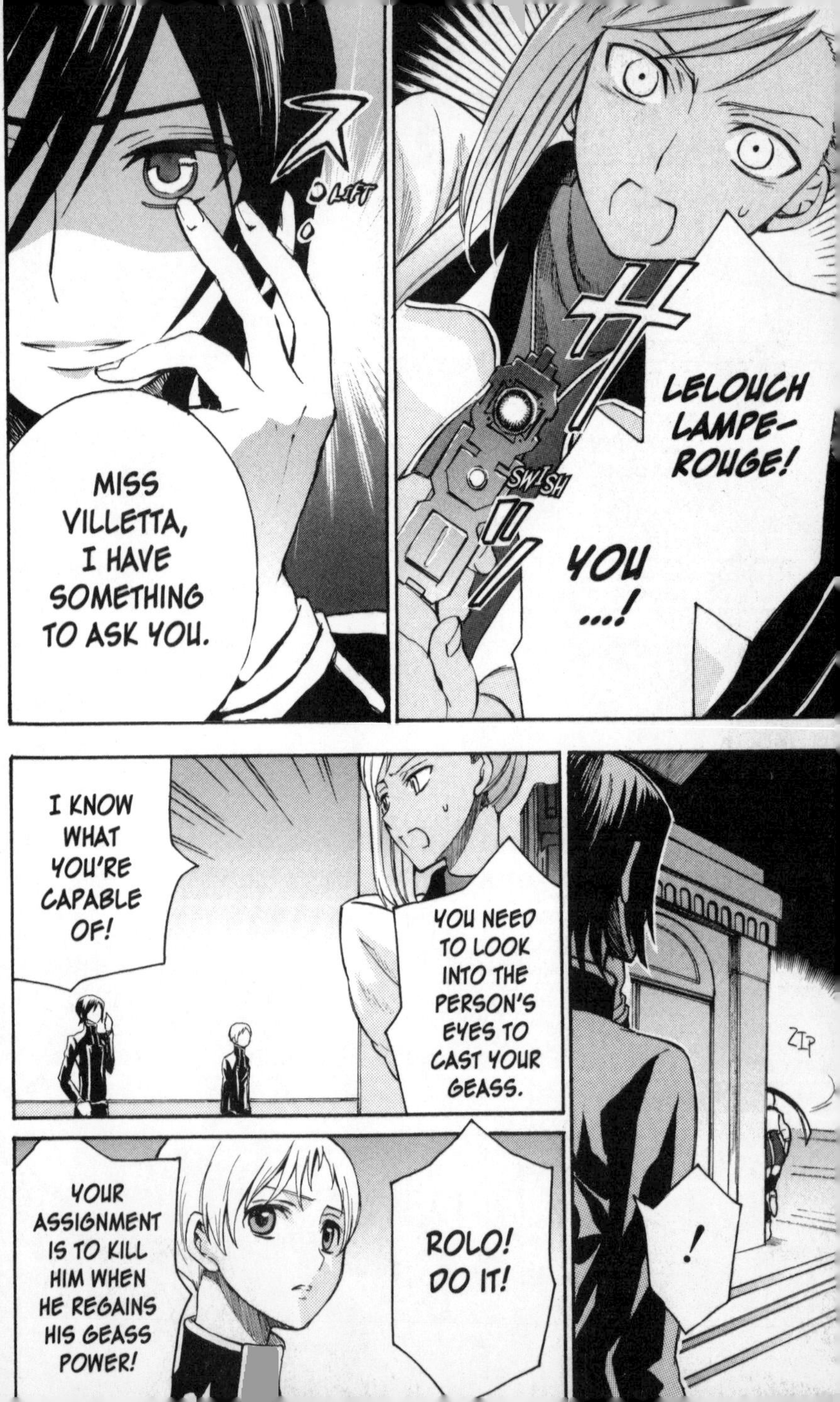
LELOUCH LAMPE-ROUGE!
SWISH
YOU ...!
LIFT
MISS VILLETTA, I HAVE SOMETHING TO ASK YOU.
ZIP
!
I KNOW WHAT YOU'RE CAPABLE OF!
YOU NEED TO LOOK INTO THE PERSON'S EYES TO CAST YOUR GEASS.
ROLO! DO IT!
YOUR ASSIGNMENT IS TO KILL HIM WHEN HE REGAINS HIS GEASS POWER!

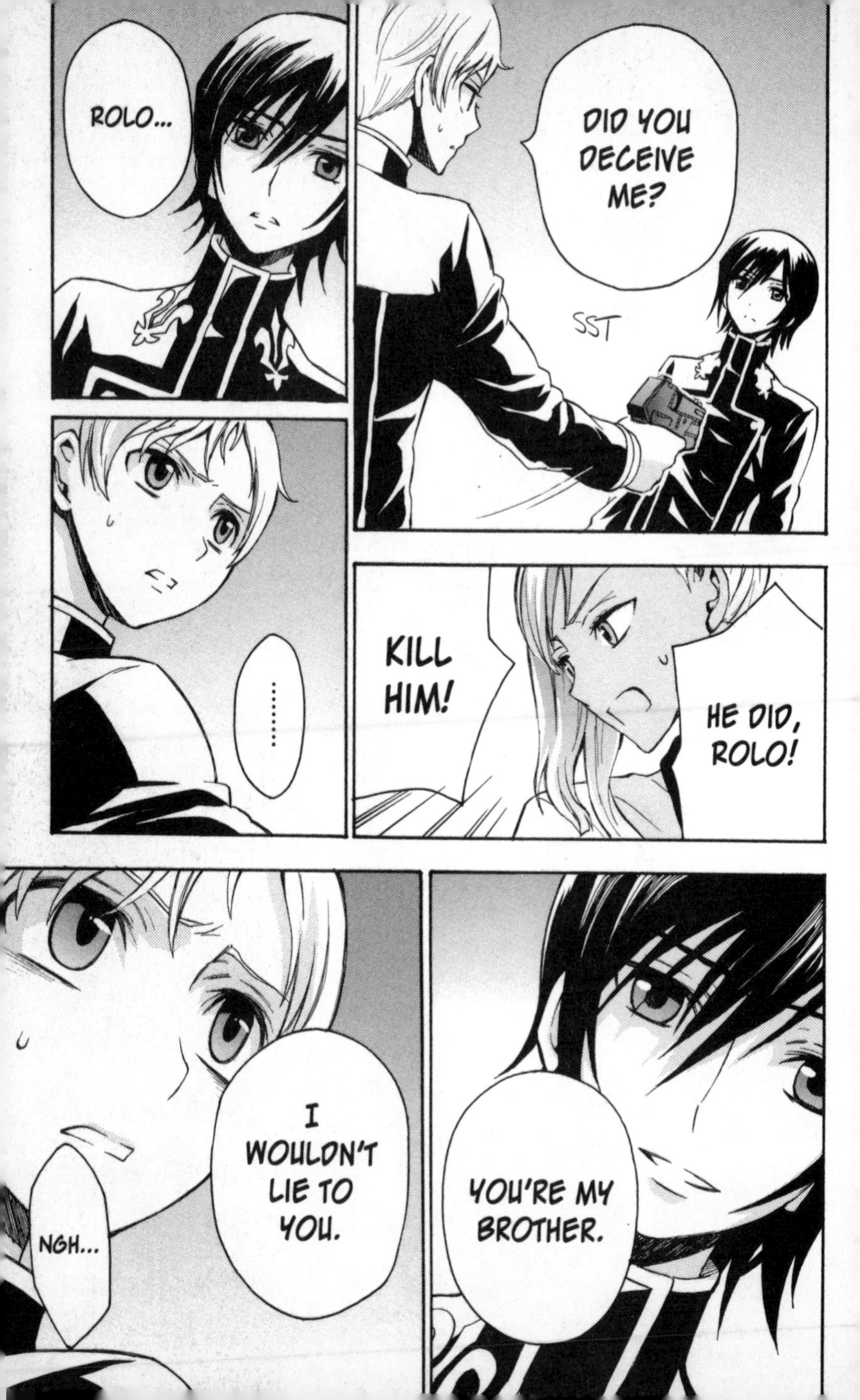
DID YOU DECEIVE ME?
SST
ROLO...
HE DID, ROLO!
KILL HIM!
......
YOU'RE MY BROTHER.
I WOULDN'T LIE TO YOU.
NGH...

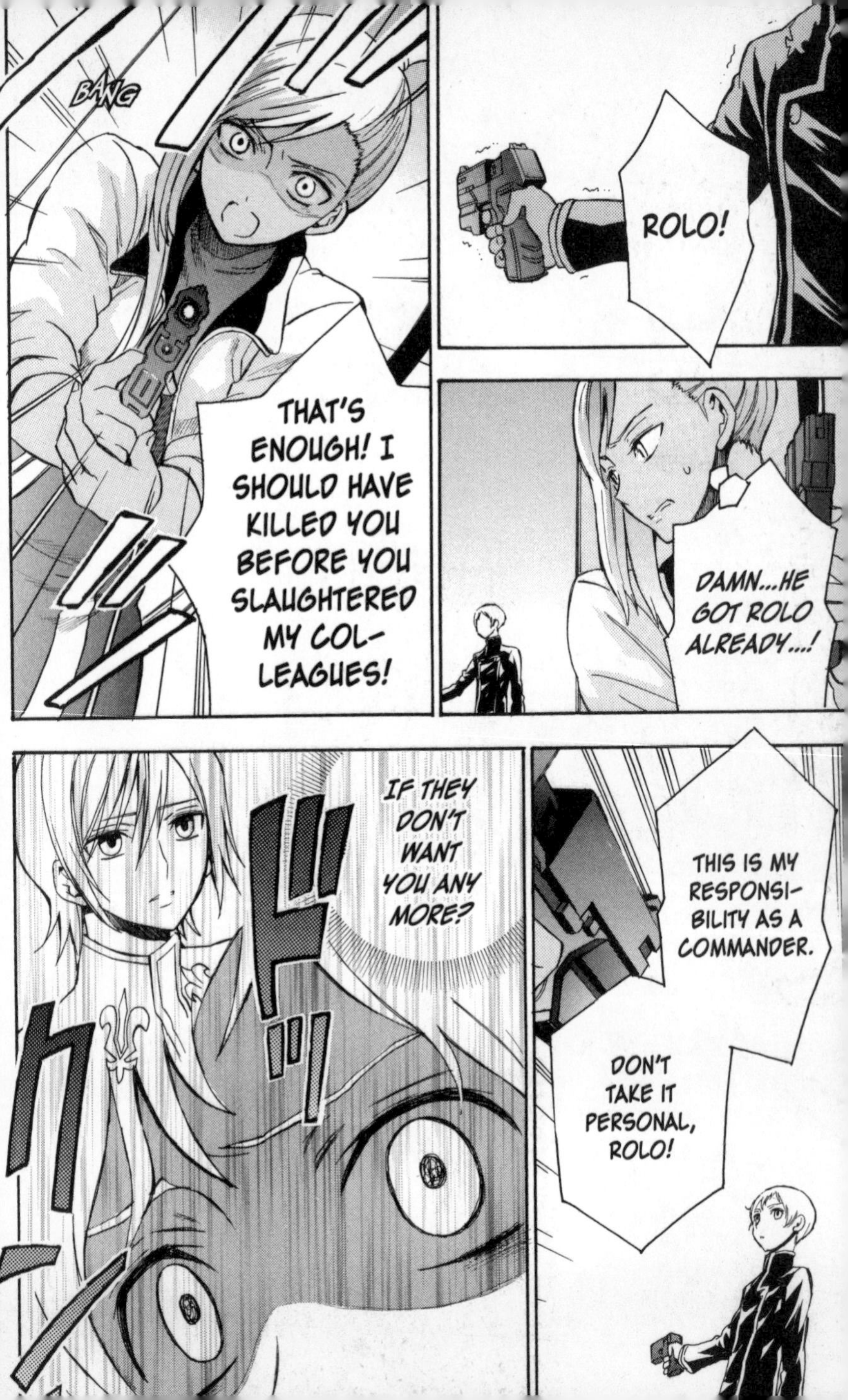
ROLO!
DAMN...HE GOT ROLO ALREADY...!
BANG
THAT'S ENOUGH! I SHOULD HAVE KILLED YOU BEFORE YOU SLAUGHTERED MY COL-LEAGUES!
THIS IS MY RESPONSI-BILITY AS A COMMANDER.
DON'T TAKE IT PERSONAL, ROLO!
IF THEY DON'T WANT YOU ANY MORE?

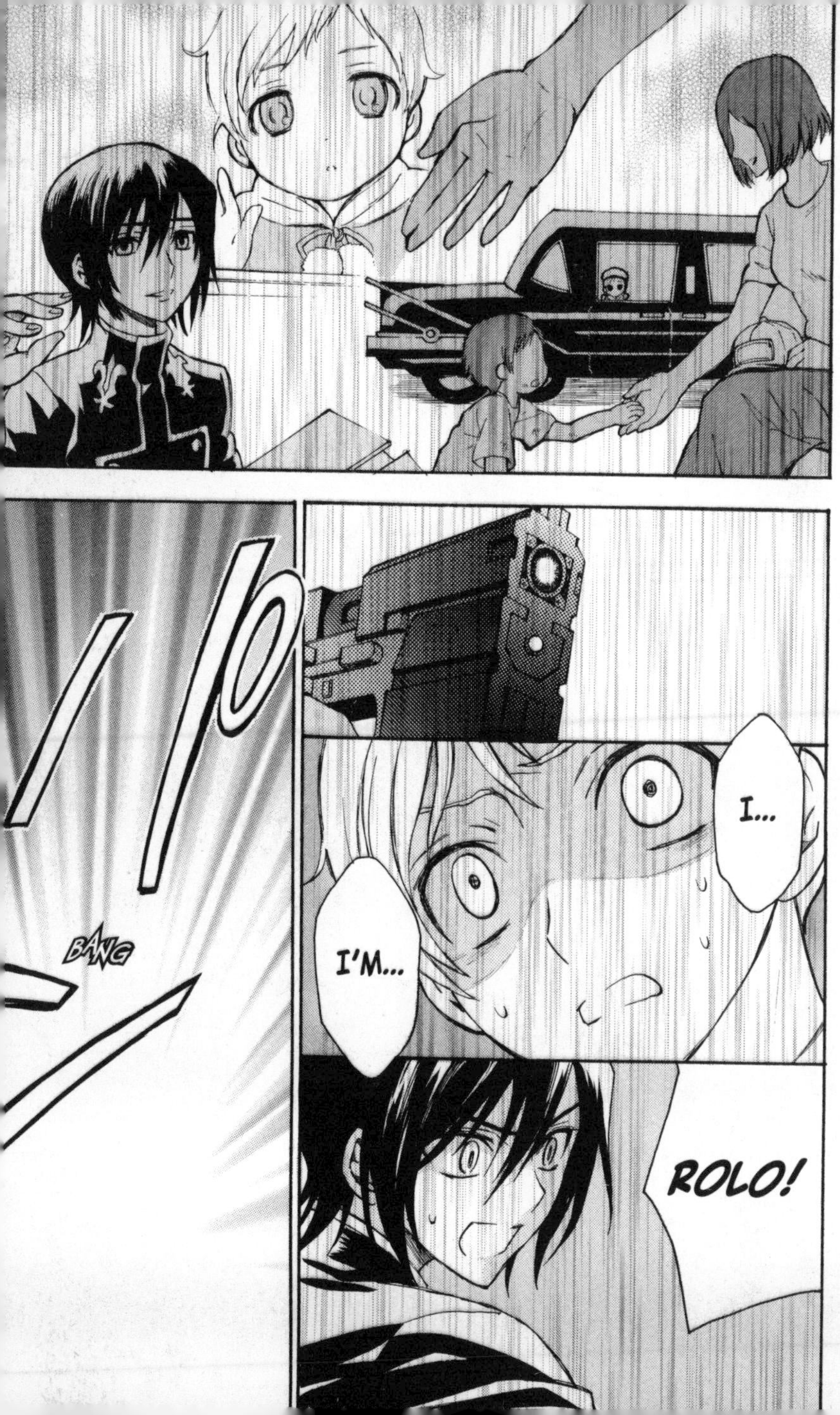
I...
I'M...
ROLO!
BANG

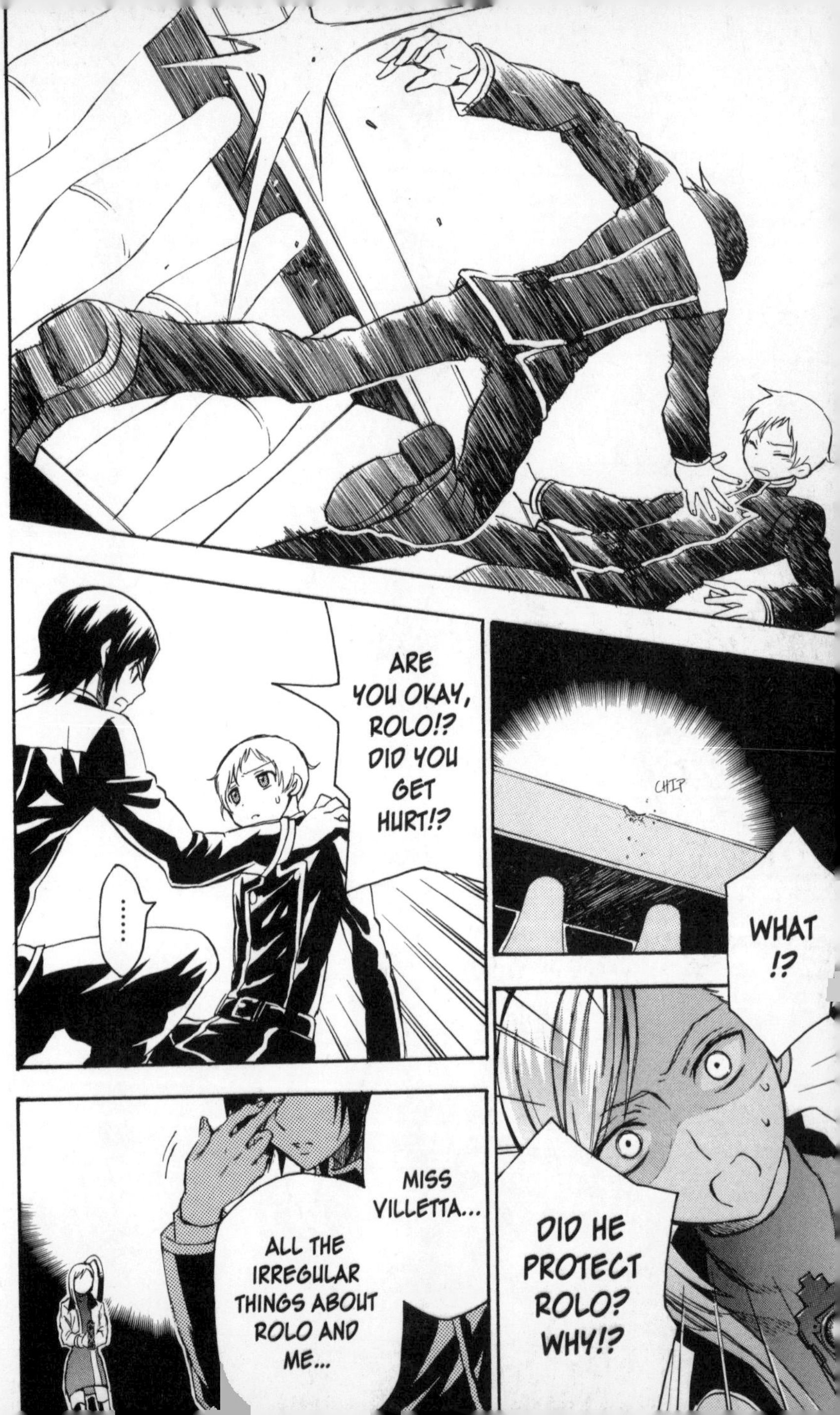
CHIP
WHAT!?
ARE YOU OKAY, ROLO!? DID YOU GET HURT!?
......
DID HE PROTECT ROLO? WHY!?
MISS VILLETTA...
ALL THE IRREGULAR THINGS ABOUT ROLO AND ME...

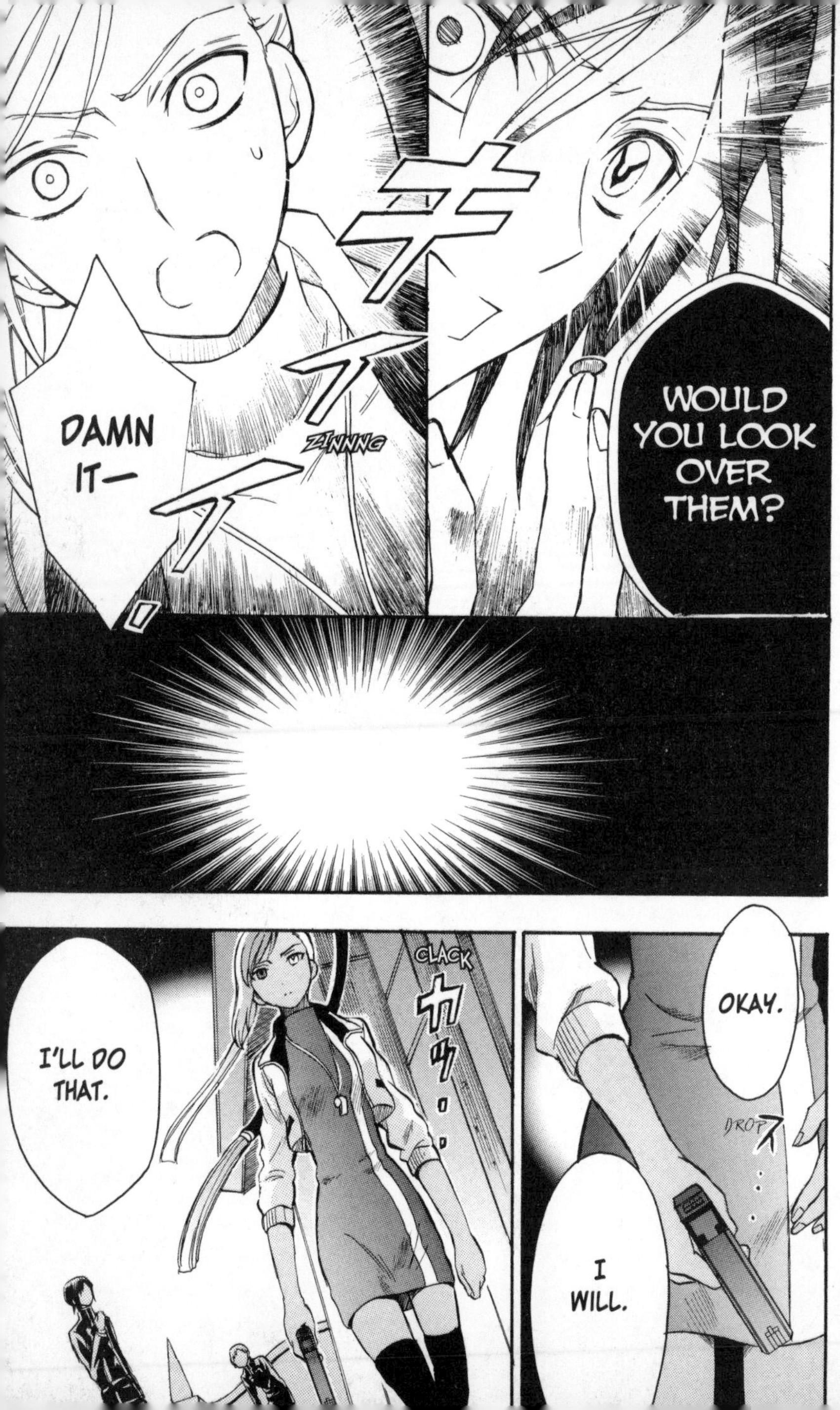
WOULD YOU LOOK OVER THEM?
ZINNNG
DAMN IT—
OKAY.
DROP
I WILL.
CLACK
I'LL DO THAT.

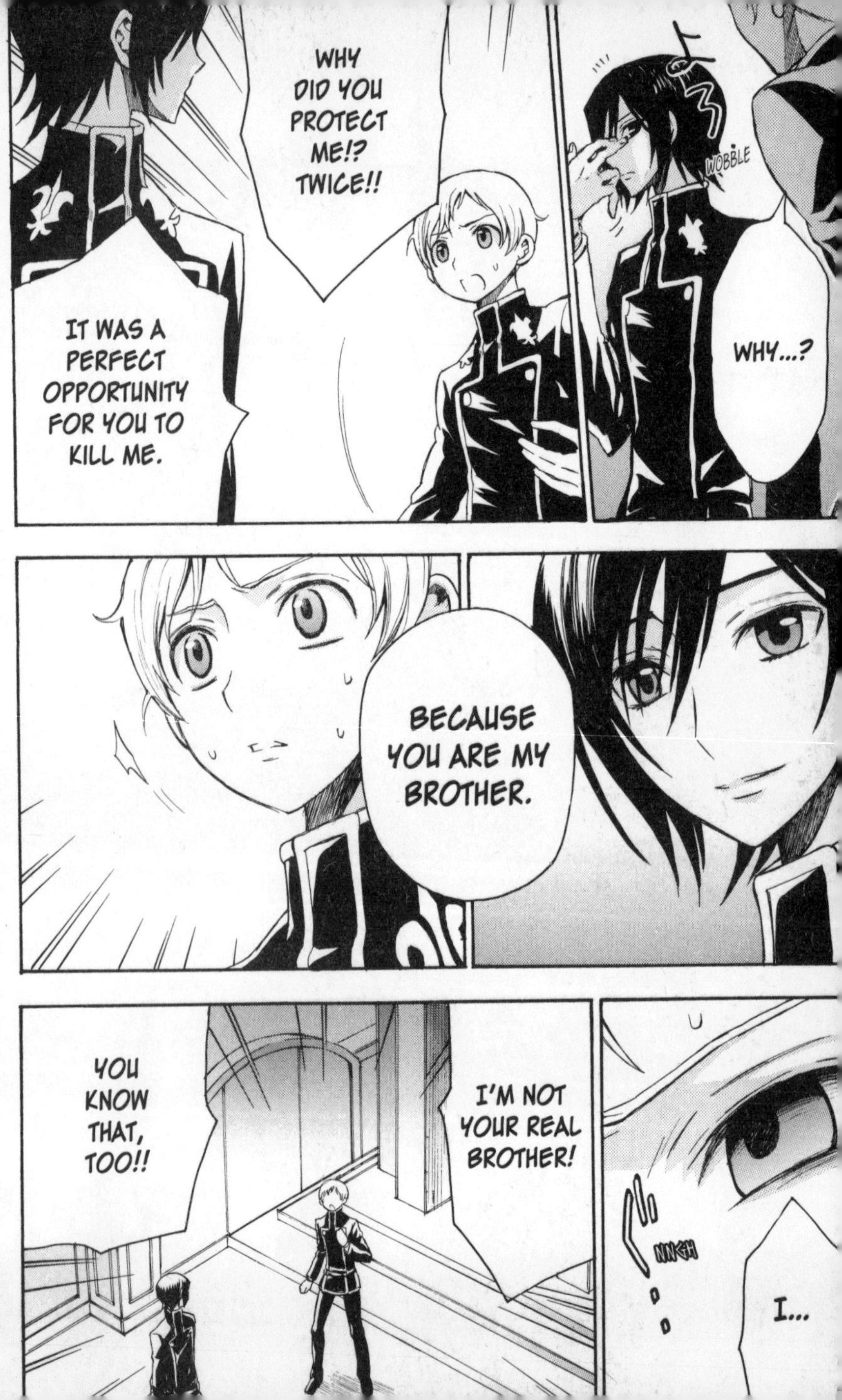
WOBBLE
WHY...?
WHY DID YOU PROTECT ME!? TWICE!!
IT WAS A PERFECT OPPORTUNITY FOR YOU TO KILL ME.
BECAUSE YOU ARE MY BROTHER.
NNGH
I...
I'M NOT YOUR REAL BROTHER!
YOU KNOW THAT, TOO!!

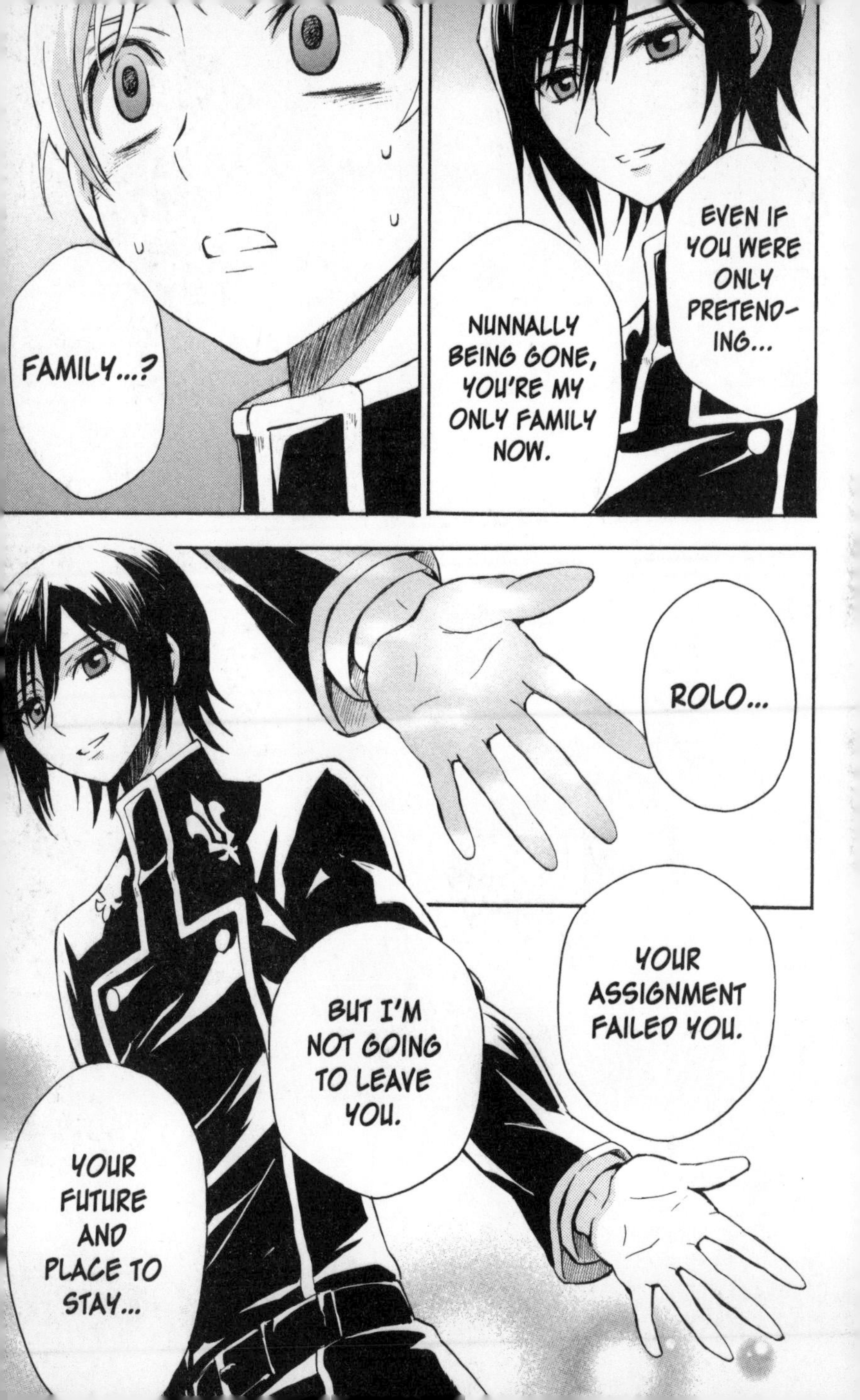
EVEN IF YOU WERE ONLY PRETENDING...
NUNNALLY BEING GONE, YOU'RE MY ONLY FAMILY NOW.
FAMILY...?
ROLO...
YOUR ASSIGNMENT FAILED YOU.
BUT I'M NOT GOING TO LEAVE YOU.
YOUR FUTURE AND PLACE TO STAY...

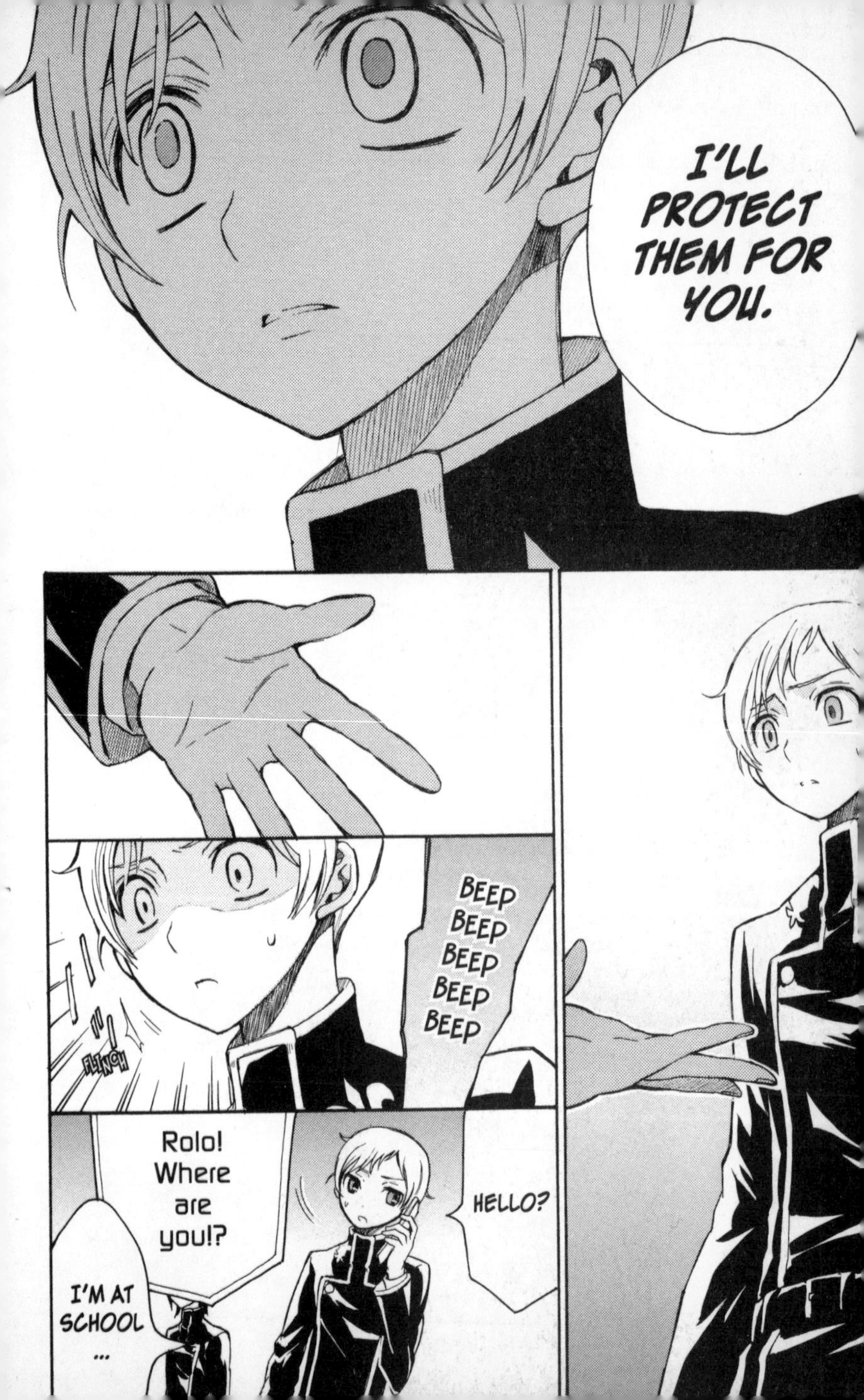
I'LL PROTECT THEM FOR YOU.
BEEP BEEP BEEP BEEP BEEP
FLINCH
HELLO?
Rolo! Where are you!?
I'M AT SCHOOL ...

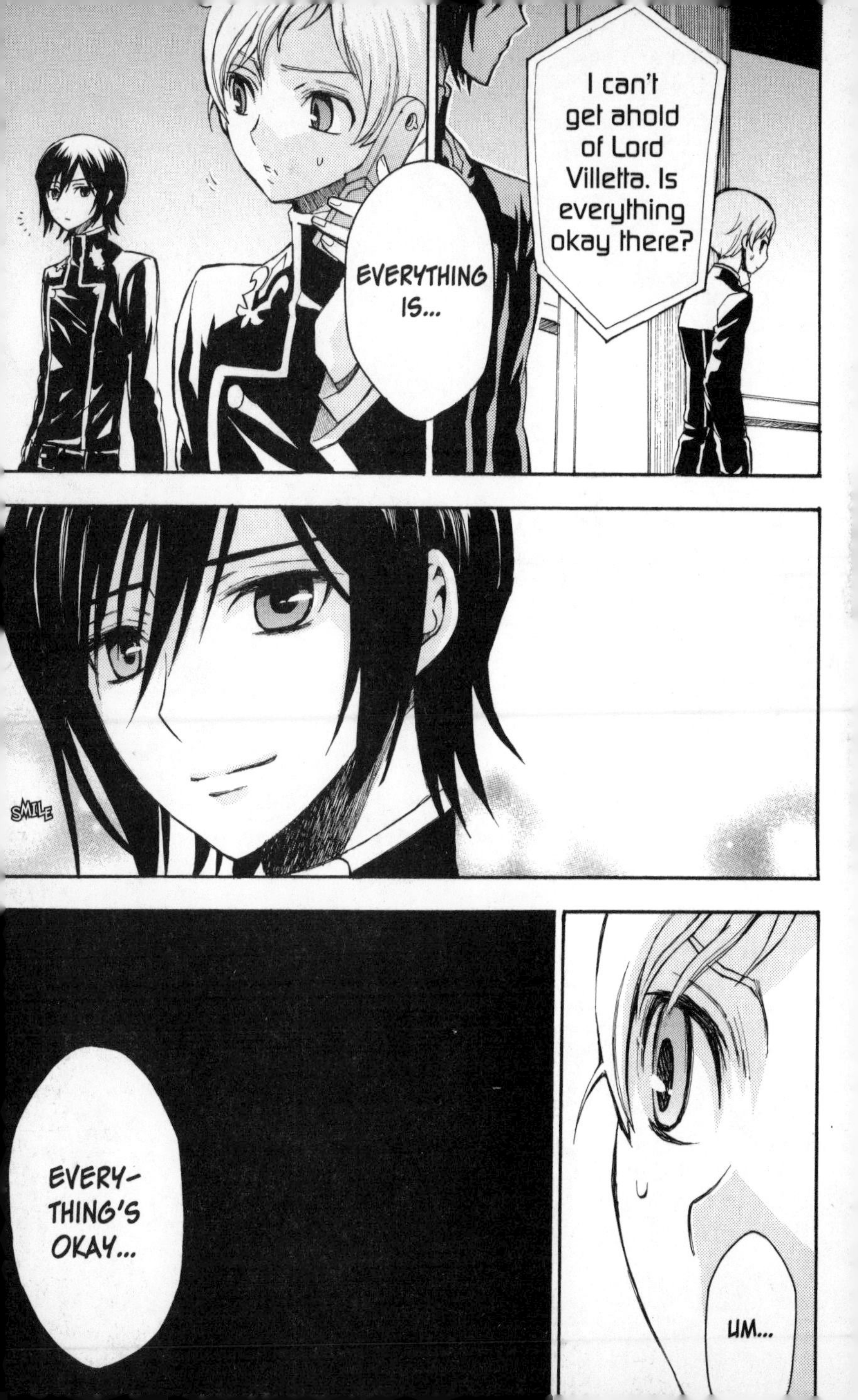
I can't get ahold of Lord Villetta. Is everything okay there?
EVERYTHING IS...
SMILE
UM...
EVERY-THING'S OKAY...

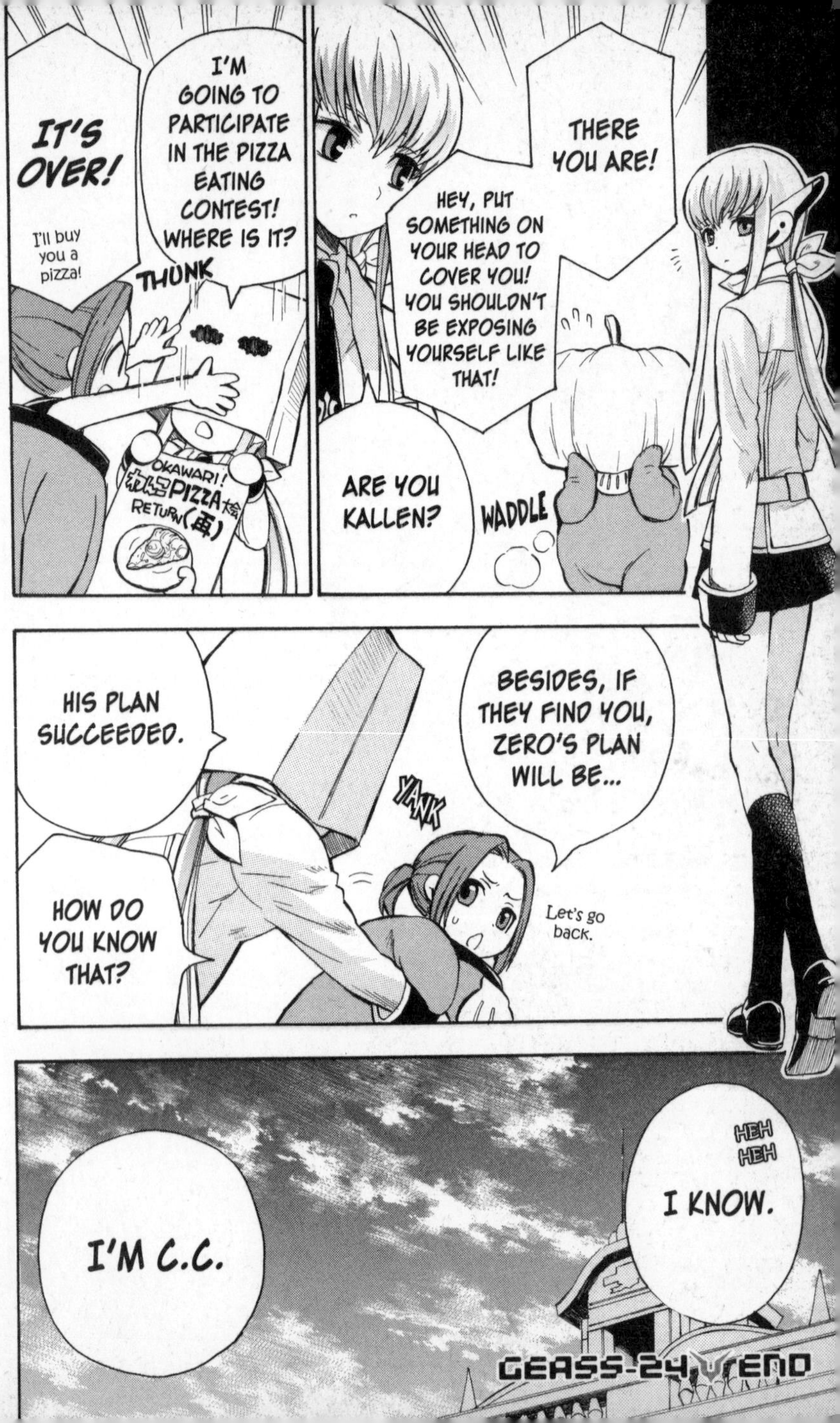
THERE YOU ARE!
HEY, PUT SOMETHING ON YOUR HEAD TO COVER YOU! YOU SHOULDN'T BE EXPOSING YOURSELF LIKE THAT!
WADDLE
ARE YOU KALLEN?
I'M GOING TO PARTICIPATE IN THE PIZZA EATING CONTEST! WHERE IS IT?
IT'S OVER!
I'll buy you a pizza!
THUNK
OKAWARI!
PIZZA
RETURN
BESIDES, IF THEY FIND YOU, ZERO'S PLAN WILL BE...
YANK
Let's go back.
HIS PLAN SUCCEEDED.
HOW DO YOU KNOW THAT?
HEH HEH
I KNOW.
I'M C.C.
GEASS-24 END

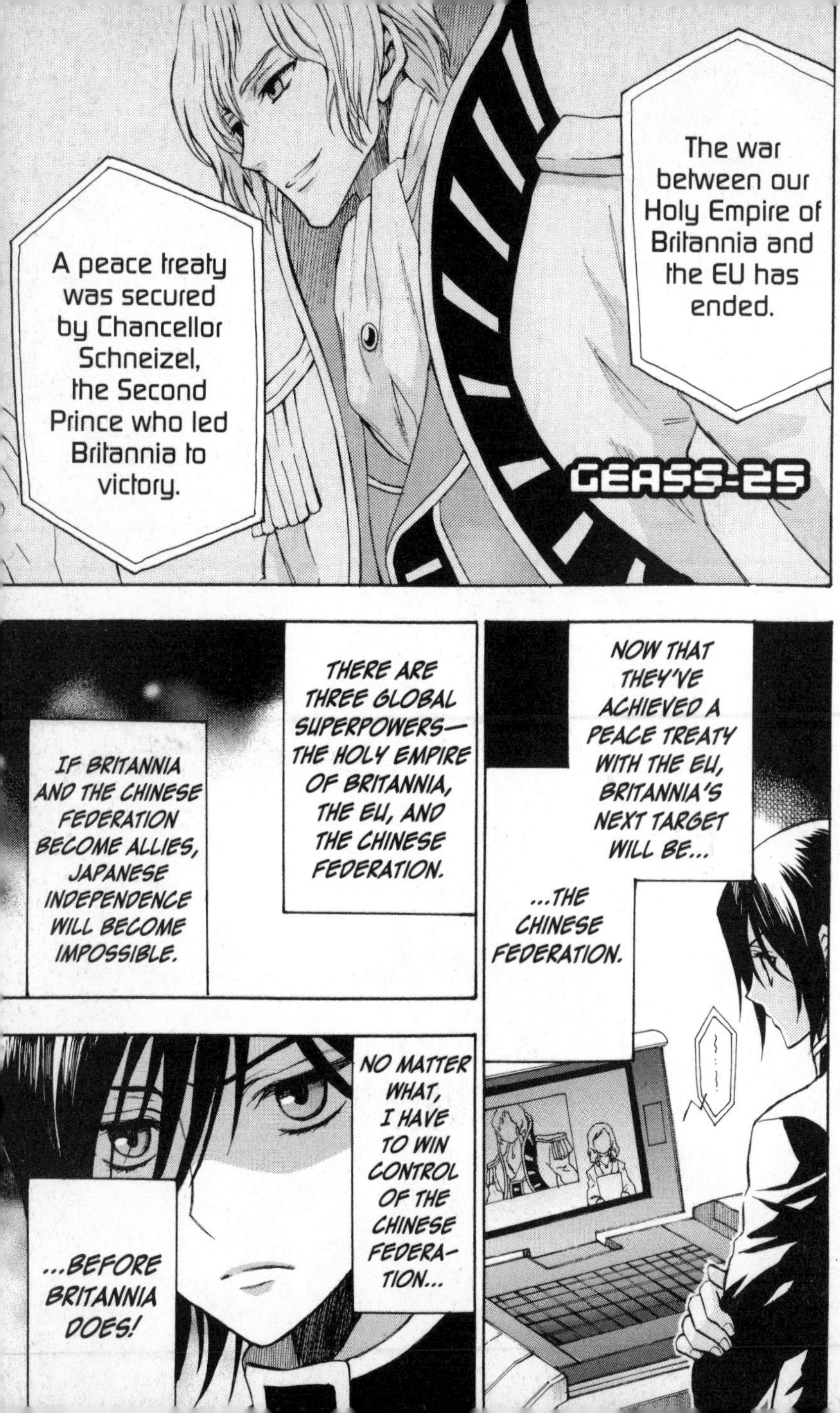
The war between our Holy Empire of Britannia and the EU has ended.
A peace treaty was secured by Chancellor Schneizel, the Second Prince who led Britannia to victory.
GEASS-25
NOW THAT THEY'VE ACHIEVED A PEACE TREATY WITH THE EU, BRITANNIA'S NEXT TARGET WILL BE...
...THE CHINESE FEDERATION.
THERE ARE THREE GLOBAL SUPERPOWERS—THE HOLY EMPIRE OF BRITANNIA, THE EU, AND THE CHINESE FEDERATION.
IF BRITANNIA AND THE CHINESE FEDERATION BECOME ALLIES, JAPANESE INDEPENDENCE WILL BECOME IMPOSSIBLE.
NO MATTER WHAT, I HAVE TO WIN CONTROL OF THE CHINESE FEDERA-TION...
...BEFORE BRITANNIA DOES!

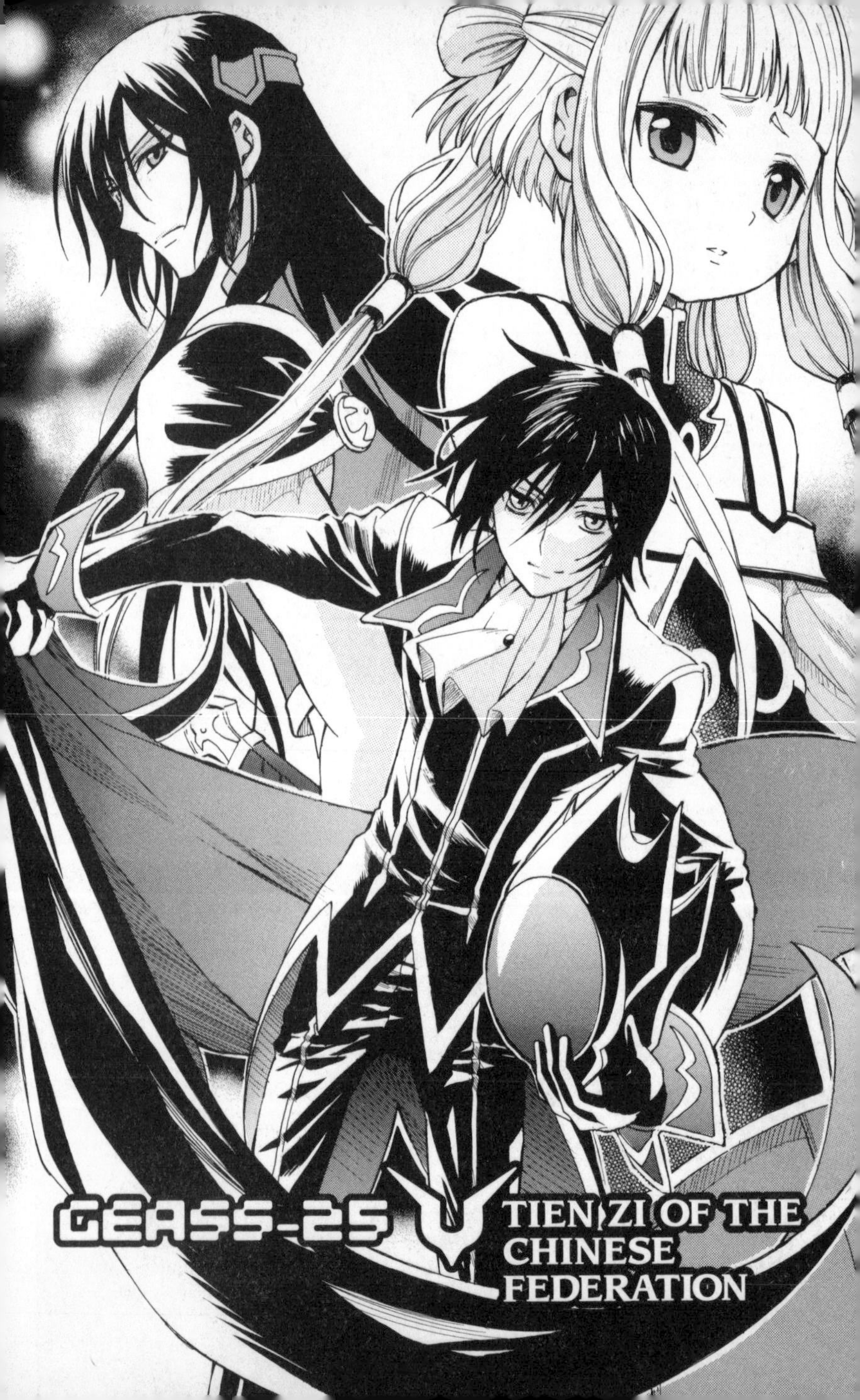
GEASS-25
TIEN ZI OF THE CHINESE FEDERATION

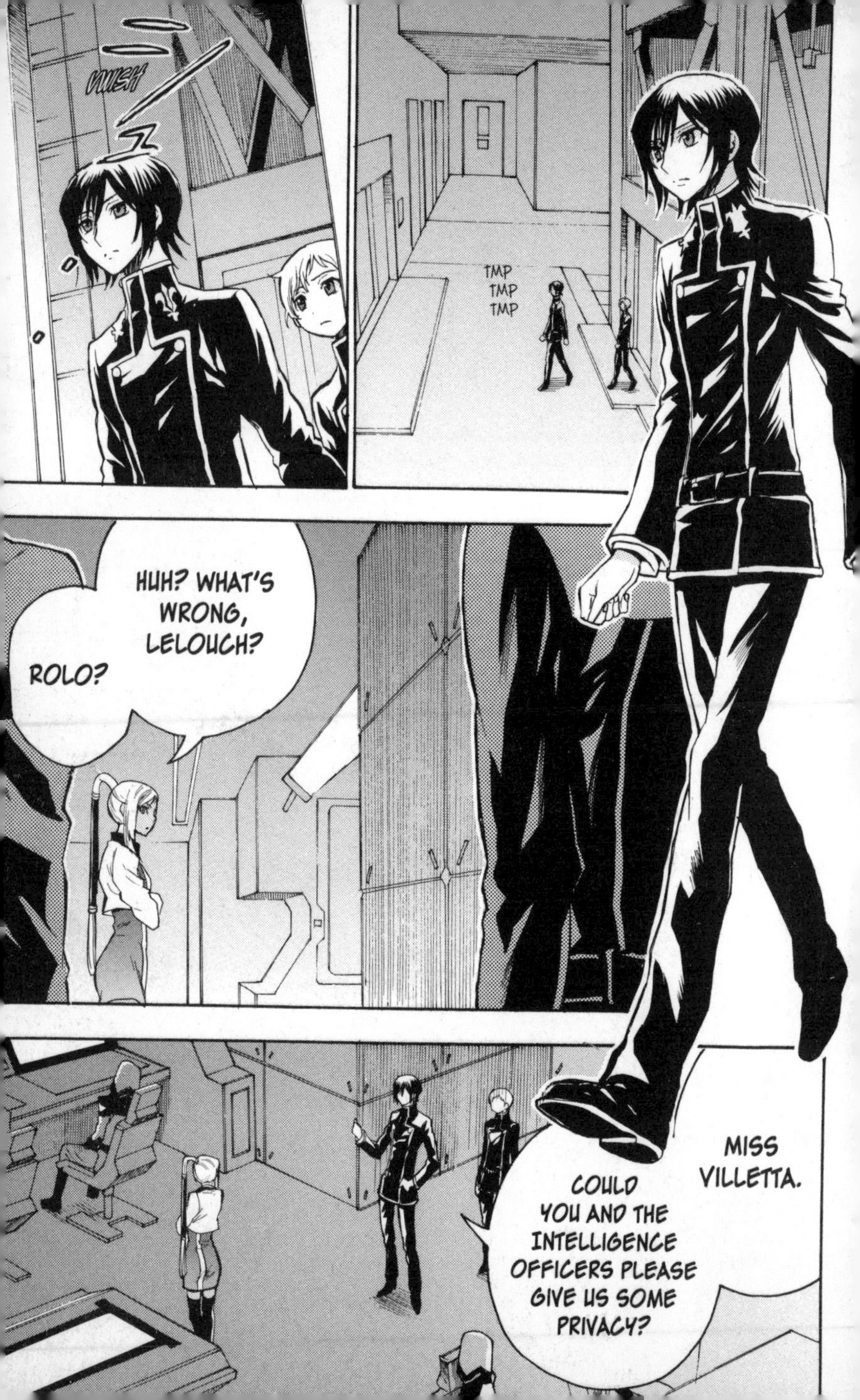
TMP
TMP
TMP
VMISH
HUH? WHAT'S WRONG, LELOUCH?
ROLO?
MISS VILLETTA.
COULD YOU AND THE INTELLIGENCE OFFICERS PLEASE GIVE US SOME PRIVACY?

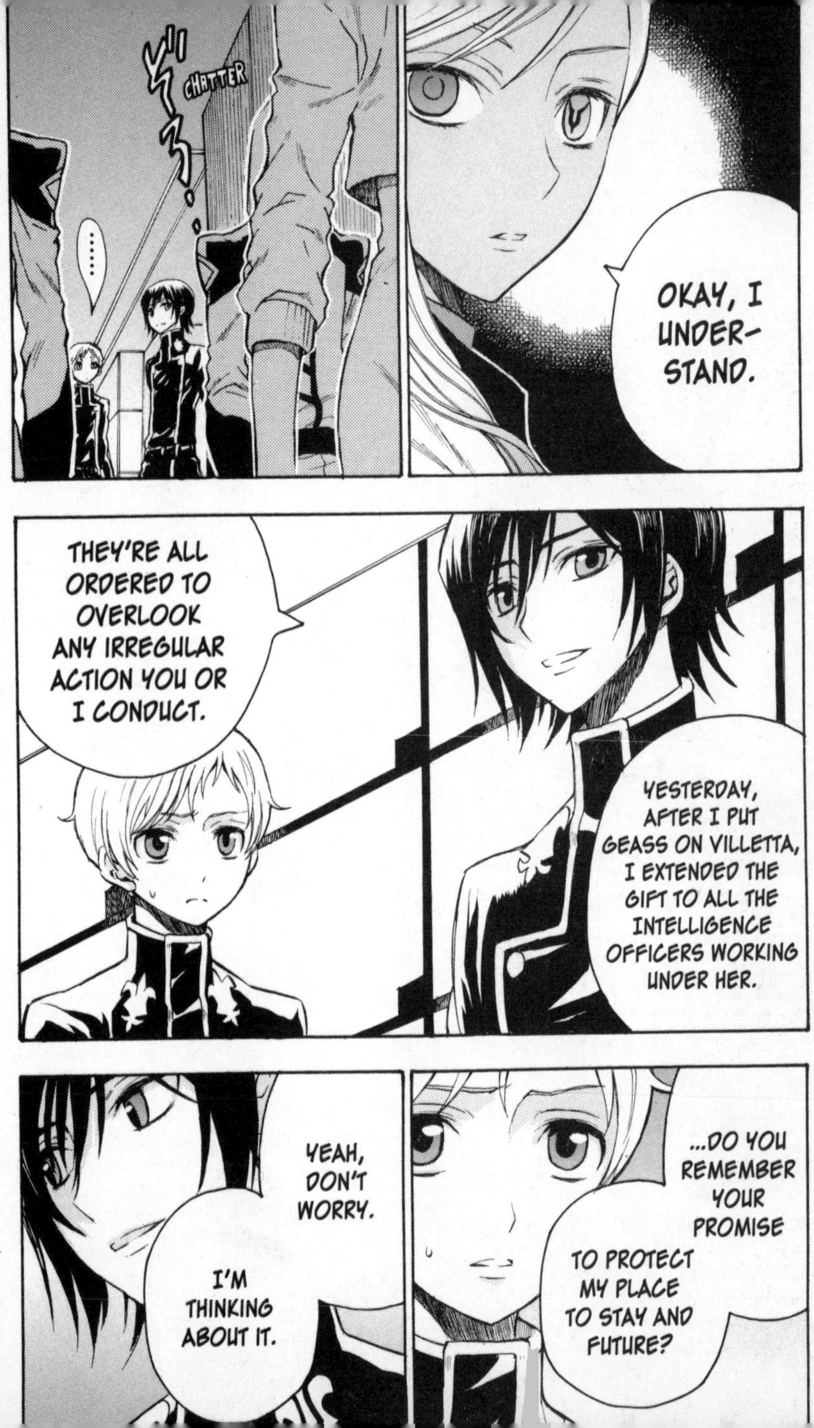
OKAY, I UNDER-STAND.
CHATTER
......
YESTERDAY, AFTER I PUT GEASS ON VILLETTA, I EXTENDED THE GIFT TO ALL THE INTELLIGENCE OFFICERS WORKING UNDER HER.
THEY'RE ALL ORDERED TO OVERLOOK ANY IRREGULAR ACTION YOU OR I CONDUCT.
...DO YOU REMEMBER YOUR PROMISE
TO PROTECT MY PLACE TO STAY AND FUTURE?
YEAH, DON'T WORRY.
I'M THINKING ABOUT IT.

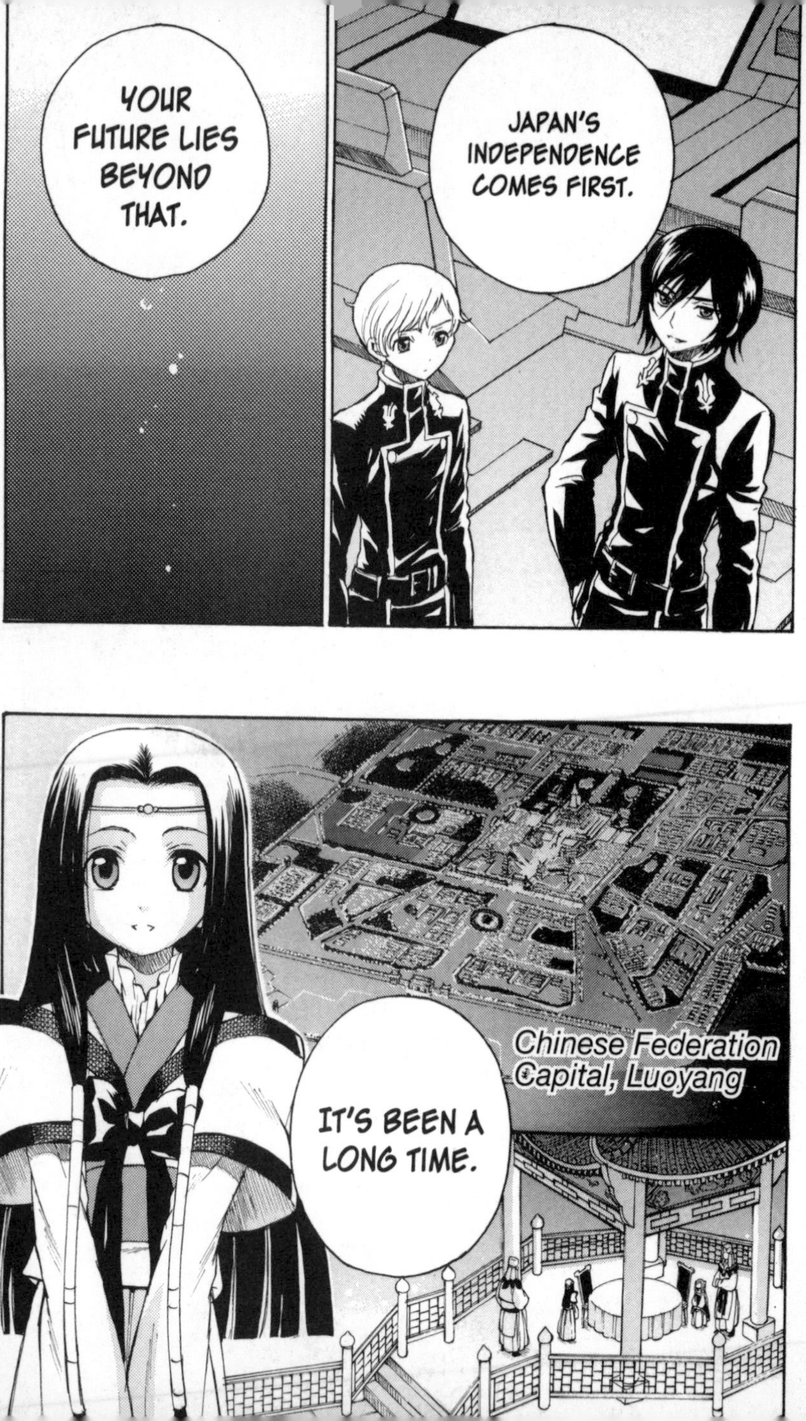
JAPAN'S INDEPENDENCE COMES FIRST.
YOUR FUTURE LIES BEYOND THAT.
Chinese Federation Capital, Luoyang
IT'S BEEN A LONG TIME.

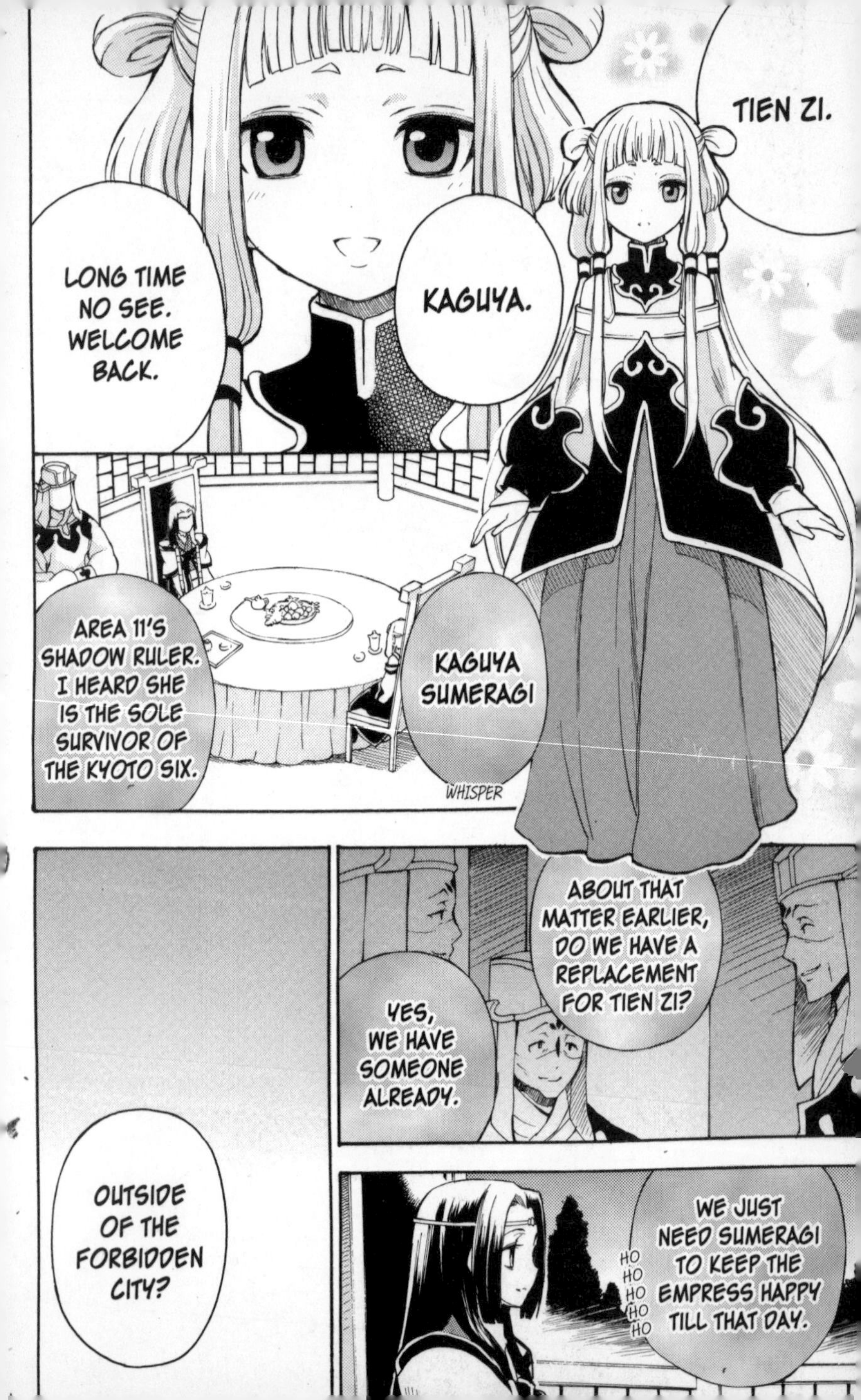
TIEN ZI.
KAGUYA.
LONG TIME NO SEE. WELCOME BACK.
KAGUYA SUMERAGI
WHISPER
AREA 11'S SHADOW RULER. I HEARD SHE IS THE SOLE SURVIVOR OF THE KYOTO SIX.
ABOUT THAT MATTER EARLIER, DO WE HAVE A REPLACEMENT FOR TIEN ZI?
YES, WE HAVE SOMEONE ALREADY.
WE JUST NEED SUMERAGI TO KEEP THE EMPRESS HAPPY TILL THAT DAY.
HO HO HO HO HO HO
OUTSIDE OF THE FORBIDDEN CITY?

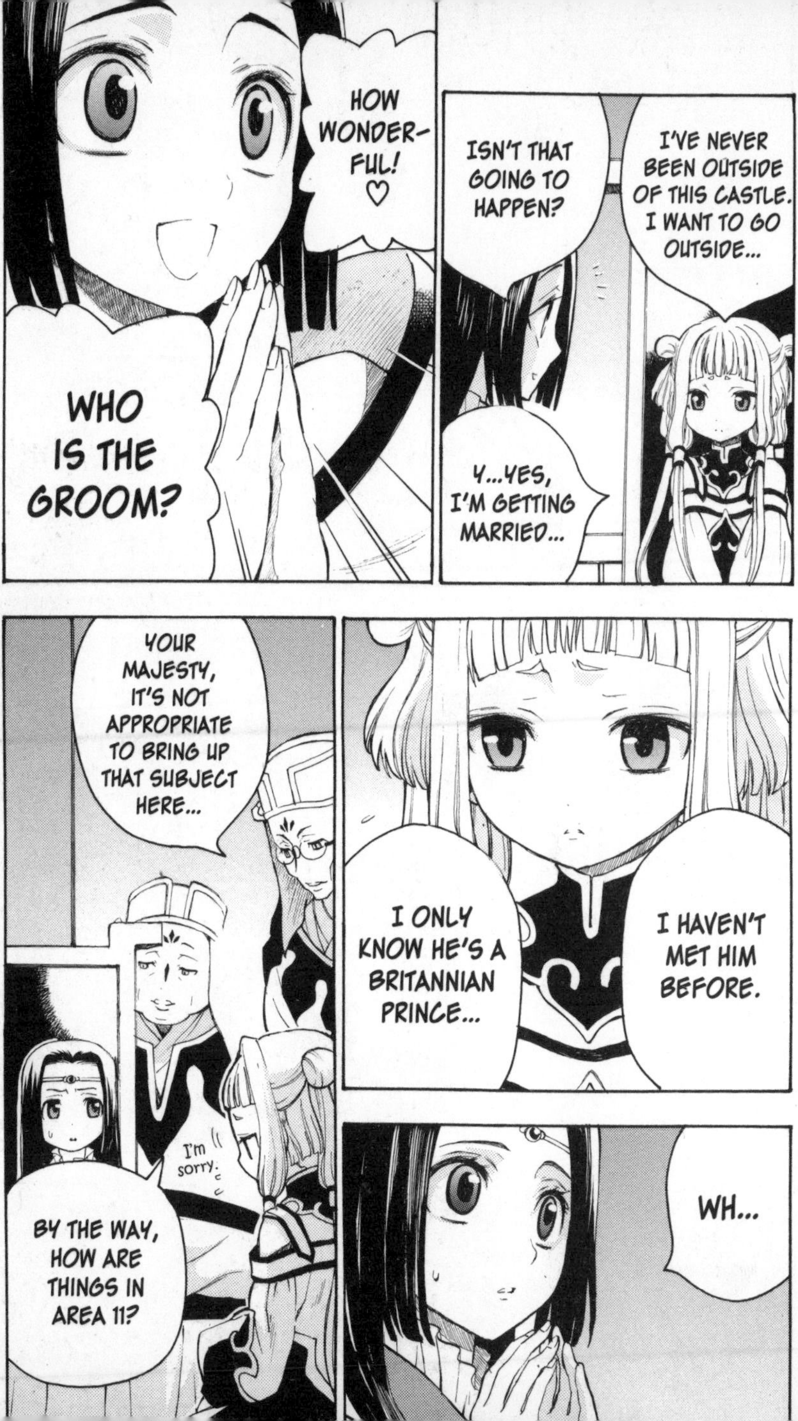
I'VE NEVER BEEN OUTSIDE OF THIS CASTLE. I WANT TO GO OUTSIDE...
ISN'T THAT GOING TO HAPPEN?
Y...YES, I'M GETTING MARRIED...
HOW WONDER-FUL! ♡
WHO IS THE GROOM?
I HAVEN'T MET HIM BEFORE.
I ONLY KNOW HE'S A BRITANNIAN PRINCE...
WH...
YOUR MAJESTY, IT'S NOT APPROPRIATE TO BRING UP THAT SUBJECT HERE...
I'm sorry.
BY THE WAY, HOW ARE THINGS IN AREA 11?

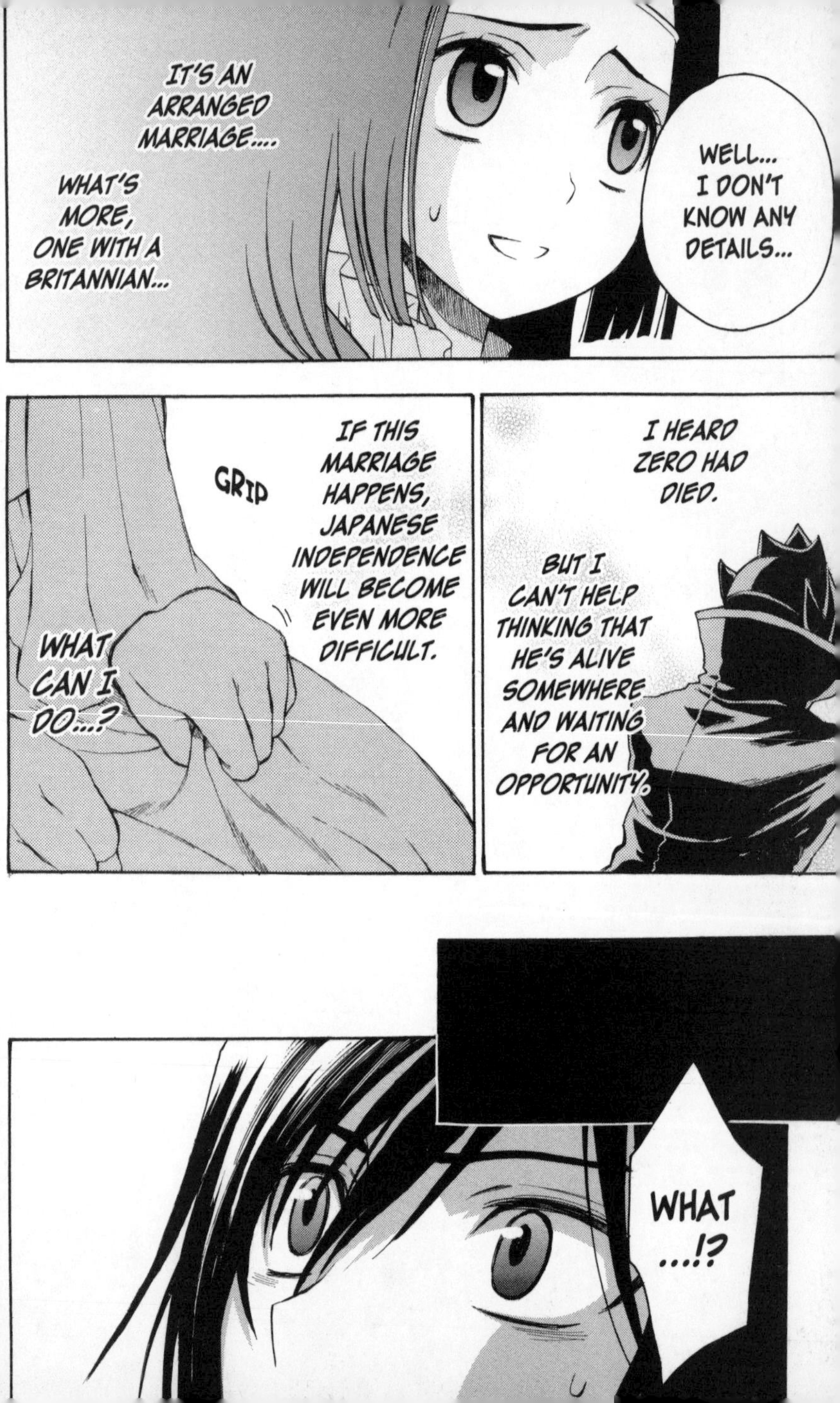
WELL... I DON'T KNOW ANY DETAILS...
IT'S AN ARRANGED MARRIAGE....
WHAT'S MORE, ONE WITH A BRITANNIAN...
I HEARD ZERO HAD DIED.
BUT I CAN'T HELP THINKING THAT HE'S ALIVE SOMEWHERE AND WAITING FOR AN OPPORTUNITY.
IF THIS MARRIAGE HAPPENS, JAPANESE INDEPENDENCE WILL BECOME EVEN MORE DIFFICULT.
GRIP
WHAT CAN I DO...?
WHAT ...!?

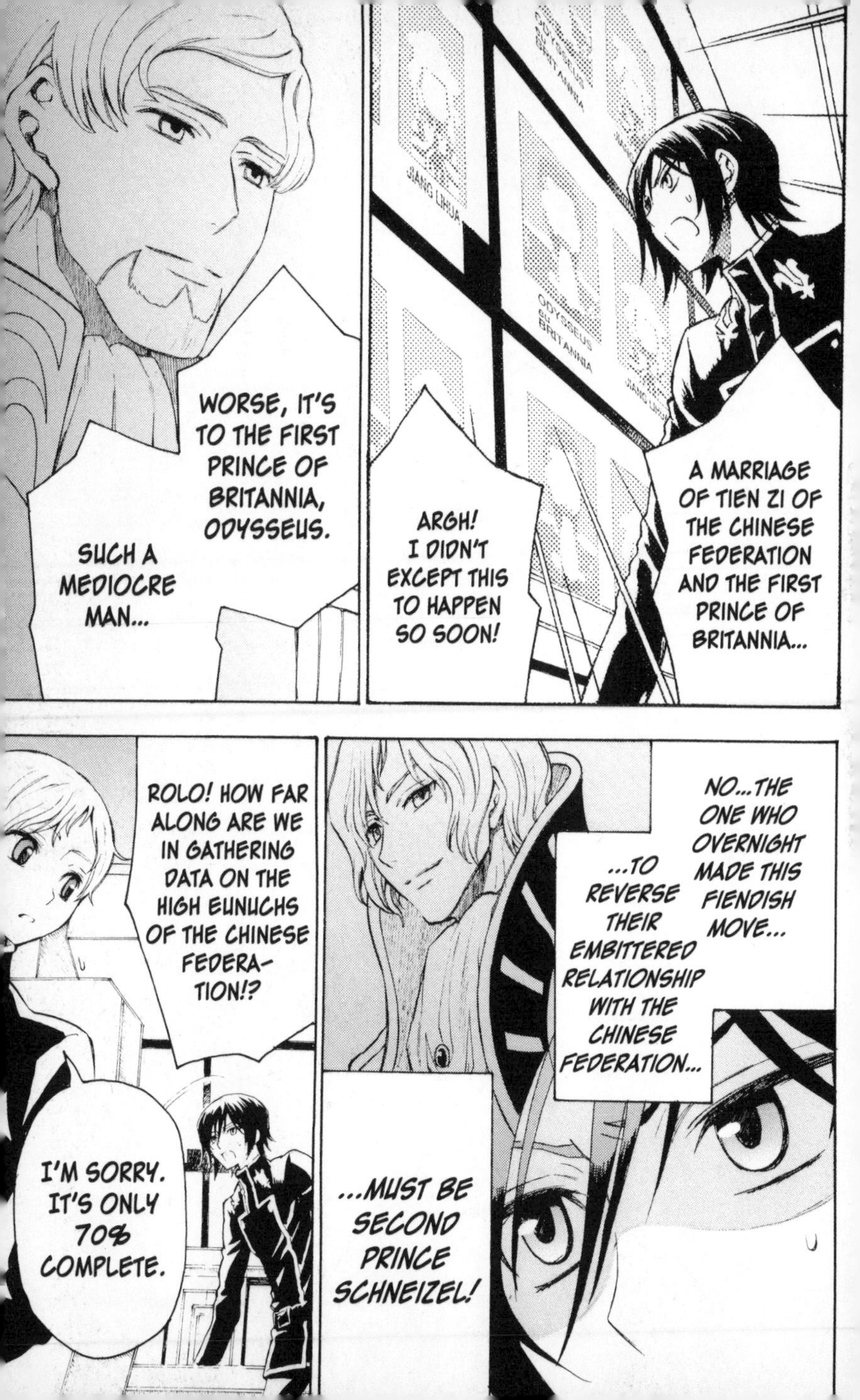

ODYSSEUS eu BRITANNIA
JIANG LIHUA
A MARRIAGE OF TIEN ZI OF THE CHINESE FEDERATION AND THE FIRST PRINCE OF BRITANNIA...
ARGH! I DIDN'T EXCEPT THIS TO HAPPEN SO SOON!
WORSE, IT'S TO THE FIRST PRINCE OF BRITANNIA, ODYSSEUS.
SUCH A MEDIOCRE MAN...
NO...THE ONE WHO OVERNIGHT MADE THIS FIENDISH MOVE...
...TO REVERSE THEIR EMBITTERED RELATIONSHIP WITH THE CHINESE FEDERATION...
...MUST BE SECOND PRINCE SCHNEIZEL!
ROLO! HOW FAR ALONG ARE WE IN GATHERING DATA ON THE HIGH EUNUCHS OF THE CHINESE FEDERA-TION!?
I'M SORRY. IT'S ONLY 70% COMPLETE.

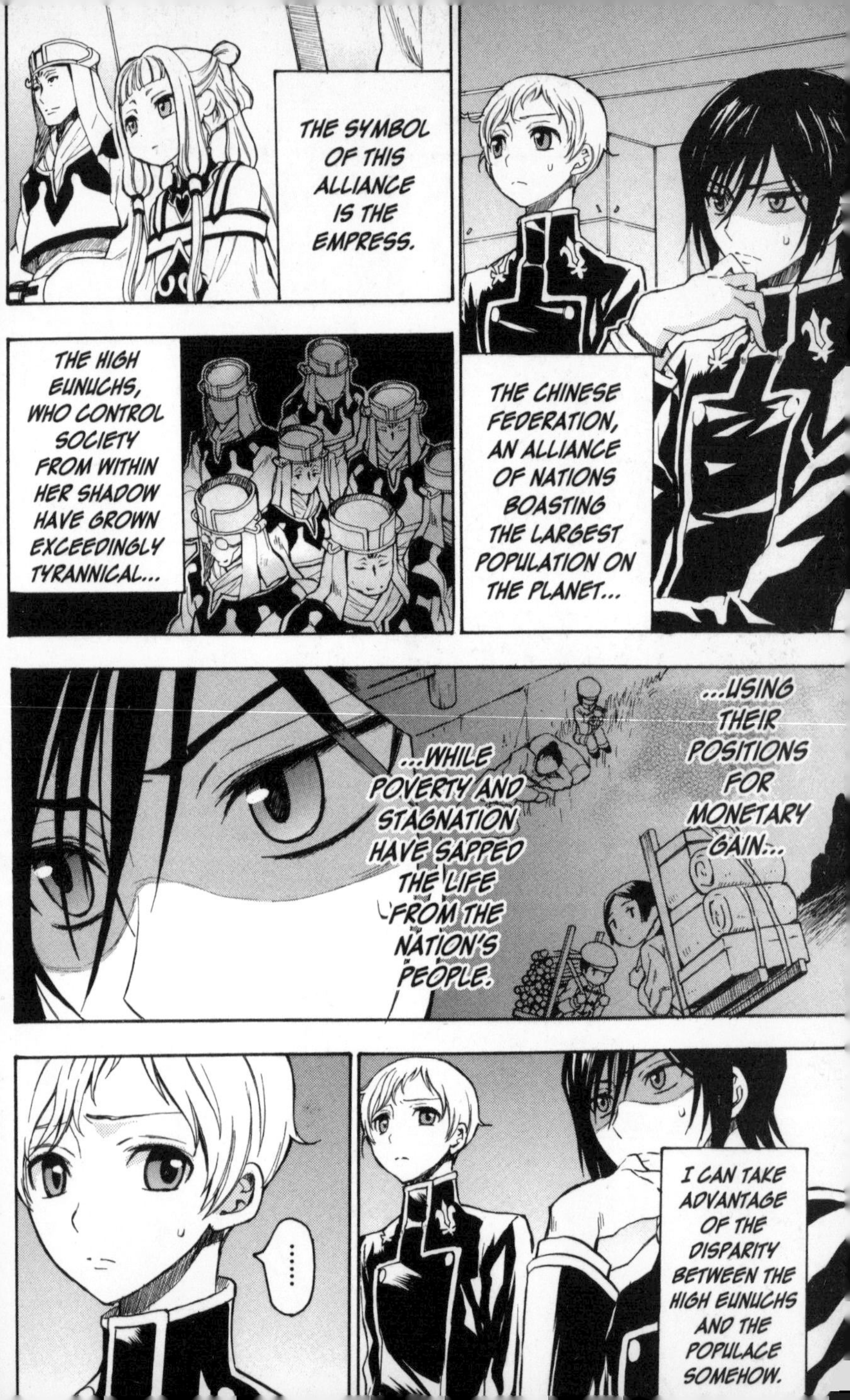
THE CHINESE FEDERATION, AN ALLIANCE OF NATIONS BOASTING THE LARGEST POPULATION ON THE PLANET...
THE SYMBOL OF THIS ALLIANCE IS THE EMPRESS.
THE HIGH EUNUCHS, WHO CONTROL SOCIETY FROM WITHIN HER SHADOW HAVE GROWN EXCEEDINGLY TYRANNICAL...
...USING THEIR POSITIONS FOR MONETARY GAIN...
...WHILE POVERTY AND STAGNATION HAVE SAPPED THE LIFE FROM THE NATION'S PEOPLE.
I CAN TAKE ADVANTAGE OF THE DISPARITY BETWEEN THE HIGH EUNUCHS AND THE POPULACE SOMEHOW.
......

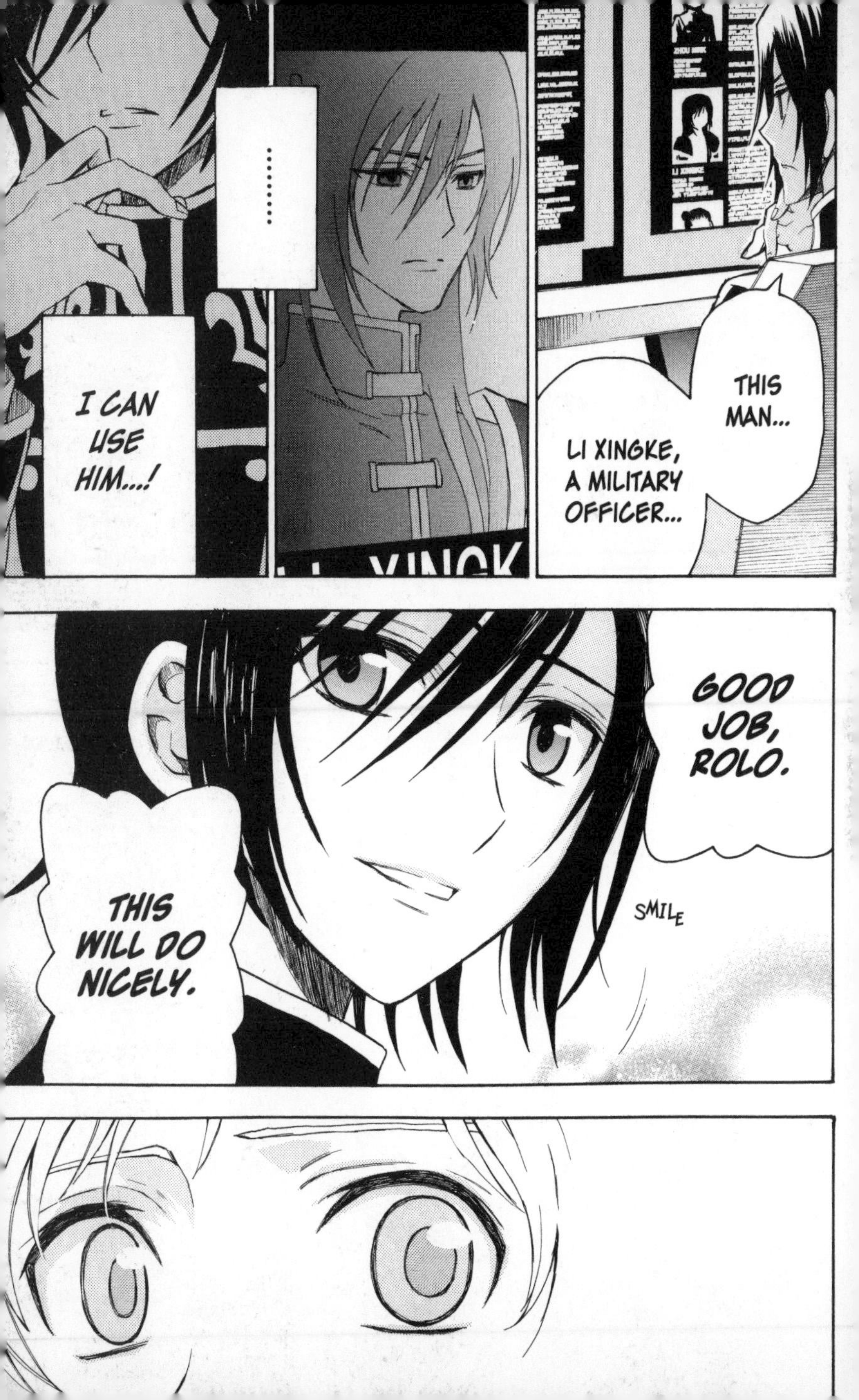
THIS MAN...
LI XINGKE, A MILITARY OFFICER...
......
I CAN USE HIM...!
GOOD JOB, ROLO.
SMILE
THIS WILL DO NICELY.

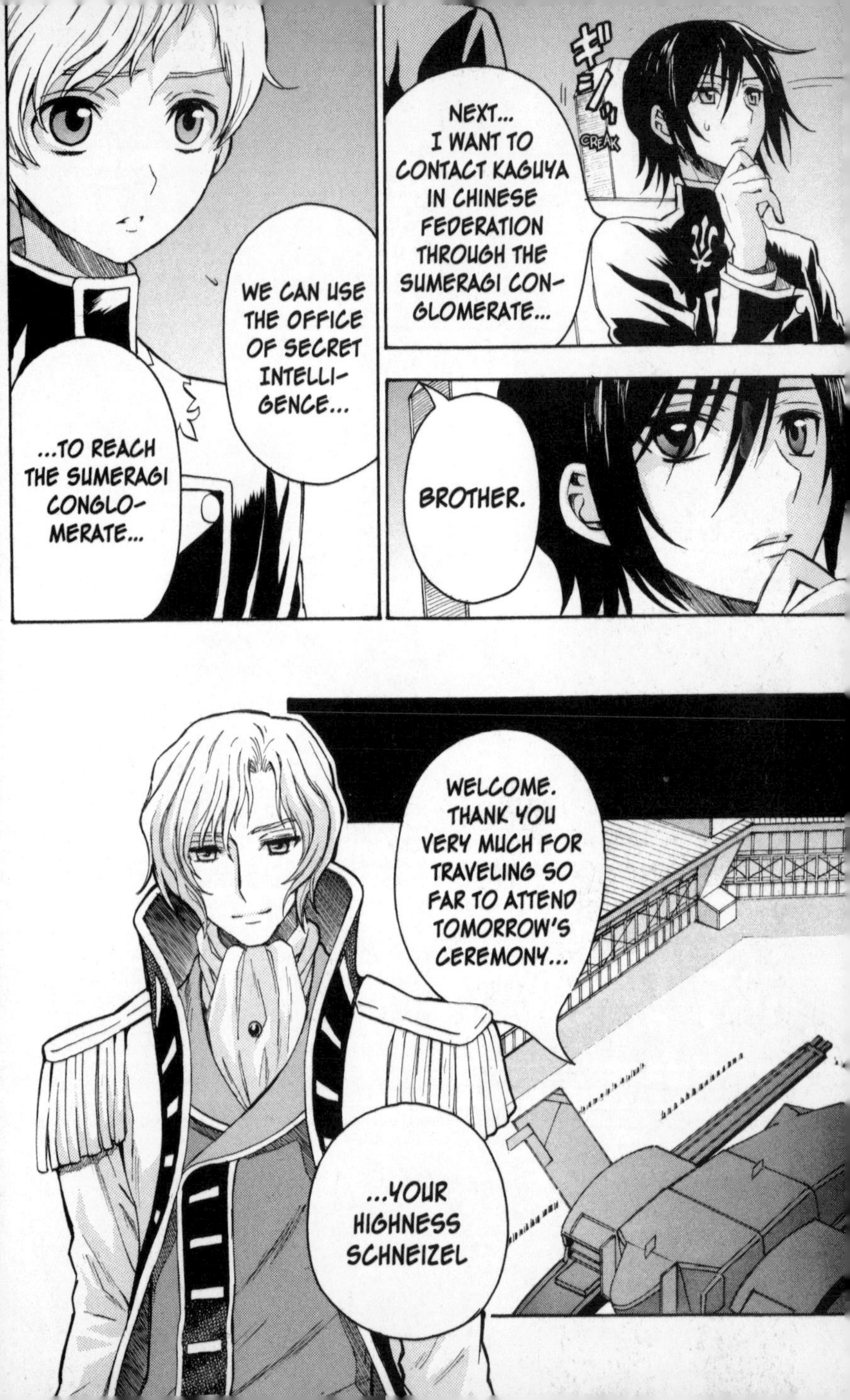
NEXT... I WANT TO CONTACT KAGUYA IN CHINESE FEDERATION THROUGH THE SUMERAGI CONGLOMERATE...
CREAK
BROTHER.
WE CAN USE THE OFFICE OF SECRET INTELLIGENCE...
...TO REACH THE SUMERAGI CONGLOMERATE...
WELCOME. THANK YOU VERY MUCH FOR TRAVELING SO FAR TO ATTEND TOMORROW'S CEREMONY...
...YOUR HIGHNESS SCHNEIZEL

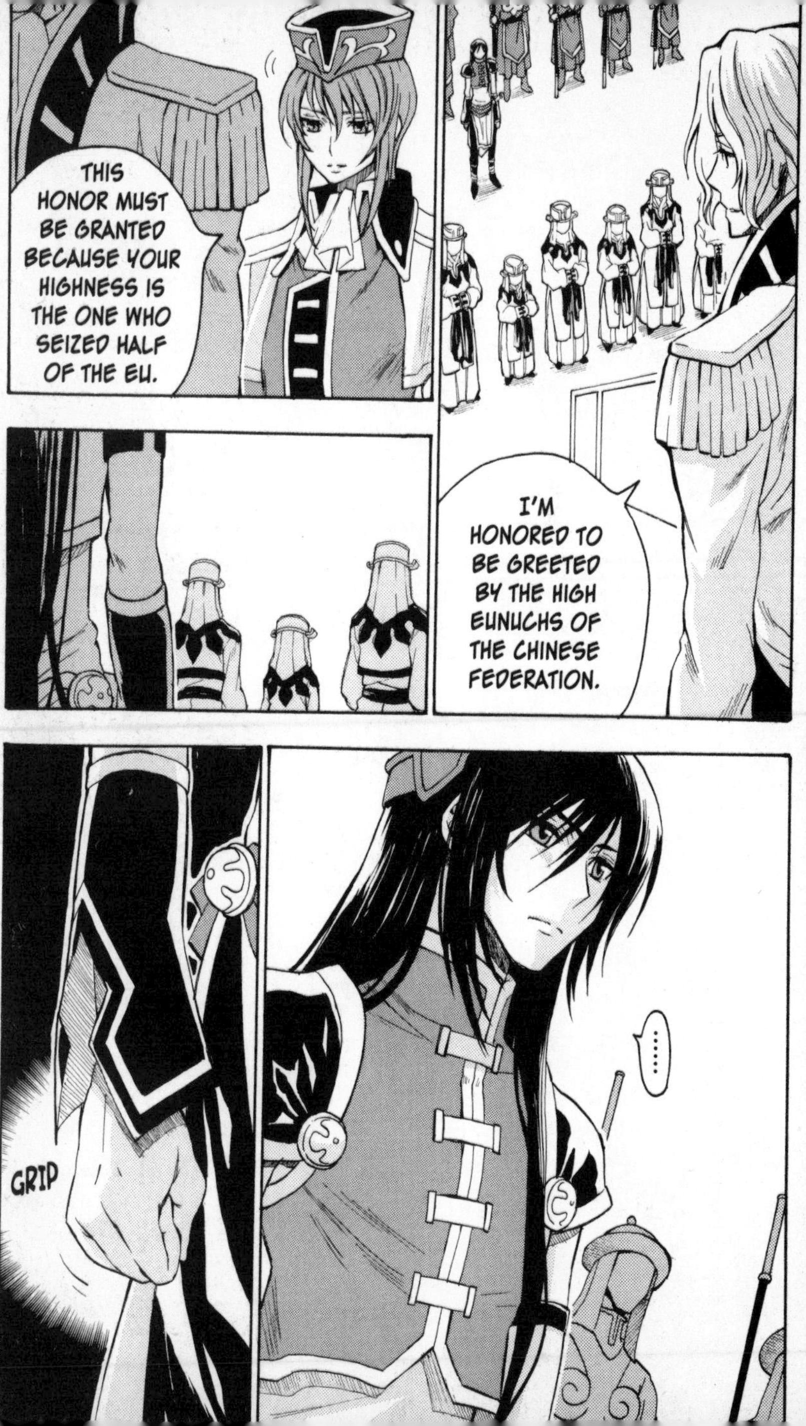
I'M HONORED TO BE GREETED BY THE HIGH EUNUCHS OF THE CHINESE FEDERATION.
THIS HONOR MUST BE GRANTED BECAUSE YOUR HIGHNESS IS THE ONE WHO SEIZED HALF OF THE EU.
......
GRIP

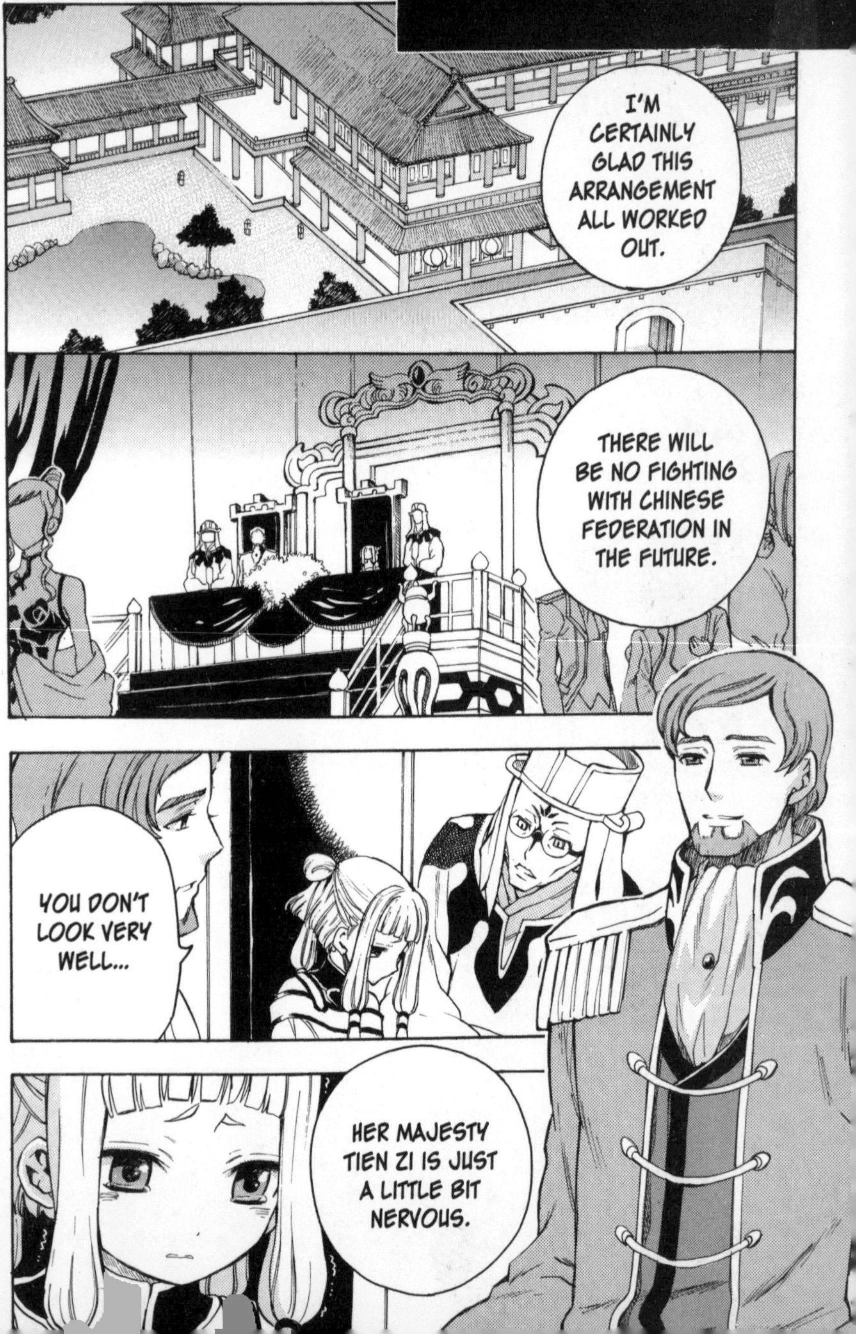
I'M CERTAINLY GLAD THIS ARRANGEMENT ALL WORKED OUT.
THERE WILL BE NO FIGHTING WITH CHINESE FEDERATION IN THE FUTURE.
YOU DON'T LOOK VERY WELL...
HER MAJESTY TIEN ZI IS JUST A LITTLE BIT NERVOUS.

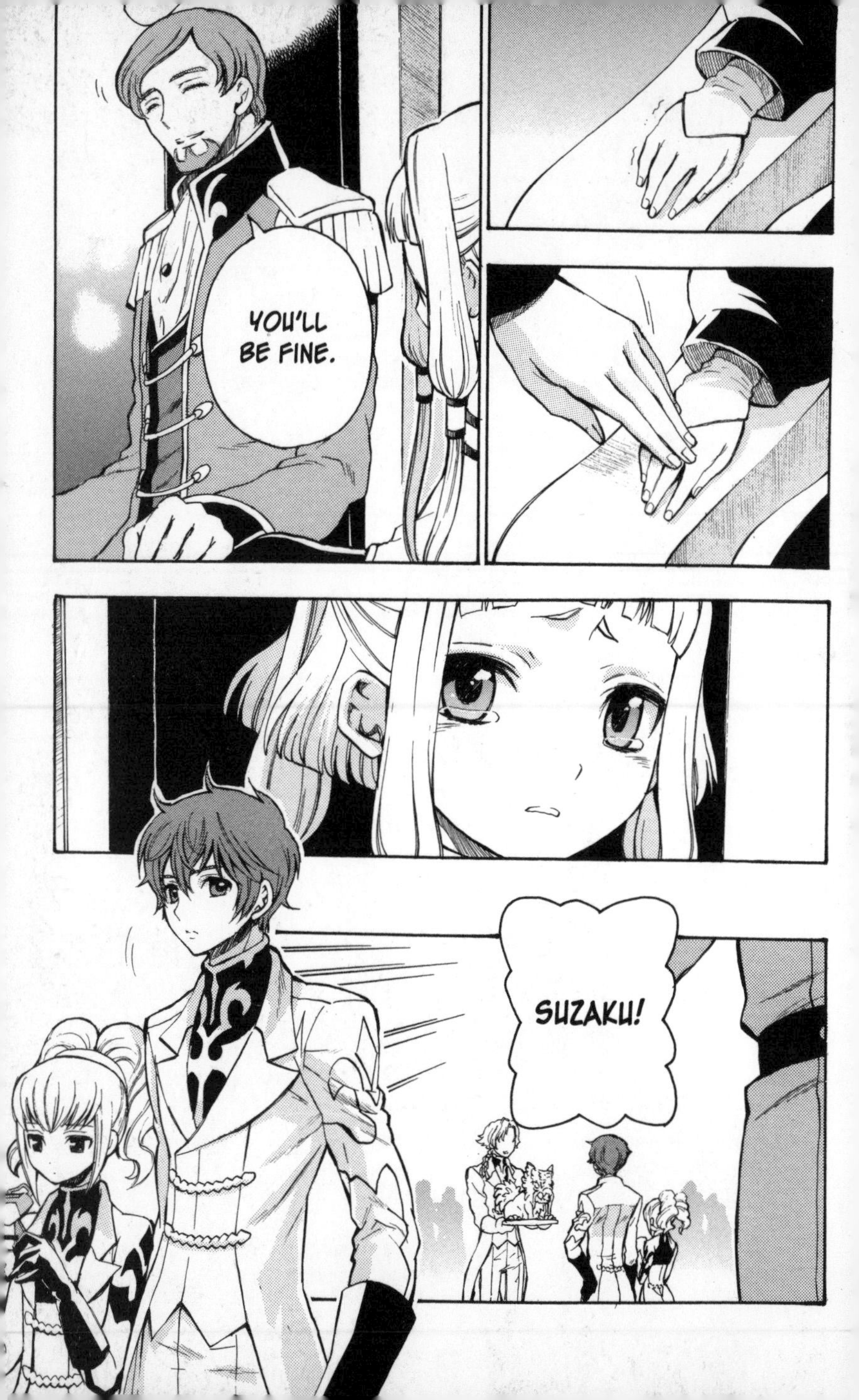
YOU'LL BE FINE.
SUZAKU!

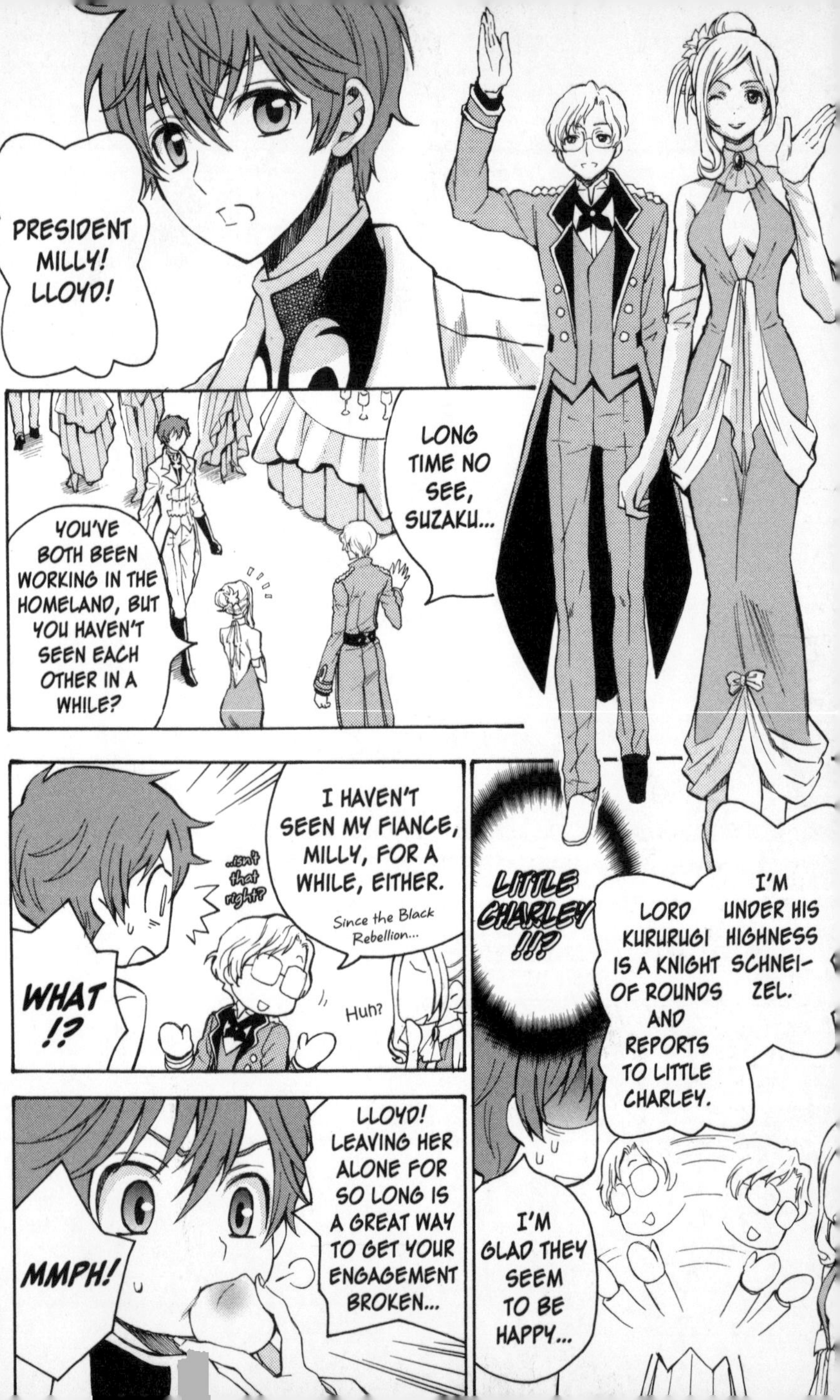
PRESIDENT MILLY! LLOYD!
LONG TIME NO SEE, SUZAKU...
YOU'VE BOTH BEEN WORKING IN THE HOMELAND, BUT YOU HAVEN'T SEEN EACH OTHER IN A WHILE?
I'M UNDER HIS HIGHNESS SCHNEI-ZEL.
LORD KURURUGI IS A KNIGHT OF ROUNDS AND REPORTS TO LITTLE CHARLEY.
LITTLE CHARLEY!!?
I'M GLAD THEY SEEM TO BE HAPPY...
I HAVEN'T SEEN MY FIANCE, MILLY, FOR A WHILE, EITHER.
Since the Black Rebellion...
...isn't that right?
Huh?
WHAT!?
LLOYD! LEAVING HER ALONE FOR SO LONG IS A GREAT WAY TO GET YOUR ENGAGEMENT BROKEN...
MMPH!

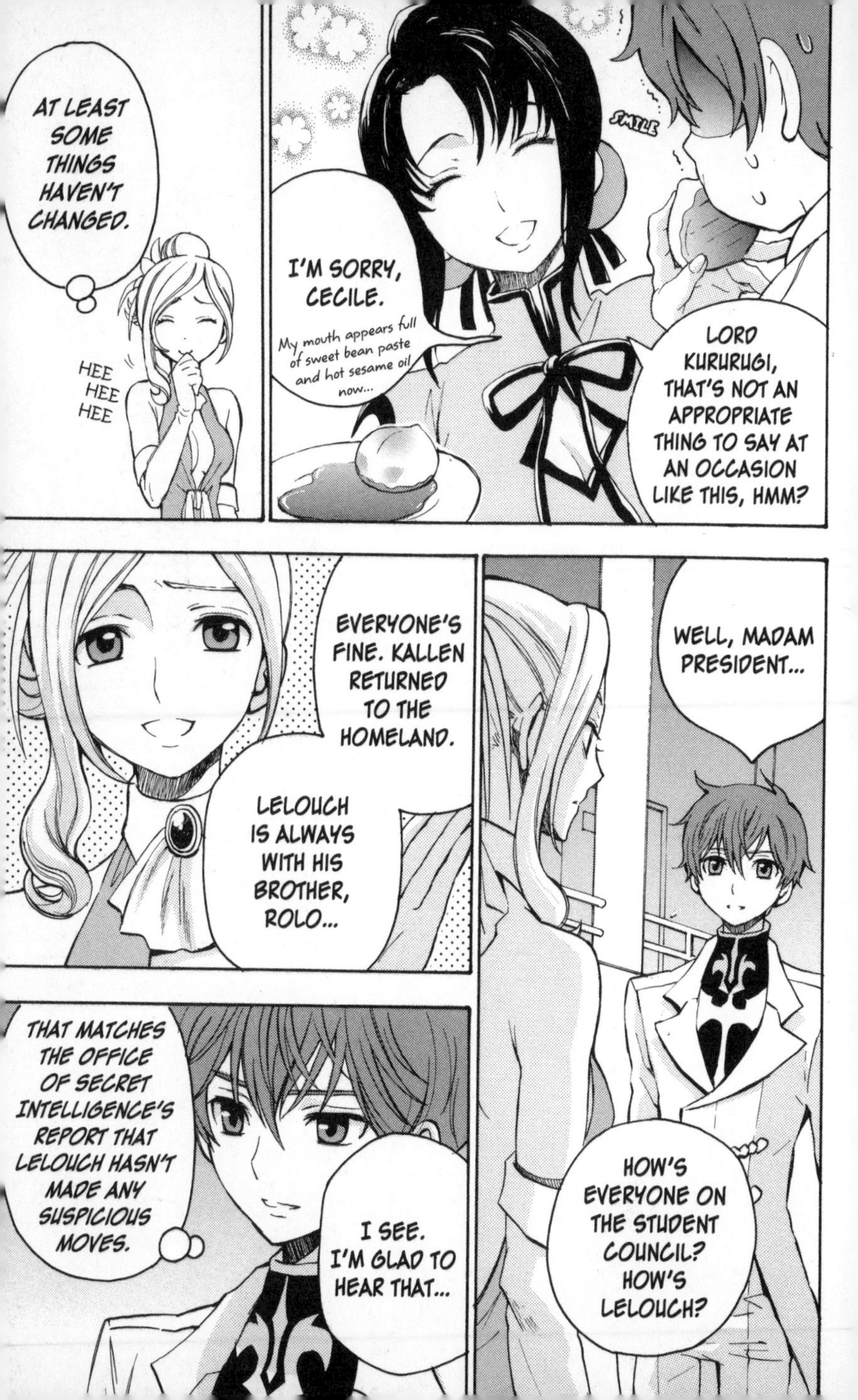
SMILE
LORD KURURUGI, THAT'S NOT AN APPROPRIATE THING TO SAY AT AN OCCASION LIKE THIS, HMM?
I'M SORRY, CECILE.
My mouth appears full of sweet bean paste and hot sesame oil now...
AT LEAST SOME THINGS HAVEN'T CHANGED.
HEE HEE HEE
WELL, MADAM PRESIDENT...
HOW'S EVERYONE ON THE STUDENT COUNCIL? HOW'S LELOUCH?
EVERYONE'S FINE. KALLEN RETURNED TO THE HOMELAND.
LELOUCH IS ALWAYS WITH HIS BROTHER, ROLO...
I SEE. I'M GLAD TO HEAR THAT...
THAT MATCHES THE OFFICE OF SECRET INTELLIGENCE'S REPORT THAT LELOUCH HASN'T MADE ANY SUSPICIOUS MOVES.

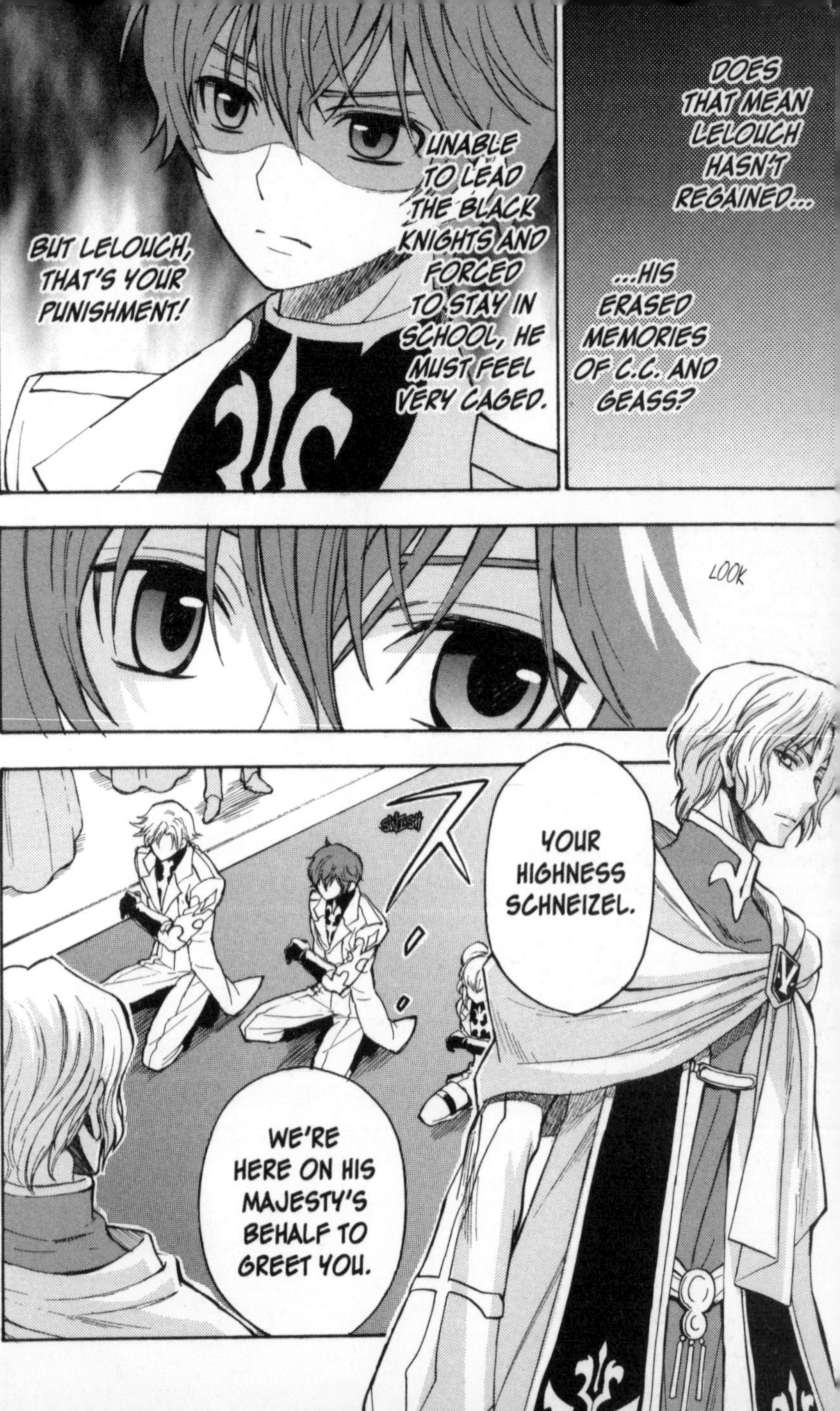
DOES THAT MEAN LELOUCH HASN'T REGAINED...
...HIS ERASED MEMORIES OF C.C. AND GEASS?
UNABLE TO LEAD THE BLACK KNIGHTS AND FORCED TO STAY IN SCHOOL, HE MUST FEEL VERY CAGED.
BUT LELOUCH, THAT'S YOUR PUNISHMENT!
LOOK
SWISH
YOUR HIGHNESS SCHNEIZEL.
WE'RE HERE ON HIS MAJESTY'S BEHALF TO GREET YOU.

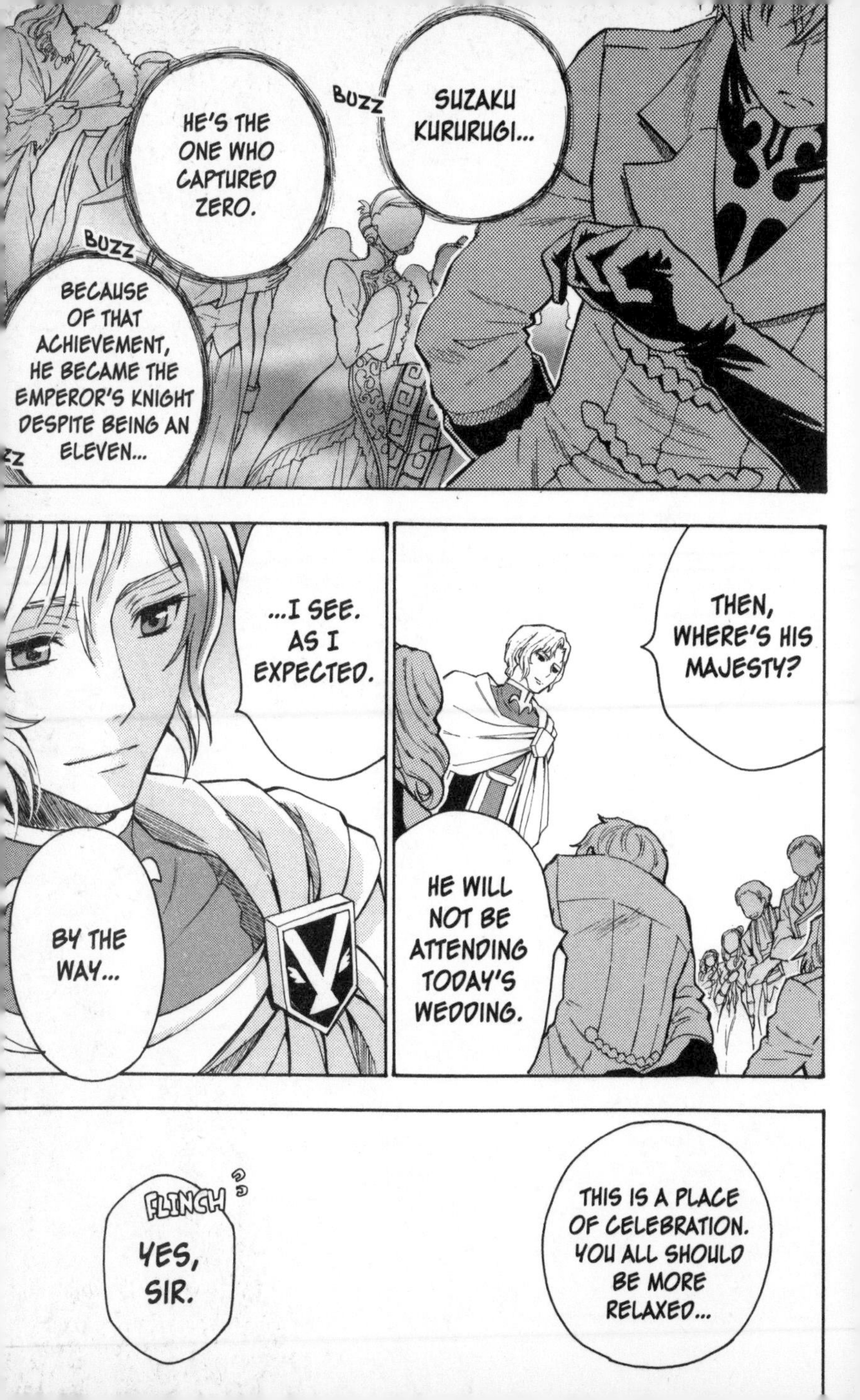
BUZZ
SUZAKU KURURUGI...
HE'S THE ONE WHO CAPTURED ZERO.
BUZZ
BECAUSE OF THAT ACHIEVEMENT, HE BECAME THE EMPEROR'S KNIGHT DESPITE BEING AN ELEVEN...
THEN, WHERE'S HIS MAJESTY?
HE WILL NOT BE ATTENDING TODAY'S WEDDING.
...I SEE. AS I EXPECTED.
BY THE WAY...
THIS IS A PLACE OF CELEBRATION. YOU ALL SHOULD BE MORE RELAXED...
FLINCH
YES, SIR.

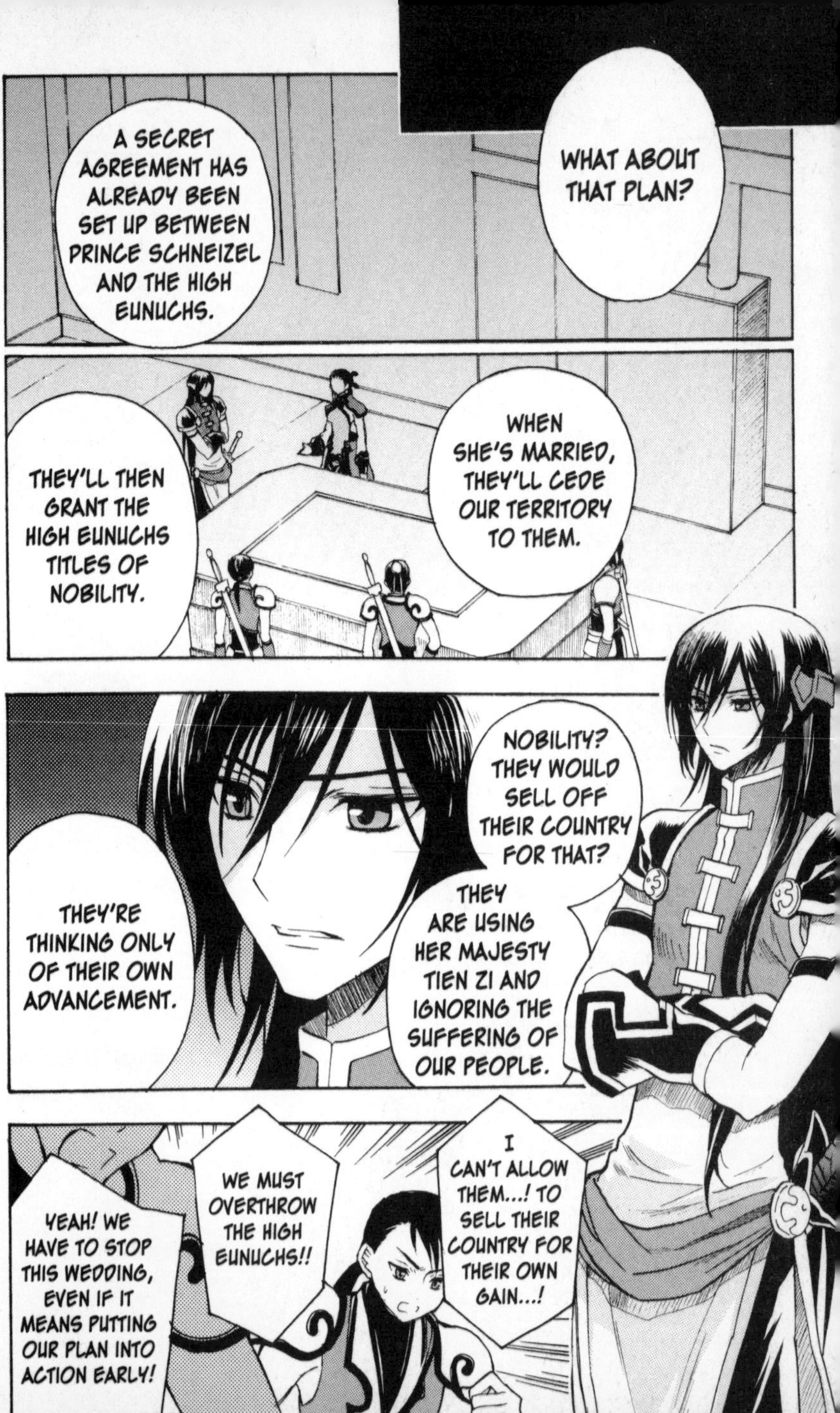
WHAT ABOUT THAT PLAN?
A SECRET AGREEMENT HAS ALREADY BEEN SET UP BETWEEN PRINCE SCHNEIZEL AND THE HIGH EUNUCHS.
WHEN SHE'S MARRIED, THEY'LL CEDE OUR TERRITORY TO THEM.
THEY'LL THEN GRANT THE HIGH EUNUCHS TITLES OF NOBILITY.
NOBILITY? THEY WOULD SELL OFF THEIR COUNTRY FOR THAT?
THEY ARE USING HER MAJESTY TIEN ZI AND IGNORING THE SUFFERING OF OUR PEOPLE.
THEY'RE THINKING ONLY OF THEIR OWN ADVANCEMENT.
I CAN'T ALLOW THEM...! TO SELL THEIR COUNTRY FOR THEIR OWN GAIN...!
WE MUST OVERTHROW THE HIGH EUNUCHS!!
YEAH! WE HAVE TO STOP THIS WEDDING, EVEN IF IT MEANS PUTTING OUR PLAN INTO ACTION EARLY!

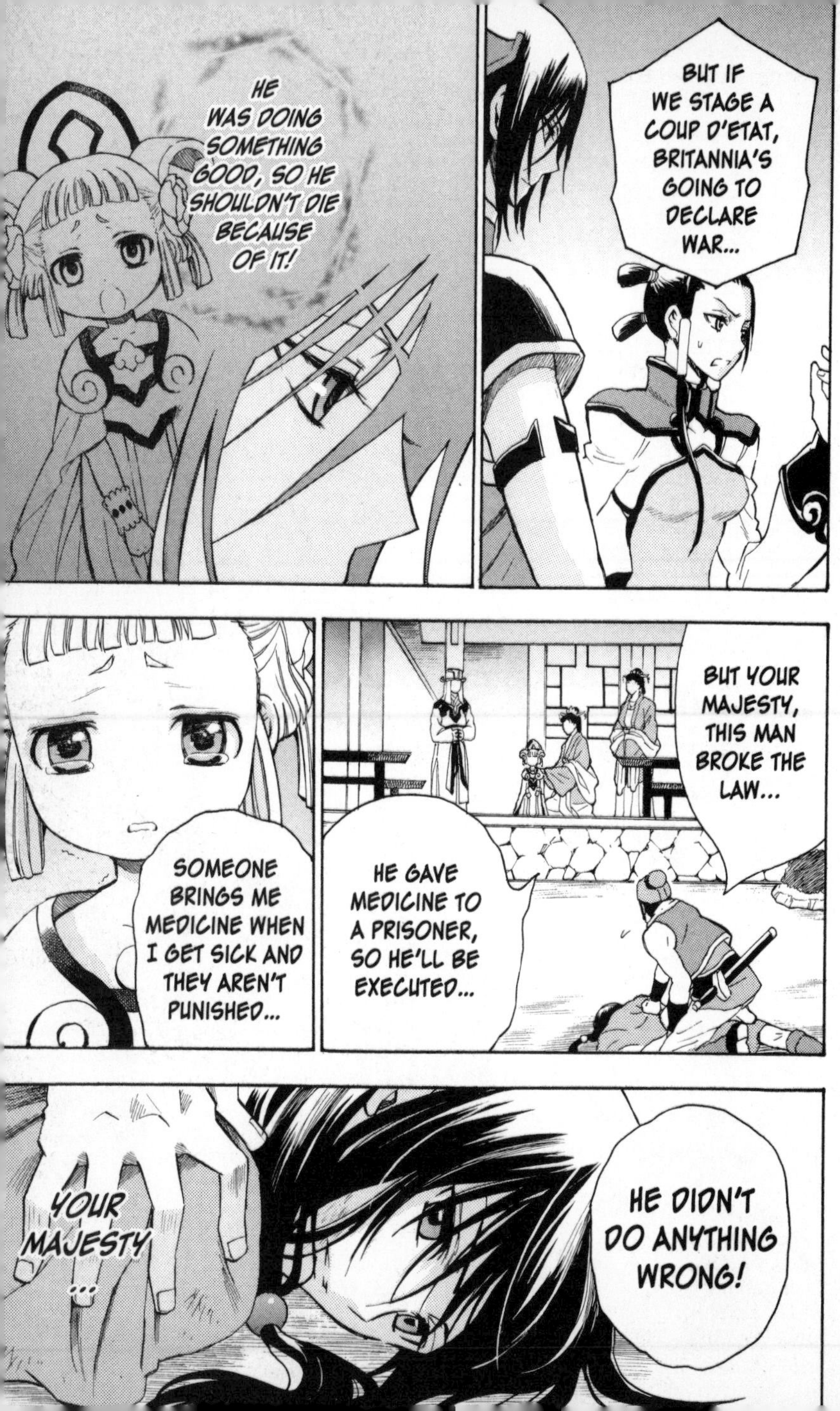
BUT IF WE STAGE A COUP D'ETAT, BRITANNIA'S GOING TO DECLARE WAR...
HE WAS DOING SOMETHING GOOD, SO HE SHOULDN'T DIE BECAUSE OF IT!
BUT YOUR MAJESTY, THIS MAN BROKE THE LAW...
HE GAVE MEDICINE TO A PRISONER, SO HE'LL BE EXECUTED...
SOMEONE BRINGS ME MEDICINE WHEN I GET SICK AND THEY AREN'T PUNISHED...
HE DIDN'T DO ANYTHING WRONG!
YOUR MAJESTY ...

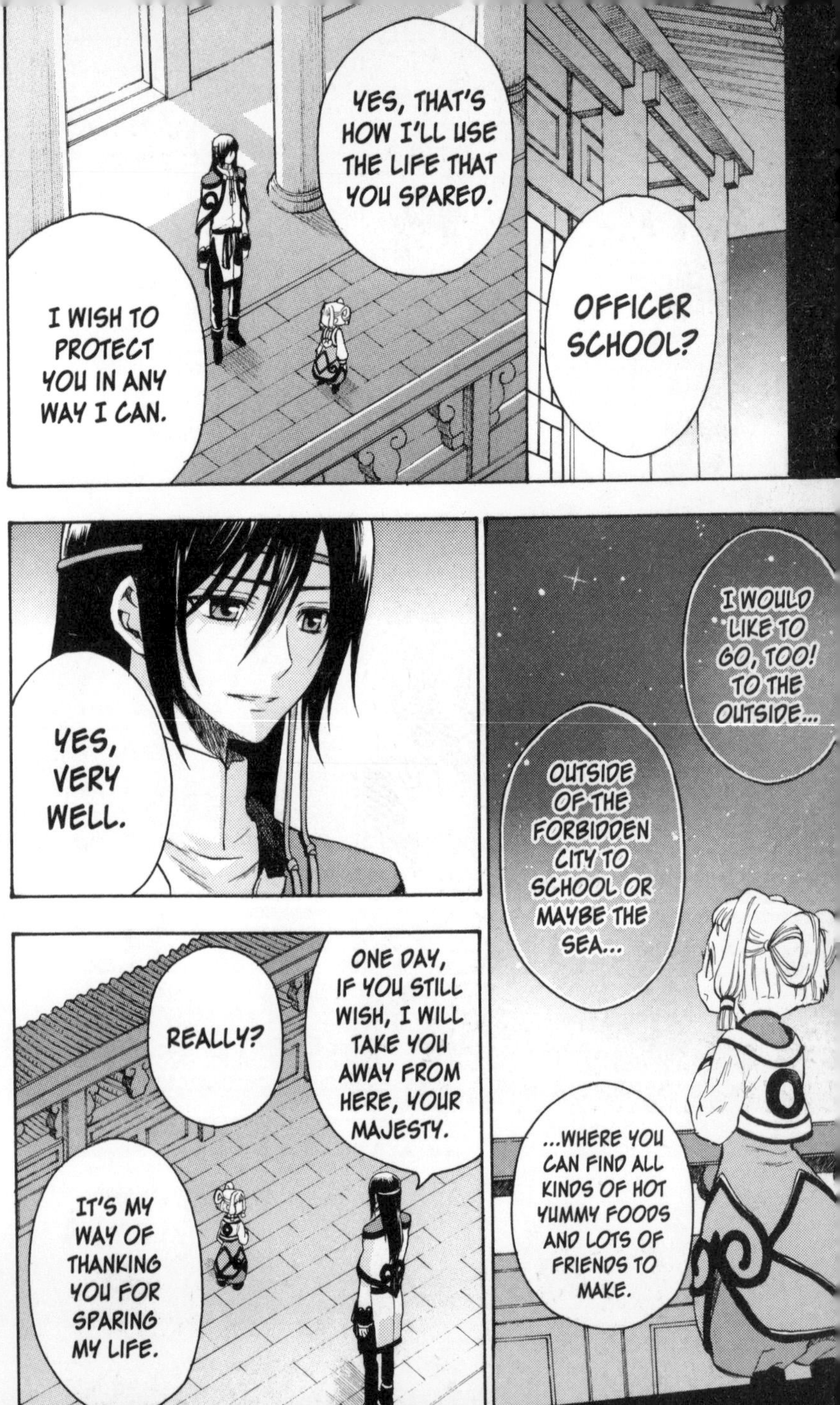
OFFICER SCHOOL?
YES, THAT'S HOW I'LL USE THE LIFE THAT YOU SPARED.
I WISH TO PROTECT YOU IN ANY WAY I CAN.
I WOULD LIKE TO GO, TOO! TO THE OUTSIDE...
OUTSIDE OF THE FORBIDDEN CITY TO SCHOOL OR MAYBE THE SEA...
...WHERE YOU CAN FIND ALL KINDS OF HOT YUMMY FOODS AND LOTS OF FRIENDS TO MAKE.
YES, VERY WELL.
ONE DAY, IF YOU STILL WISH, I WILL TAKE YOU AWAY FROM HERE, YOUR MAJESTY.
REALLY?
IT'S MY WAY OF THANKING YOU FOR SPARING MY LIFE.

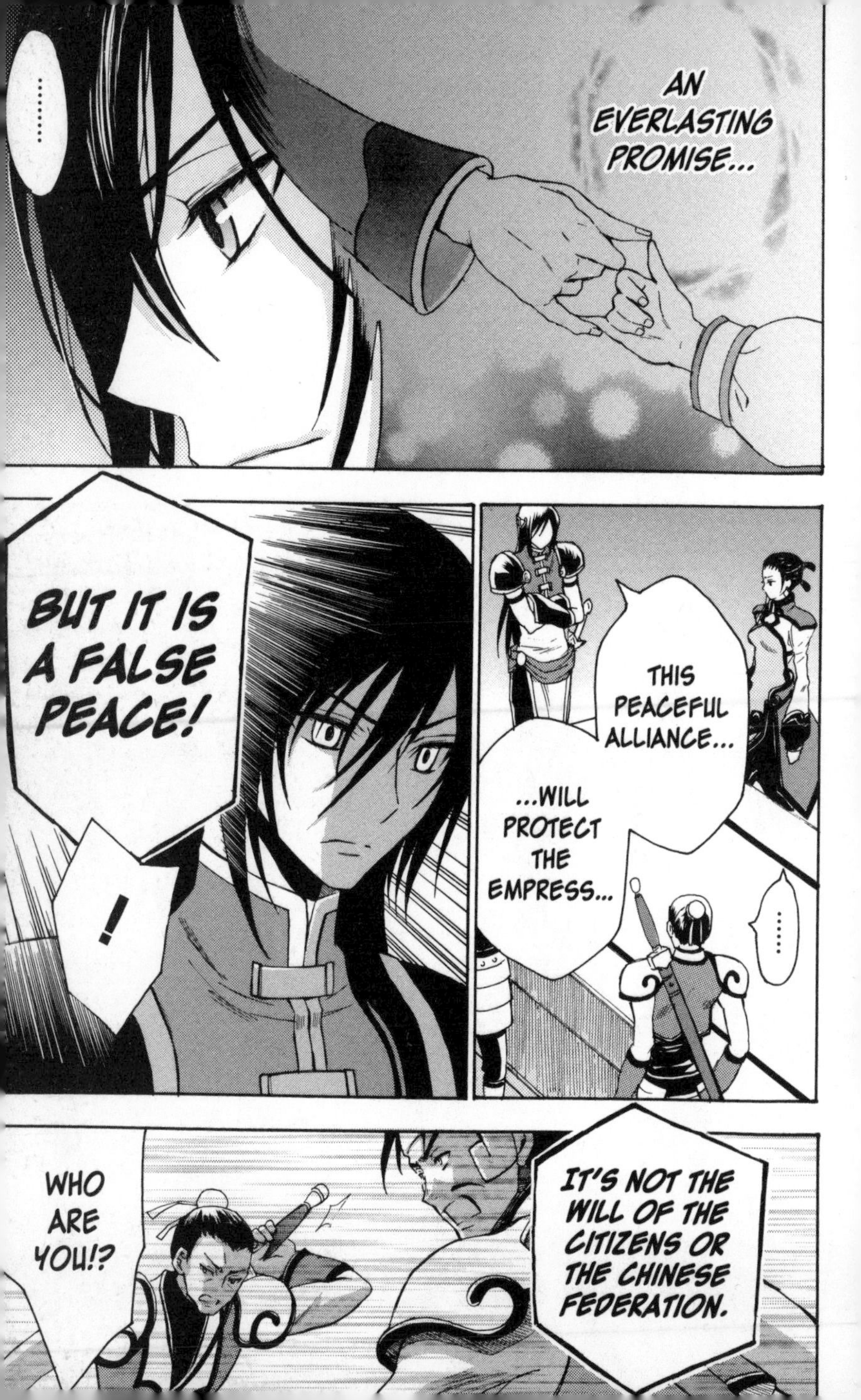
AN EVERLASTING PROMISE...
......
THIS PEACEFUL ALLIANCE...
...WILL PROTECT THE EMPRESS...
......
BUT IT IS A FALSE PEACE!
!
IT'S NOT THE WILL OF THE CITIZENS OR THE CHINESE FEDERATION.
WHO ARE YOU!?

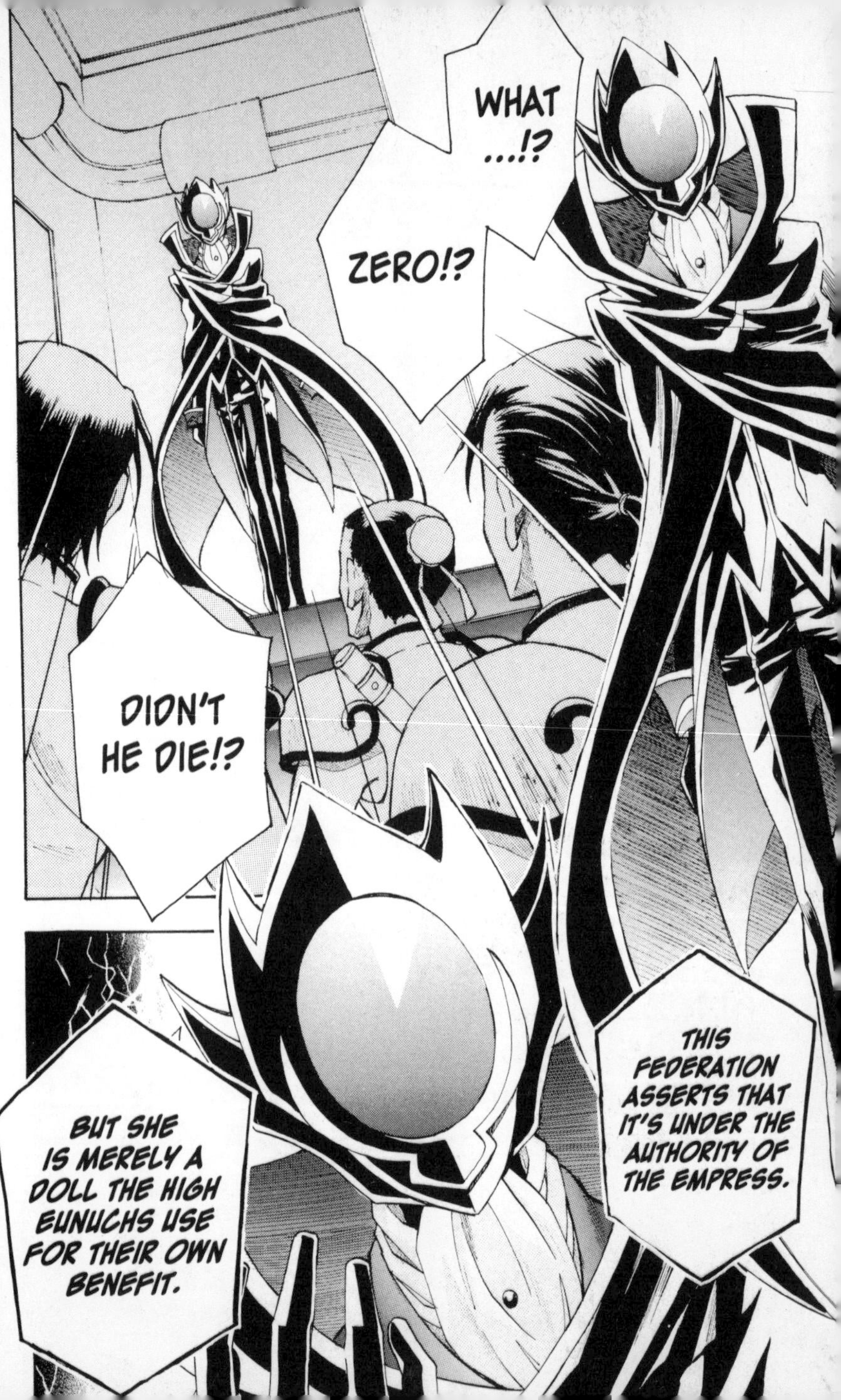
WHAT ...!?
ZERO!?
DIDN'T HE DIE!?
THIS FEDERATION ASSERTS THAT IT'S UNDER THE AUTHORITY OF THE EMPRESS.
BUT SHE IS MERELY A DOLL THE HIGH EUNUCHS USE FOR THEIR OWN BENEFIT.

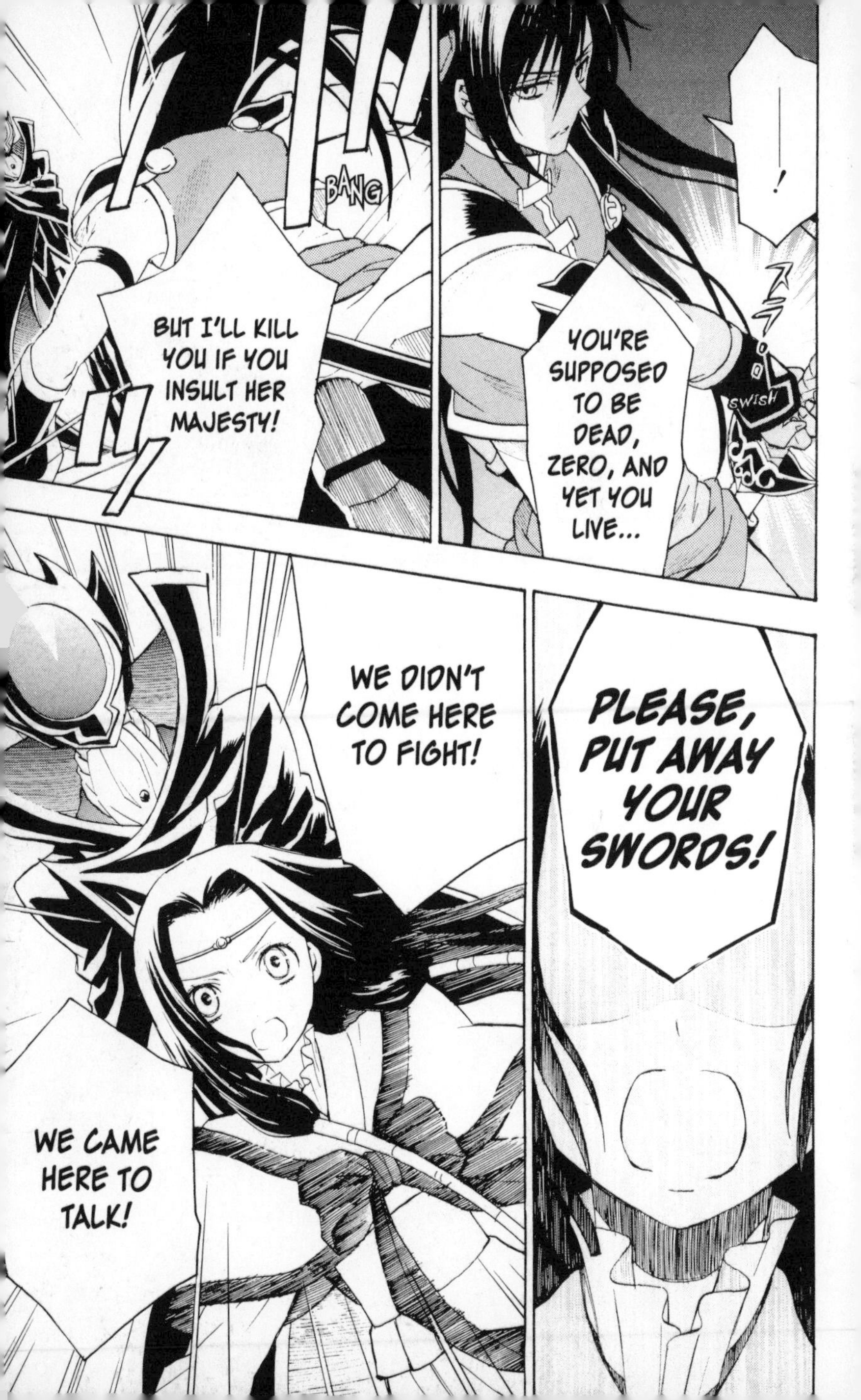
!
SWISH
YOU'RE SUPPOSED TO BE DEAD, ZERO, AND YET YOU LIVE...
BANG
BUT I'LL KILL YOU IF YOU INSULT HER MAJESTY!
PLEASE, PUT AWAY YOUR SWORDS!
WE DIDN'T COME HERE TO FIGHT!
WE CAME HERE TO TALK!

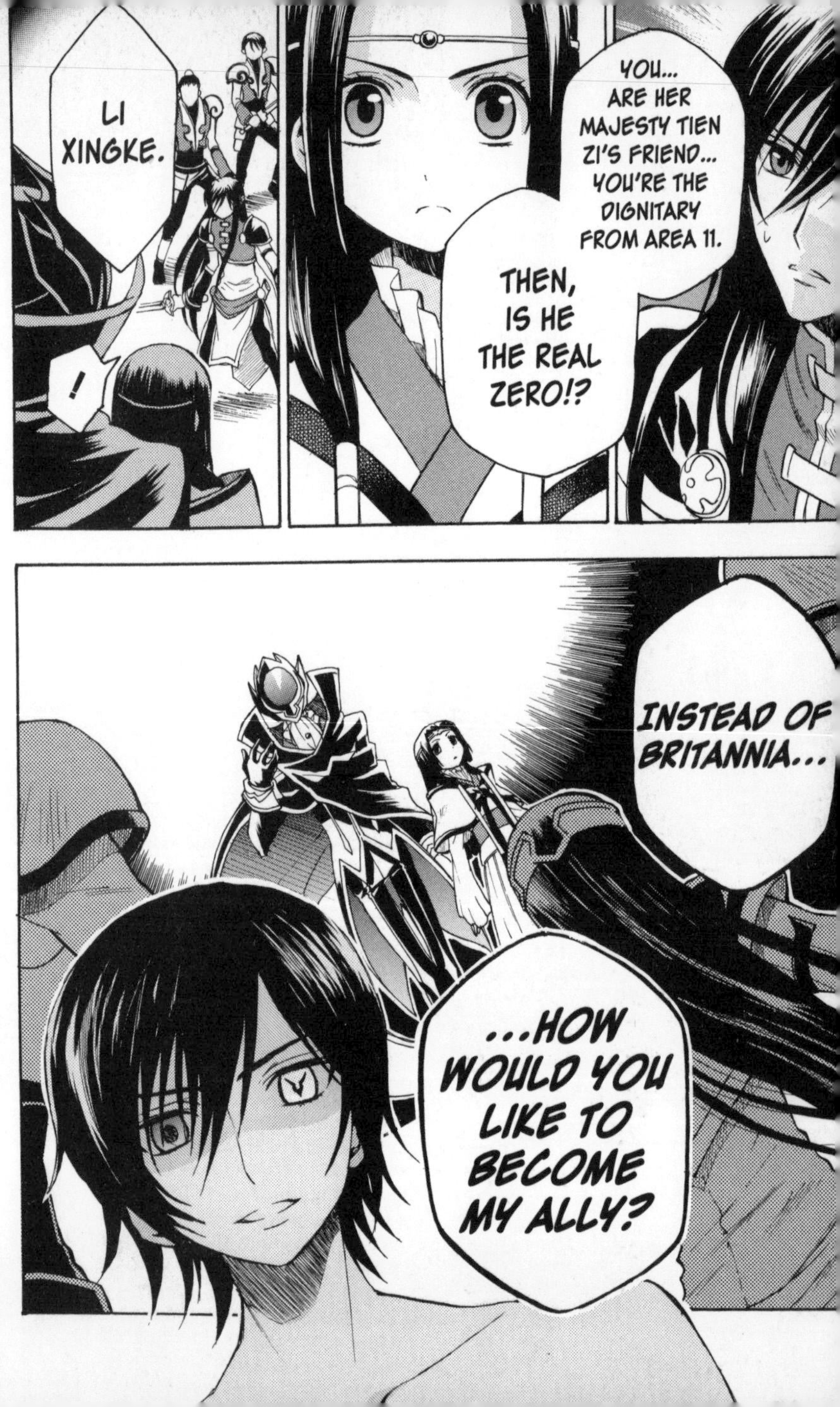
YOU... ARE HER MAJESTY TIEN ZI'S FRIEND... YOU'RE THE DIGNITARY FROM AREA 11.
THEN, IS HE THE REAL ZERO!?
LI XINGKE.
!
INSTEAD OF BRITANNIA...
...HOW WOULD YOU LIKE TO BECOME MY ALLY?

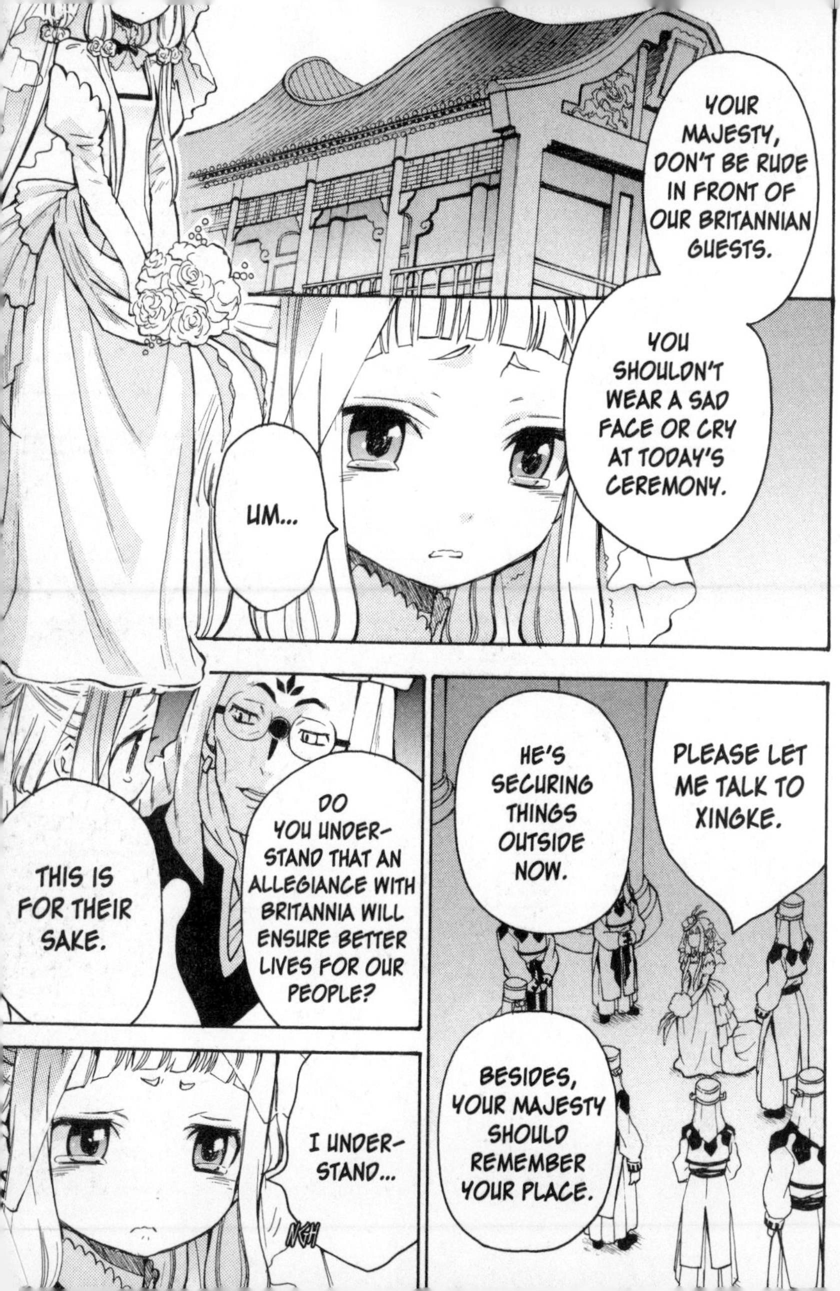
YOUR MAJESTY, DON'T BE RUDE IN FRONT OF OUR BRITANNIAN GUESTS.
YOU SHOULDN'T WEAR A SAD FACE OR CRY AT TODAY'S CEREMONY.
UM...
PLEASE LET ME TALK TO XINGKE.
HE'S SECURING THINGS OUTSIDE NOW.
BESIDES, YOUR MAJESTY SHOULD REMEMBER YOUR PLACE.
DO YOU UNDERSTAND THAT AN ALLEGIANCE WITH BRITANNIA WILL ENSURE BETTER LIVES FOR OUR PEOPLE?
THIS IS FOR THEIR SAKE.
I UNDERSTAND...
NGH

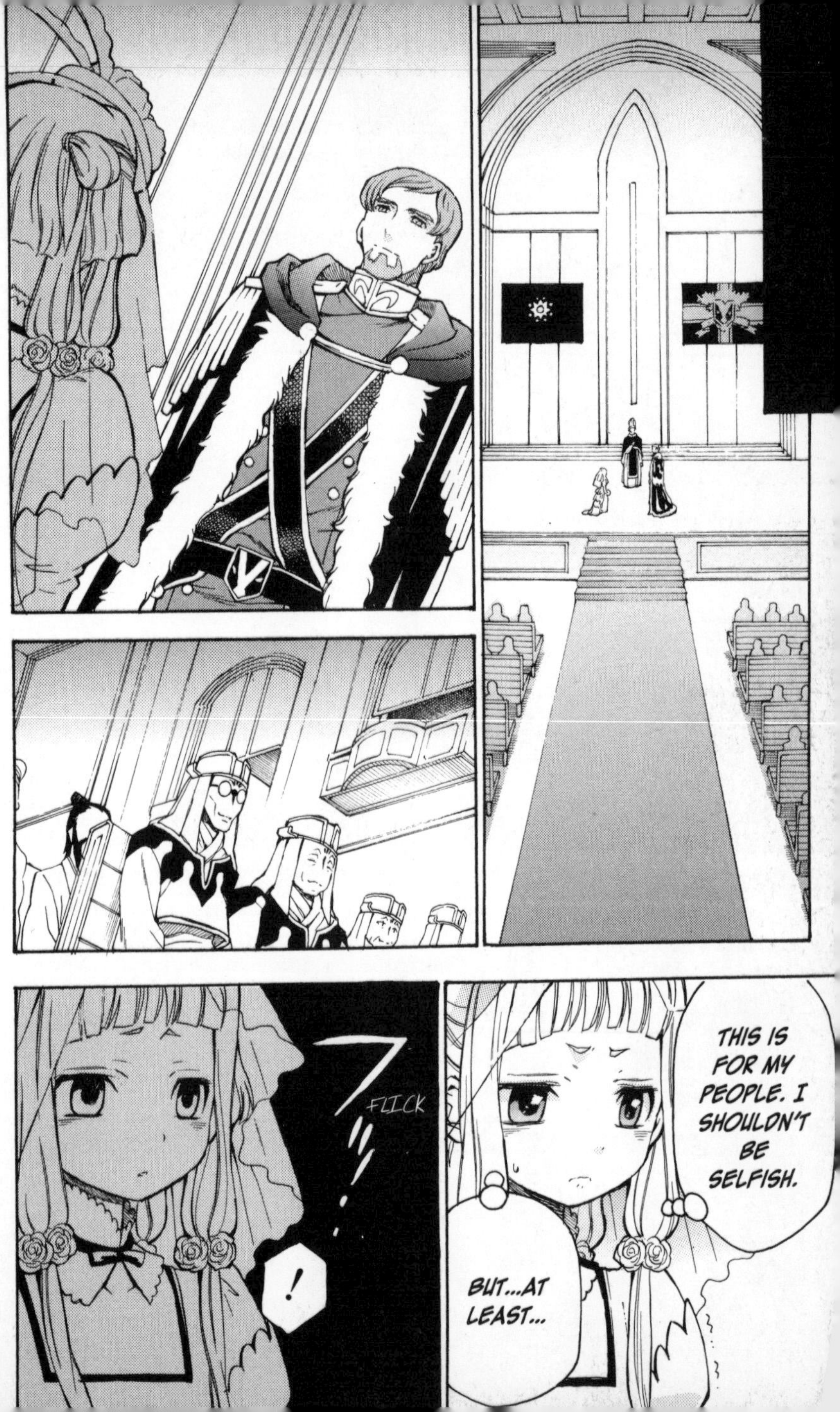
THIS IS FOR MY PEOPLE. I SHOULDN'T BE SELFISH.
BUT...AT LEAST...
FLICK
!

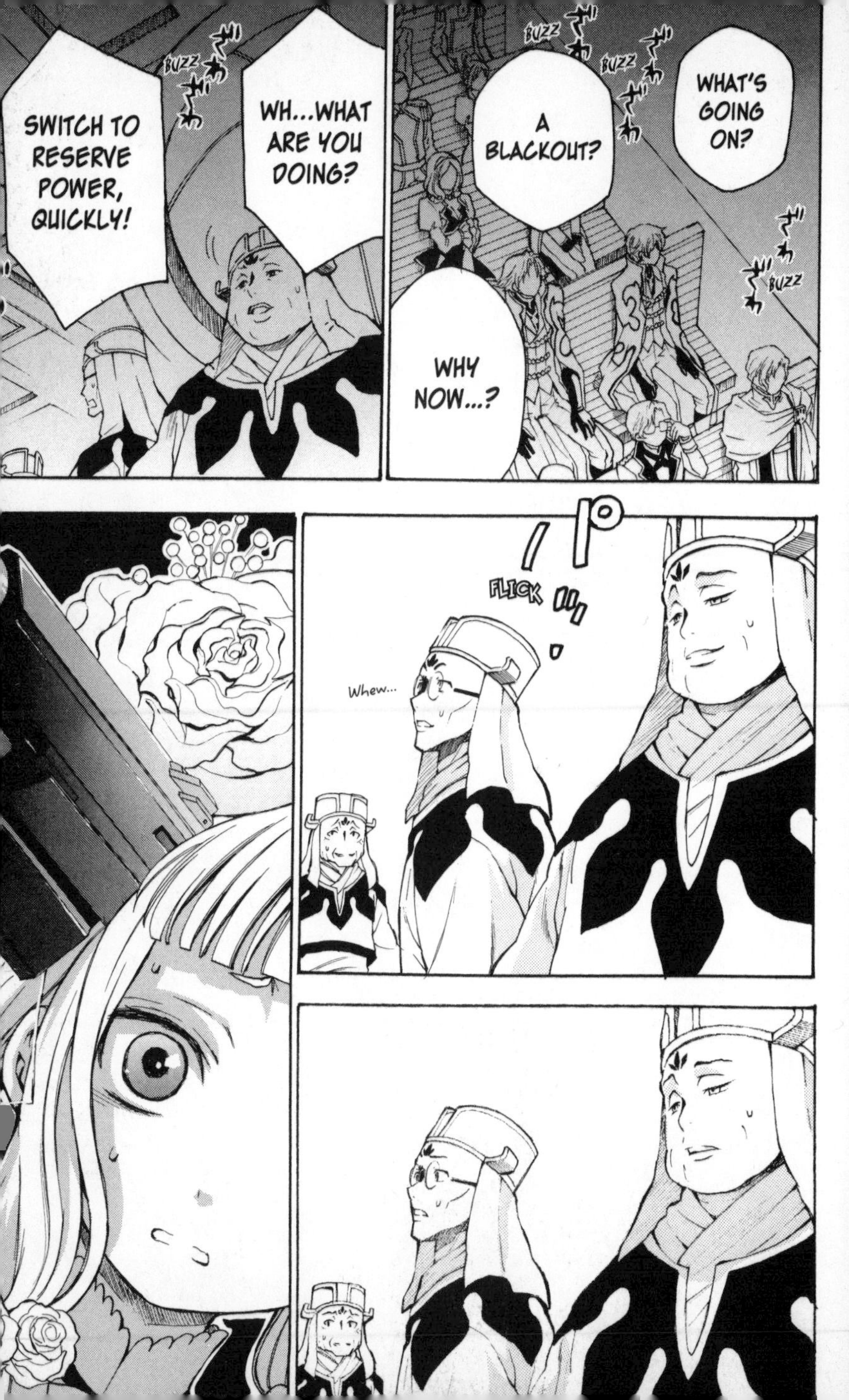
WHAT'S GOING ON?
BUZZ
BUZZ
A BLACKOUT?
BUZZ
WHY NOW...?
BUZZ
WH...WHAT ARE YOU DOING?
SWITCH TO RESERVE POWER, QUICKLY!
FLICK
Whew...

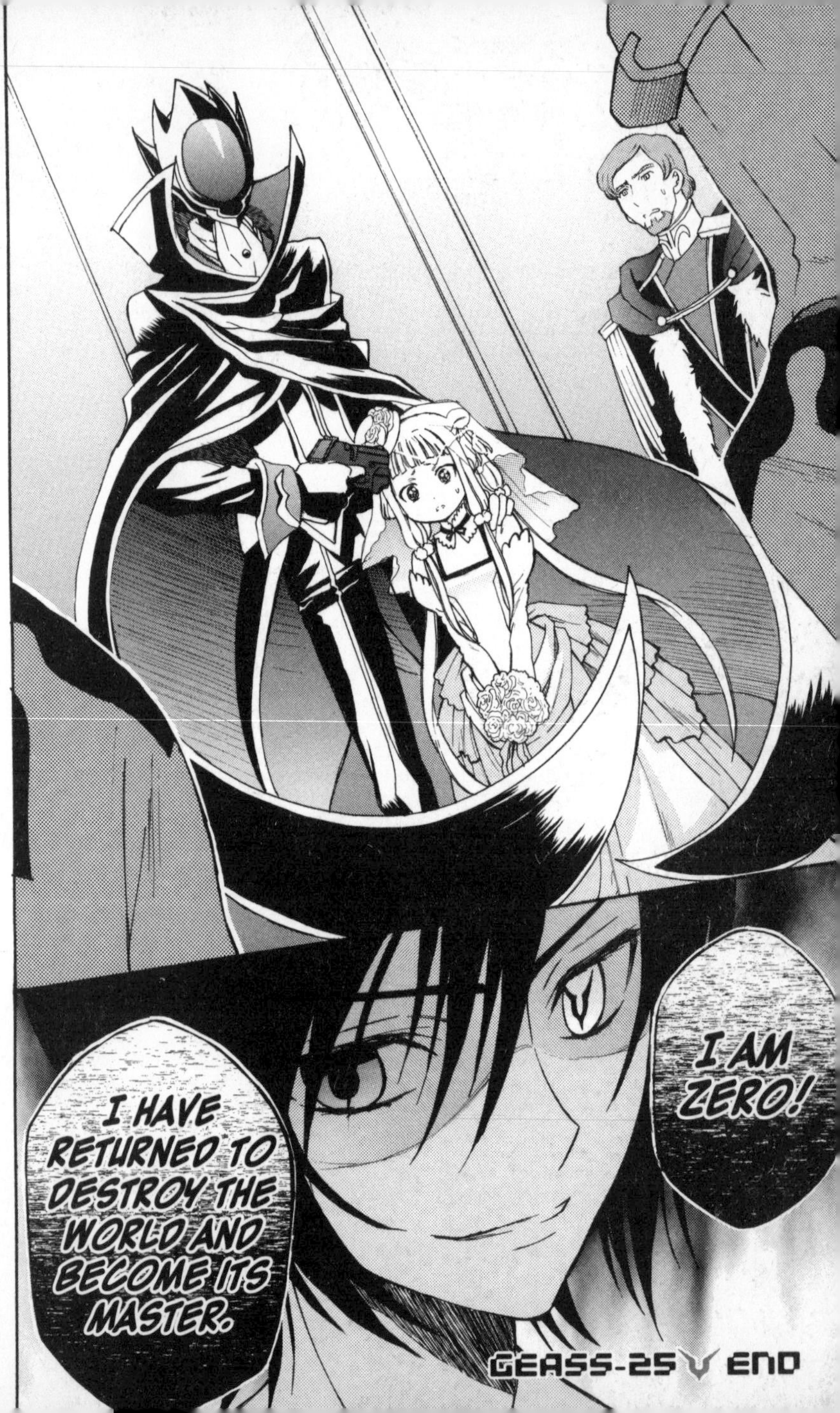
I AM ZERO!
I HAVE RETURNED TO DESTROY THE WORLD AND BECOME ITS MASTER.
GEASS-25 END

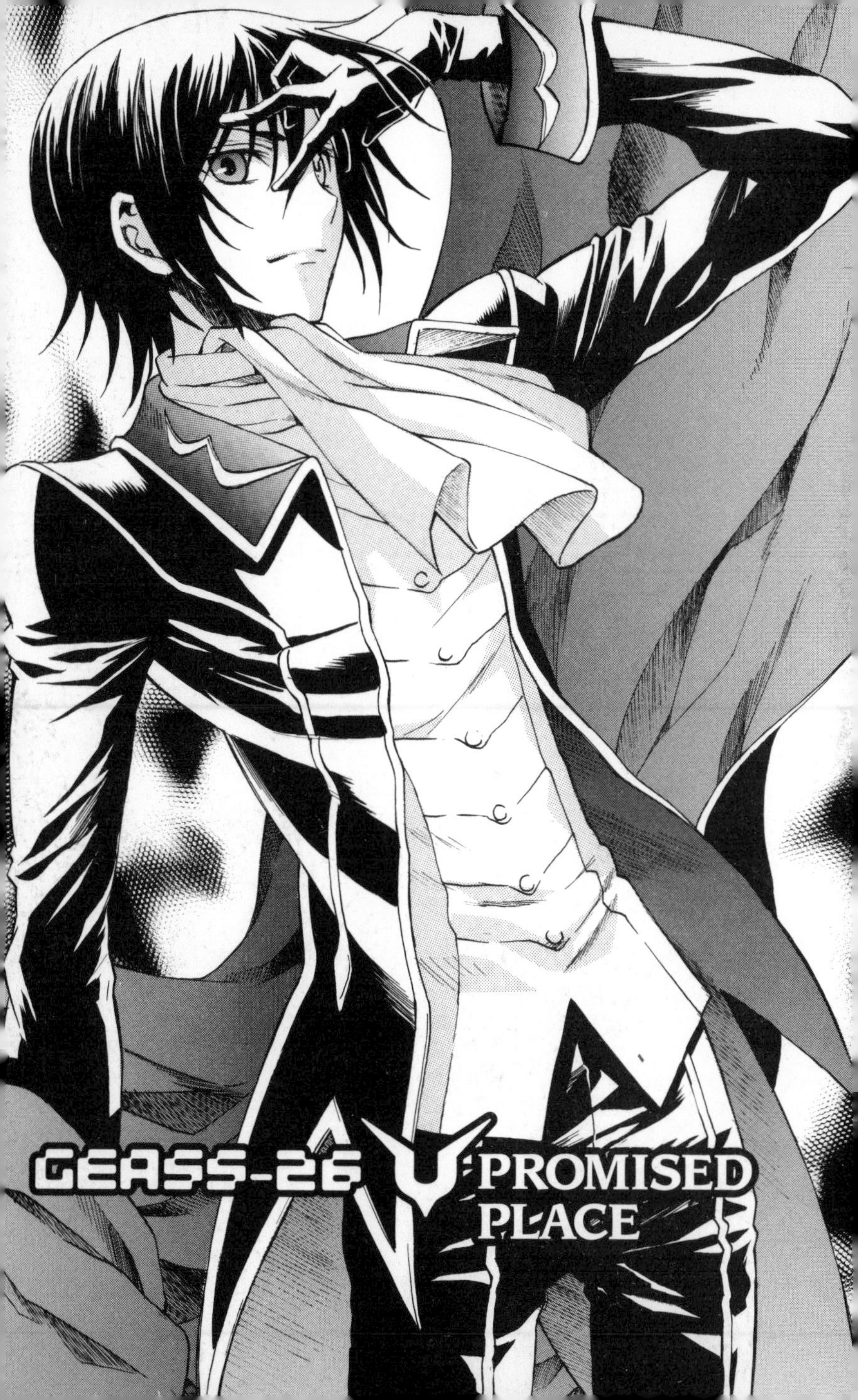
GEASS-26
PROMISED PLACE

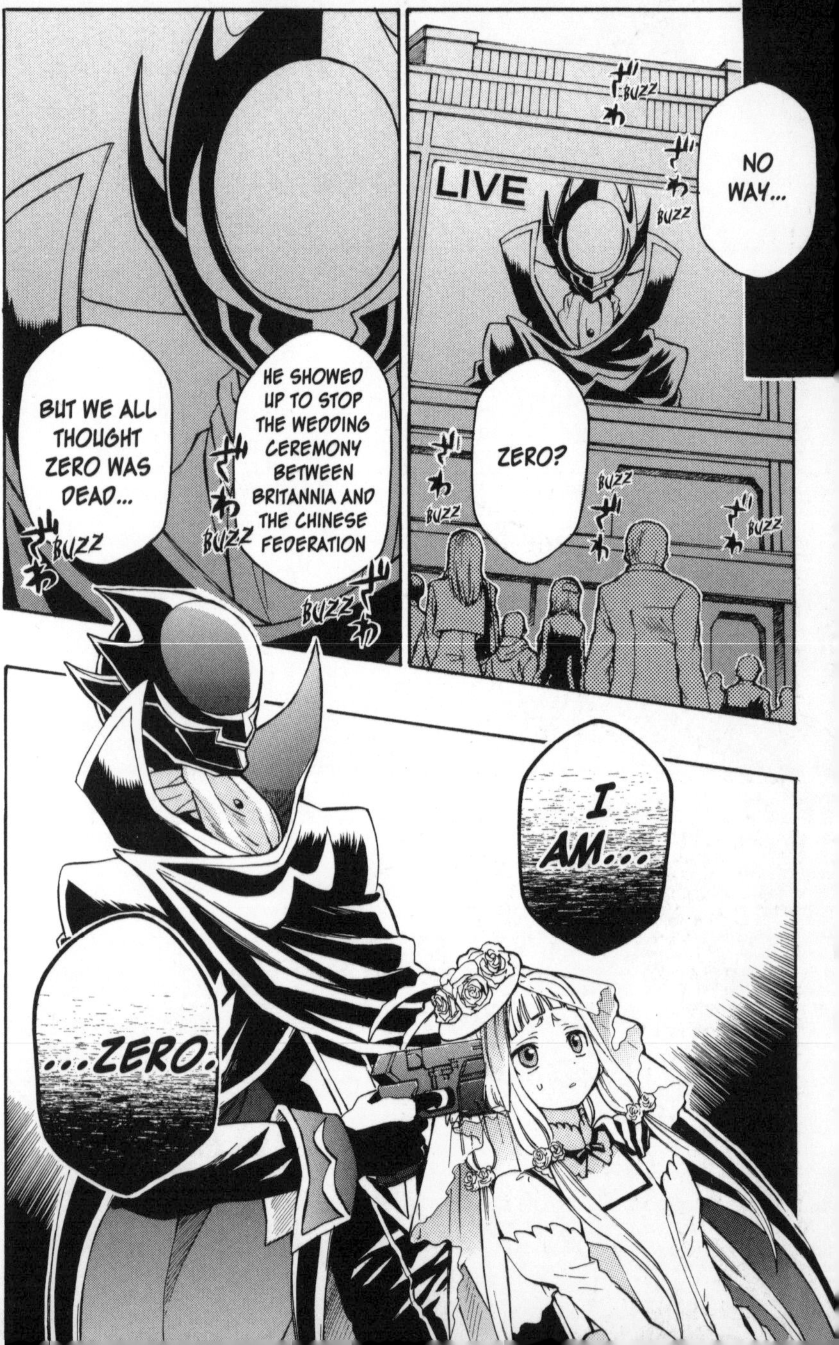
NO WAY...
ざわ BUZZ
ざわ BUZZ
LIVE
ZERO?
ざわ BUZZ
ざわ BUZZ
ざわ BUZZ
HE SHOWED UP TO STOP THE WEDDING CEREMONY BETWEEN BRITANNIA AND THE CHINESE FEDERATION
ざわ BUZZ
ざわ BUZZ
BUT WE ALL THOUGHT ZERO WAS DEAD...
ざわ BUZZ
I AM...
...ZERO.

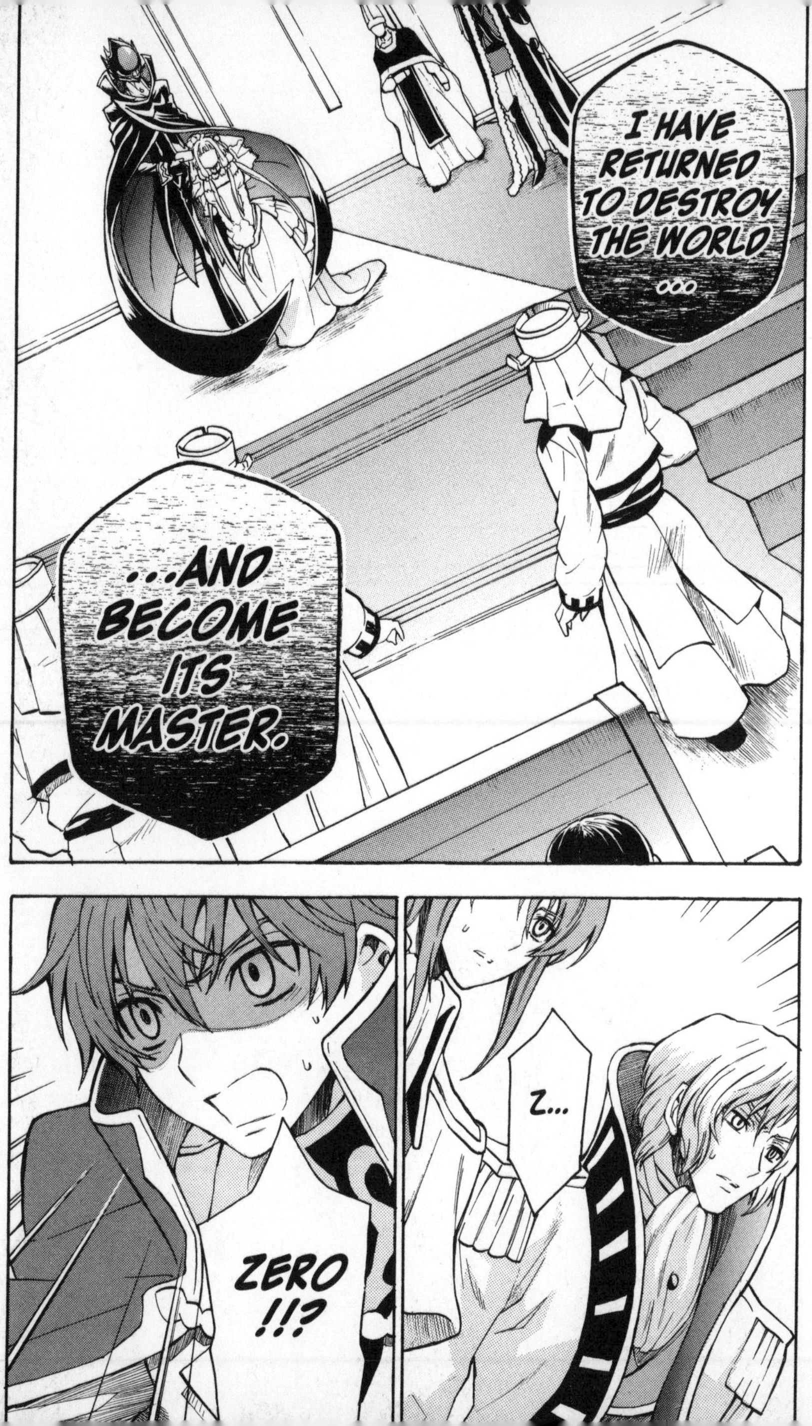
I HAVE RETURNED TO DESTROY THE WORLD ...
...AND BECOME ITS MASTER.
Z...
ZERO !!?

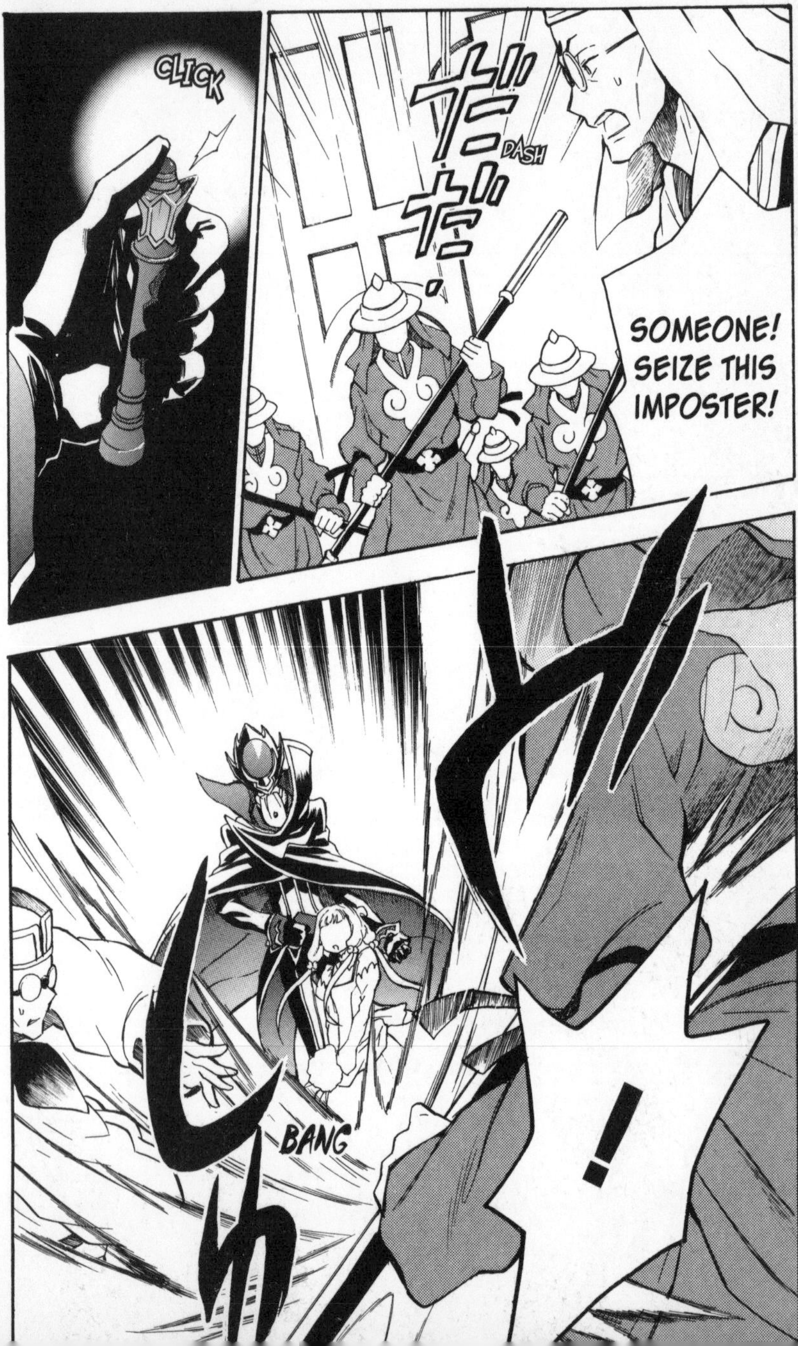
DASH
SOMEONE! SEIZE THIS IMPOSTER!
CLICK
BANG
!

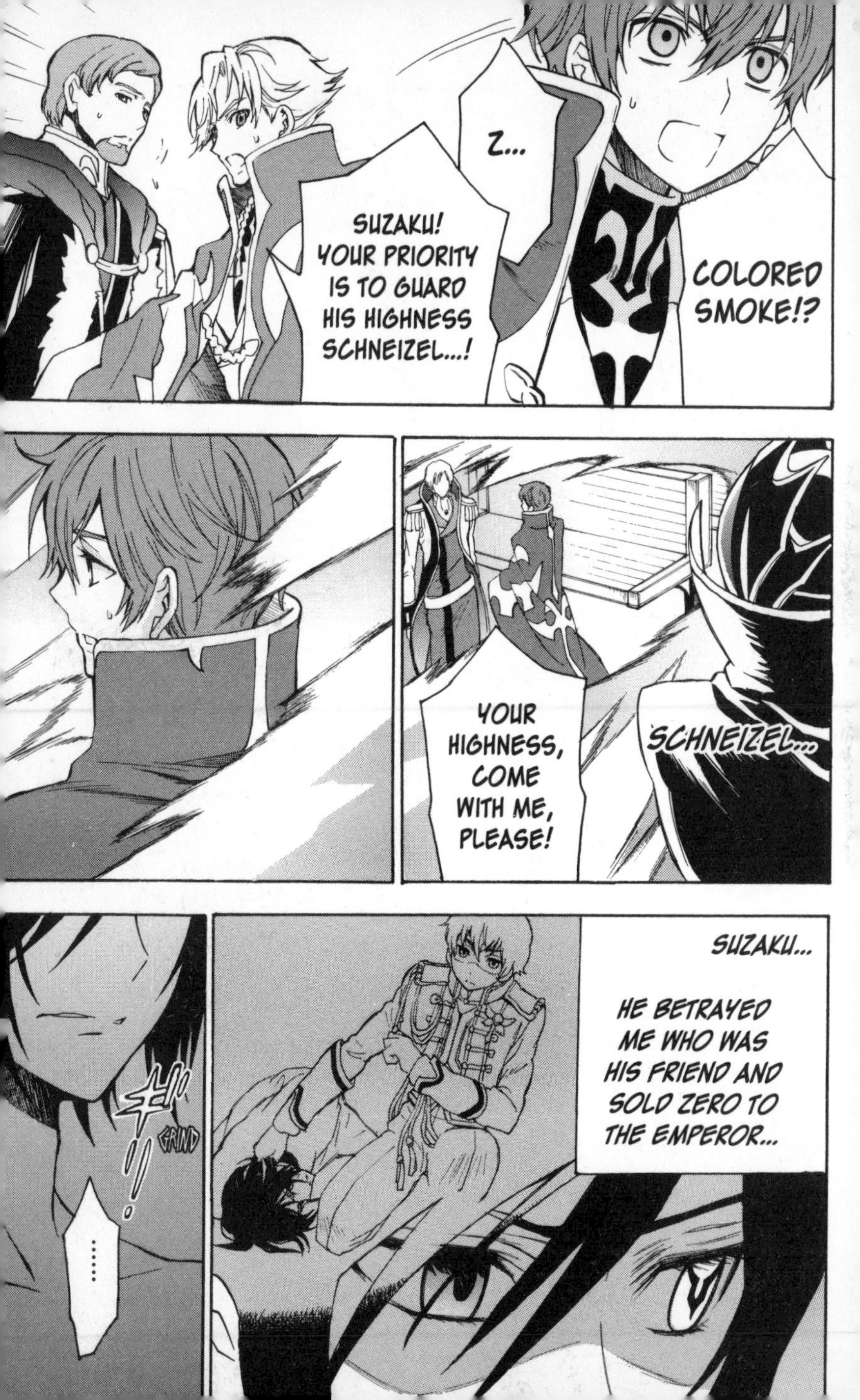
Z...
COLORED SMOKE!?
SUZAKU! YOUR PRIORITY IS TO GUARD HIS HIGHNESS SCHNEIZEL...!
SCHNEIZEL...
YOUR HIGHNESS, COME WITH ME, PLEASE!
SUZAKU...
HE BETRAYED ME WHO WAS HIS FRIEND AND SOLD ZERO TO THE EMPEROR...
GRIND
......

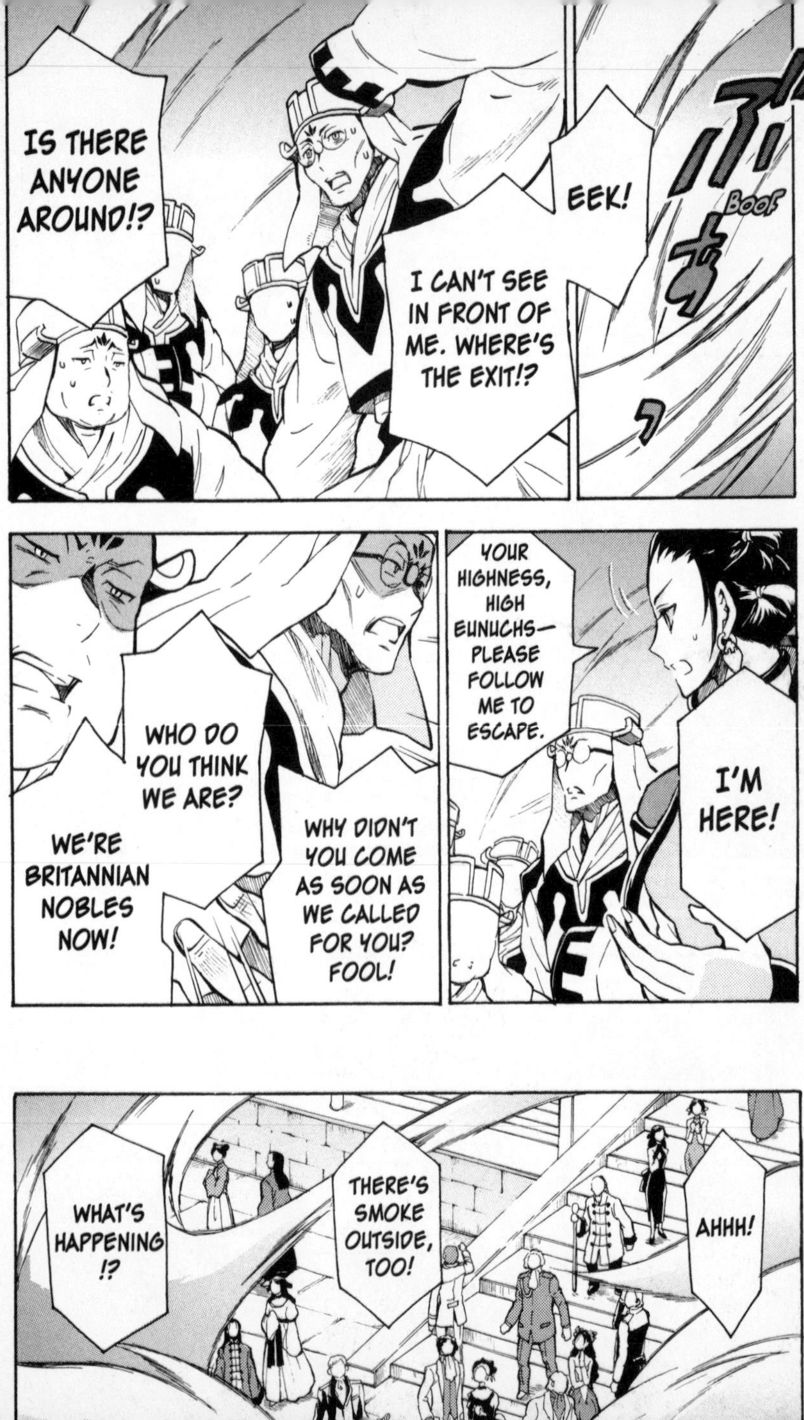
Boof
EEK!
IS THERE ANYONE AROUND!?
I CAN'T SEE IN FRONT OF ME. WHERE'S THE EXIT!?
I'M HERE!
YOUR HIGHNESS, HIGH EUNUCHS—PLEASE FOLLOW ME TO ESCAPE.
WHY DIDN'T YOU COME AS SOON AS WE CALLED FOR YOU? FOOL!
WHO DO YOU THINK WE ARE?
WE'RE BRITANNIAN NOBLES NOW!
AHHH!
THERE'S SMOKE OUTSIDE, TOO!
WHAT'S HAPPENING!?

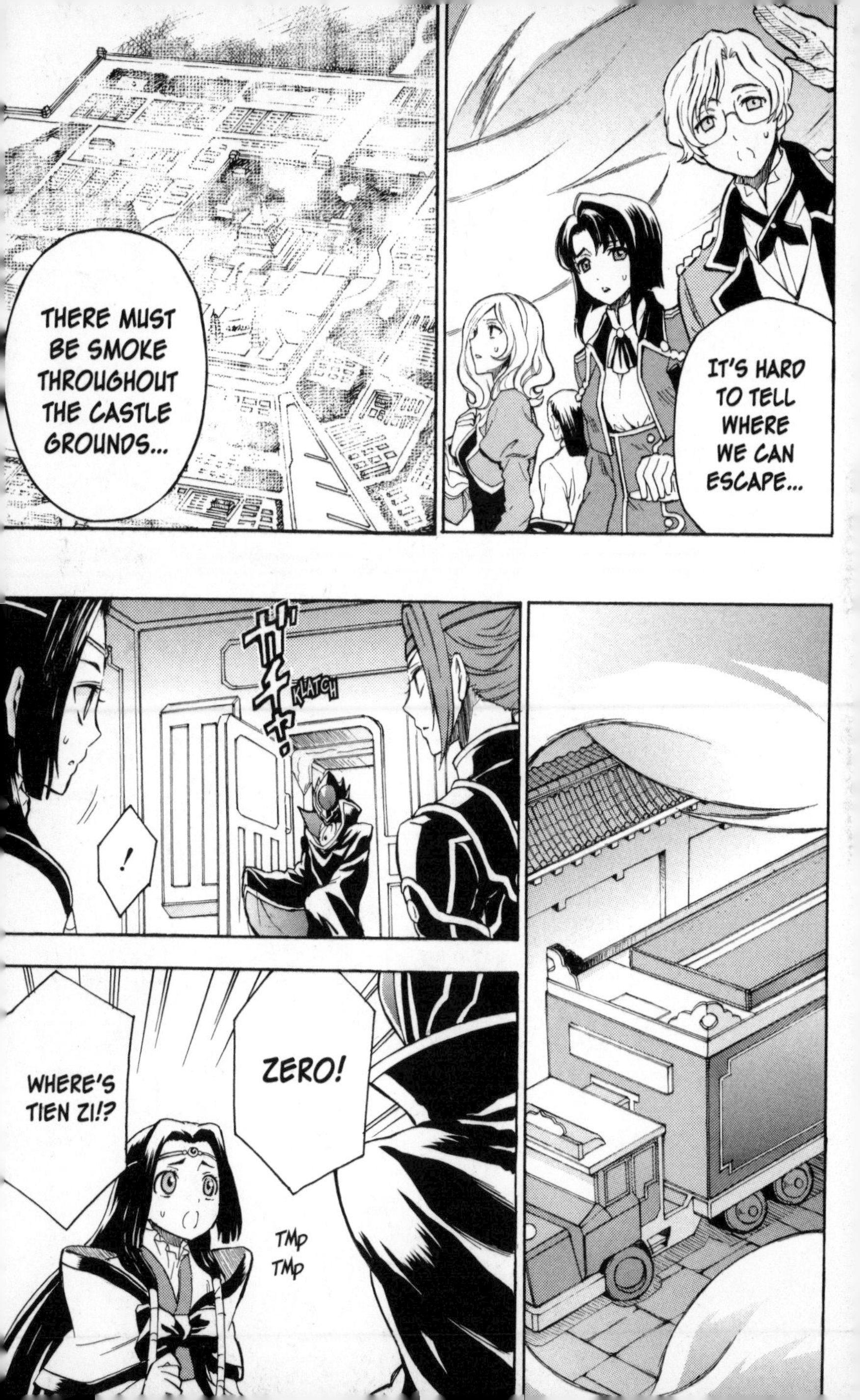
IT'S HARD TO TELL WHERE WE CAN ESCAPE...
THERE MUST BE SMOKE THROUGHOUT THE CASTLE GROUNDS...
ガチャ
KLATCH
!
ZERO!
WHERE'S TIEN ZI!?
TMP TMP

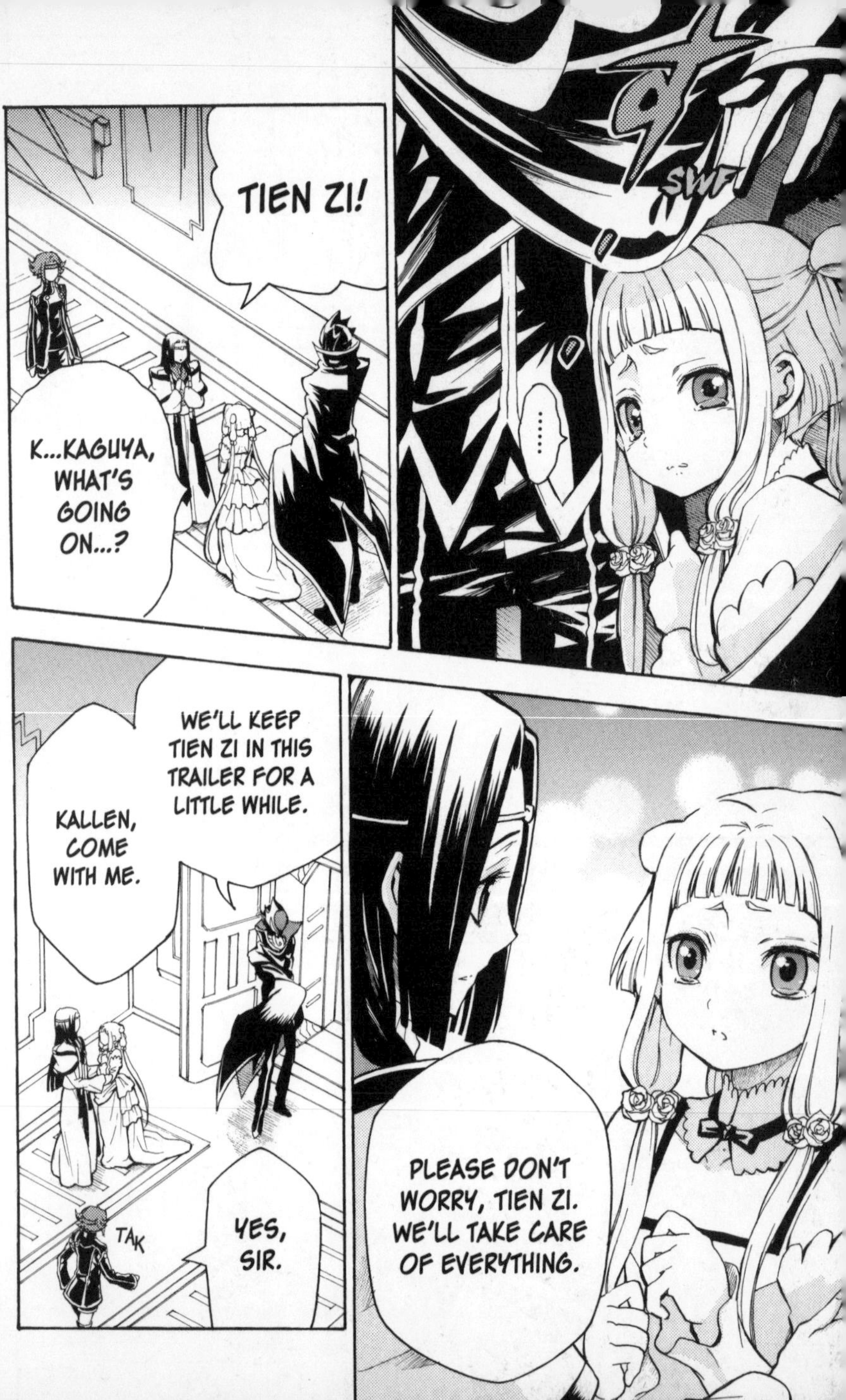
SWF
......
TIEN ZI!
K...KAGUYA, WHAT'S GOING ON...?
PLEASE DON'T WORRY, TIEN ZI. WE'LL TAKE CARE OF EVERYTHING.
WE'LL KEEP TIEN ZI IN THIS TRAILER FOR A LITTLE WHILE.
KALLEN, COME WITH ME.
YES, SIR.
TAK

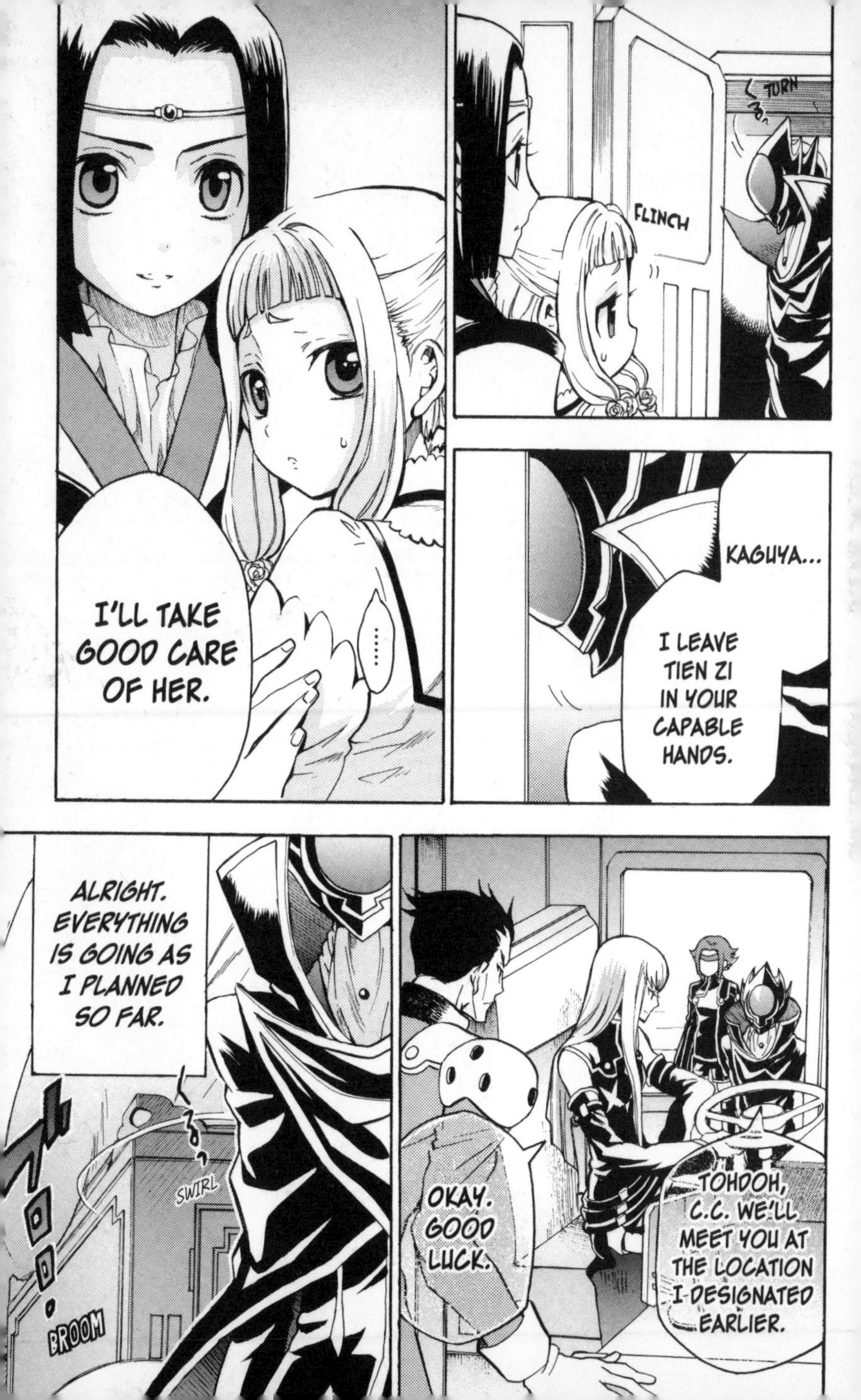
TURN
FLINCH
KAGUYA...
I LEAVE TIEN ZI IN YOUR CAPABLE HANDS.
......
I'LL TAKE GOOD CARE OF HER.
TOHDOH, C.C. WE'LL MEET YOU AT THE LOCATION I DESIGNATED EARLIER.
OKAY. GOOD LUCK.
ALRIGHT. EVERYTHING IS GOING AS I PLANNED SO FAR.
SWIRL
BROOM

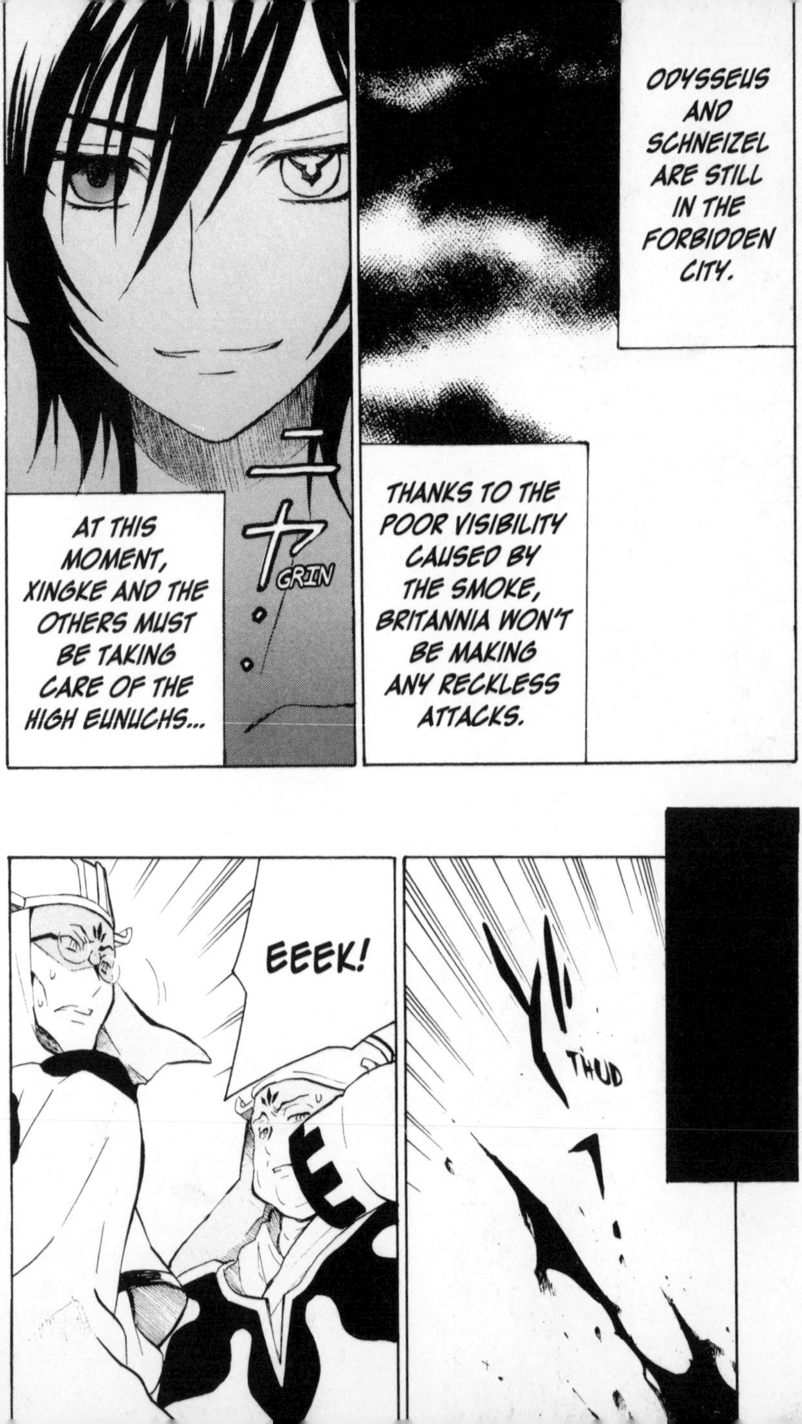
ODYSSEUS AND SCHNEIZEL ARE STILL IN THE FORBIDDEN CITY.
THANKS TO THE POOR VISIBILITY CAUSED BY THE SMOKE, BRITANNIA WON'T BE MAKING ANY RECKLESS ATTACKS.
AT THIS MOMENT, XINGKE AND THE OTHERS MUST BE TAKING CARE OF THE HIGH EUNUCHS...
GRIN
THUD
EEEK!

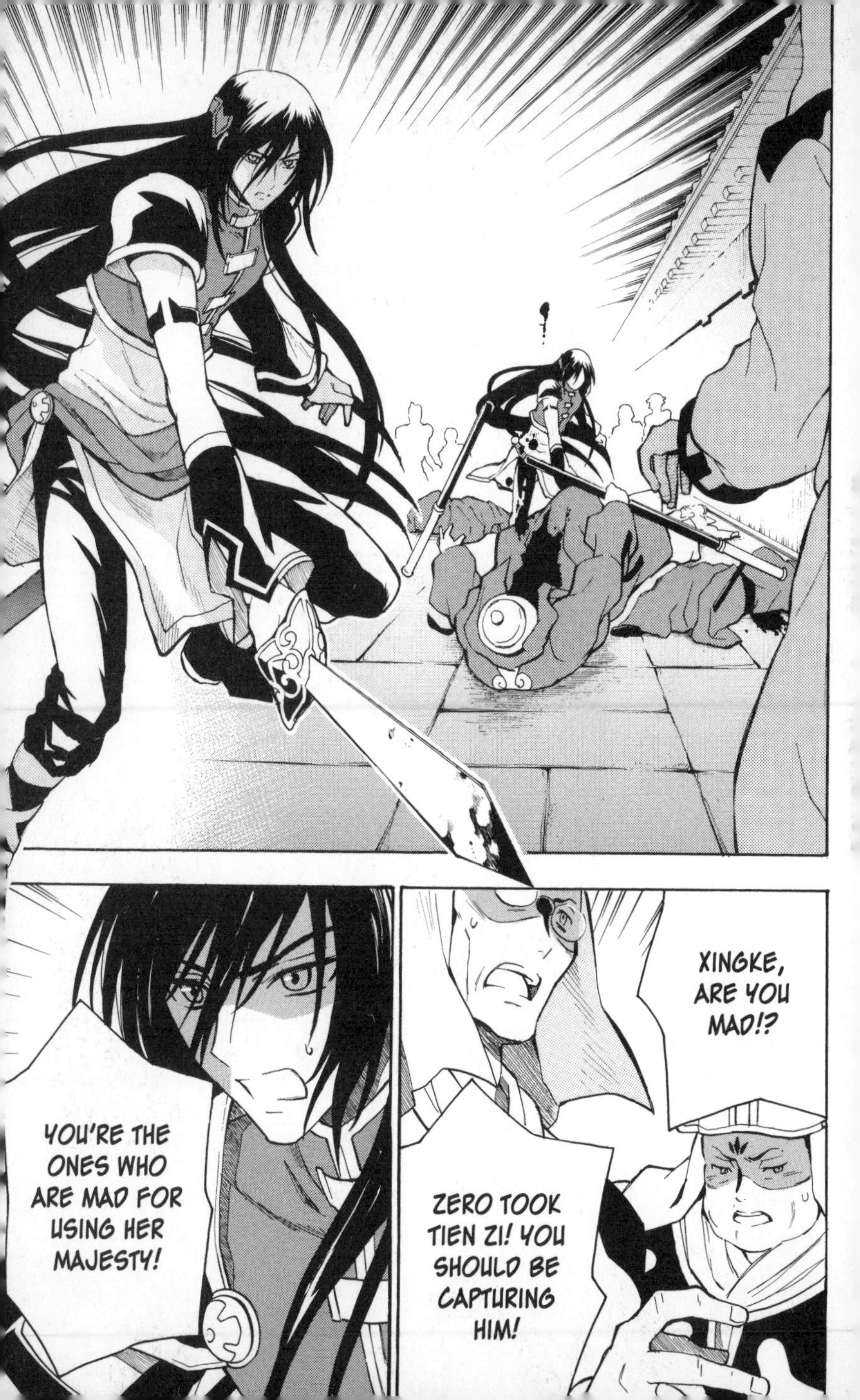
XINGKE, ARE YOU MAD!?
ZERO TOOK TIEN ZI! YOU SHOULD BE CAPTURING HIM!
YOU'RE THE ONES WHO ARE MAD FOR USING HER MAJESTY!

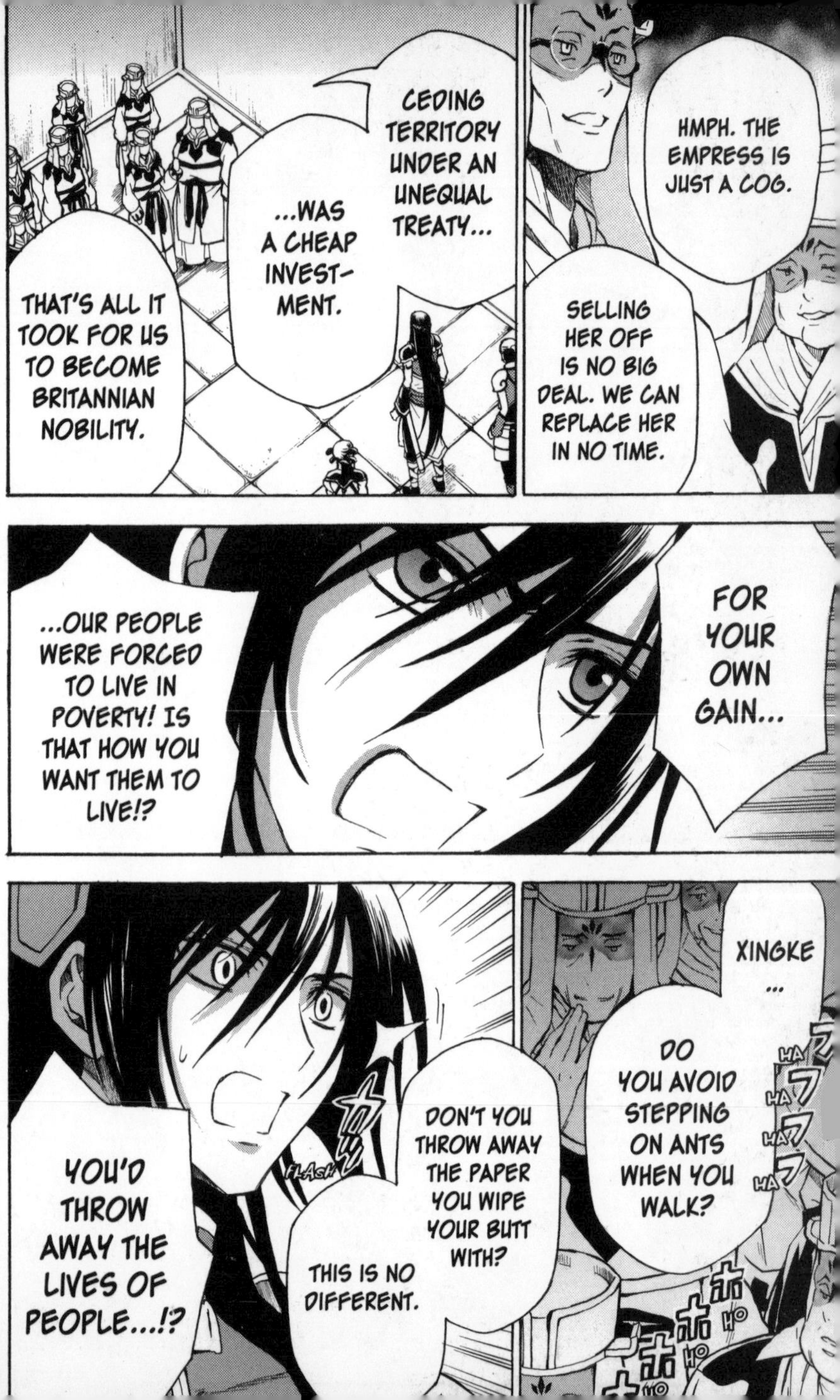
HMPH. THE EMPRESS IS JUST A COG.
SELLING HER OFF IS NO BIG DEAL. WE CAN REPLACE HER IN NO TIME.
CEDING TERRITORY UNDER AN UNEQUAL TREATY...
...WAS A CHEAP INVEST-MENT.
THAT'S ALL IT TOOK FOR US TO BECOME BRITANNIAN NOBILITY.
FOR YOUR OWN GAIN...
...OUR PEOPLE WERE FORCED TO LIVE IN POVERTY! IS THAT HOW YOU WANT THEM TO LIVE!?
XINGKE ...
DO YOU AVOID STEPPING ON ANTS WHEN YOU WALK?
HA HA HA HA
HO HO HO HO
FLASH
DON'T YOU THROW AWAY THE PAPER YOU WIPE YOUR BUTT WITH?
THIS IS NO DIFFERENT.
YOU'D THROW AWAY THE LIVES OF PEOPLE...!?

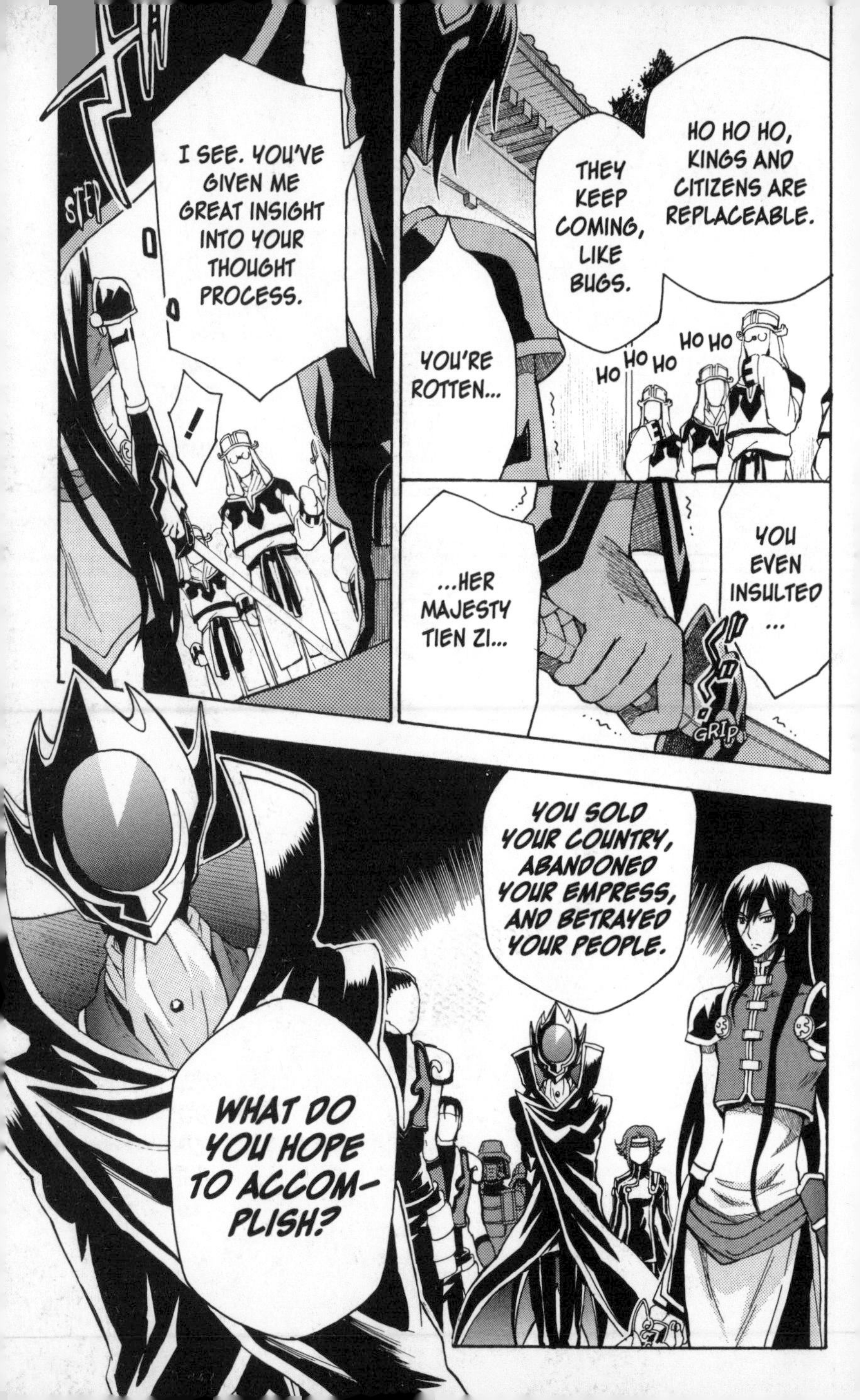
HO HO HO, KINGS AND CITIZENS ARE REPLACEABLE.
THEY KEEP COMING, LIKE BUGS.
HO HO HO HO HO
YOU'RE ROTTEN...
YOU EVEN INSULTED...
...HER MAJESTY TIEN ZI...
GRIP
STEP
I SEE. YOU'VE GIVEN ME GREAT INSIGHT INTO YOUR THOUGHT PROCESS.
!
YOU SOLD YOUR COUNTRY, ABANDONED YOUR EMPRESS, AND BETRAYED YOUR PEOPLE.
WHAT DO YOU HOPE TO ACCOMPLISH?

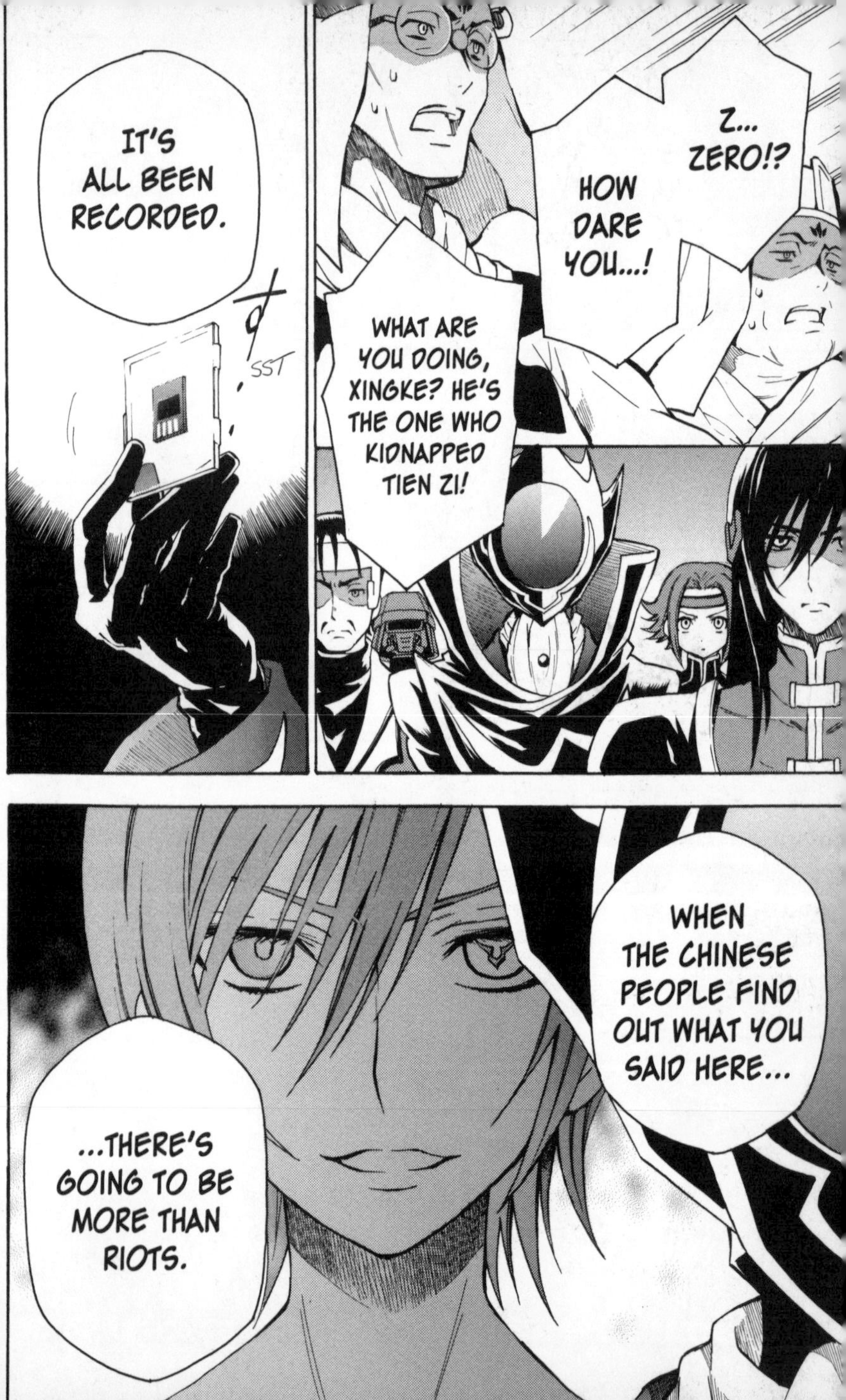
Z... ZERO!?
HOW DARE YOU...!
WHAT ARE YOU DOING, XINGKE? HE'S THE ONE WHO KIDNAPPED TIEN ZI!
IT'S ALL BEEN RECORDED.
SST
WHEN THE CHINESE PEOPLE FIND OUT WHAT YOU SAID HERE...
...THERE'S GOING TO BE MORE THAN RIOTS.

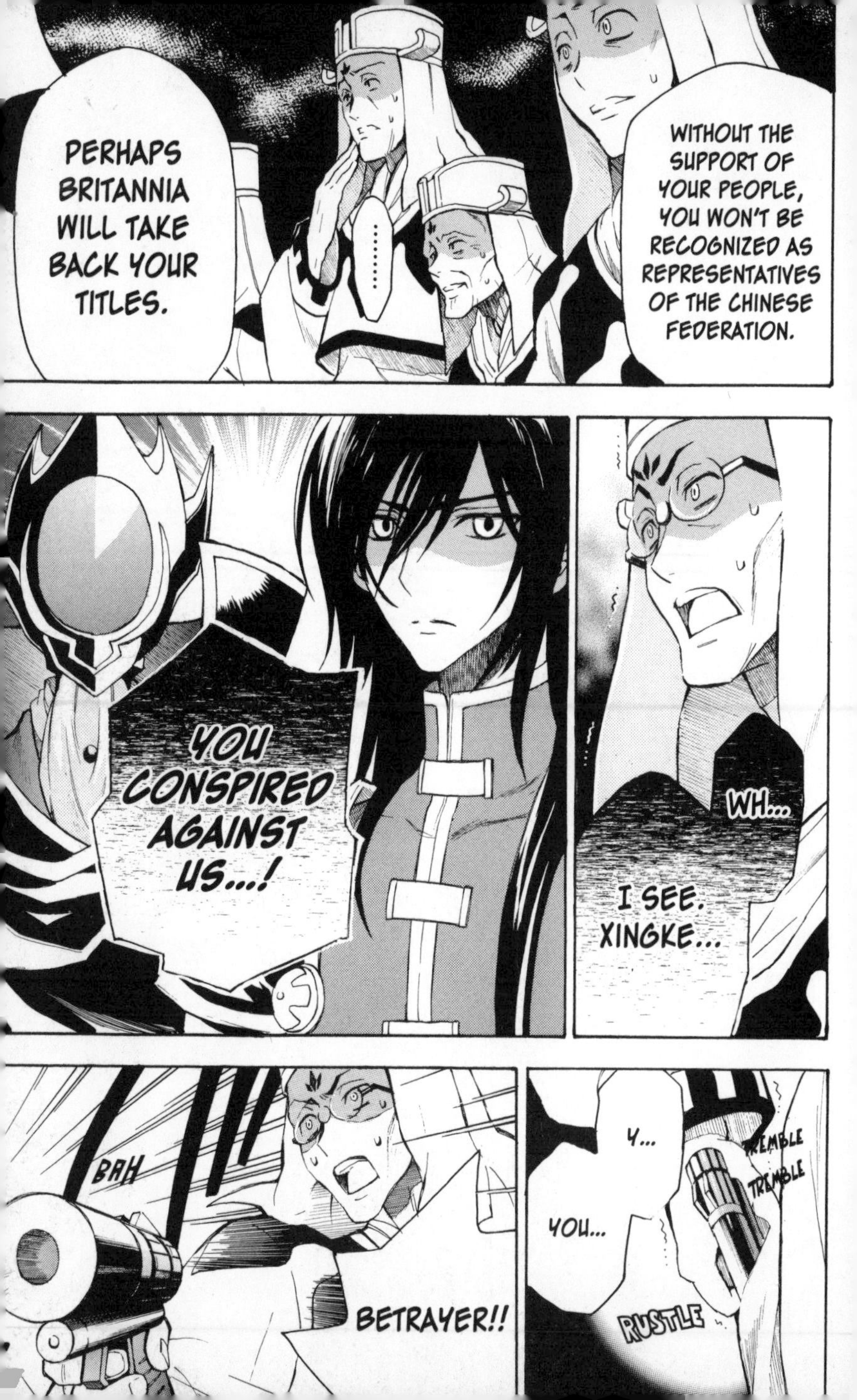
WITHOUT THE SUPPORT OF YOUR PEOPLE, YOU WON'T BE RECOGNIZED AS REPRESENTATIVES OF THE CHINESE FEDERATION.
......
PERHAPS BRITANNIA WILL TAKE BACK YOUR TITLES.
WH...
I SEE. XINGKE...
YOU CONSPIRED AGAINST US...!
Y...
TREMBLE
TREMBLE
YOU...
RUSTLE
BAH
BETRAYER!!

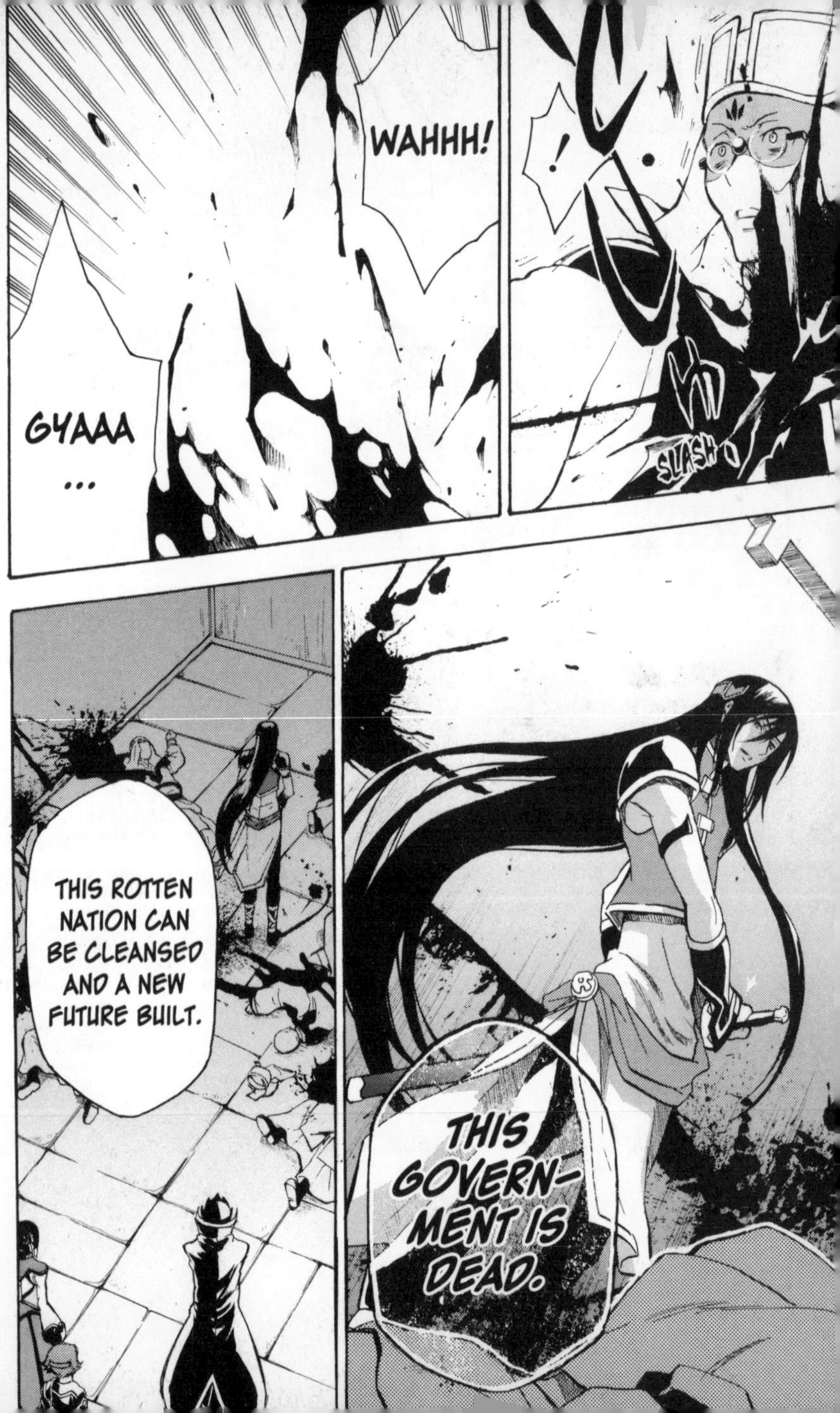
!
SLASH
WAHHH!
GYAAA
...
THIS GOVERNMENT IS DEAD.
THIS ROTTEN NATION CAN BE CLEANSED AND A NEW FUTURE BUILT.

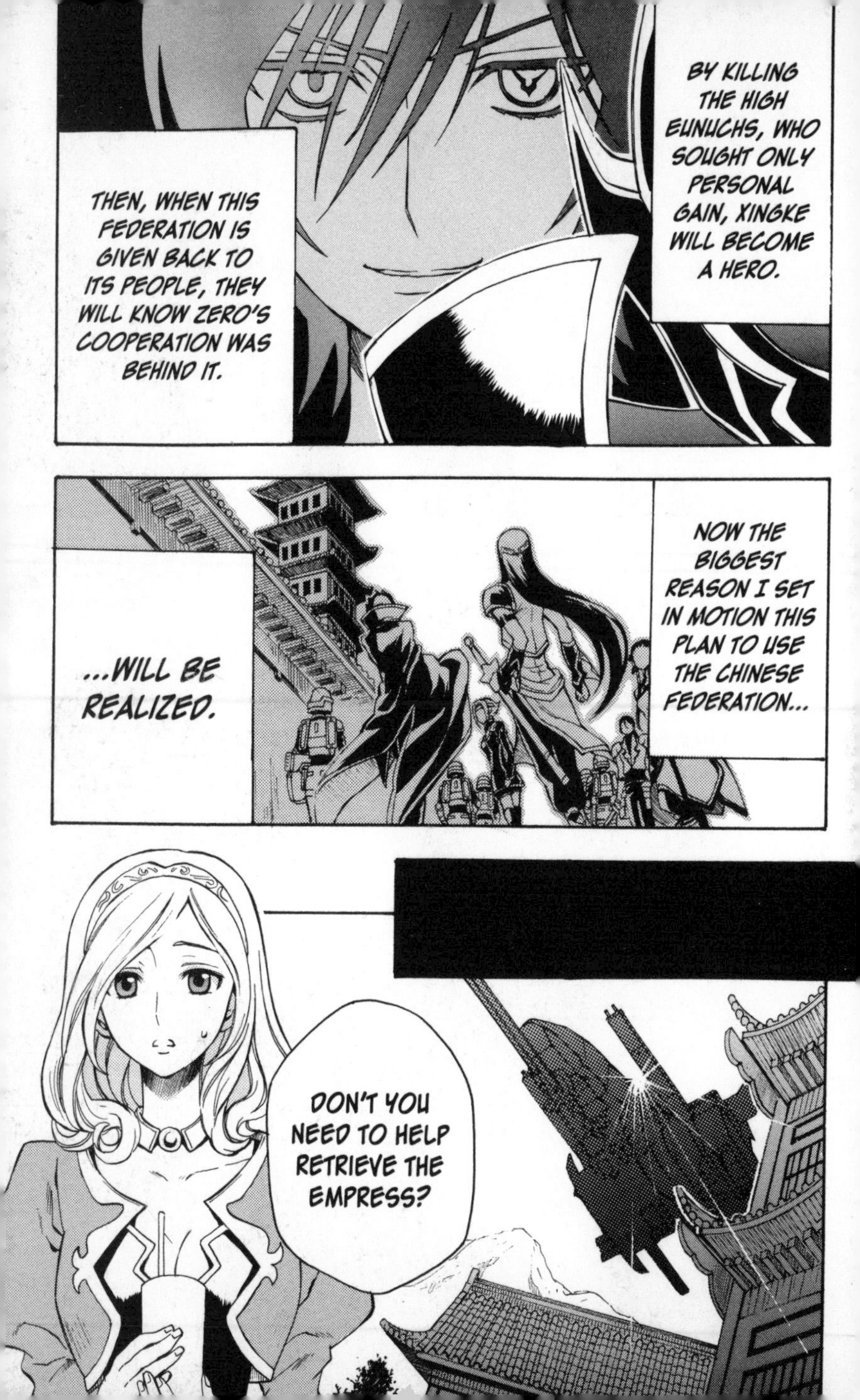
BY KILLING THE HIGH EUNUCHS, WHO SOUGHT ONLY PERSONAL GAIN, XINGKE WILL BECOME A HERO.
THEN, WHEN THIS FEDERATION IS GIVEN BACK TO ITS PEOPLE, THEY WILL KNOW ZERO'S COOPERATION WAS BEHIND IT.
NOW THE BIGGEST REASON I SET IN MOTION THIS PLAN TO USE THE CHINESE FEDERATION...
...WILL BE REALIZED.
DON'T YOU NEED TO HELP RETRIEVE THE EMPRESS?

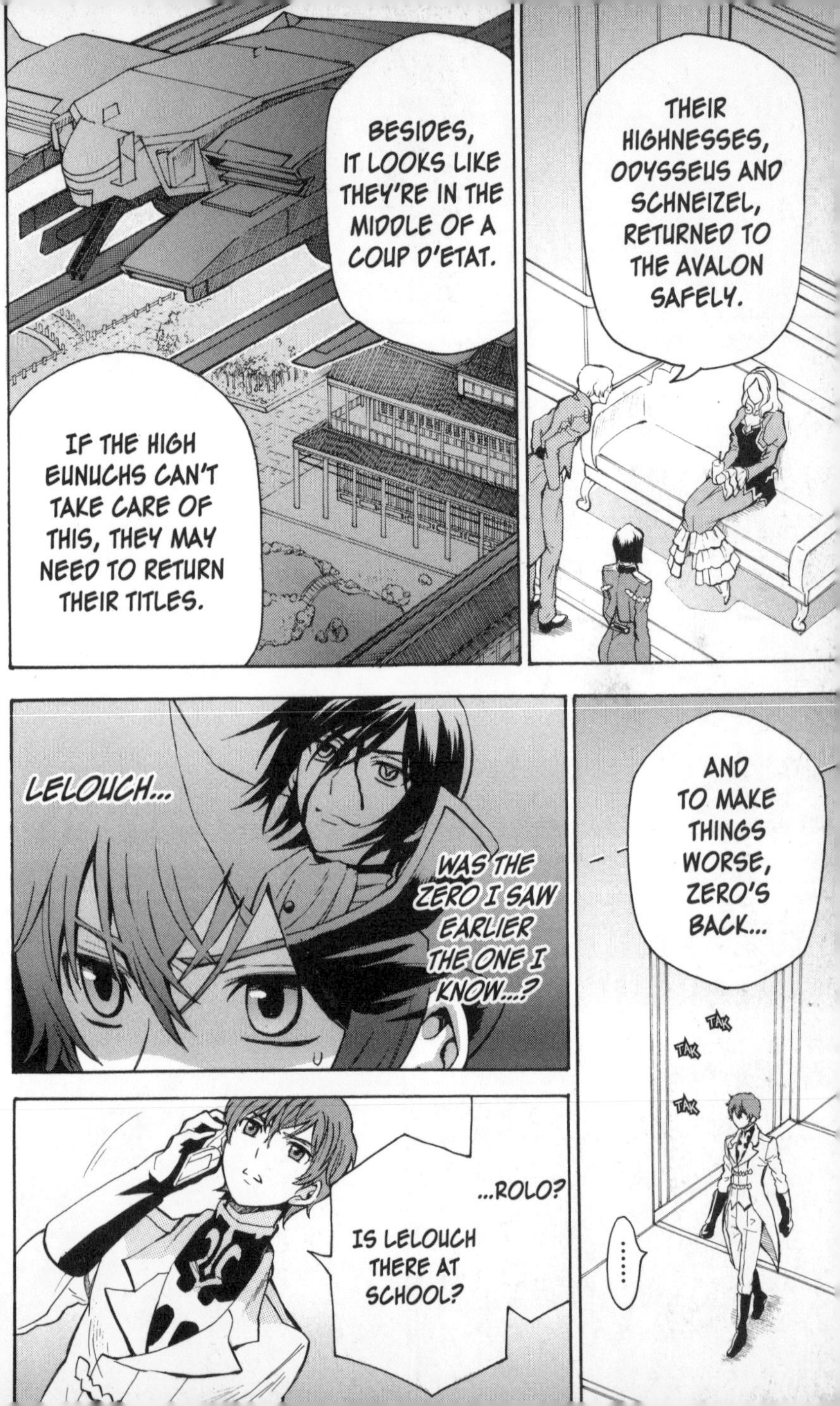
THEIR HIGHNESSES, ODYSSEUS AND SCHNEIZEL, RETURNED TO THE AVALON SAFELY.
BESIDES, IT LOOKS LIKE THEY'RE IN THE MIDDLE OF A COUP D'ETAT.
IF THE HIGH EUNUCHS CAN'T TAKE CARE OF THIS, THEY MAY NEED TO RETURN THEIR TITLES.
AND TO MAKE THINGS WORSE, ZERO'S BACK...
TAK
TAK
TAK
......
LELOUCH...
WAS THE ZERO I SAW EARLIER THE ONE I KNOW...?
...ROLO?
IS LELOUCH THERE AT SCHOOL?

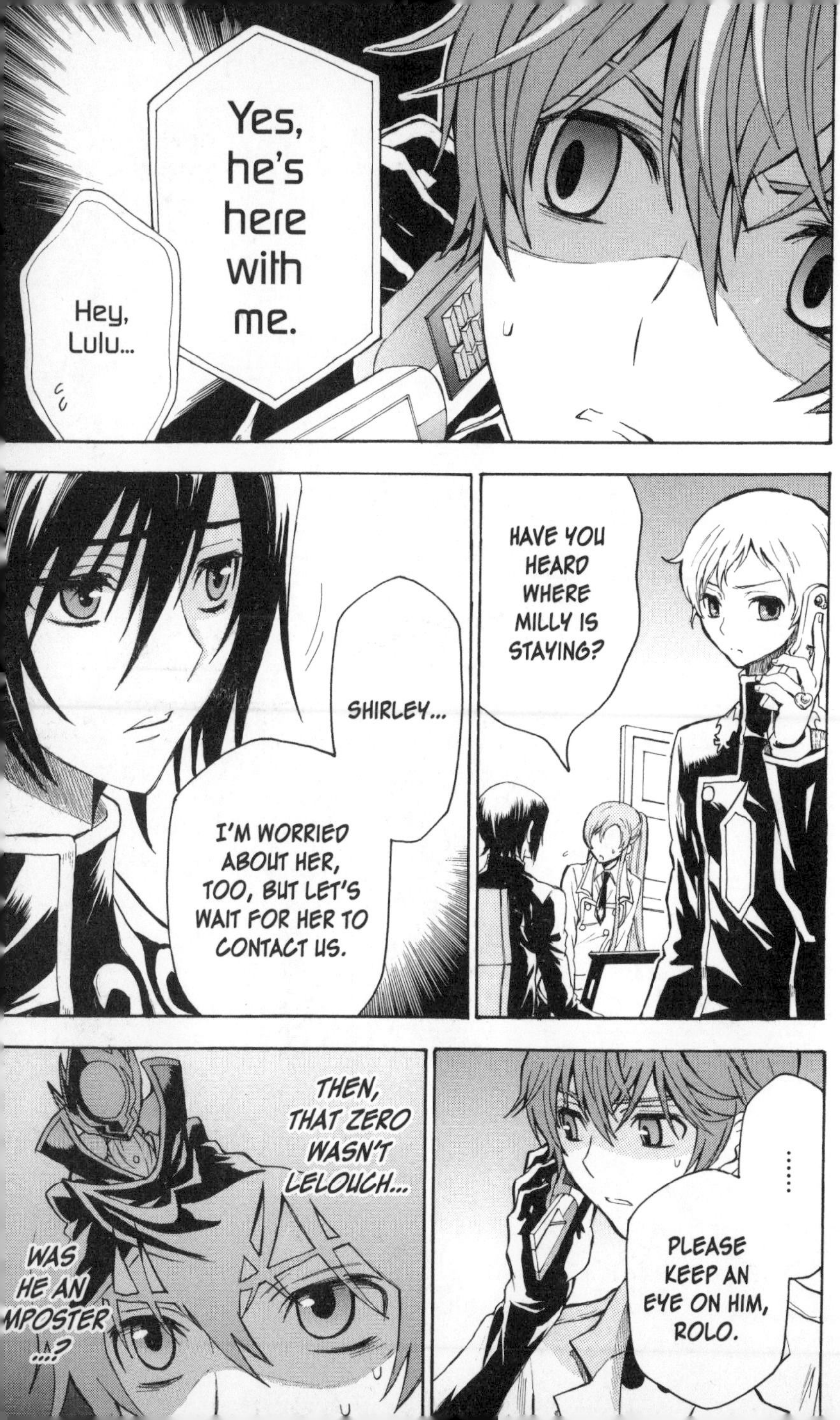
Yes, he's here with me.
Hey, Lulu...
HAVE YOU HEARD WHERE MILLY IS STAYING?
SHIRLEY...
I'M WORRIED ABOUT HER, TOO, BUT LET'S WAIT FOR HER TO CONTACT US.
......
PLEASE KEEP AN EYE ON HIM, ROLO.
THEN, THAT ZERO WASN'T LELOUCH...
WAS HE AN MPOSTER ...?

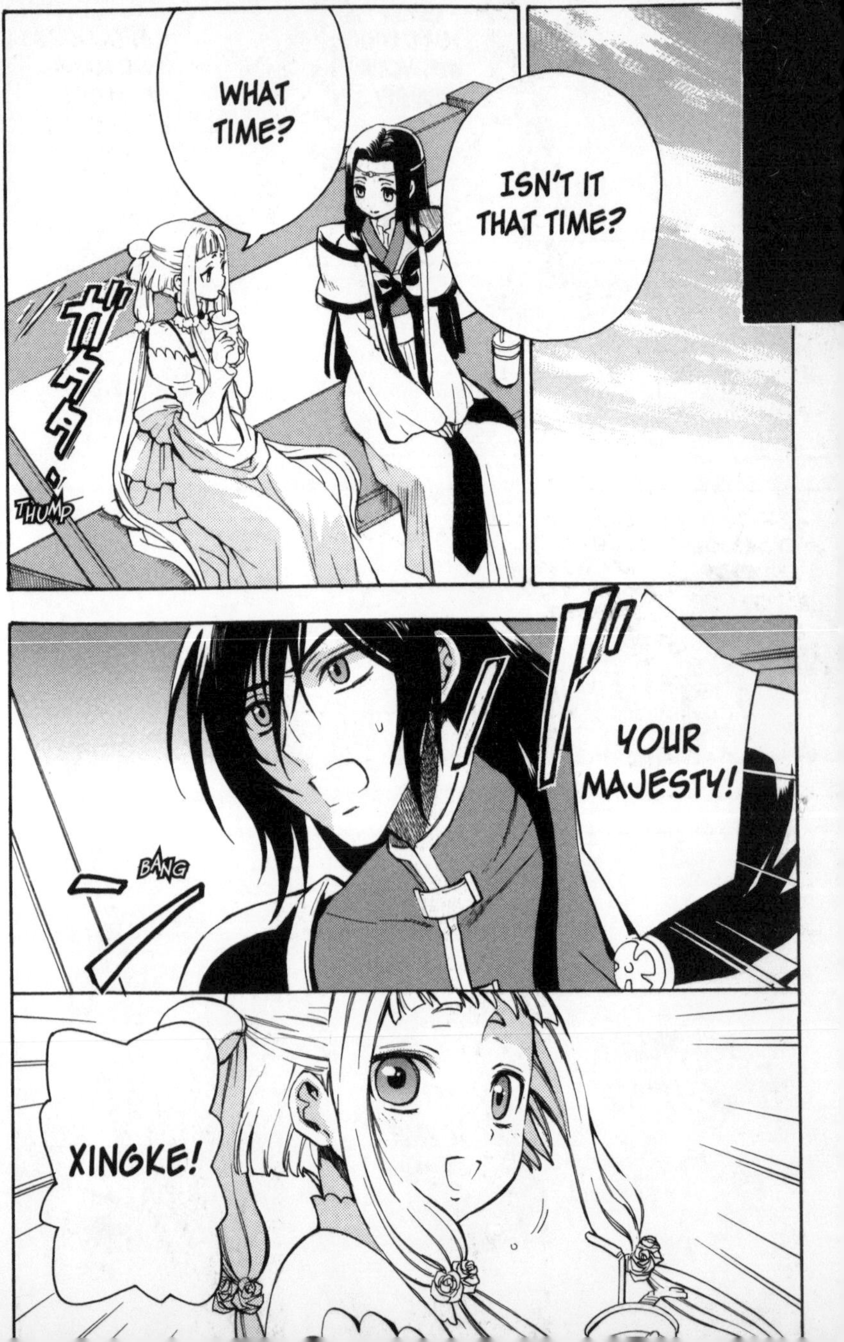
ISN'T IT THAT TIME?
WHAT TIME?
ガタッ
THUMP
YOUR MAJESTY!
BANG
XINGKE!

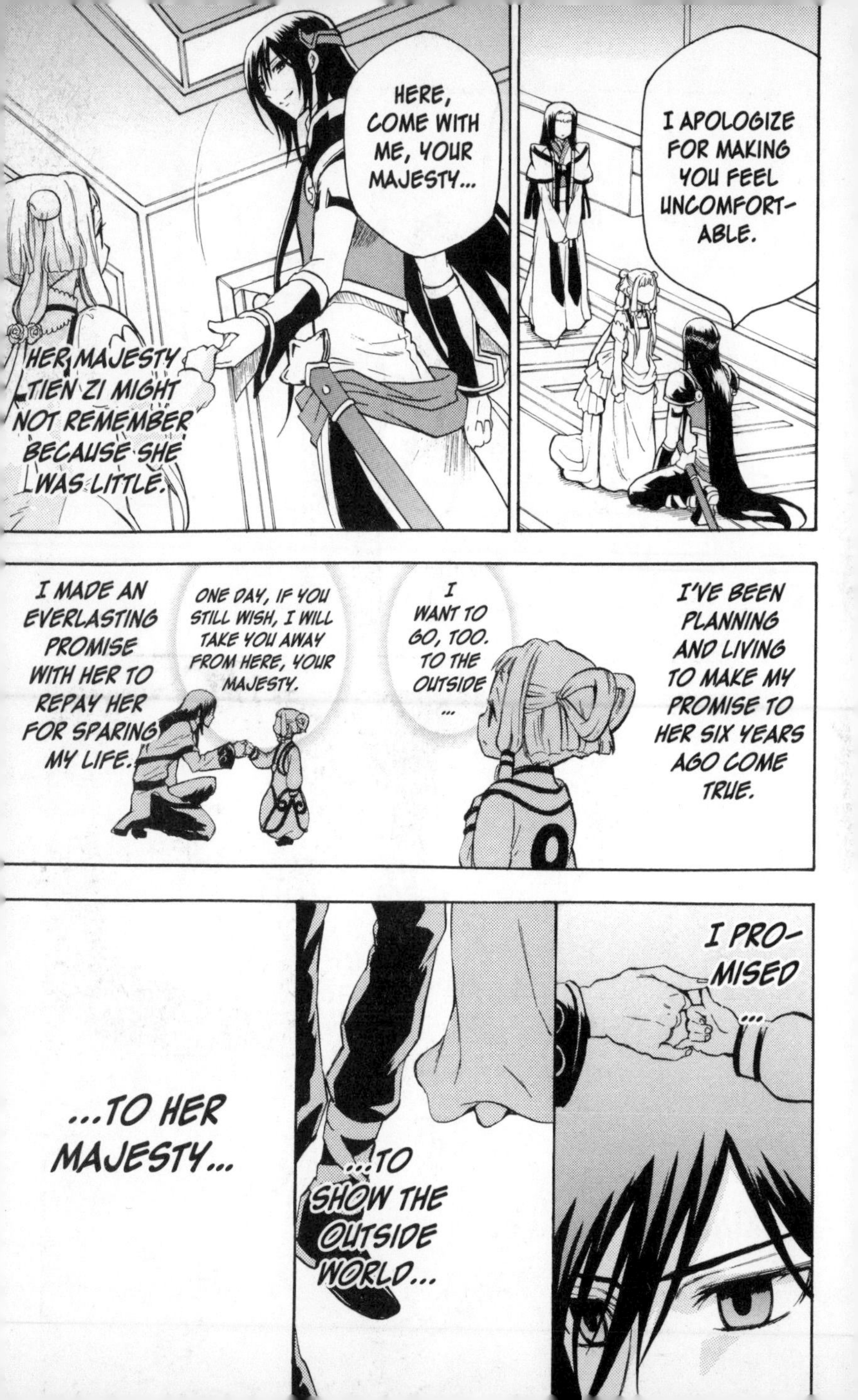
I APOLOGIZE FOR MAKING YOU FEEL UNCOMFORT-ABLE.
HERE, COME WITH ME, YOUR MAJESTY...
HER MAJESTY TIEN ZI MIGHT NOT REMEMBER BECAUSE SHE WAS LITTLE.
I'VE BEEN PLANNING AND LIVING TO MAKE MY PROMISE TO HER SIX YEARS AGO COME TRUE.
I WANT TO GO, TOO. TO THE OUTSIDE ...
ONE DAY, IF YOU STILL WISH, I WILL TAKE YOU AWAY FROM HERE, YOUR MAJESTY.
I MADE AN EVERLASTING PROMISE WITH HER TO REPAY HER FOR SPARING MY LIFE.
I PRO-MISED ...
...TO SHOW THE OUTSIDE WORLD...
...TO HER MAJESTY...

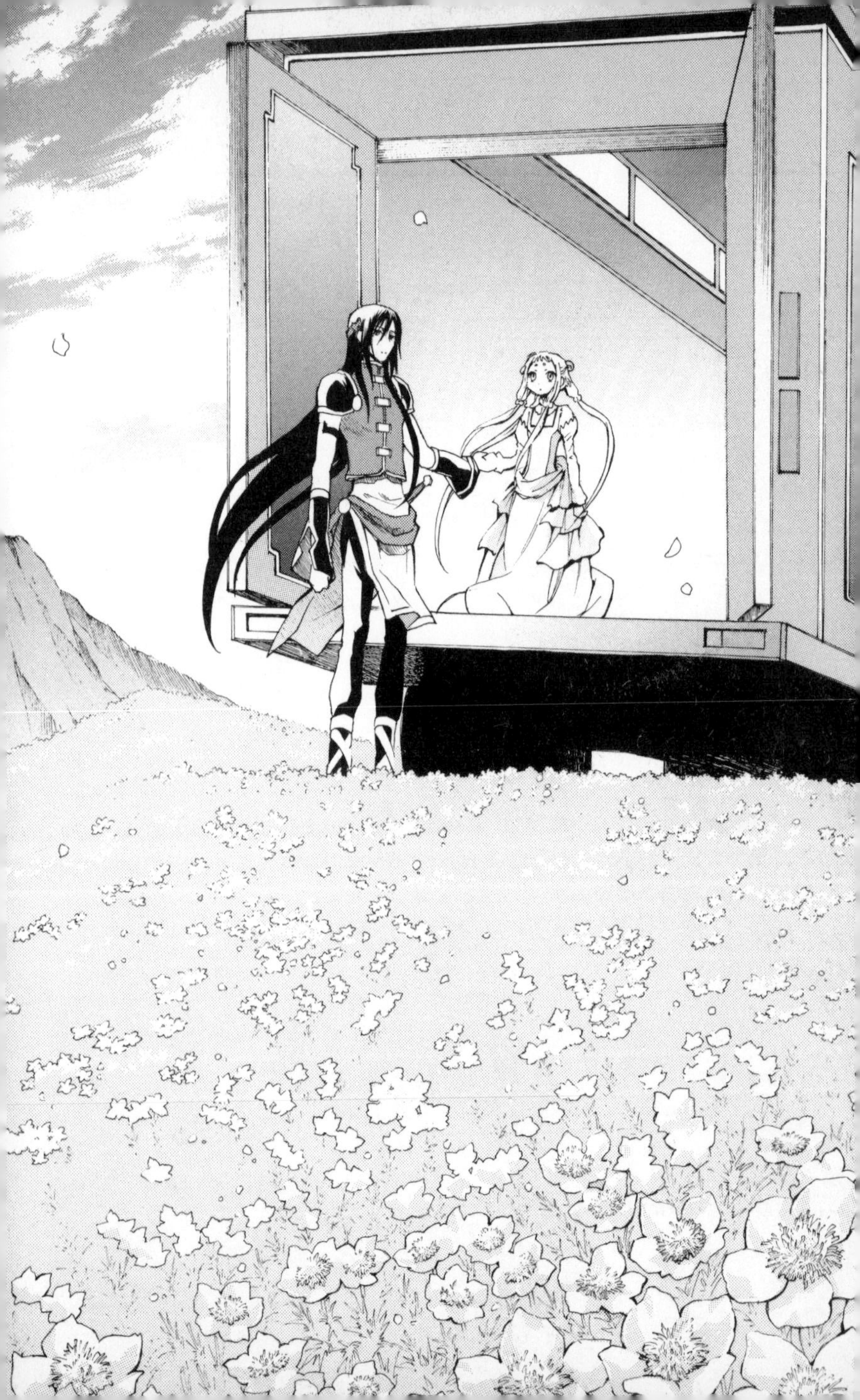

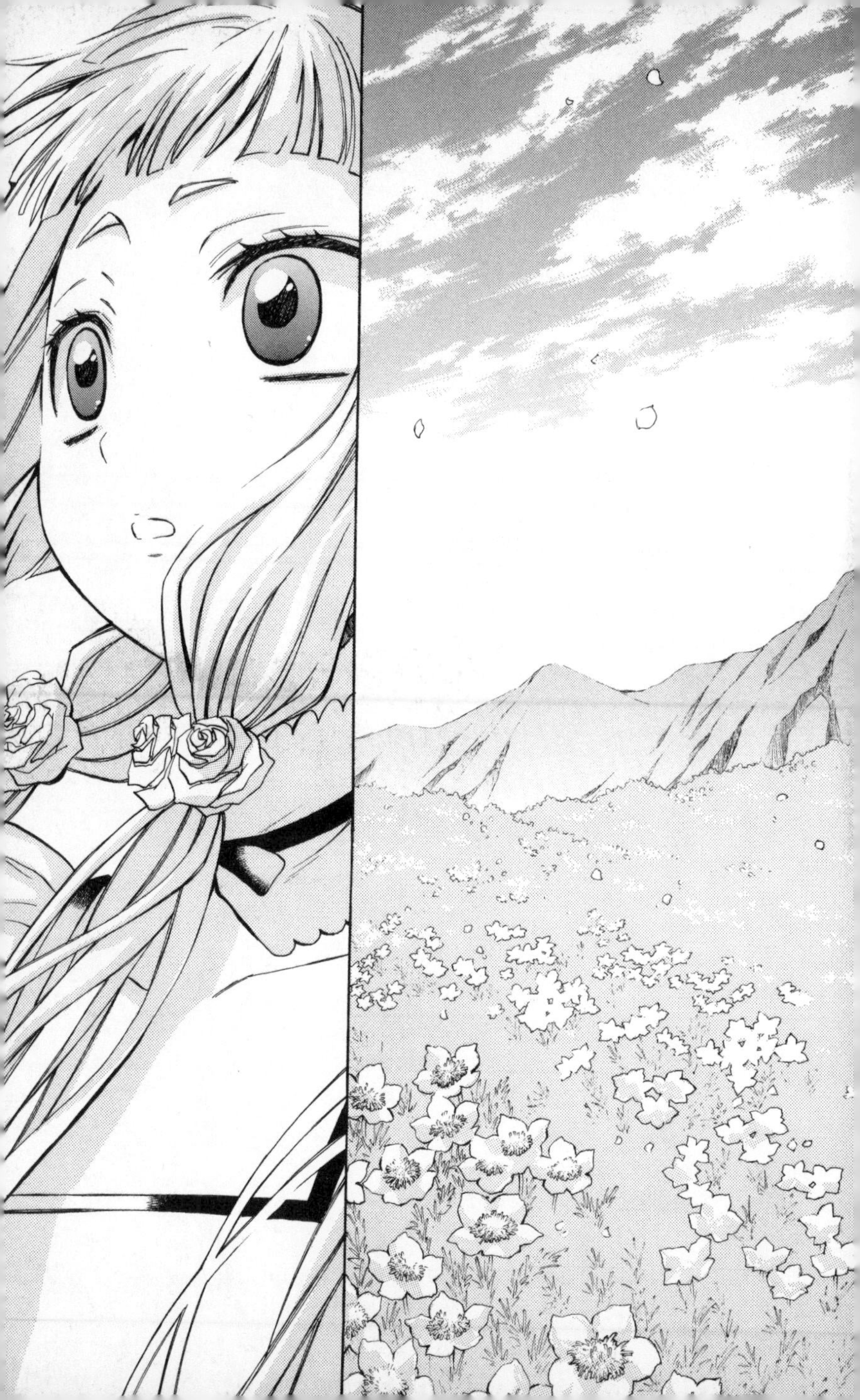

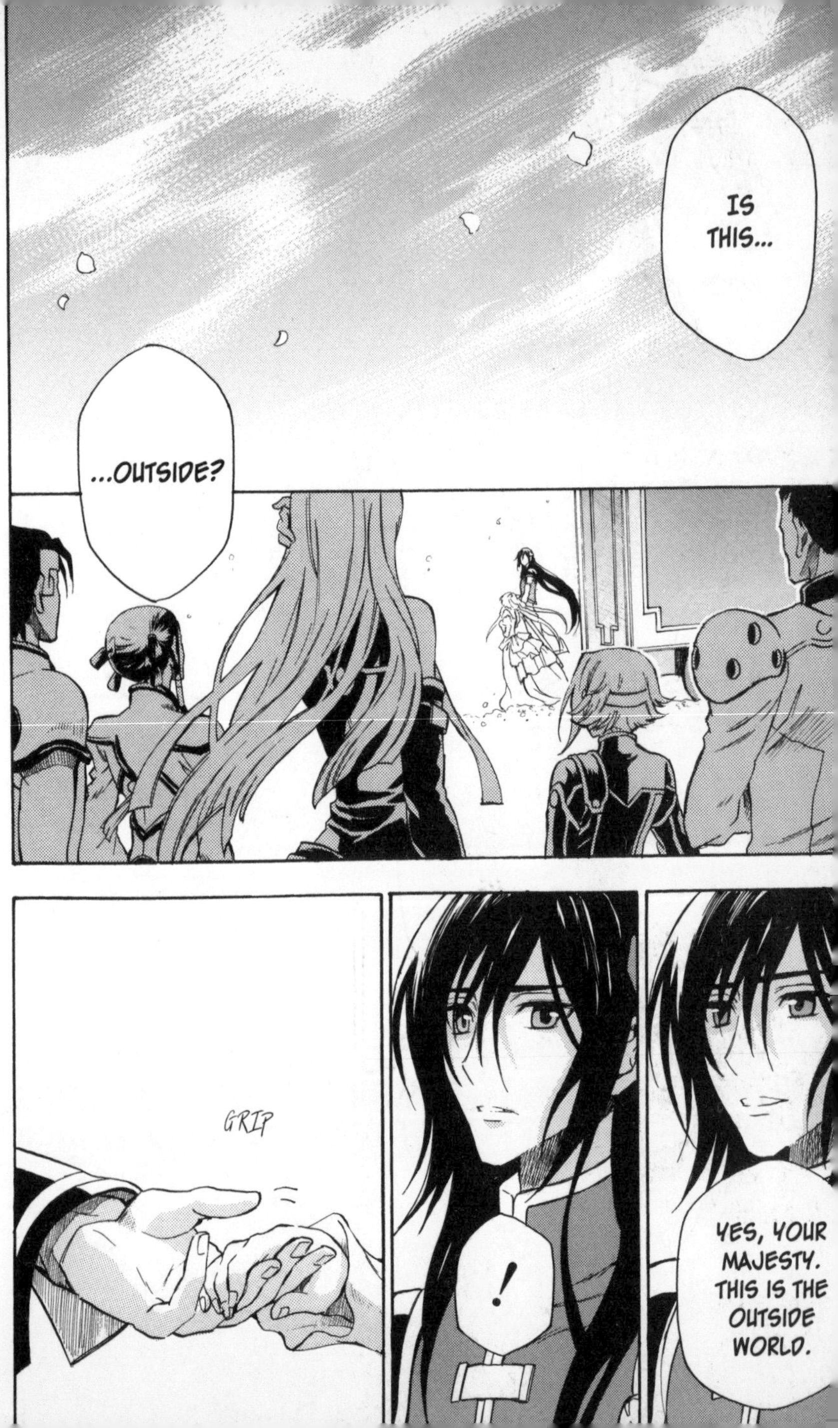
IS THIS...
...OUTSIDE?
YES, YOUR MAJESTY. THIS IS THE OUTSIDE WORLD.
!
GRIP

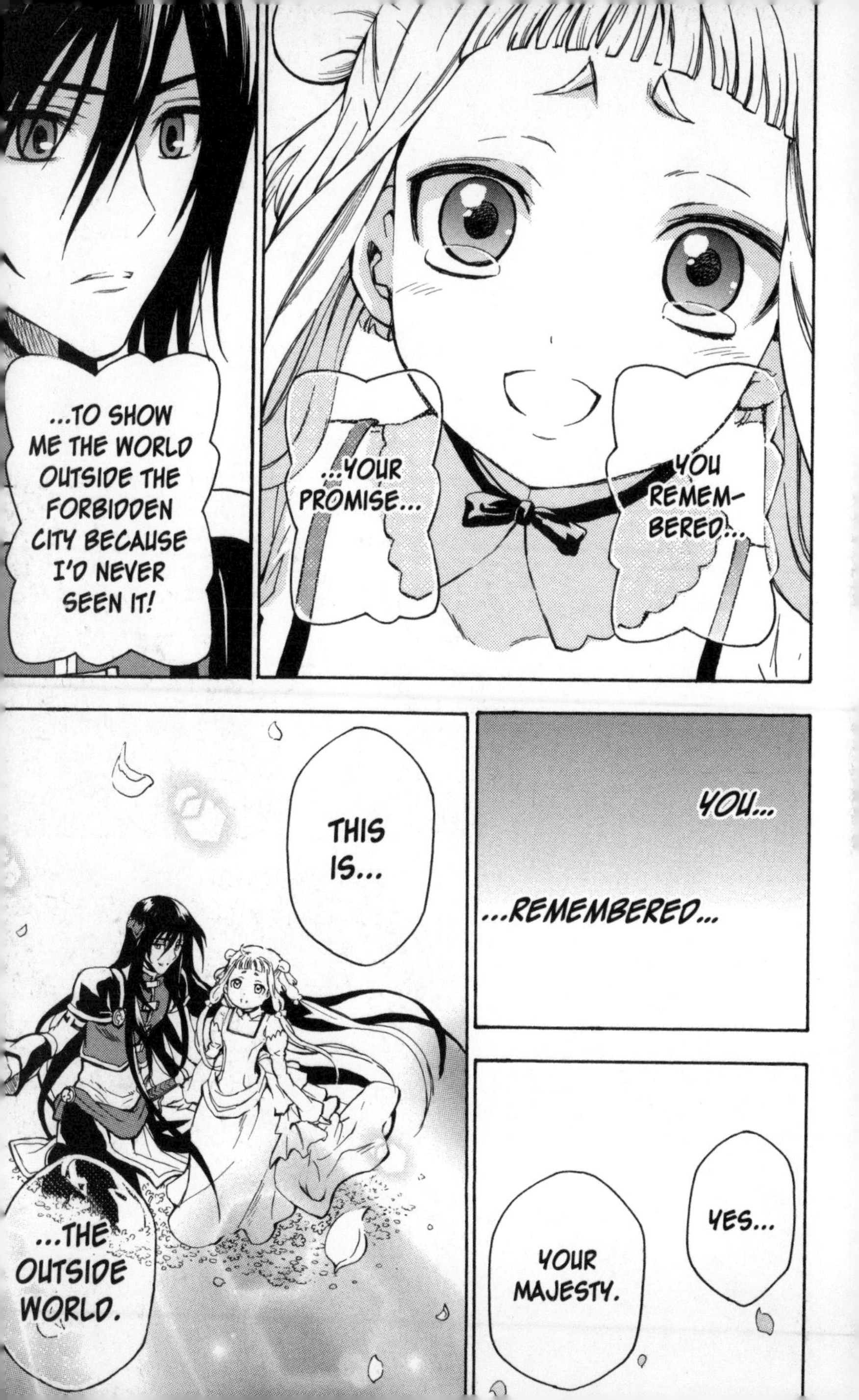
YOU REMEMBERED...
...YOUR PROMISE...
...TO SHOW ME THE WORLD OUTSIDE THE FORBIDDEN CITY BECAUSE I'D NEVER SEEN IT!
YOU...
...REMEMBERED...
YES...
YOUR MAJESTY.
THIS IS...
...THE OUTSIDE WORLD.

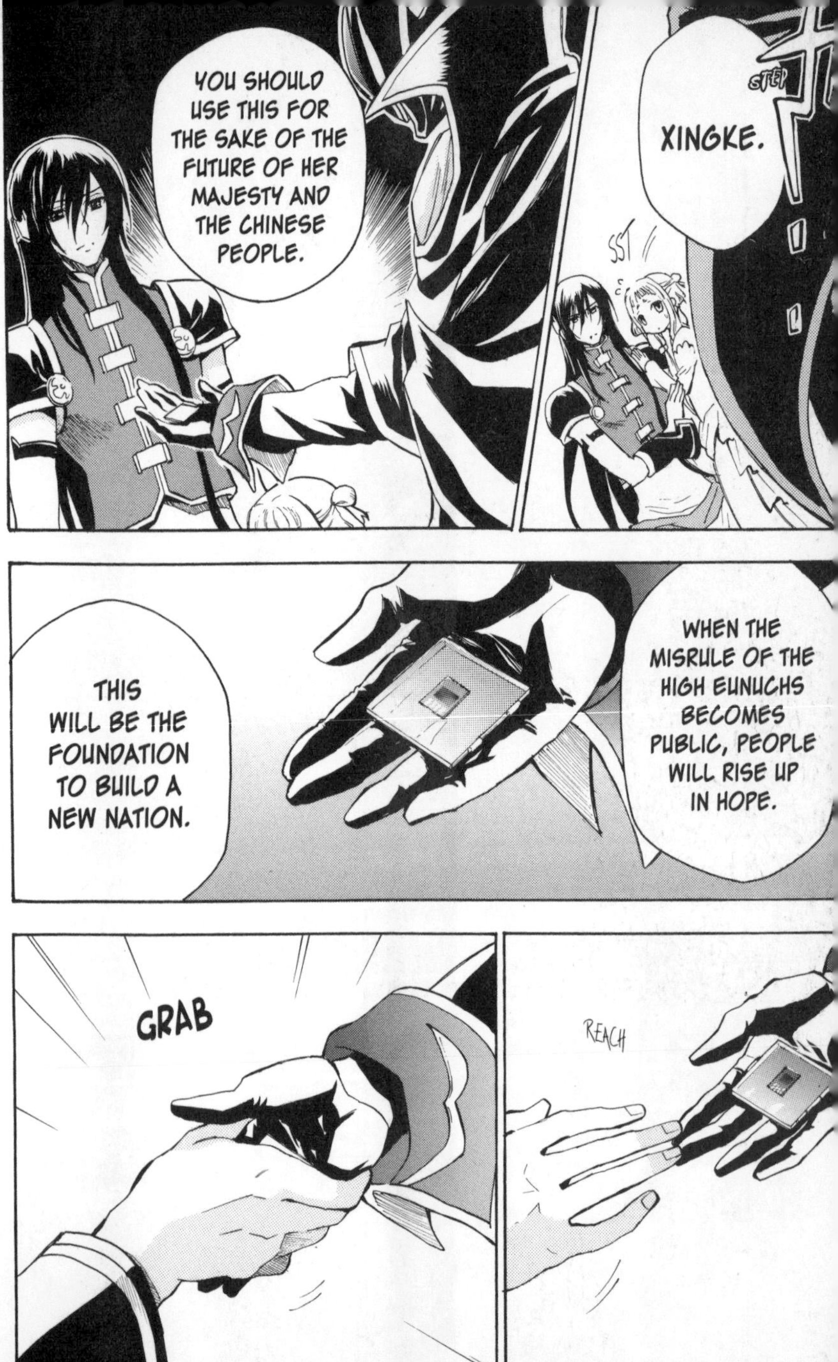
STEP
XINGKE.
SST
YOU SHOULD USE THIS FOR THE SAKE OF THE FUTURE OF HER MAJESTY AND THE CHINESE PEOPLE.
WHEN THE MISRULE OF THE HIGH EUNUCHS BECOMES PUBLIC, PEOPLE WILL RISE UP IN HOPE.
THIS WILL BE THE FOUNDATION TO BUILD A NEW NATION.
REACH
GRAB

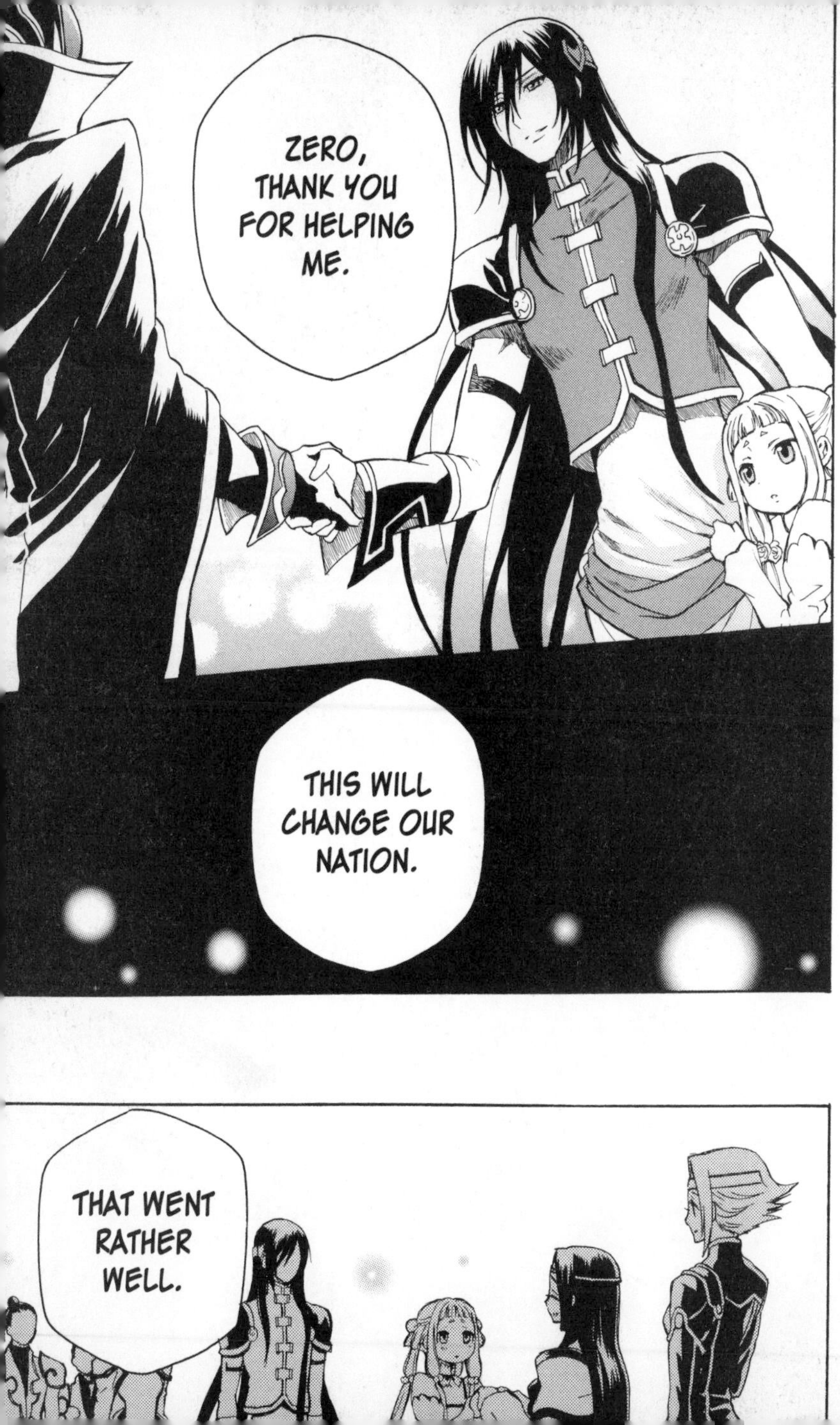
ZERO, THANK YOU FOR HELPING ME.
THIS WILL CHANGE OUR NATION.
THAT WENT RATHER WELL.

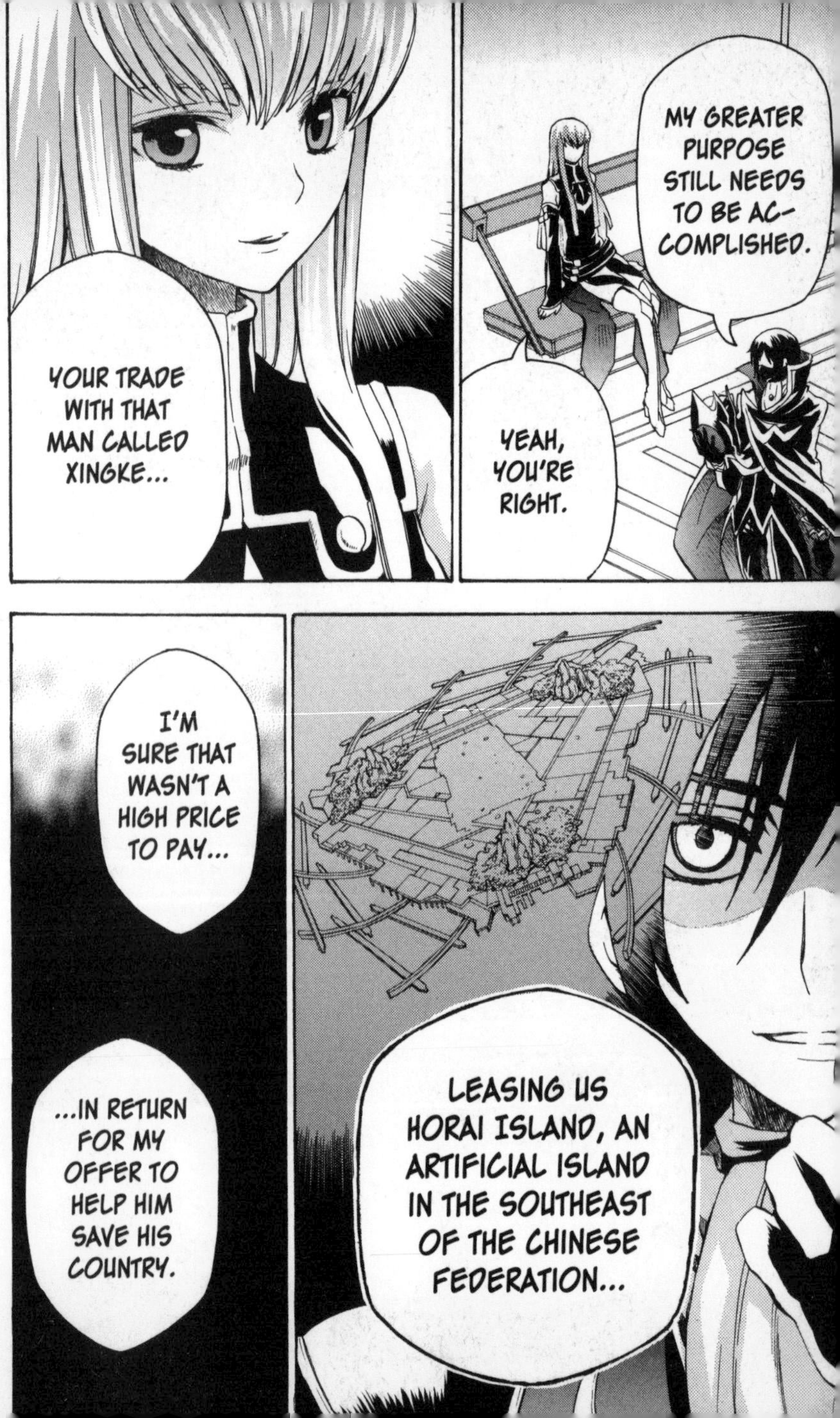
MY GREATER PURPOSE STILL NEEDS TO BE AC-COMPLISHED.
YEAH, YOU'RE RIGHT.
YOUR TRADE WITH THAT MAN CALLED XINGKE...
LEASING US HORAI ISLAND, AN ARTIFICIAL ISLAND IN THE SOUTHEAST OF THE CHINESE FEDERATION...
I'M SURE THAT WASN'T A HIGH PRICE TO PAY...
...IN RETURN FOR MY OFFER TO HELP HIM SAVE HIS COUNTRY.

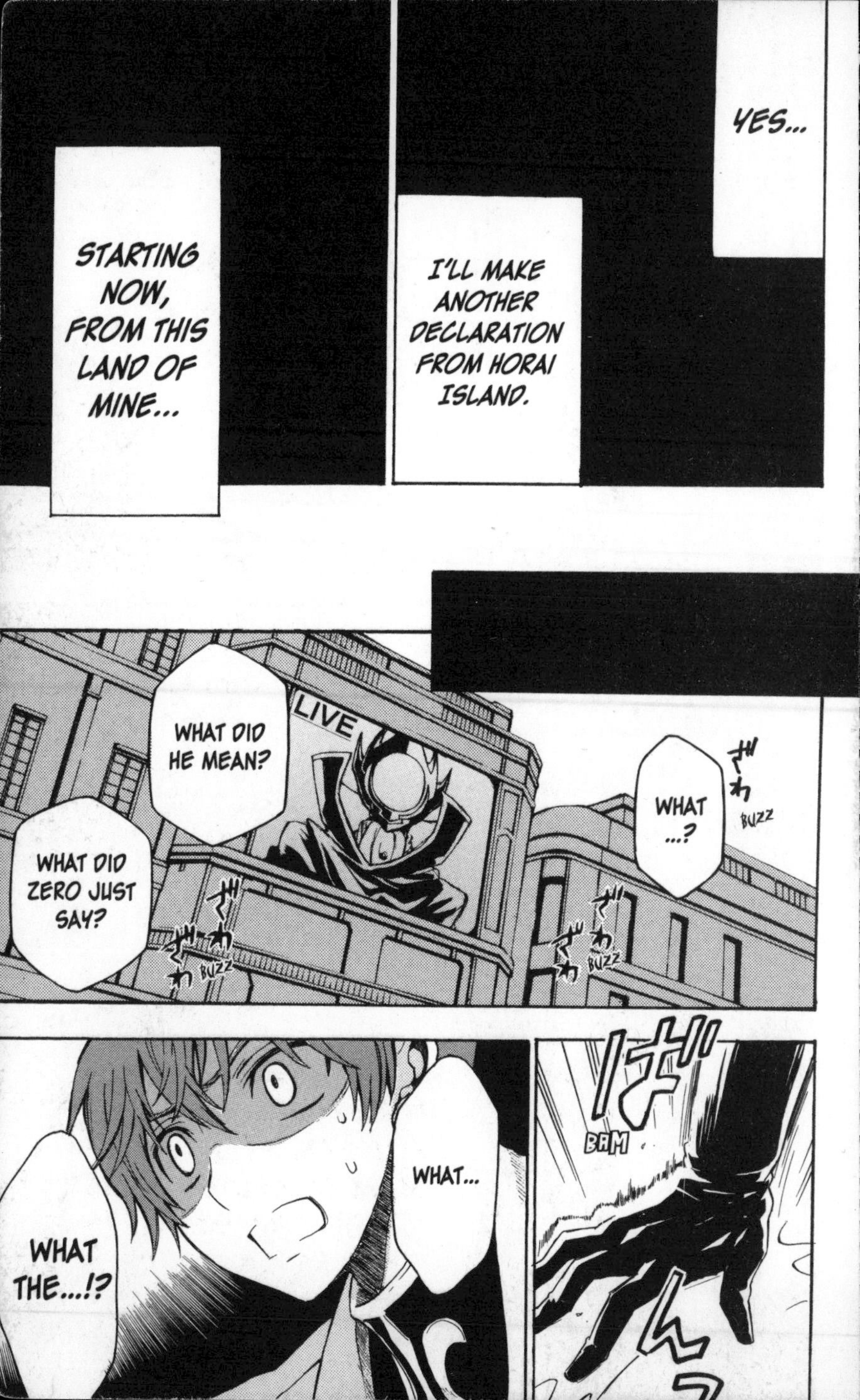
YES...
I'LL MAKE ANOTHER DECLARATION FROM HORAI ISLAND.
STARTING NOW, FROM THIS LAND OF MINE...
ざわ
BUZZ
WHAT ...?
WHAT DID HE MEAN?
LIVE
WHAT DID ZERO JUST SAY?
ざわ ざわ
BUZZ
ざわ ざわ
BUZZ
ばっ
BAM
WHAT...
WHAT THE...!?

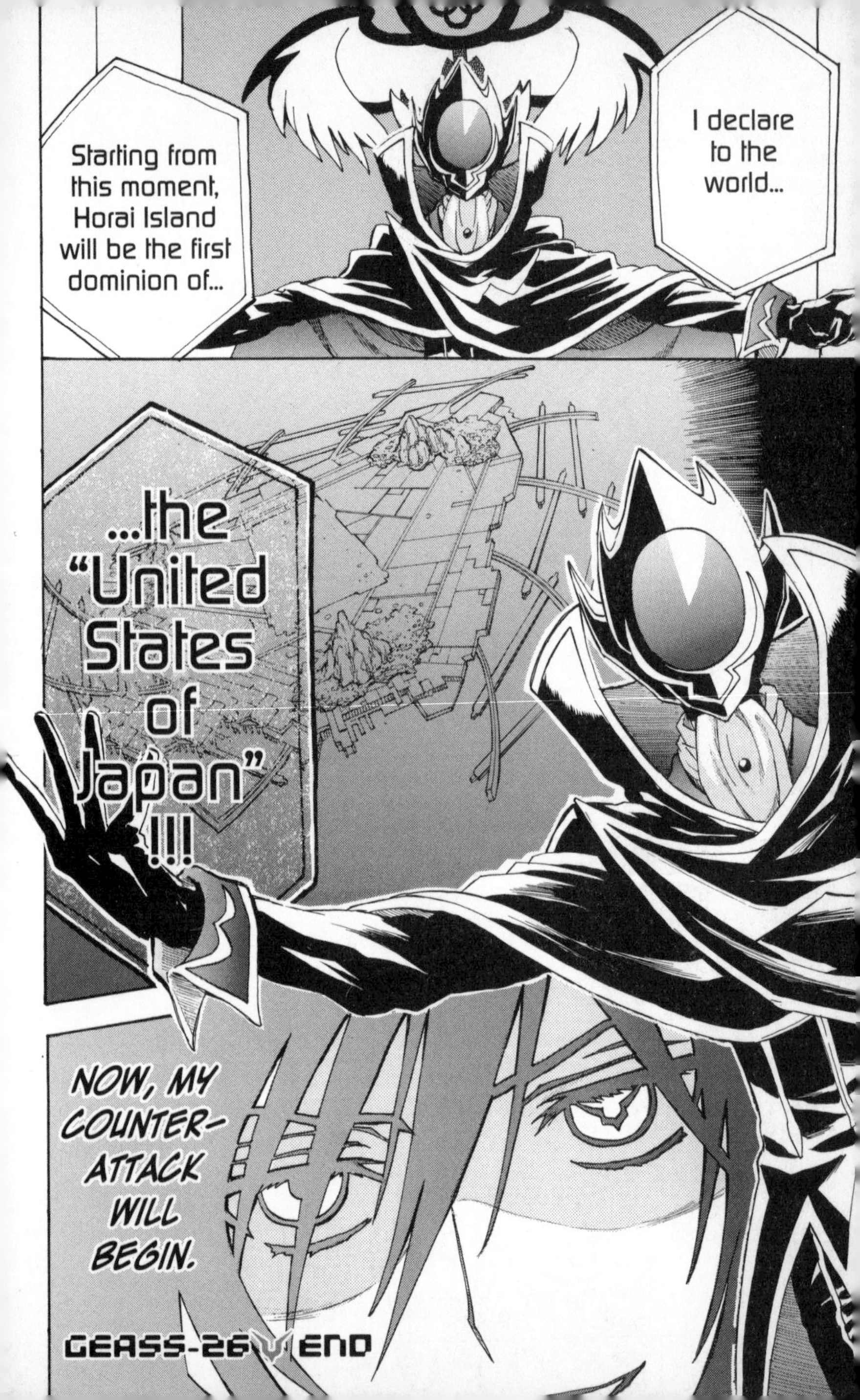
I declare to the world...
Starting from this moment, Horai Island will be the first dominion of...
...the "United States of Japan" !!!
NOW, MY COUNTER-ATTACK WILL BEGIN.
GEASS-26 END

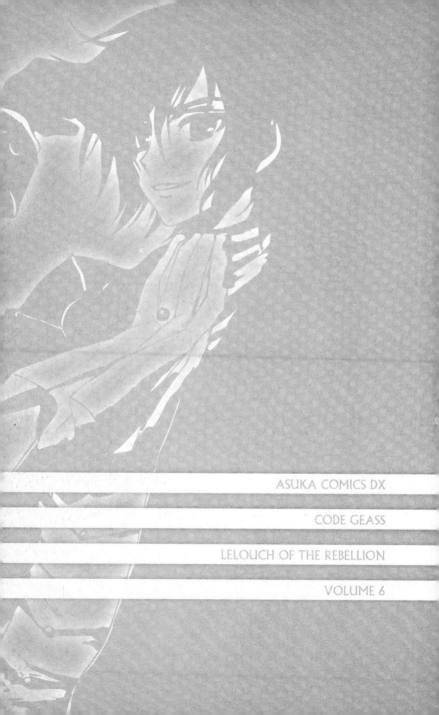

ASUKA COMICS DX

CODE GEASS

LELOUCH OF THE REBELLION

VOLUME 6

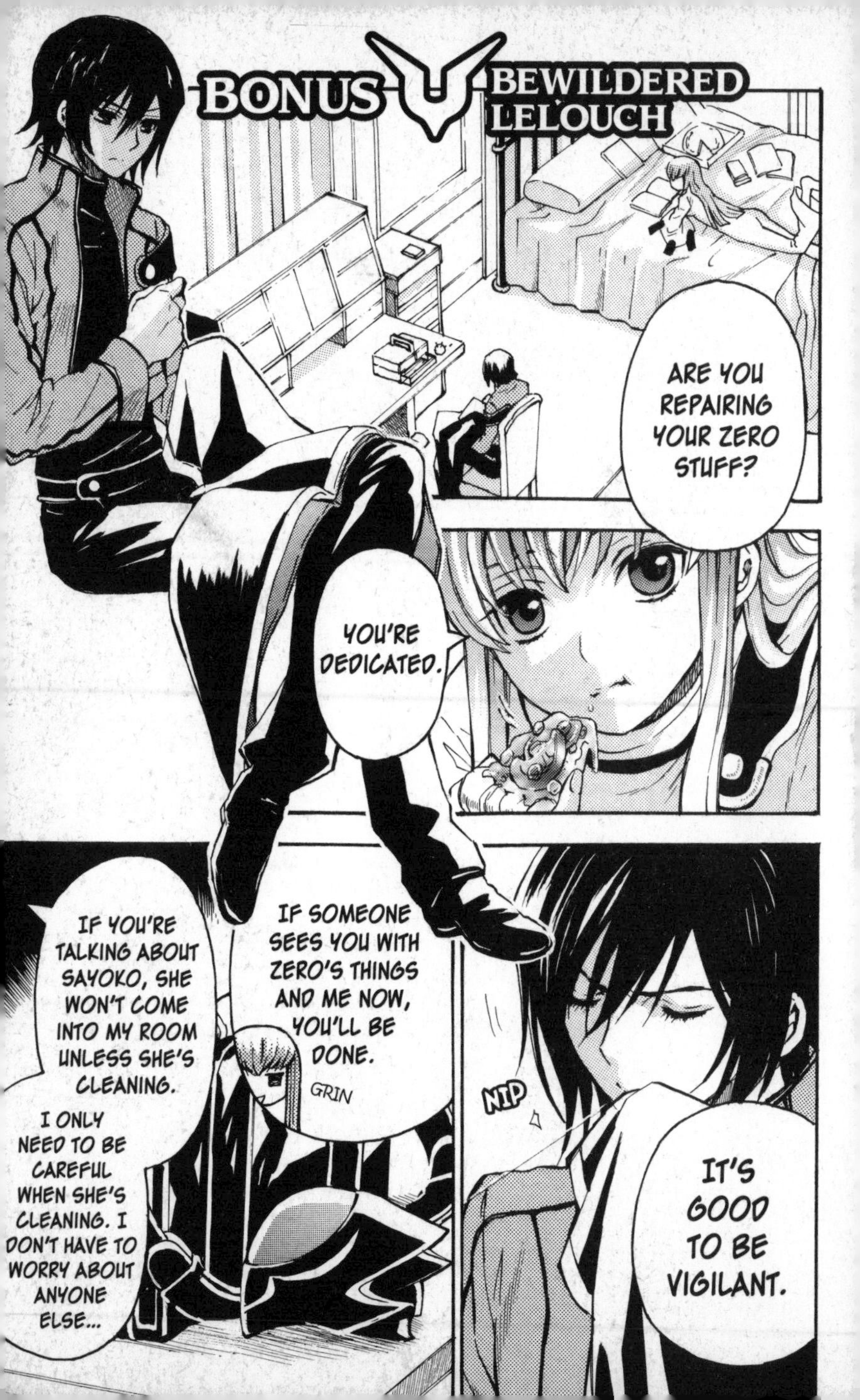
BONUS BEWILDERED LELOUCH
ARE YOU REPAIRING YOUR ZERO STUFF?
YOU'RE DEDICATED.
NIP
IT'S GOOD TO BE VIGILANT.
IF SOMEONE SEES YOU WITH ZERO'S THINGS AND ME NOW, YOU'LL BE DONE.
GRIN
IF YOU'RE TALKING ABOUT SAYOKO, SHE WON'T COME INTO MY ROOM UNLESS SHE'S CLEANING.
I ONLY NEED TO BE CAREFUL WHEN SHE'S CLEANING. I DON'T HAVE TO WORRY ABOUT ANYONE ELSE...

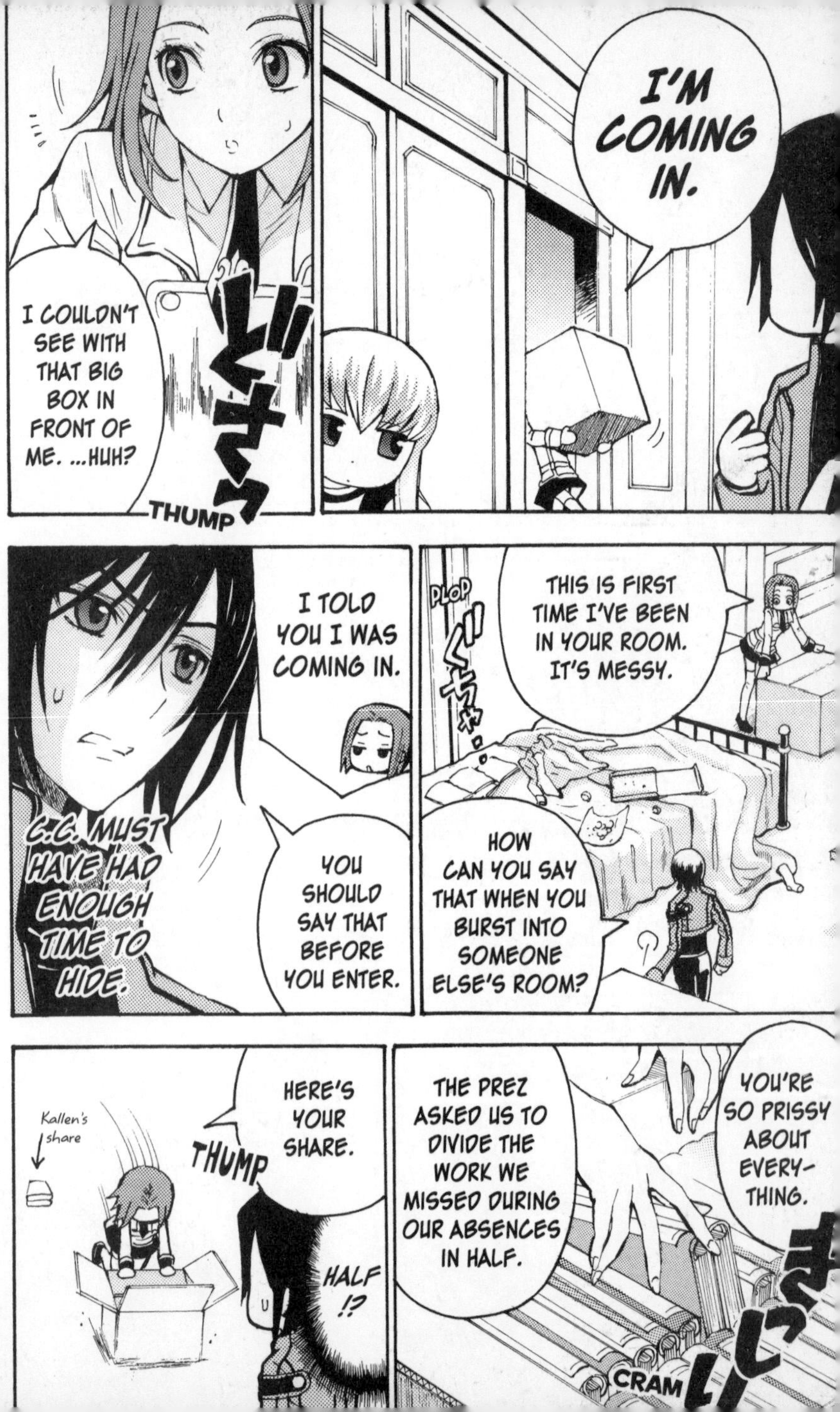
I'M COMING IN.
I COULDN'T SEE WITH THAT BIG BOX IN FRONT OF ME. ...HUH?
THUMP
THIS IS FIRST TIME I'VE BEEN IN YOUR ROOM. IT'S MESSY.
PLOP
HOW CAN YOU SAY THAT WHEN YOU BURST INTO SOMEONE ELSE'S ROOM?
I TOLD YOU I WAS COMING IN.
YOU SHOULD SAY THAT BEFORE YOU ENTER.
C.C. MUST HAVE HAD ENOUGH TIME TO HIDE.
YOU'RE SO PRISSY ABOUT EVERY-THING.
THE PREZ ASKED US TO DIVIDE THE WORK WE MISSED DURING OUR ABSENCES IN HALF.
CRAM
HERE'S YOUR SHARE.
THUMP
HALF !?
Kallen's share

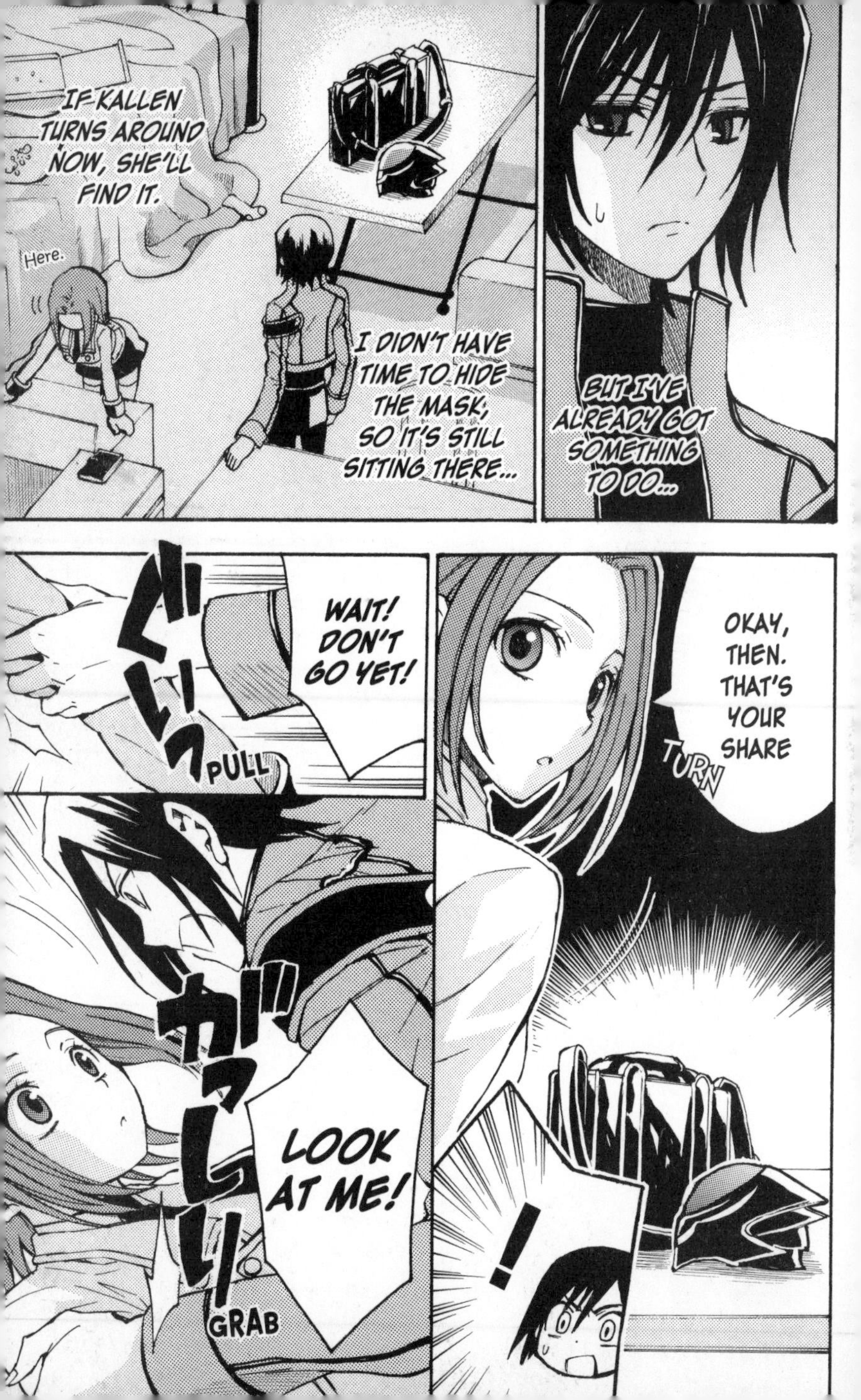

BUT I'VE ALREADY GOT SOMETHING TO DO...
I DIDN'T HAVE TIME TO HIDE THE MASK, SO IT'S STILL SITTING THERE...
IF KALLEN TURNS AROUND NOW, SHE'LL FIND IT.
Here.
OKAY, THEN. THAT'S YOUR SHARE
TURN
!
WAIT! DON'T GO YET!
PULL
LOOK AT ME!
GRAB

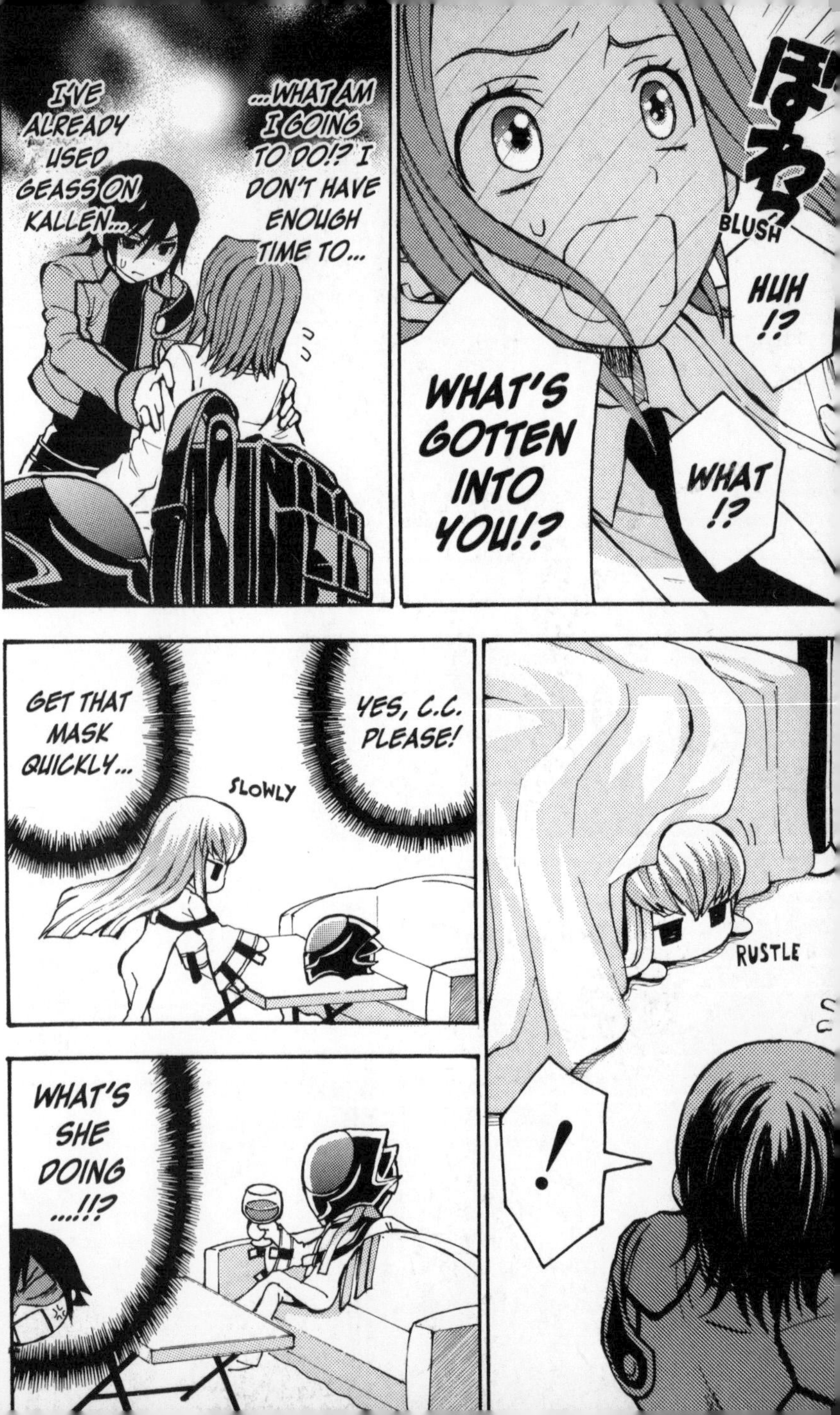
BLUSH
HUH!?
WHAT!?
WHAT'S GOTTEN INTO YOU!?
...WHAT AM I GOING TO DO!? I DON'T HAVE ENOUGH TIME TO...
I'VE ALREADY USED GEASS ON KALLEN...
RUSTLE
!
YES, C.C. PLEASE!
GET THAT MASK QUICKLY...
SLOWLY
WHAT'S SHE DOING ...!!?

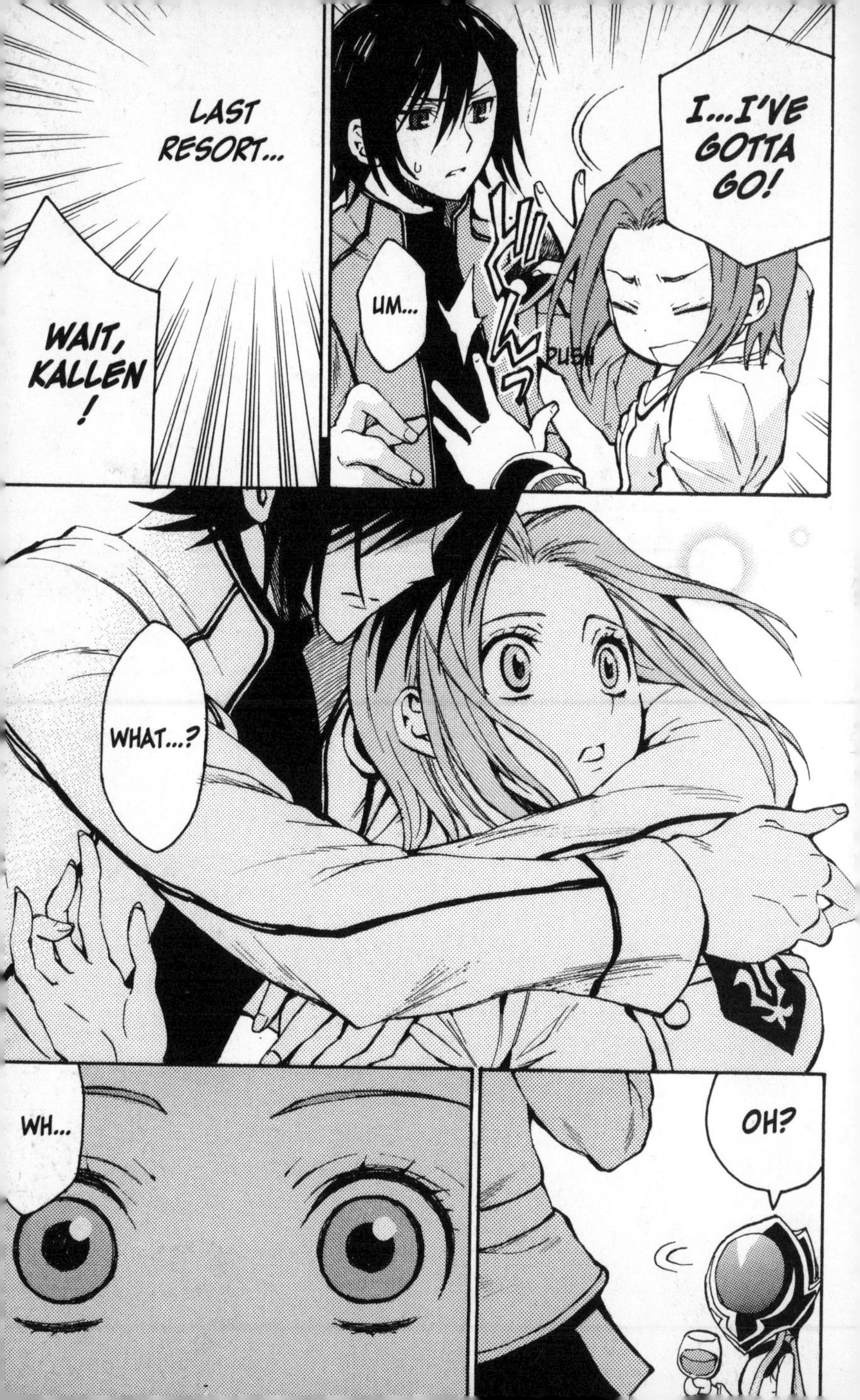
I...I'VE GOTTA GO!
PUSH
UM...
LAST RESORT...
WAIT, KALLEN!
WHAT...?
OH?
WH...

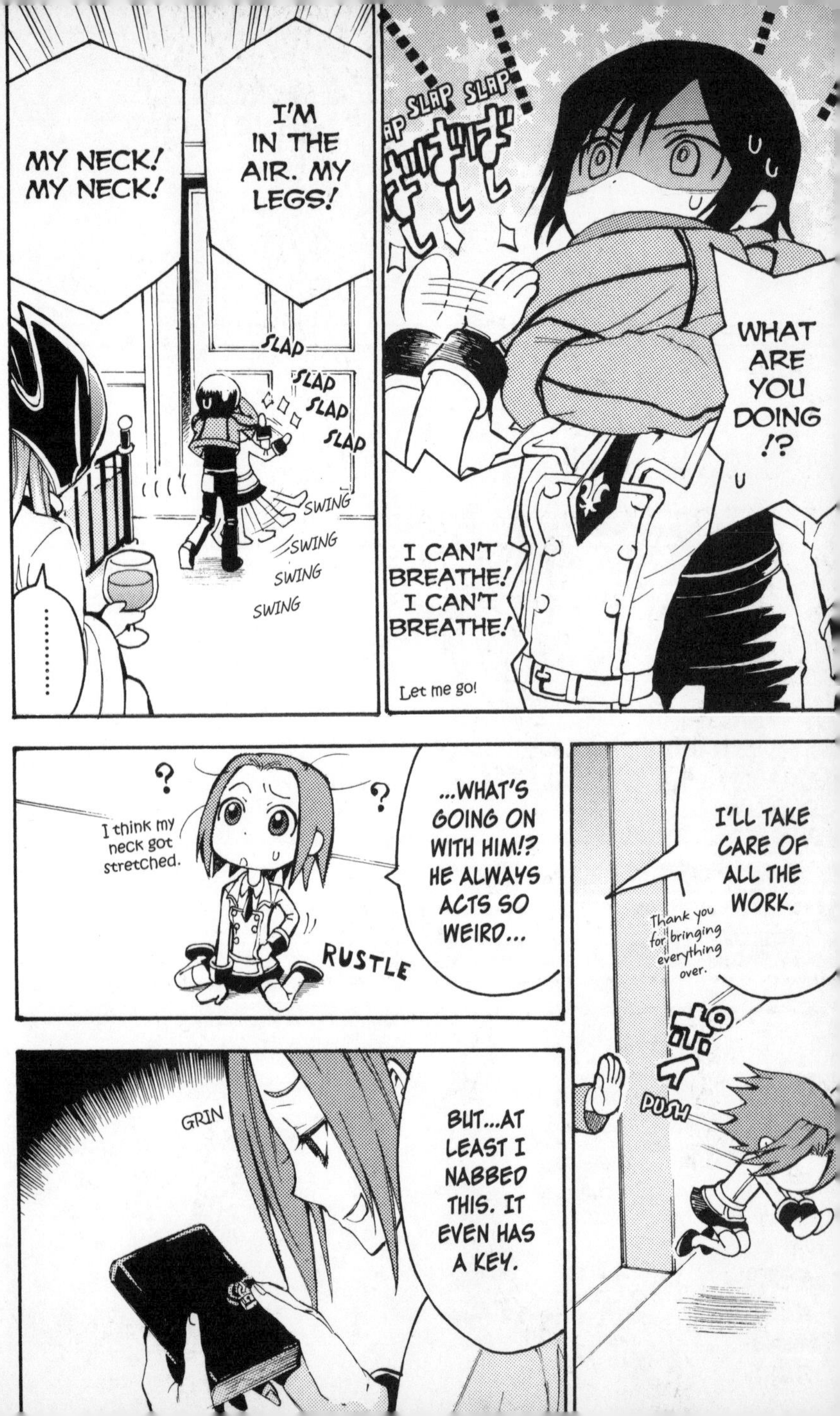
SLAP SLAP SLAP
WHAT ARE YOU DOING !?
I CAN'T BREATHE! I CAN'T BREATHE!
Let me go!
I'M IN THE AIR. MY LEGS!
MY NECK! MY NECK!
SLAP
SLAP
SLAP
SLAP
SWING
SWING
SWING
SWING
....
I'LL TAKE CARE OF ALL THE WORK.
Thank you for bringing everything over.
ポイ
PUSH
...WHAT'S GOING ON WITH HIM!? HE ALWAYS ACTS SO WEIRD...
I think my neck got stretched.
RUSTLE
BUT...AT LEAST I NABBED THIS. IT EVEN HAS A KEY.
GRIN

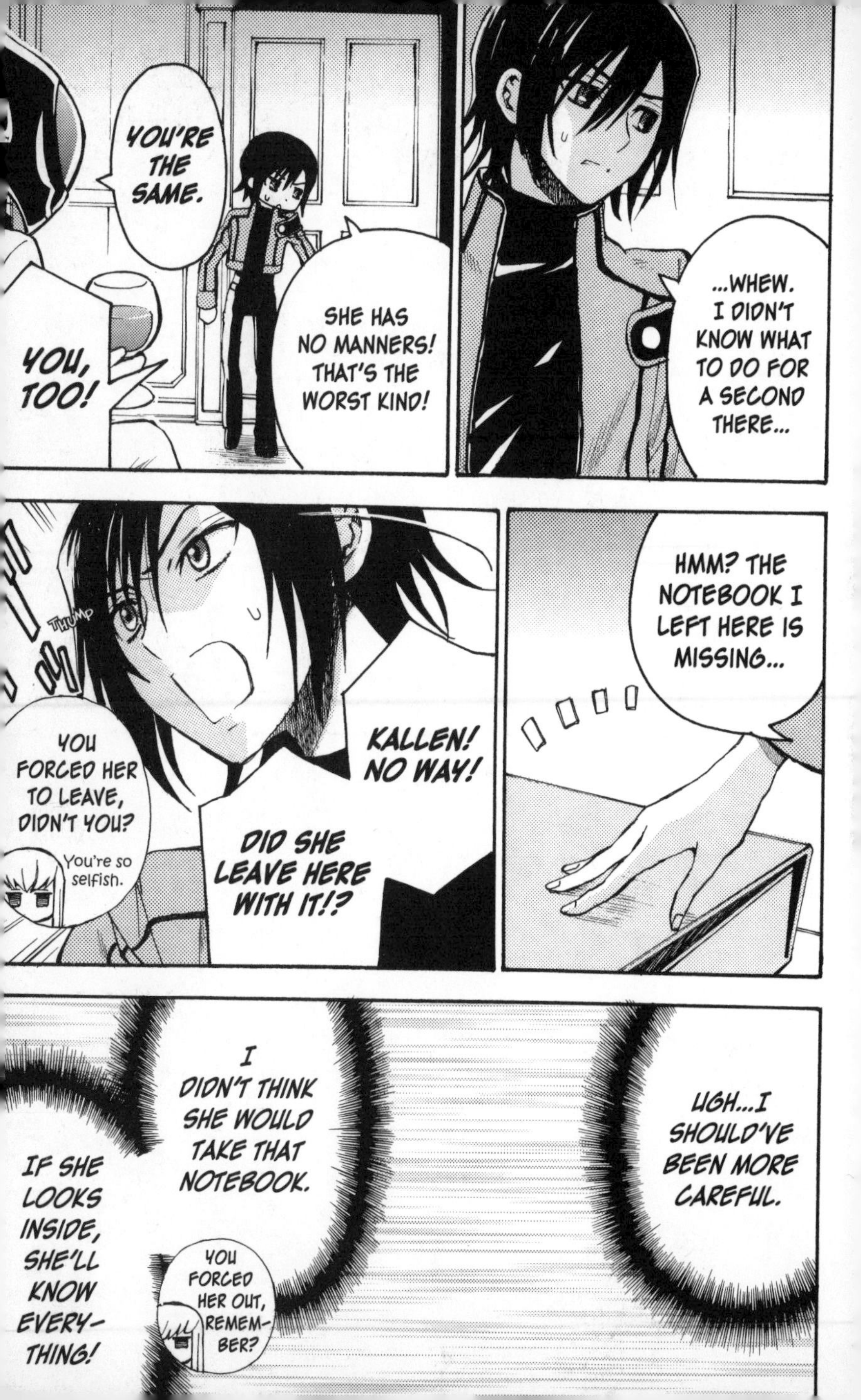
...WHEW. I DIDN'T KNOW WHAT TO DO FOR A SECOND THERE...
SHE HAS NO MANNERS! THAT'S THE WORST KIND!
YOU'RE THE SAME.
YOU, TOO!
HMM? THE NOTEBOOK I LEFT HERE IS MISSING...
KALLEN! NO WAY!
DID SHE LEAVE HERE WITH IT!?
THUMP
YOU FORCED HER TO LEAVE, DIDN'T YOU?
You're so selfish.
UGH...I SHOULD'VE BEEN MORE CAREFUL.
I DIDN'T THINK SHE WOULD TAKE THAT NOTEBOOK.
IF SHE LOOKS INSIDE, SHE'LL KNOW EVERY-THING!
YOU FORCED HER OUT, REMEM-BER?

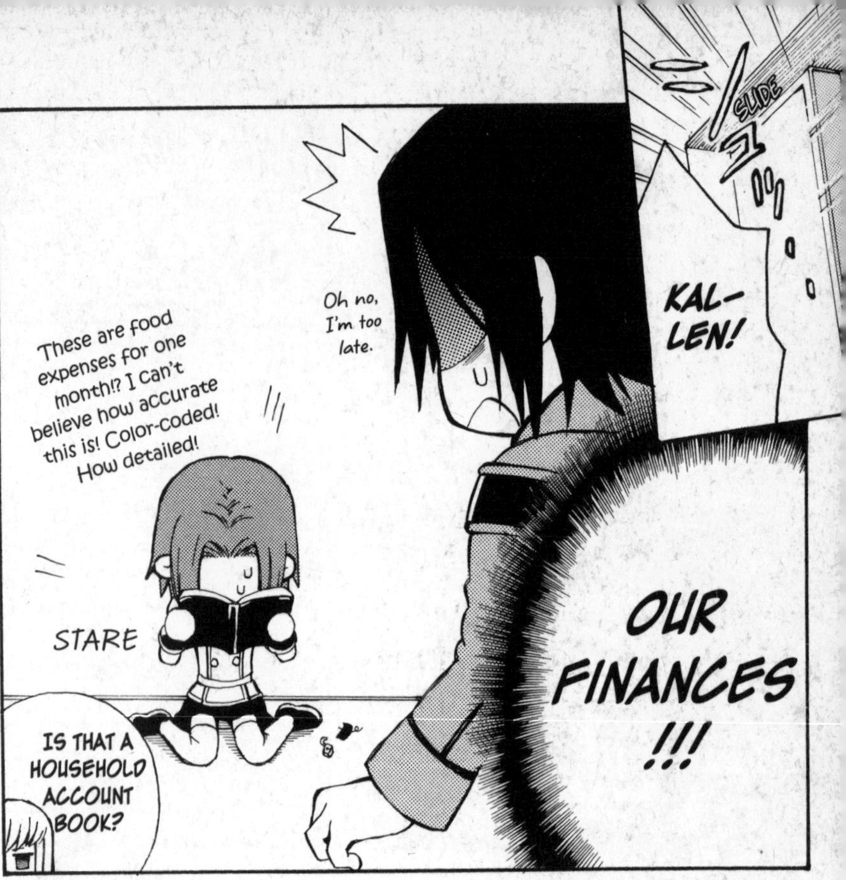
SLIDE
KAL-LEN!
OUR FINANCES!!!
Oh no, I'm too late.
These are food expenses for one month!? I can't believe how accurate this is! Color-coded! How detailed!
STARE
IS THAT A HOUSEHOLD ACCOUNT BOOK?

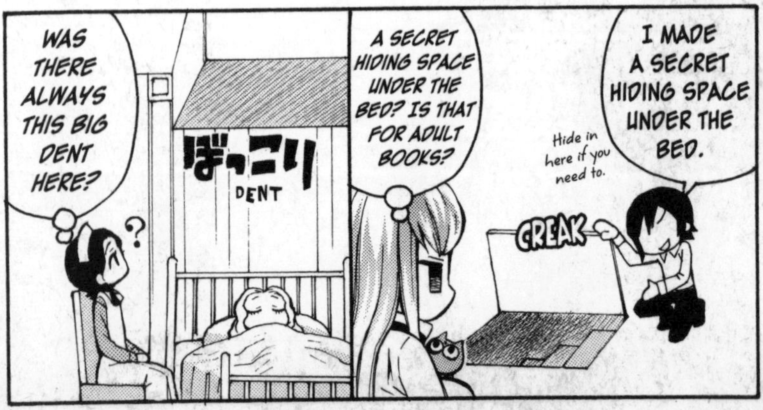
I MADE A SECRET HIDING SPACE UNDER THE BED.
Hide in here if you need to.
CREAK
A SECRET HIDING SPACE UNDER THE BED? IS THAT FOR ADULT BOOKS?
WAS THERE ALWAYS THIS BIG DENT HERE?
ぼっこり
DENT

BONUS END

After two years of working, I got a vacation and went to a famous theme park.

I'd never been there and it was my dream to go. So, I was very glad that my wish came true.

However, it was a particularly crowded day, and the wait times for some attractions were seven hours long even with the fast pass... ☺

When I've reached my next big deadline, I would like to go there again.

I want to go there when there are not so many people next time... ☺

MAJIKO!

Thank you!
Mr. Ichirou Ohkouchi, Mr. Goro Taniguchi, Mr. S-mura,
Mr. Y-moto and Producer Mr. Kawaguchi

My editors Mr. Mr. M-shita, Mr. K-da

ASSISTANTS:
Nagase Ueda

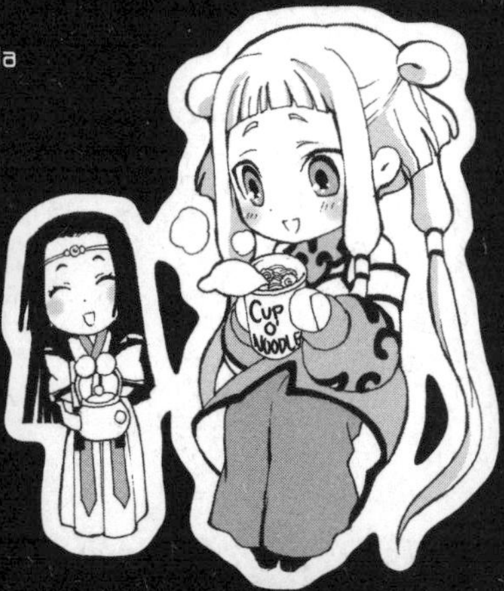
Cup O' NOODLE

CODE GEASS
コードギアス
反逆のルルーシュ Lelouch
of the Rebellion

MANGA	Majiko!
ORIGINAL STORY	Ichirou Ohkouchi
	Goro Taniguchi

ENGLISH PRODUCTION CREDITS

TRANSLATION	KURO UZU
LETTERING	Keiran O'Leary
EDITOR	Robert Place Napton
PUBLISHER	Ken Iyadomi

Code Geass Lelouch of the Rebellion Vol. 6
©Majiko! 2009
©2006-2009 SUNRISE/PROJECT GEASS, MBS
Character Design ©2006 CLAMP

Originally published in Japan in 2009 by KADOKAWA SHOTEN PUBLISHING CO., LTD., Tokyo.
English translation published by Bandai Entertainment Inc. under the license from Sunrise Inc.

ISBN-13: 978-1-60496-160-7